FIREWORKS MX FUNDAMENTALS

BY

Abigail Rudner

With contributions by

Lori Denning

Steven Grosvenor

Lise LaTorre

Mary Rich

201 West 103rd Street, Indianapolis, Indiana 46290

An Imprint of Pearson Education

Boston • Indianapolis • London • Munich • New York • San Francisco

Fireworks® MX Fundamentals

Copyright © 2003 by New Riders Publishing

International Standard Book Number: 0-7357-1153-4

Library of Congress Catalog Card Number: 20-01089193

Printed in the United States of America

First Printing: August 2002

06 05 04 03 02   7 6 5 4 3 2 1

Interpretation of the printing code: The rightmost double-digit number is the year of the book's printing; the rightmost single-digit number is the number of the book's printing. For example, the printing code 02-1 shows that the first printing of the book occurred in 2002.

Trademarks

Warning and Disclaimer

Publisher
David Dwyer

Associate Publisher
Stephanie Wall

Production Manager
Gina Kanouse

Managing Editor
Kristy Knoop

Senior Acquisitions Editor
Linda Anne Bump

Development Editor
Jennifer Eberhardt

Senior Marketing Manager
Tammy Detrich

Publicity Manager
Susan Nixon

Copy Editor
Sheri Cain

Indexer
Becky Hornyak

Manufacturing Coordinator
Jim Conway

Cover Designer
Aren Howell

Composition
Jeff Bredensteiner

Media Developer
Jay Payne

Contents At A Glance

Introduction

Part IV   Appendix

Table of Contents

5 Working with Color Fills and Strokes   121

About the Author

 **Abigail Rudner** is a dynamic educator and artist. She is Principle Visual Designer and Creative Director of her little company, BIG FUN Designs, in Oakland, California.

With a wealth of knowledge in marketing, advertising, interactive digital media design, and production, Abigail and her team of experts have produced an amazing array of content for a wide range of interactive, animated, web, and print design projects since 1990. BIG FUN clients include PeopleSoft, Levi's, Wells Fargo, Dow Jones, America Online, Absolut Vodka, The SYDA Foundation, Amgen, Apple Computers, Microsoft, and Radius. Abigail's illustration has been published in *FAD* and *Publish* magazines.

An early adopter of digital design tools, Abigail has been teaching web design, web graphics, illustration, and photo illustration courses with love and enthusiasm across the USA since 1991. Using a synthesis of design methodology, visual thinking, and computer-graphics tools and techniques, Abigail inspires and teaches students how to design and produce with purpose.

Abigail is a graduate of Parsons School of Design, with a BFA in Communication Design and Photography. She is a five-year Associate Design veteran (1984-89) of Campbells' Soup International, where she was one of three junior designers chosen to spearhead Campbells' conversion to electronic design in 1987.

She is a certified trainer (through CompTIA International) in the following: Macromedia Certified in Flash, Fireworks, and Dreamweaver, and an Adobe Certified Product Expert for Photoshop 6.

Abigail's dream is to work with young people in a museum setting with corporate dollars, building an international interactive young people's creative forum on the web. Got any ideas or want to participate creatively or financially? Check out Abigail's web site at www.rudner.com or e-mail her at abigail@rudner.com.

Contributing Authors

Lori Denning started her design career where all designers begin: in the chemistry lab. Realizing that she was ill-suited to be a research scientist, she bounced around until she found marketing and design. Her eclectic tastes include sports (especially fencing), reading sci-fi, traveling, and playing computer games. She currently works as a director of marketing in Northern California.

Steven Grosvenor is co-founder of phireworx.com (`www.phireworx.com`), a Fireworks resource site; co-author of *Dreamweaver MX Expert Edge* (McGraw-Hill/Osborne, July 2002); and Senior Systems Architect for a managed internet security company in the United Kingdom. Steven's background is in cross-platform systems integration, interface design, interaction, and architecture design.

Demand from users for a customized, interactive experience led him to develop and create many timesaving and creative commands and behaviors for Dreamweaver, vastly reducing deployment time for corporate sites and increasing their portability and scalability. His drive to increase team productivity led him to develop extensibility add-ons for other products in the Macromedia web suite including Dreamweaver MX, Fireworks MX, and Flash MX.

One of the new breed of commands for Fireworks MX, "Twist and Fade 3.0," which was created by Steven, had the accolade of shipping with Fireworks MX. His other publications include several Fireworks MX and Dreamweaver MX tutorials, which can be found at Macromedia (`www.macromedia.com`).

Lise LaTorre is a founding partner and Production Director of InMotionMedia.net, a small web design shop focused on supporting community through bringing small businesses and non-profit organizations online. Lise graduated from UC Berkeley with degrees in Psychology and Linguistics, which turned out to be the perfect foundation for developing information architecture, data models, and user interface, as well as the use of programming languages. She leaves the pretty stuff to Abigail and her partner in IMM, Liz Goh.

Mary Rich began her career as an insurance agent. She switched to become a programming trainee, found out what programmers did, and fell in love. The affair continued through mainframes and midrange systems and peaked when the first IBM PCs arrived. Mary eventually became involved with various graphics programs, then web sites. A firm believer in Macromedia products, she found Dreamweaver and Fireworks to answer her prayers for productivity. She provides consulting and training in many different areas to organizations in the Los Angeles area and—through the Internet—to the world. She has a BA degree from Brown University and is working on a certificate in computer graphics from UCLA. Mary's cat, Friday, lets her live with him in El Segundo, CA.

About the Technical Reviewers

These reviewers contributed their considerable hands-on expertise to the entire development process for *Fireworks MX Fundamentals* As the book was being written, these dedicated professionals reviewed all the material for technical content, organization, and flow. Their feedback was critical to ensuring that *Fireworks MX Fundamentals* fits our readers' need for the highest-quality technical information.

 **Mark Haynes** is the Fireworks Product Team liaison for Macromedia Customer Care. He has served as the product's Technical Support Team Lead since the early days of Fireworks 1, and is a prolific poster boy for the Fireworks Online Forum, the Fireworks-L listserv, and the FreeHand-L listserv. (A recent search on Groups.Google.com turned up more than 31,100 posts with his name in them.) Mark has also supported FreeHand, xRes, SoundEdit 16, DeckII, Director, and Dreamweaver as a technical support engineer at Macromedia. He is responsible for writing, editing, and reviewing hundreds of TechNotes on the Macromedia web site, and his broad knowledge of Macromedia products, specifically Fireworks, has enabled him to help educate and enlighten the Fireworks user community.

Mark lives in Allen, Texas (home of a famous T.V. dinosaur known to children worldwide) with his wife and four children. (Another child is coming in August 2002, so he thanks you for buying this book.) As a University of North Texas Music School graduate, he suffers from a lingering addiction to jazz music, and, in between book reviews, forum posts, and replies to emails, he can occasionally be heard playing "As Time Goes By," "Scrapple from the Apple," "I Wish You Love," or any number of other standards on one of his guitars.

 **Ram Ganesh** is an international award-winning design consultant. He has spoken in various conferences and product launches worldwide (including InternetWorld, Sydney). Ram has been an advisor for Fireworks since v1.0 and has won awards, including the latest Macromedia eLearning Innovators Award. He graduated with a master's in Design from IIT Bombay, India, with a 99.2 percentile and has been featured in the *IT* Who's Who List 2001. He loves to travel and has explored planet Earth from the top of the Swiss Alps to the Malaysian rainforests. In 2001, he did a five-country road trip in his new Beamer throughout Europe.

Acknowledgments

A special thanks to all the wonderful and loving people who have helped me, directly and indirectly, with this book. Each contribution was unique, subtle, and important. Your support of me and my work is not taken for granted.

With great love, gratitude, and respect to:

My parents, Michael and Ruth Rudner.

Aaron Rudner, my first best friend and #1 member of our mutual admiration society!

Jennifer Michals, my best friend with benefits. Thank you for sharing your heart, your humor, your strong support, your patience, and your vision.

My contributing authors and editors: Lise LaTorre, Lori Denning and Mary Rich, and Steven Grosvenor. Thank you for your excellent and hard work, and for caring as much as I do about sharing knowledge.

A special thank you to my technical editors, Mark Haynes and Ram Ganesh, for your incredible knowledge and guidance. You are so great!

David Morris and The Macromedia Fireworks MX team: Thanks for your brilliance and hard work to create a product that allows me to say, "I love my work!"

To Diana Smedley for saying something good about me to the right person at the right time so that I eventually wound up here!

The folks at New Riders Publishing, including Linda Bump, John Rahm, Victoria Elzey, and Jennifer Eberhardt. Thank you for the opportunity to learn, teach, and write about my passion in the form of this book. I will say another big thank you in advance for all that I do not know will come from this work in the future!

Sally Smith of Connect Learning for empowering me to self leadership, for inspiring me in so many ways, for countless amazing and wonderful hours of your time, and for believing in me.

The folks at Ciber Training: Lesley Grizzell, Bill Ramirez, Amy Shen, and Jennifer Murray. Thank you for your support, encouragement, and for believing in me.

My friends and associates, Steve McGuire, John Ulliman, Jennifer Gertz, Pippa Green, Kathy Klein, Fred Delisios, Carl Merchant, deAnna Harper, Lisa Kaplan, Dr. Lenny Cocco, and Patricia McDade.

My grandparents, Abraham Binder and Golda Riva Goldstein Binder Klein, and Hanna Garber Rudner and Harry Rudner.

Dana Hope Margolis, for your support, coaching, guidance, love, and for helping me to "be" in the best way possible.

My beloved Guru Mayi, Baba and Bagawan for your grace, compassion, guidance, protection, and for giving me the inner knowledge, vision, and experience of Muktananda and Chidvilasananda. I will never stop thanking your golden heart and laying my head at your lotus feet.

Dedication

For my father, Michael M. Rudner, who taught me how to write, to be open to possibilities, to see beauty in the sublime, to use a camera, and to love my work.

For my mother, Ruth Rachel Binder Rudner, who held me like a precious treasure inside of her, knows the difference between honey and vinegar, and who—with my father—taught me to play, see, draw, paint, make pottery, build, grow, and love.

Tell Us What You Think

As the reader of this book, you are the most important critic and commentator. We value your opinion and want to know what we're doing right, what we could do better, what areas you'd like to see us publish in, and any other words of wisdom you're willing to pass our way.

As the Associate Publisher for New Riders Publishing, I welcome your comments. You can fax, email, or write me directly to let me know what you did or didn't like about this book—as well as what we can do to make our books stronger.

Please note that I cannot help you with technical problems related to the topic of this book, and that due to the high volume of mail I receive, I might not be able to reply to every message.

When you write, please be sure to include this book's title and author, as well as your name and phone or fax number. I will carefully review your comments and share them with the author and editors who worked on the book.

Fax: 317-581-4663

Email: stephanie.wall@newriders.com

Mail: Stephanie Wall
               Associate Publisher
               New Riders Publishing
               201 West 103rd Street
               Indianapolis, IN 46290 USA

Introduction

Why This Book?

Cut to the chase. That was what motivated me to write this book. As a student, I know when someone is teaching me well and when I "get" it. As a teacher, I strive to understand what my students need to know and how they need it presented to them. I know that students don't need another book filled with fluff that's not relevant to their goals. This book's goal is to give design students and designers a clear and comprehensive reference and tutorial information on how to use the finest web-graphics tool on the planet.

- Fireworks is incredibly underused by design community.
- It's a best-kept secret that shouldn't be kept secret.
- Fireworks is a phenomenal tool.
- It's the only tool truly designed for making flawless graphics because it has, hands down, the best feature set and interface.
- As you'll discover in this book, it's the only program that seamlessly combines bitmap- and vector-art creation.
- With the new MX products, we're likely to see people migrating to other tools.
- Awesome power lies in the ability to integrate code bits and graphics with Dreamweaver and Flash from Fireworks MX.
- This book demystifies the program's awesome power.
- The highest gift that you can give is knowledge. Share the joy by ushering people to use this amazing tool.

Who This Book Is For

Fireworks MX Fundamentals is for beginning users. The language and exercises presented in this book meet you at your level. Clear and concise explanation and instruction make learning easier, and we throw in some of the most relevant and meaningful tutorials in town.

Who This Book Is Not For

Let's face it: You're not reading this book if you're already a Fireworks superexpert. You also don't want to read this book if you're a brand-new computer user.

How to Use This Book

Like me, this book is straightforward. Here's the method:

Want to learn about animation? Just jump to that chapter.

Want to learn the whole enchilada? Start at the beginning and read until the end (preferably with bathroom breaks). You'll get it.

So now you're thinking, "Cut to the chase? I'm holding this big, fat book. How can this be cutting to the chase?" Ah ha. You just grasped the paradox of Fireworks. So simple, yet so in depth.

Overview

Part I of this book gets you up to speed, which is why it's called "Getting Up to Speed." In this part, you learn all the basics, including what Fireworks is, how to navigate the workspace, and you get a handle on using all the tools that are in the Tools panel.

Part II, "The Meat of the Matter," teaches you about vector drawing, how to control your color, fills and strokes, and the ins and outs of working with text. You also enter the wonderful world of live effects, scale the learning curve of bitmap painting, and master masking techniques.

Part III, "Getting It Out There," discusses, obviously, how to get your work out there. The chapters in this part include creating image maps, proper optimization techniques, and the oh-so-important intricacies of exporting your files to most every file format imaginable, plus two or three.

Part III also includes information about interactivity, behaviors, and automation. This is the part where, if you haven't already fallen in love with Fireworks, you become love struck. Up until now, you were only infatuated. After this part, you become a true disciple because you'll see beyond the cool features and tricks and realize the true driving power beneath what is too often seen as a mere graphical production-tool exterior. Wow.

Part IV, "Appendix," includes the chapter "What's on the CD-ROM." Be aware that certain projects may call for a particular font. The font being used is for illustration purposes only. You may substitute a different font, as the font selected is not the important part of the project.

The grand finale is an appendix that explains how to work with the CD-ROM. the book also includes an index, so if you're looking for a quick fix, you can locate a specific topic, quickly learn that topic, and get back to your project.

A Final Thought

Fireworks is really, we mean, *really* fun. It's *big fun*. So, put your tray tables up and your chairs in the upright position because we're taking off.

Part I

Getting Up
to Speed

Chapter 1

What's New and Different in Fireworks MX

What Is Fireworks?

Until now, Fireworks was unique among graphics applications because, not only was it specifically designed for creating and exporting web graphics, but it combines both types of computer graphics into one program.

Those of us who have been around the block a few times (like myself) and are familiar with tools such as Adobe Illustrator, Macromedia Freehand, PaintShop Pro, and Adobe Photoshop will be used to working with tools like those found in Fireworks. Fireworks combines the main aspects of both vector and bitmap (otherwise known as raster graphics) programs into one program.

Fireworks Is a Graphics Development Application

There are two types, or modes, of computer graphics: vector graphics and bitmap graphics. Computers can display graphics in either vector or bitmap format. Fireworks uses both types of graphics, which gives you amazing drawing, designing, and editing capabilities.

Each mode is radically different from the other. Vectors are mathematical equations that describe a line as it passes between two points in space. *Vector graphic* equations describe the length, direction, end point, and other attributes of a vector object.

Bitmap images are just what they sound like—a map, or grid, that's filled in with bits (color or not). The bits mesh to form an image, similar to a television. (Get dangerously close to a T.V. and all you see is colored dots.) We'll get to the details in a minute, so don't worry about the technical definitions just yet.

Some Background on Vector and Bitmap

Technically, what you see when you look at a computer screen is a bitmap. Both bitmap and vector graphics are translated into pixels to be viewed on a monitor. This process is known as *rasterizing*. Vector objects are actually never displayed as vectors, but as pixel representations that are rasterized to the screen. Even a high-quality PostScript printer is a rasterized, or rendering of, the vectors in the file. Vector graphics came of age for computers when CAD programs allowed users to plot coordinates on a grid and define the lines that pass through those coordinates as mathematical equations. It's similar to what we do in algebra and geometry.

Note

Pierre Bezier, a French scientist, developed a theory of how the lines, or paths, pass through plotted points and are controlled by invisible handles that are known as Bezier control handles. The process of drawing, or creating images with the vector tool set in Fireworks uses a technique that allows you to draw and modify the shape of objects by creating and moving a series of anchor points to connect vector lines and to control the shape of the lines with Bezier handles.

Vector graphics came of age commercially when Adobe Systems developed the PostScript printing language, which allowed printers to take advantage of the smaller and faster vector data, rendering it at high quality on high-resolution Raster Image Processors (RIPs). So, vector data is never really seen onscreen. It is rasterized and rendered onscreen.

Vector Art

Vector art is extremely scalable, whereas bitmap art isn't. Because the rendered pixels of vector objects in Fireworks are controlled by the position of the vector paths, what you see is mostly what you get.

For most people, this method of graphics creation makes creating web graphics fluid and natural. It is "always editable, all the time."

Traditionally, vector artwork is known as *drawing* and bitmap artwork is known as *painting*. Conventionally, there's been a separation between vector and bitmap programs. If you worked with programs such as FreeHand or Illustrator, you've worked with vectors. If you worked primarily with Photoshop or PaintShop Pro, you've worked in bitmap or pixel-based format.

Bitmap Graphics and Digital Paint

Images, such as photographs or other continuous-tone artwork that originates from either a scan or from a digital camera, are bitmap images. They are comprised of *pixels*.

The word *pixel* is a combination of "pix," meaning picture and "el," meaning element. So, a pixel is a picture element. A pixel is, in fact, the smallest image element that a bitmap image can contain. Each little square, or pixel, is a container that stores data. This information is basically a color or a representation of dark and light. As previously mentioned, when working with bitmap programs, you are creating a digital painting. When you paint in or on an image, you're not using vector equations; you're changing the color of, copying, modifying, adjusting, rearranging, and duplicating pixels.

To do this, you use digital paint and digital paintbrushes. This mode of computer graphics relies heavily on the use of alpha channels to render pixel transparency, or opacity. This technique is commonly referred to as *masking*, which is discussed in Chapter 9, "Masking."

Tool Behaviors and Shifting Modes

Although Fireworks is a powerful web-design program, it has an arsenal of excellent image-editing tools. Fireworks, in truth, is a vector-drawing program that creates natural-looking bitmap images because it rastorizes (or renders) your vector art to the screen as you create it with the vector tools. This is advantageous for all web designers.

As previously mentioned, Fireworks is both a vector and a bitmap-editing program. For this reason, Fireworks offers two awesome sets of tools: One set allows you to work in vector mode, and the other set is for working in bitmap mode.

Although Fireworks offers two sets of tools, Fireworks also contains some shared tools whose functions differ, depending on in which tool set you are currently working. When you are working with the Fireworks vector tools, you can tell Fireworks to change to bitmap mode by selecting and using a bitmap-editing tool. When you do this, Fireworks automatically shifts over to bitmap mode. Then, when you pick a vector-editing tool and begin working, the program automatically shifts back into vector mode. Sometimes, choosing a tool from the mode in which you are *not* working generates a mode-shift warning. The warning alerts you that the option you are selecting requires Fireworks to shift modes. This is helpful in case you accidentally choose the wrong tool. If this is the case, you can click Cancel and remain in the current mode.

You can also convert vector images into bitmaps within Fireworks. You cannot, however, do the opposite.

Although more aspects of working with bitmaps are covered in Chapter 8, "Working with Bitmaps," you must understand one more distinction about how bitmaps work in Fireworks: Bitmaps act like objects when you are in vector mode.

What Is a Fireworks Object?

In Fireworks terms, an *object* is a generic term for any individual entity, be it a bitmap image, a text element, a path, a composite path, a group, a mask group, and so on. This means that any object can be selected with the Pointer tool and then transformed in many ways. It can be moved, scaled, skewed, rotated, or flipped. To further enhance your art, you can also apply customizable effects to it.

Fireworks Is a Web-Site Production Application

Fireworks is a special tool in the process of web-site development. In terms of file size and web-page download time, Fireworks is an excellent resource for the creation of multiple file formats with optimal compression. But that's just the beginning. Using the Fireworks Export tools (described in Chapter 14, "Exporting"), right along with your web graphics, you can also create the HTML, JavaScript, and XHTML that you need to display those images as static or interactive web pages. Although complete upon export, these pages can also be opened in other production applications for further development. In particular, the tight integration between Fireworks and other Macromedia programs, such as Dreamweaver and Homesite, allows for easy editing back and forth until you create the perfect page.

What's New in Fireworks MX?

Fireworks MX is the latest incarnation in the Fireworks series. In the course of creating this version, the Macromedia Fireworks development team did scads and scads of research. They spoke to designers, production artists, and new users. A great deal of care was taken to understand what users need to make Fireworks approachable, creative, and interactive. This means that Fireworks strives to provide professionals, new developers, and designers with an environment that's easy to learn and use.

This section provides an overview of the new and brilliant features that make Fireworks MX so great. For in-depth exploration of these features and how they work in conjunction with the rest of the Fireworks package, see the appropriate chapters. The new features, the redesign, and the increased usability of existing features and processes render Fireworks a more creative and fluid application. For designers, the new tools improve your experience in designing graphics, user interface, and animation. For web developers and site producers, Fireworks has evolved into a powerful tool for slicing the work of designers from any standard design application, compressing those images and creating the HTML code that you need to display those images, and the JavaScript to make them interactive. Additionally, new export features allow for easier integration with other applications for further development.

The Macromedia Fireworks development team targeted enhancements in four areas:

- Workspace and workflow
- Graphic development
- Code creation
- Integration with other applications

A Flexible and Intuitive Workspace

Macromedia has developed Fireworks MX to be powerful enough to cover the needs of the experienced professional designer, yet accessible enough that a novice can design and build an entire web site. An in-depth description of how to use these new workflow tools are peppered throughout this book, where they are related to the task at hand. Figure 1.1 shows the Fireworks MX workspace.

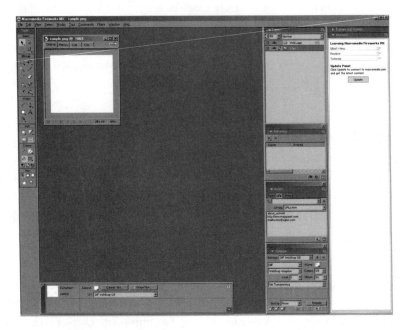

Figure 1.1   The Fireworks MX workspace.

The Answers Panel

First and foremost, Macromedia has made it easier to get help. The Answers panel, new to Fireworks MX, Dreamweaver MX, and Flash MX, is a link to help-related materials on the web. When you are connected to the Internet, you can click the Update button in the workspace and download the latest information from Macromedia, or search online help databases, such as TechNotes, for documentation.

Improved Panel Management

Now you can make a cleaner, less distracting workspace by grouping your panels. After they're grouped, the panels can be collpased so that only the panel group title bar is visible, docked in one of the panel docking areas, or attached anywhere you want.

The Divided Toolbox

The toolbox is clearly divided into tool types. In fact, when you work in Fireworks now, you don't have to consciously think to switch modes. Formerly, a set of tools was used in vector mode, and another set of tools was used in bitmap mode. Now, mode switching is invisible. If you are a new Fireworks user, this change is transparent to you, but old users can see that, when you create art with either the bitmap tools or the vector tools, you see virtually no change to your Document window—no more bold, highlighted outline. The new toolbar is divided into the select tools, the bitmap tools, the vector tools, and web tools, colors, and view. This change makes Fireworks basically modeless to its users.

Variable Zooming

To determine a precise degree of magnification, you can now drag the Magnify tool from the Tools panel. The level of magnification can then be seen and adjusted in the Set Magnification text box at the bottom of the document.

Spell-Checker

Fireworks MX has a built-in spell-checker that searches every text block in your document. When it finds a word that it doesn't recognize, the spell-checker offers suggestions for correcting it or allows you to add it to your dictionary.

More Interactivity

The new version of Fireworks is more interactive. The most amazing new interactive feature is the Reconstitute Tables feature. It works like this: Say that your HTML author was vaporized by aliens and you don't know how she created some of the old HTML files in your archive. Well, you can take an HTML file that has working links to its images, perhaps in an image file, and open HTML in Fireworks. This means that, in a sense, Fireworks turns an HTML file into a PNG file, which gives you the ability to see all the table structures as slices and slice guides. It also allows you to redesign and adjust the way that the page is written by adjusting the position of slices.

Finally, even interactive features, such as image rollovers, are imported as JavaScript behaviors attached to the correct slices. (For more informtion, see Chapter 11, "Working with Behaviors.") That's truly amazing!

Slice Table Layout

You can easily adjust pages that have already been sliced, or imported (see Chapter 11), simply by dragging the slice guides. All related slices are automatically resided, added, or deleted.

Create Panels and Dialog Boxes

The ultimate in workspace flexibility is the ability to actually create elements for the workspace itself. Now, hard-core developers can create their own JavaScript commands using Macromedia Flash MX components and ActionScript to make Fireworks MX panels and dialog boxes. Non-hard-core users can also take advantage of this new feature by using commands created by other users in the online exchange community. Additionally, Fireworks MX ships with several of these commands in the Commands menu.

Additional Workspace Enhancements

Additional approachability features include *smart window maximizing*, which allows you to resize your window without having your document window covered by panels.

On a Mac, there's now the option for recent files. New browse buttons are next to URL fields, whereas in the previous version of Fireworks, there were only file folders.

There is now auto-scrolling in the Layers panel, which means that you can click and drag a layer and not have to drop it there and rescroll. When you move past what you are currently viewing, the Layers panel scrolls automatically.

You can also make use of the Extensions Manager menu item.

The Property Inspector

The new Property Inspector minimizes the number of onscreen panels. It includes and displays options for fill, stroke, effect, object, info, and other various tool options. Similar tools that originally appeared in two different modes, such as the knife and eraser, have been separated into their own, specific tool—the eraser for bitmap and the knife for vector mode.

The seamless switching of tool modes is done by dropping your current selection as you switch tools instead of when you use a tool. When you choose a tool from the vector tools while you have been drawing with bitmap, the vector becomes deselected; when you switch back to a bitmap tool, the vector automatically becomes deselected.

Bitmap tools do not have selection properties. The Effects panel is also now eliminated and has become a button for launching effects properties from the Property Inspector. In the Property Inspector, you can find the following:

- Tool options
- Text properties
- Button properties

Creative Features

When you create a new bitmap through a copy and paste, the new bitmap pastes into its own layer instead of into the same layer (as it previously did). Now, marquee selections move between objects. Selections can be retained and used on another bitmap layer. The new seamless mode-switching feature allows you to move between modes without exiting or reentering modes. This makes the design experience more fluid. A new merge-down feature allows you to move objects on separate layers into one layer.

Handy Code Generation on Export

Fireworks has become a tool for production and design. The following enhancements have enabled developers to generate code. In particular, the latest version of Fireworks makes for easy manipulation of complex interactivity including four-state buttons, navigational bars, and pop-up menus. To learn how to specify the format of this code, and for an introduction to HTML itself, refer to Chapter 14 "Exporting." For in-depth instruction on assigning interactivity to web objects, see Chapter 11 "Working with Behaviors."

Instance-Level Properties on Buttons

Another great improvement is *instance-level button properties*. This means that, within the instance, sublevel properties can be altered, such as the name on a button, without prompting the Change Text in Other Instances dialog box. The pop-up menu now also has horizontal pop-up menus; pop-up menu positioning is relative to the button that you create it for as opposed to the browser window. The `table` attributes of pop-up menus are now customizable, and editing pop-up menu entries is simplified and redesigned. Plus, submenu positioning is added.

The Nav Bar Builder

Fireworks MX contains a *Nav Bar Builder* to automate the process of building navigation bars out of button symbols. You can select an instance of a button symbol, and choose the number of copies to add to the bar, vertical or horizontal orientation and spacing, and associated actions and URLs.

The Pop-Up Menu Editor

Because pop-up menus have become popular among Fireworks users, the Macromedia Fireworks development team expanded this feature to greatly increase your options. Now you can select alignment, border characteristics, cell spacing and size, and placement in the document relative to the trigger object.

The Data-Driven Graphics Wizard

To generate mulitple documents from your source file, each with its own text, image, hotspot and slice variables, you can now use the data-driven Graphics Wizard. This enhancement is particularly helpful for new users.

Smoother Transfer of Files Between Applications

In both design and development, many users want to move files back and forth, into additional applications. The Macromedia Fireworks team has responded to this tendency by creating easy integration with other applications, including non-Macromedia programs.

The Quick Export Button

The Quick Export button, located conveniently in the workspace, allows you to simplify your exporting process. When you click this button, you are presented with a menu that you can choose from—Dreamweaver, Flash, Director, and so on—that allows you to select specific properties appropriate to the desired target application.

XHTML

Developers wanting to meet the latest W3-complaint XHTML can now select to export in this format rather than Fireworks HTML. This code can also be exported for editing in Dreamweaver, Homesite, and other web editors.

Round-Trip Development: Working with Other Software

You can now write directly onscreen by using the onscreen text feature, which also includes UTF8 font encoding. This feature allows XHTML text to be exported from Fireworks to Dreamweaver and exports HTML to GoLive and FrontPage. When Dreamweaver sees XHTML code, it sends back XHTML code to Fireworks for updates, changes, and fixes, and resends the correct code to Dreamweaver when doing round-trip edits between Fireworks and Dreamweaver. Note that there is also Windows XP and Mac OS X support.

FrontPage

A new feature allows Fireworks to install round-trip table editing for FrontPage. Flyout tools now have labels and shortcut keys and, within the Button editor, you can find a function to insert clip art so that you can choose from many existing clip-art buttons. The clip-art buttons are cool for non-designers because they can quickly create great-looking pages without creating their own buttons or artwork.

Photoshop

Fireworks MX now has Photoshop text support, which means that you have round-trip Photoshop text. When Photoshop text is saved, a cache of the text is saved in the file. Fireworks can open text objects that are created in Photoshop and keep them editable. It also saves its own bitmap cache for text that opens in Photoshop, and allows for files to go from a PC to a Mac and vice versa. This makes it easy for people to share files without turning text to paths.

Dreamweaver

With the release of Dreamweaver MX, you find several improvements, including those made to masking features. Now, the Mask icon indicates black for hiding objects and white for revealing objects instead of the other way around. A variable zoom feature lets you zoom in to the exact percentage that you want, instead of snapping to the zoom presets. Image placeholders, like a for-position-only object, allows you to mock up an idea in Dreamweaver where a graphic is needed and, by placing this image placeholder and clicking it, you can export it into Fireworks, where you can design an image at the exact size. Now, there is slice-level HTML cell properties, which means any changes that you make to your table from Fireworks into Dreamweaver, and any changes that you make inside of the TD tag, are maintained when you edit the table into Fireworks and then return to Dreamweaver.

Another Dreamweaver update that impacts Fireworks is *automatic checkout*. Automatic checkout allows graphics to be fixed without re-exporting the entire batch. Fireworks now sports gradient transparency that allows gradient areas to be added to the color ramp, which is similar to the way a new color is added to the ramp (by using a gradient transparency well). The new version of Fireworks opens Freehand 10 files. There is also a new control for paragraph spacing within the text editor. A new tool for blur and sharpen is now in the bitmap tools area, and there is also text-image caching. Previously, Fireworks did not recognize or correctly work with Photoshop 6 plug-ins. Photoshop 6 plug-ins no longer appear as a choice, as opposed to appearing and not working. You can now set a choice of pixel versus percentage letting when you design type.

Another feature, called *Spacebar Move While Dragging*, allows you to click and drag a marquee selection with the bitmap tools while holding the spacebar to reposition the marquee and then removing your finger from the spacebar to continue drawing the marquee. Some style enhancements have been added, including gradient direction of text and the ability to save more detailed text styles.

At the bottom of the Tools panel, the addition to view buttons in the toolbar has been made. You can now look at your document with the menus turned off in a gray or black mat. The import of Photoshop-layered files has also been improved to better support Photoshop layer groups.

Fireworks now maintains the appearance of all text in a document regardless of fonts installed on the current system. *Cross-Platform Font Caching* now makes it easy to share files among work groups and clients without worrying about cross-platform font issues.

Summary

Fireworks MX represents a great advance in the areas of design and web-site creation. With tools that enhance the development of images in multiple formats, and settings to generate code for optimal viewing on the Web, all in an easy-to-use workspace, users no longer need to work in multiple applications. However, elaborate integration with Macromedia and non-Macromedia applications alike means that you can choose to develop your project further for ulitimate control. This book attempts to maximize this experience, whether you are a novice Fireworks user or a faithful fan looking to make the most of the Fireworks MX enhancements.

Chapter 2

Interface, Tools, and Workspace Overview

When you enter the Fireworks MX workspace for the first time, you are presented with its elegant new interface. This new look is not only better organized, but it is also consistent with the other applications in the Macromedia Studio MX.

Fireworks MX is now easier to use, and it has more power than before. This makes it easier for you to create gorgeous graphics and gives you increased power to build your web site's interactivity. Fireworks MX is for anyone who needs to develop or work with graphics-rich, interactive web pages. It is the brilliant coding behind the interface of Fireworks MX that allows you to do this whether or not you have coding and JavaScript knowledge. Hats off to the geniuses at Macromedia.

Upon your first launch of Fireworks MX, you are greeted by the Welcome screen at the center of the workspace (see Figure 2.1). The Fireworks menu and the Tools panel are nested at the left the Property Inspector, and numerous control panels are nested on the right.

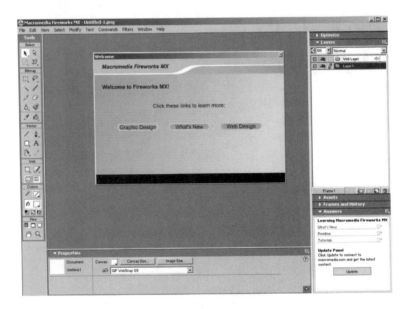

Figure 2.1   The new Fireworks MX interface.

Note

On the Windows platform, the Fireworks interface inherits the colors currently selected in the appearance settings. Your screen probably looks a bit different because it reflects your particular settings.

On the Windows platform, the main interface window (or program window) of Fireworks contains an additional two toolbars that you can open and dock. These are the main toolbar and the modify toolbar. These toolbars give you single-click ability to four of the commonly used types of image modifications. (See Figure 2.2.)

Figure 2.2   Windows' main and modify toolbars. The main toolbar buttons, from left to right: New, Open, Save, Import, Export, Print, Undo, Redo, Cut, Copy, and Paste. The Modify toolbar buttons, from left to right: Group, Ungroup, Join, Split, Bring to Front, Bring Forward, Send Backward, Send to Back, Align, Rotate (90 degrees CW and CCW), and Flip (horizontal and vertical).

Getting Started with the Welcome Panel

You can dive into the Welcome panel and immediately start learning Fireworks by choosing one of the three tutorial options: Graphic Design, What's New, and Web Design.

If you're new to creating graphics in Fireworks, you might want to check out the Graphic Design tutorial. It shows you around Fireworks MX and gets you started working in this terrific program.

In What's New, you can find out about all the features of Fireworks MX. This tutorial contains a great deal of exciting information about the new MX interface for both new users and veterans.

The Web Design tutorial allows you to create a web page with interactive buttons and pop-up menus, which you can then optimize and export for the web. This tutorial reveals the foundation of the power behind the Fireworks Web Design process flow.

After you close the Welcome panel, you can always access it by choosing Help, Welcome from the Fireworks menu at the top of the screen.

The New Property Inspector

The Property Inspector and the Multitab panel groups modify and adjust various aspects of bitmap and vector artwork created in Fireworks.

The new Property Inspector displays options and information that change according to the tool or object that's currently selected. In a sense, this is the new helm of the Fireworks MX command and control center.

The Options Panel Is No More

Depending on the tool that you are using, the Property Inspector allows you to see and set different properties for the way you want your tools to work. First and foremost, it tells you what you have selected. This is one of the most important tools for troubleshooting problems in Fireworks.

The Property Inspector reflects the current attributes of the selected object and allows you to interact with it:

- **Path**—Displayed when an ungrouped vector object is selected (see Figure 2.3). Buttons to choose stroke placement (how the selected brush pixels are to be rendered to the path) are available from the Stroke Color box, which reveals the Color pop-up window from this panel, as well as fill over stroke (which makes the fill overlap the inside part of the stroke around the filled object). (The stroke placement settings work only for closed paths.)

Figure 2.3   The Property Inspector with Path properties displayed.

- **Rectangle**—When a rectangle object is selected, the roundness setting is available for changing rectangle corners (see Figure 2.4). Rectangles are grouped objects. Ungroup the rectangle to use the Freeform or Reshape Area tools on the rectangle.

Figure 2.4   The Property Inspector with Rectangle properties displayed.

- **Text**—When text is selected, the Property Inspector displays all the typographical controls that you would normally see in a professional text-editing program, such as kerning, leading, paragraph indent, spacing, and various alignment controls. From here, you can also select from four anti-aliasing settings.

Figure 2.5   The Property Inspector with Text properties displayed.

- **Text on a Path**—This panel is identical to the Text properties, but you can also set and offset along the path value in pixels.
- **Bitmap**—When bitmapped objects are selected, the Property Inspector indicates that the object is indeed a bitmap object (see Figure 2.6).

Figure 2.6   The Property Inspector with Bitmap properties displayed.

- **Bitmap Mask and Vector Mask**—When an object with a bitmap mask is selected, you can choose to apply the mask using its alpha channel or its actual appearance converted to grayscale (see Figure 2.7).

  When an object with a vector mask is selected, you can select to apply the mask using the grayscale appearance of the mask object or the path outline. (This is commonly known as a *clipping path*).

Figure 2.7   The Property Inspector with Mask properties displayed.

- **Slice**—When a slice is selected, the Property Inspector enables you to select whether the contents of the exported table cell will be an image or HTML text. You can also select from preset optimization settings; set a URL link, Alt tag, and target; set the slice's overlay color; and name the image(s) that will be exported from that slice (see Figure 2.8). Hotspots can be converted to slices, but slices cannot be converted to hotspots. If you select a slice and choose Insert, Hotspot, a slice still remains under the hotspot. On the other hand, if you select a hotspot and choose Insert, Slice, the hotspot is replaced by a slice of the same shape as the hotspot.

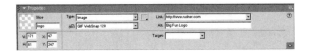

Figure 2.8   The Property Inspector with Slice properties displayed.

- **Hotspot**—You can set the shape for the hotspot to rectangle, oval, or polygon (see Figure 2.9), and assign a URL link, Alt tag, and target information.

Figure 2.9   The Property Inspector with Hotspot properties displayed.

- **Symbols**—For each of the three symbol types, you can set the following by using the Property Inspector:
  - **Graphic Symbol**—Name, Size, Position, Transparency, and Effect (see Figure 2.10).

Figure 2.10   The Property Inspector with Graphic Symbol properties displayed.

  - **Button Symbol**—Size, Name, Position, Text, Export options, Link, Alt, Target, Effects, and Show Down on Load (see Figure 2.11).

Figure 2.11   The Property Inspector with Button Symbol properties displayed.

  - **Animation Symbol**—Size, Name, Position, Frames, Scaling, Opacity, and Rotation (see Figure 2.12).

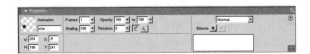

Figure 2.12   The Property Inspector with Animation Symbol properties displayed.

Tool Behavior

You can set the behavior of your tools with the options found in the Property Inspector. Each specific tool has setting that you can modify in Fireworks to meet your needs. (We cover each tool's options and behaviors where they apply throughout the exercises in each chapter.)

The Effects Panel Is No More

In Fireworks MX, the Effects panel has merged into the Property Inspector (see Figure 2.13).

Figure 2.13   The Property Inspector with Effects properties displayed.

When I first started doing multimedia and interactive design, it took many steps to make the kinds of things that you can make with the Effect panel. The effects that you apply are considered "live." This means that you can update, turn on, turn off, apply, reapply, and adjust the values of your effects immediately and infinitely because the effects are being rendered and stored in Fireworks.

You can apply an effect to the currently selected object by choosing an effect from the Add Effects button on the Property Inspector. After the effect is applied to the selection, it appears in the active list with a check by it in the Effects panel. You can turn the check on and off to toggle the effect.

A small blue circle with a white letter "i" appears in the next column in the Effects panel. Clicking this icon enables you to modify the settings of a particular effect. Each effect has its own pop-up edit window with which to modify its particular settings. After you create a combination of settings that you like, Fireworks allows you to save them as a style and reuse them in your current project (or in another project).

The Fill Panel Is No More

The Property Inspector now contains the controls for setting and creating fills in Fireworks MX. You can do much more than just fill objects with a solid color here. You can also control the application of gradients, patterns, web dither, intensity, texture, transparency, and the object's edge feather. Seven main controls are found in the Fill panel:

- **Fill Category**—Enables you to set the fill to None, Solid, Web Dither, and Pattern, as well as Gradient options (see Figure 2.14). The Edit button lets users access the Gradient color ramp and set colors for the gradient, as well as add transparency to the ramp (not just texture transparency, but alpha).

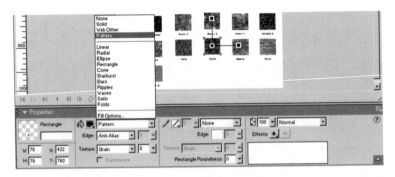

Figure 2.14   The Property Inspector with Fill properties and Fill Category displayed.

- **Pattern or Gradient Color Scheme**—After a pattern or gradient option is selected, a second option list appears with another level of modifications to apply to those options.
- **Fill Edge**—The edge of the object itself can be set to any of theses three options: Hard, Anti-Alias, and Feathered.
- **Degree of Feathering**—Specifies the amount of feather with slider or enter a numeric value into the text box.
- **Fill Texture**—Includes the same options as the Stroke panel.
- **Degree of Texture**—Controls the transparency and opacity of the selected texture.
- **Transparency of Texture**—When the transparency check box is clicked on, the lighter parts of the texture become transparent.

You can find out more about all these options in Chapter 5, "Working with Color Fills and Strokes."

The Stroke Panel Is No More

The Property Inspector now contains the controls for setting and creating strokes in Fireworks MX (see Figure 2.15).

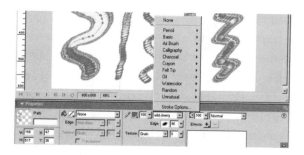

Figure 2.15 The Property Inspector with Stroke properties and Stroke Category displayed.

What is traditionally known as an outline around a vector object is referred to as a *stroke* in Fireworks. The stroke controls on the Property Inspector offer such amazing effects that it transcends what we think a stroke can do. Fireworks contains an array of preset stroke settings that you can access through the Stroke panel. This is also the place where you can modify existing settings and save custom settings for strokes. This is one of the features that blurs the line between vectors and bitmaps in that the strokes in Fireworks render automatically to screen even though they appear to be painted brushstrokes (hence, the term *stroke* instead of *path*).

There are 12 main categories of strokes in the Stroke Name pop-up control on the Property Inspector: None, Pencil, Basic, Air Brush, Calligraphy, Charcoal, Crayon, Felt Tip, Oil, Water Color, Random, and Unnatural. Within each category are these additional settings:

- **Stroke Color**—Click the Color box to select your color preference or to choose No Stroke.

- **Stroke Edge**—Controls the softness or hardness of a given selected stroke. Sliding the slider from bottom to top increases the softness, and sliding the slider from top to bottom makes the stroke edge harder.

- **Stroke Size**—Controls the value of the stroke from 1 to 100 pixels.

- **Stroke Texture**—You can add 26 different stroke textures to customize your stroke. Other textures can be added to enhance your design capabilities in Fireworks.

- **Degree of Stroke Texture**—Alters the degree or opacity that the stroke texture is applied to the stroke.

Repositioning the Property Inspector

If you like, you can tear the Property Inspector from its docked position and place it elsewhere on your screen. To do this, just click and drag on its title bar and move it to where you want. To return the Property Inspector to its original location, drag the side bar to the bottom of the screen (Windows only). When you drag a panel or Inspector into a docking area, and the panel comes over a dockable area of the user interface, you see a light blue highlight around the area in which the panel is about to dock.

Clicking the expander arrow in the lower-right corner lets you display the Property Inspector at half its height and view two rows of properties (see Figure 2.16). At full height, it displays four rows of properties. You can also fully collapse it to maximize your workspace.

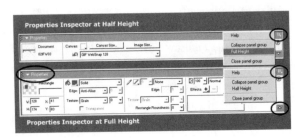

Figure 2.16   The Property Inspector title bar with the gripper, the expander arrows circled, and the Options menu opened.

If you close the Property Inspector, you can open it by choosing Window, Properties from the main menu.

Panels and Panel Groups

The new panel management system allows you the ability to place panels in groups and then collapse the groups. In this way, only the panel group title bar is visible until you need to use the panels. You can dock the panel groups in the panel docking area to organize your workspace, and you can drag groups or individual panels anywhere in the workspace.

Now we'll look at default set of panels docked to the right of the work area. We'll go over them from top to bottom.

The Optimize Panel

You use the Optimize panel's powerful features to make your graphics clean and download-friendly (see Figure 2.17). The Optimize panel's settings contain file format including JPEG, GIF, PNG, and a range of other settings.

The optimization process allows you to set image file sizes so they load quickly when viewed on the web. The Optimize panel can be used while comparing the quality of the graphics in the Preview, 2-Up, or 4-Up view in the workspace.

Figure 2.17
The Optimize panel.

The Layers Panel

The Layers panel is the command and control center for your artwork objects in Fireworks (see Figure 2.18). It is easy to create many objects within layers quickly. As you create each object—whether it is a rectangle, circle, complex shape, piece of type, or bitmap—they are created inside the current layer. Fortunately, layers behave like folders in the Finder when you view them as a list (Macintosh), or they behave like the left-side hierarchical layout in Windows Explorer. Within these folders, you can organize different elements of your artwork. This comes in handy when you are making complex layouts within Fireworks, or even when you're making specialty logos or artwork for animations. Each layer has its own name, and each object within each layer can also have its own name. Plus, each object contains a thumbnail version of that object.

With the Layer panel's controls, you can get a handle on managing complex artwork. The Layer panel's controls allow you expand and collapse layers, which are similar to folders; show and hide layers; lock and unlock layers; and create, delete, duplicate, and add masks to layers. The new Bitmap Image button creates an empty bitmap object within a layer.

The Layers panel also contains the Layers panel's Options menu, which can be activated by clicking the arrow at the top right. It contains the following commands: New Image, New Layer, Duplicate Layer, Share This Layer, Single Layer Editing, Delete Layer, Hide All, Show All, Lock All, Unlock All, Add Mask, Edit Mask, Disable Mask, Delete Mask, and Thumbnail Options.

Figure 2.18
The Layers panel.

The Assets Panel

Within the Assets panel, there are three other panels—Styles, Symbols, and URLs:

Yet another amazing bell (or is it whistle?) in Fireworks, the Styles panel is an array of attributes that you can apply to any object (see Figure 2.19). This group of styles presets is displayed as large graphic buttons and text within the Styles panel. You can compose a series of fills, strokes, gradients, effects, and the like to a selected object, and you can save these properties as a style. You can give it a name and reuse it at any time in any file. This makes it easy to apply a consistent look and feel across objects within your web project.

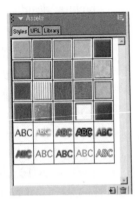

Figure 2.19
The Assets panel with the Styles panel displayed.

The Styles panel pop-up menu commands are New Style, Edit Style, Delete Styles, Import Styles, Export Styles, Reset Styles, and Large Icon.

The Library Panel

You can create and save objects by using the Library panel (see Figure 2.20). These items are known as *symbols*. The three types of symbols are Graphic, Button, and Animation. Each type has its own unique characteristics for its specific use.

Symbols are used when you want to reuse a graphic element. You can place instances in multiple Fireworks documents and keep the association with the orignal symbol. Symbols are great for creating buttons and animating objects across multiple frames. Symbols can be handy for elements, such as logos or buttons, that appear or reappear throughout a web site's pages.

Figure 2.20
The Assets panel with the Library panel displayed.

The Library panel's Options pop-up menu commands include New Symbol, Duplicate, Delete, Edit Symbol, Properties, Select Unused Items, Update, Play, Import Symbols, and Export Symbols.

The URL Panel

You guessed it! URLs are stored in the URL panel (see Figure 2.21). *URL* (short for Uniform Resource Locator), is the address of a specific page or file on the Internet. You use the URL panel to assign a URL to a slice. This allows users to click the element and go to the web address that you assigned.

You can create groups of URLs in libraries with the URL panel. You can save your URL libraries for use on multiple projects. This is particularly handy when you have an extremely long URL.

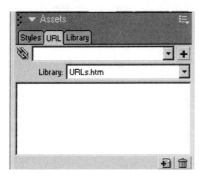

Figure 2.21   The Assets panel with the URL panel displayed.

The Frames Panel

When you are first working with Fireworks, it can be easy to confuse the functions of layers and frames. Frames have some similarities to layers, but they actually have two main functions that make them different from layers.

In Fireworks, frames correspond to frames in an animation. You use the Frames panel (see Figure 2.22) to set up animations and rollovers. When you think about it, rollovers are really manually triggered animations. The Frames panel lets you create and control the frames of your animation and the states of rollovers.

The Frames panel's Options menu commands include Add Frames, Duplicate Frame, Delete Frame, Copy to Frame, Distribute to Frames, Auto Crop, Auto Difference, and Properties.

Figure 2.22
The Frames panel.

The History Panel

This is the magical, mystical, multiple Undo command in Fireworks (see Figure 2.23). The History panel contains a sliding pointer, known as the *Undo Marker*, that you can drag up to your preceding steps and roll back time. As you work, the History panel tracks your actions and allows you to step back through them.

You can set the number of undo steps up to 1,009, but you'd better have the memory and scratch disk space to handle it. The mystical part of the History panel is that it allows you to save and replay your steps as commands. This feature automates Fireworks and helps you reduce tedious tasks.

The History panel's commands include Replay Selected Steps, Copy Steps, Save as Command, and Clear History. When you save your document, its history is cleared.

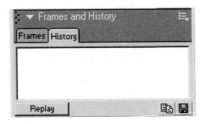

Figure 2.23   The History panel.

The Answers Panel

The Answers panel is a central location where you can find tutorials, TechNotes, and the most up-to-date information about Fireworks all in one place (see Figure 2.24). This dynamic panel updates with just the click of a button, dowloading you the latest updates and information about Fireworks directly from Macromedia.

Figure 2.24   The Answers panel.

More Panels, More Control

You can select, access, use, and dock several other panels that are located in the Window menu. These panels are discussed in this section.

The Color Mixer Panel

The Color Mixer panel offers a more loose and spontaneous way for web designers to work with color in Fireworks (see Figure 2.25). This color mixer allows you to select the color mode with which you're most familiar, and allows you to choose modes that serve print, TV, and multimedia design well, not only web imagery.

Figure 2.25   The Color Mixer panel.

You can select color fill and stroke within the Color Mixer panel by clicking the color boxes next to the pencil and paint bucket. The Color Mixer panel sports a color ramp that provides the full-spectrum preview color model, plus one more way to mix colors—color-component sliders for RGB, hexadecimal, CMY and HSB, and grayscale.

The Color Mixer panel contains a default color button for restoring your chosen preset stroke and fill color. It also contains the Swap Color button. These items also appear on the Tools panel. You can set both fill and stroke colors to None.

The Swatches Panel

In Fireworks, the Swatches panel is a powerful little arsenal of color tools (see Figure 2.26). This panel allows you to view palettes by type, sort palettes, add colors, remove colors, change and recall custom palettes, and access the current palette and export palettes. The Swatches panel contains nine powerful commands that enable you to manage sets of colors effectively: Add Swatches, Replace Swatches, Save Swatches, Clear Swatches, Macintosh System, Windows Systems, Grayscale, Current Export Palette, and Sort By Color. This panel gives the designer precise control over choosing specific colors from specific palettes.

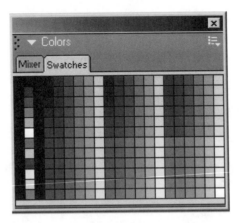

Figure 2.26   The Swatches panel.

The Info Panel

The Info panel is not a natural tool for some people to get used to, but after you give it a try, it's hard to give up. The Info panel is a feedback panel that offers you information on an object's size or position while you're creating it (see Figure 2.27). You can also determine the cursor location and the color value of any object on the canvas in any of the modes specified in the Options menu.

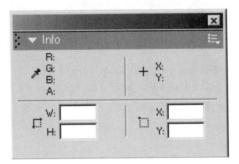

Figure 2.27   The Info panel.

You can also select objects and type in numeric values and, therefore, change the width, height, and x and y coordinates of your objects precisely. The Info panel enables you to alter and set the following options: Width, Height, X and Y Coordinates, Rotation, Scaling, and Distortion.

You can do this by selecting and object, typing in the fields of the Info panel, and pressing the Enter key.

The Info panel also has the following Options pop-up menu commands for altering the color model and measurement system from the Info panel's pop-up menu. These options are Hexadecimal, RGB, CMY, HSB, Pixels, Inches, Centimeters, and Scale Attributes.

The Behaviors Panel

Yet another shining jewel in the crown of Fireworks is the Behaviors panel (see Figure 2.28). It is what makes your Fireworks web pages and objects loop the loop. You apply behaviors to slices, hotspots, and buttons by using the Behaviors panel. You cannot, however, apply a behavior directly to an image. The JavaScript code is exported out along with your Fireworks HTML and your graphics. This code enables interactive web behaviors, including rollovers, swap images, setting pop-up menus, setting the text of a status bar, and setting the Navigation Bar.

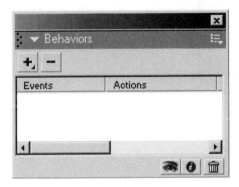

Figure 2.28   The Behaviors panel.

To set up a behavior with the Behaviors panel, you need a web object, such as a hotspot slice or a button. After the web object is selected, assign a behavior by choosing the Add Behavior button from the Behaviors panel.

Fireworks contains five main groups of behaviors, including Simple Roll-Over, Swap Image, Set Navigation Bar Image, Set Pop-up Menu, and Set Text of Status Bar. You can remove a behavior by selecting it and choosing the Remove Behavior button (the minus sign) from the Behaviors panel. You can also select a behavior and delete it with the Delete key or all the behaviors at once from a web object.

The Behaviors panel's pop-up menu commands are Edit, Delete, Delete All, Show All, and Ungroup.

The Project Log Panel

Here is where Fireworks' automation and power can really pack a punch. The Project Log panel contains detailed information on each change that takes place in your document (see Figure 2.29). It can also make it easy for you to open a group of files by using the Add Files to Log command and then enables you to make changes easily and then re-export them with the settings they were previously using.

The Project Log's Options menu commands are Export Again, Add Files to Log, Clear Selection, and Clear All.

Figure 2.29 The Project panel.

The Find and Replace Panel

The Find and Replace panel allows you to search for and replace elements, including making text changes, font, color, and URL (see Figure 2.30). The Find and Replace panel can search within the current working document or multiple files. As you work, Fireworks tracks and stores a log of the changes that you make in the Project Log panel.

Note

Find and Replace works only in Fireworks PNG files or in files that contain vector objects, such as FreeHand, Illustrator, and uncompressed CorelDRAW files.

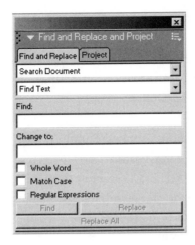

Figure 2.30   The Find and Replace panel.

The Align Panel

The Align panel in Fireworks is new, unique, and special (see Figure 2.31). Actually, it is an example of a Flash movie used as a panel. Using Flash, you can now create SWF movies that contain JavaScript code. These amazing movies can be used as Fireworks commands that are accessible from the Commands menu. This panel was developed by Kleanthis Econemu. You can find more of his commands at www.projectfireworks.com.

Figure 2.31   The Align panel.

Customizing Panels

When you first start working with a program that has as many panels as Fireworks, it can seem overwhelming. After you get the hang of how to use them and rearrange their placement, however, you learn to love the interchangeability with which you can customize your workspace in Fireworks.

Grouping and Ungrouping Docked Panels

Grouping and ungrouping docked panels is easy. To remove a panel from its group, simply click the tab of a panel and drag it from its current group. To add or move a panel between groups, drag it to the edge of the target panel until you see the heavy black line around the target panel. When you see the heavy black line, release the panel. The panel is then added to the panel group.

Panels can also snap to the edges of your document window or to the edges of other floating panels. This feature makes it easy to neatly arrange your floating panels.

Saving Panel Layouts

When I retouch photographs, I set up my work area with the Swatches, Colors, and Layers panels grouped and visible and all others hidden (see Figure 2.32).

Figure 2.32   My custom panel that's set for photo retouching.

You can save a panel layout as what's called a *Panel Layout Set*. This is useful for optimizing your screen real estate based on specific work tasks. The following steps show you how to do this:

1. Arrange your floating panels the way you like them for your general working environment or for specific tasks.

2. Choose the command Panel Layout.

   A JavaScript dialog box appears. (JavaScript is used by Fireworks to build commands.)

3. Enter the name for your new Panel Layout Set and click OK.

   This arrangement is saved as a new Panel Layout Set and is added to the command's Panel Layout Set submenu. In this way, you can rearrange your screen and then reset your screen to your different Panel Layout Set choices. You can use the keyboard shortcut settings to call your Panel Layout Set by using a simple keyboard stroke combination.

To reset your panels to one of the default sets, choose Commands, Panel Layout Sets, and choose the Panel Layout Set that you want to display.

Hiding and Showing Panels

Although it's great that panels are mobile and interchangeable in Fireworks, sometimes you just don't want to see them at all. The following list shows a few ways to hide the panels and tools:

- Choose View, Hide Panels to toggle the panels off and on.
- Use the official keyboard shortcut, F-4.
- Press the tab key to toggle panels on and off.
- Double-click the title bar on both Macintosh and Windows machines to hide and show all but the title bar of panels.

More Fireworks MX Interface Goodies

Now for a bit of the nitty-gritty details. I know how much you love pushing buttons, right? Well, here's the rundown of common Fireworks interface elements:

- **Tabs**—Tabs are handles for panels and reside at the top of every panel, just under the title bars (see Figure 2.33).

Figure 2.33   Panel tabs.

- **Pop-up menus**—Pop-up menus appear on panels that offer a number of different options for a particular preference (see Figure 2.34).

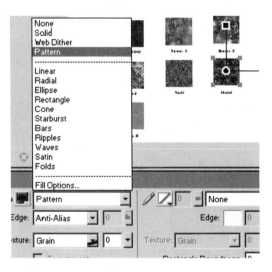

Figure 2.34   Pop-up menu.

Note

This is not to be confused with the JavaScript behavior "Set Pop-up Menu."

- **Help button**—When you click the Help button on floating
  panels, the Fireworks Help System launches and opens a
  page that describes how to use the features on the currently
  selected panel (see Figure 2.35).

Figure 2.35
The Help button.

- **Check boxes**—You can enable and disable options by clicking on and clicking off the check boxes (see Figure 2.36).

Figure 2.36   The Checkbox button.

- **Numeric sliders**—Change numbers by clicking and dragging the arrow up and down (see Figure 2.37).

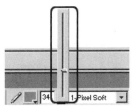

Figure 2.37   The numeric slider.

- **Color boxes**—Click directly on the Color box to bring up a pop-up window, which is known as the Color pop-up window, and choose a color (see Figure 2.38).

Figure 2.38   The Color box.

Select a new color by moving the cursor around within the window or by using the eyedropper cursor that appears when the Color pop-up window is open. Or access the system color picker by clicking the multicolored circle at the top right of the window, or type a hexadecimal color into the field at the top of the window. You can choose no color by clicking the box with the red line passing diagonally through it.

You can also click the Color Picker button to open the operating system's color palette. There is also an option for no color represented by a white square with a red line passing diagonally through it.

- **Text boxes**—As previously mentioned, you can enter values directly into the text boxes (see Figure 2.39). Always make sure that you press Enter to tell Fireworks to accept the input you type; otherwise, it won't be applied.

Figure 2.39   The Text Entry box.

- **Option lists**—To select an option out of the available choices, click the current panel's Options pop-up menu's arrow button to view the options from which you can now select (see Figure 2.40).

Figure 2.40   The Layers panel option list.

Summary

This chapter covered many features of the new Fireworks MX interface, including the improved Property Inspector and its associated panels, as well as ways to customize panel layouts. The remainder of the interface, which includes the menus, is explained in context within the upcoming chapters, exercises, and tutorials.

Chapter 3

Setting Up a New Document and Navigating the Workspace

This chapter covers the oh-so-important intricacies of working with your documents and setting up your workspace. Just as you wouldn't move all of your furniture into a room before you paint the walls or add carpet, you wouldn't want to jump into your Fireworks files without having your files set up properly.

In this chapter, you learn the best methods for creating, saving, and closing new documents. Additionally, this chapter covers working with the Fireworks features that you'll use throughout this book: setting measurement preferences, using guides and grids, working with layers, and more.

Creating New Documents

Creating a new document in Fireworks is easy. Just follow these steps:

1. Launch the program. Simply choose File, New or click the New button on the main toolbar. You can also press the keyboard shortcut: Ctrl-N for Windows or Command-N for Macintosh.

   The New Document dialog box appears, requesting input for the size and resolution of the document (see Figure 3.1).

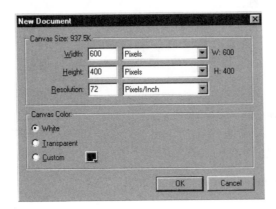

Figure 3.1 The New Document dialog box.

2. Type the width and height to set the width and height of the canvas.

3. Choose the unit of measurement by using the pop-up menus. You can choose between pixels, inches, or centimeters.

4. Set the resolution to 72 pixels/inch, which is the resolution to create web and multimedia screen graphics.

   Higher resolutions are needed to create print graphics. If you don't know what resolution to choose for your project's output type, ask your service bureau or printer for their recommendation.

5. Set the canvas color by clicking one the radio buttons (White, Transparent, or Custom).

Choose the Custom radio button and click the Color box to open the color pop-up window, which is set to Color Cubes by default. This palette contains the web-safe palette and some duplicates. Move your eyedropper tool around the panel to choose a color. You can also choose from any color on your monitor screen.

Click the arrow at the top right of the color pop-up window to choose a different color panel arrangement. These include the Swatches Panel, Color Cubes, Continuous Tone, Windows OS, Mac OS, Gray Scale, or Snap to Web Colors (see Figure 3.2).

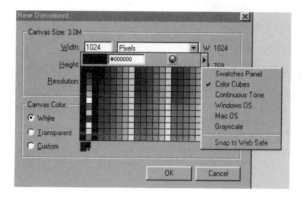

Figure 3.2   The New Document dialog box with the color box selected and the color panel arrangements revealed.

You can also click the small color wheel, which launches the System Color Picker. You can mix colors through two models: Hue, Saturation, Luminance or Red, Green, Blue (see Figure 3.3). (On a Macintosh, you can use the HTML System Color Picker.)

6. Click OK to set up your new document. It is named untitled.png by default.

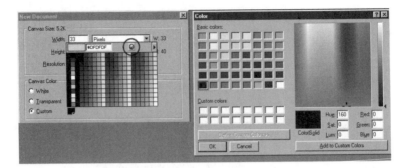

Figure 3.3   The New Document dialog box with Color Wheel button and System Color
Picker revealed.

Opening Existing Documents

To open an existing document, simply choose File, Open and navigate to the directory
where your file resides. Select the file and click Open.

Fireworks contains an option that enables you to protect your original file when opening existing files. The feature, Open File as Untitled Document, enables you to protect
your existing document because the document is given a name of "untitled" until it's
saved. An asterisk appears to the right of the filename in the title bar of the document
window if the file has been edited but not saved.

Follow these steps to open an existing document as untitled:

1. Choose File, Open and navigate to find an existing Fireworks File.

2. Click Open as Untitled and click Open.

    Your document appears as an untitled version of the original (see Figure 3.4).

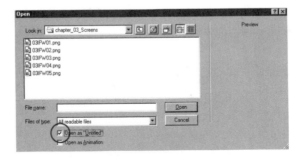

Figure 3.4   The Open dialog box with the Open as Untitled check box selected.

Note

Any changes that you make to the untitled file need to be saved as a new file. The file itself, as untitled, is not saved.

Opening Documents of Various Formats

Fireworks allows you to open a wide range of file formats. This is great if you are already working with computer graphics and not with Fireworks. When you open files in Fireworks, it retains the layers and gives you the option to either maintain your text as editable text or to rasterize your text. If you create text in a file that's not currently loaded into your system, Fireworks rasterizes the text so that you can maintain the "look and feel" of your original (see Figure 3.5).

Figure 3.5   The Replace Fonts dialog box allows you to maintain the "look and feel" of your original document.

Fireworks handles vector file formats, such as Macromedia FreeHand, Adobe Illustrator 7 and 8, and CorelDRAW differently. To work with CorelDRAW, however, files must be saved as uncompressed.

When you open these file formats in Fireworks, the Vector File Options dialog box appears (see Figure 3.6). This dialog box allows you to set vector file options, such as the following:

Scale	Anti-Alias
Width	Paths
Height	Text
Resolution	Edge smoothing

The File Conversion options consist of Include Invisible Layers, Include Background Layers, and Render as Images.

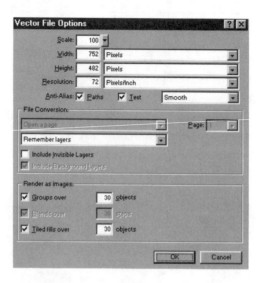

Figure 3.6   The Vector File Options dialog box.

In Fireworks, you can open an existing file created in another graphics application the same way you open a Fireworks file:

1. Choose File, Open or use the keyboard shortcut: Ctrl-O (Windows) and Command-O (Macintosh). Windows users can also choose the Open button from the main toolbar.

2. Select the desired file in the Open dialog box. To the right, Fireworks displays a preview of the file for certain image types and identifies the file format and file size (see Figure 3.7).

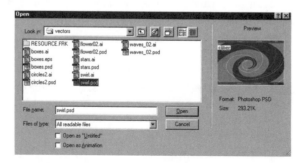

Figure 3.7   The Open dialog box with File Preview, File Format, and File Size displayed.

Opening Photoshop Files

Fireworks opens Photoshop files seamlessly. Photoshop layers are editable in Fireworks—Photoshop layers appear as Fireworks Objects on Layer 1. Photoshop masks are converted to mask groups in Fireworks. Photoshop layer effects are converted to editable Fireworks live effects. You can also distribute the objects to layers and name the layers after the objects to achieve more parity with Photoshop. Text also appears as editable text in Fireworks MX.

Opening Multiple Image Files

The fact that Fireworks allows web designers to open multiple image files speaks to the concerns and work style of web designers. Because many web designers need to work with multiple files simultaneously, Fireworks provides a number of ways to open multiple Fireworks documents.

To open multiple files, follow these steps:

1. Select File, Open or use the keyboard shortcut (Ctrl-O for Windows and Command-O for Macintosh).

   The Open dialog box appears.

2. Select all the files that you want to open (see Figure 3.8) and click Open.

Note

To deselect a file that you chose by mistake, press and hold Ctrl (for Windows) or Command (for Macintosh) and re-click the file so that's it's no longer highlighted.

Note

Macintosh users can also open multiple image files from the Finder by selecting them within the Finder and then either choosing Command-O; File, Open; double-clicking them; or dragging and dropping them onto the Fireworks program icon.

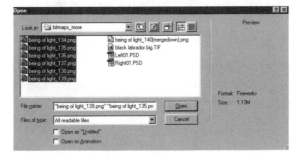

Figure 3.8   Multiple files are selected in the Open dialog box.

Saving Files

You must understand the file-saving options in Fireworks. First of all, when you create a Fireworks file and save it to the native Fireworks format, you are saving it in Portable Networks Graphics (.png) format. This file acts as the parent file; it is from this file that your final files will be exported. Saving your file in .png format allows your Fireworks document to remain infinitely editable.

> **Note**
> Saving a file differs from file exporting. The complete range of exporting files is explored in Chapter 14, "Exporting."

Saving a file is as easy as choosing File, Save. You can also use the keyboard shortcut Ctrl-S (Windows) or Command-S (Macintosh). Windows users can also click the Save button on the main toolbar.

If the file has never been saved, you can give the file a title. If the file is in progress, you cannot see the naming dialog box because saving a file after making changes to it over-writes the existing file.

Saving Multiple Versions of a Document

If you want to store multiple versions of your file, Fireworks provides you with two options for doing this: Save As and Save a Copy. Save As enables you to rename your file. Save a Copy enables you to store a backup file of your original in another folder. (It does this without saving the current document under its own name as well.) Both of these options are selected in the following manner:

1. Choose File, Save as, or File, Save as Copy to open the Save dialog box.
2. Enter your new filename and, if you desire, browse into the folder where you want resave that file. Click Save.

When either option is selected, the Save dialog box opens automatically.

Closing Files

You can close a file after you finish it by choosing File, Close. If the file has not been saved since the last change, Fireworks prompts you with a dialog box that asks if you want to save your file before closing it (see Figure 3.9).

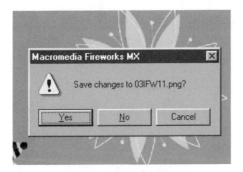

Figure 3.9   The Save Changes dialog box.

Other ways to close a file include using the keyboard shortcuts Ctrl-W (for Windows) or Command-W (for Macintosh), Ctrl-F4, and clicking the Close button (which looks like a big X) on the document window (see Figure 3.10).

If you click the Close button before saving the last change, Fireworks displays a dialog box that asks if you want to save your changes.

Figure 3.10
The document Close button.

The Dirty File Asterisk

Check this out: If you create a new file, name it, and save it, you might notice that the title bar of that document displays the filename. If you select a tool, such as the Rectangle tool, and click and drag a small rectangle onto the screen, a small asterisk appears to the right of the filename and magnification size (see Figure 3.11).

This asterisk indicates that the file has been worked on—or dirt-ied—since the last time it was saved. In another words, the dirty asterisk indicates that your file has unsaved changes. Documents that don't show the dirty asterisk in the title bar are exactly the same as their last-saved version.

Figure 3.11
The dirty mark asterisk.

Reverting to Saved Files

The Revert command is a real lifesaver. Sometimes, you might want to return to an original file although you made a number of changes to it since opening the file. Choosing File, Revert prompts the confirmation dialog box that asks you whether you want to proceed and replace the current version with the last-saved version.

After you create a document, you are not locked into the current size or color of canvas. The following section details how you can alter these elements.

Changing the Canvas Color and Size

To change your canvas color, choose Modify, Canvas Color. The Canvas Color dialog box appears. You have the option to choose a White, Transparent, or Custom canvas:

- **White**—Sets your canvas to white.

- **Transparent**—Sets your background to transparent, as indicated by the alternating gray and white squares on the canvas. This indicates that background has no color and is invisible.

- **Custom**—The Custom dialog box looks similar to the color choice of the New dialog box. If you click the Custom radio button and click the color box, you can choose a specific color as noted in the Creating a New Document dialog box (see Figure 3.12).

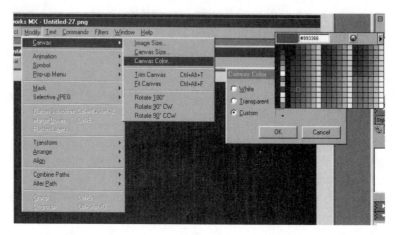

Figure 3.12   The Modify menu with Canvas Color selected, Custom selected, and the Color Cube displayed.

To change the canvas size, choose Modify, Canvas, Canvas Size. The Canvas Size dialog box appears. Enter the new width and height for your document, then click one of the anchor buttons to anchor the existing canvas. Be sure to indicate the position of the current document to which you are adding the canvas. Click OK.

You can also change the canvas size by using the Crop tool from the Tools panel. To do this, follow these steps:

1. Select the Crop tool from the Tools panel.

2. Click and drag the Crop tool to create a bounding box around the portion of the document that you want to keep (see Figure 3.13).

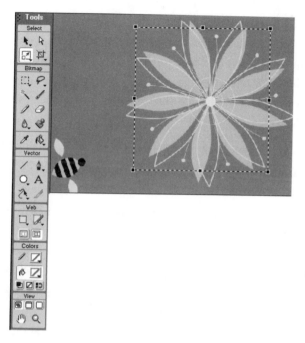

Figure 3.13   The Crop tool is selected in the Tools panel, and the crop box is drawn around the portion that will be cropped.

3. Double-click inside the cropped area to apply the cropping. Alternatively, you can double-click outside the crop area and then choose a new tool to continue without cropping the document.

4. Drag the crop outside the document window and into the gray area.

5. When you release the Crop tool, place the cursor in the center of the crop area and double-click. The area of the crop becomes the new document's new canvas size.

   You can click and drag the crop area on the canvas to reshape and define the area that you want to crop.

Note

Sometimes, when you crop a document, visible objects that you created on the canvas are now not in the visible artwork. At this point, you can either discard those objects by throwing away their layers or choose to move them into your document view. You can use the Editing section of the Preferences. Depending on whether Delete Objects When Cropping is turned on, your objects outside the crop area might or might not be deleted when you crop your document.

Changing a Document's Image Size

Canvas size and image size are different. Changing the canvas size either increases or decreases the amount of canvas on which you have to create. The image size changes the size of the actual image by resampling the image. *Resampling* is the process of adding or subtracting pixels of an existing file. To change a document's image size, follow these steps:

1. Choose Modify, Canvas, Image Size to open the Image Size dialog box.

2. Use the pixel Height and Width fields to set the width and height of the document in use.

   If the Resample Image check box is not selected, the pixel dimensions are not available. In that case, use the print size Height and Width fields to change the size of the image. You can also click the pop-up menu for pixels or inches to change the size of the document by percentage. Notice that when you alter the print size, the resolution changes because the actual number of pixels does not change unless you check the Resample Image check box.

   Selecting the Constrain Proportions option keeps the image at the same aspect ratio.

   Use the Resolution field when you want to change the image size by increasing or reducing the number of pixels per inch.

   The Interpolation pop-up menu is located in the bottom portion of the Image Size dialog box. It contains the following four choices:

   - **Bicubic**—Generally used for photographs. It usually gives the sharpest and highest quality results. This is the default setting.
   - **Nearest Neighbor**—Generally used for images with straight lines and text, such as screen shots. Using Nearest Neighbor can result in jagged edges because it closely resembles a zoomed-in screen shot.
   - **Bilinear** and **Soft**—Used as an additional alternative if you do not like the results achieved with Bicubic or Nearest Neighbor. Bilinear gives you sharper results than Soft interpolation, but it is not as sharp as Bicubic.

   If you are thinking on a scale of sharpness, Nearest Neighbor gives the sharpest contrast, Bicubic is the next best, Bilinear is okay, and Soft interpolation should be used last. Depending on the kind of artwork you are resizing, one of these four methods should be the best for you.

Working with Ruler Guides

Fireworks provides you with horizontal and vertical rulers to help you work precisely within your document. To choose your rulers and make them visible, select View, Rulers. The rulers appear at the top and left side of the document window.

After your rulers are visible, notice that as you move your cursor around the document, two lines appear on the rulers (see Figure 3.14). One line is on the horizontal ruler, and another line appears on the vertical ruler. This is how Fireworks provides you with the x and y coordinates of your cursor position. The upper-right area of the Info panel also displays the exact pixel location of the cursor.

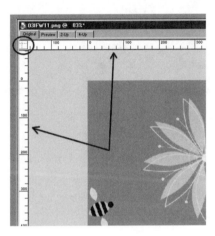

Figure 3.14   The rulers are showing, and the rulers origin point is circled.

Setting Measurement Preferences

The default unit of measurement for Fireworks is *pixels*. You can, however, change the unit of measurement to either inches or centimeters, and then change back to pixels if you prefer. To set your measurement preferences, follow these steps:

1. Choose Window, Info to make the Info panel appear (see Figure 3.15). Setting the units in the Info panel does *not* change the units on the rulers; it only changes the way that the Info panel displays information. The rulers are always displayed in pixels.

2. Use the Info panel menu to choose a new unit of measurement by clicking the right-pointing arrow or the flyaway menu from the Info panel.

3. Scroll down to either pixels, inches, or centimeters, and click the display unit of measurement that you want. That's all there is to it!

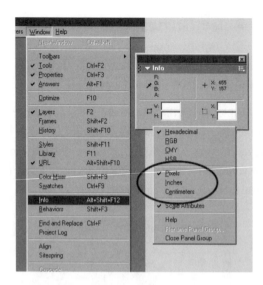

Figure 3.15   The Window menu and the Info panel with the measurement options circled.

Changing the Zero Point

The rulers have a natural zero (0) point, which is the origin point of the rulers. The zero point is located in the upper left-hand corner of the document (refer to the circled dotted lines in Figure 3.14). You can change your rulers' zero point on a document-by-document basis by following these steps:

1. Click the zero point crosshairs and drag the zero point somewhere else within the document.

   This assigns the zero, or the beginning of the rulers, to the place where you release the crosshairs.

2. Double-click the zero crosshairs in the corner of the document window to reset them to the original zero point.

I think that the best thing that you can do with your rulers is use them to create guides. *Guides* allow you to place lines that do not print or show up in your final document, but you can use them to align objects within your art. The important thing about guides is that they aid you in positioning and laying out objects on the page, including slices. When you export, you can also specify Slice Along Guides rather than Use Slice Objects.

Using Guides

To create guides, make sure that your rulers are visible and then do the following:

1. Click inside your horizontal ruler and drag down from the ruler onto the canvas to create a horizontal guide.

   You cannot set a guide off the canvas. You must be over the canvas when you release the guide or you won't not see it in your document.

2. Release the mouse button within the canvas to position it (see Figure 3.16).

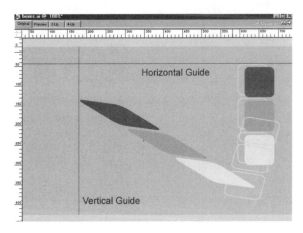

Figure 3.16   Horizontal and vertical guides are created by dragging the rulers out into the canvas.

3. Click and drag from the left ruler to create a vertical guide. Again, you must to be over the canvas when you release the guide or you won't see it.

4. Release the mouse button inside the canvas to place the guide (see Figure 3.16).

You can do this as many times as you like and add as many guides as you need within your artwork. You can also drag a guide over the canvas to check object alignment and release it by dragging it over the gray area outside the canvas (in case you do not want to set the guide permanently).

Repositioning Guides

You can reposition guides by clicking them directly and dragging them from left to right or up and down:

1. Select the Pointer tool from the Tools panel.

2. Double-click a guide to open the Move Guide dialog box (see Figure 3.17).

3. Enter the exact position for your guide.

Figure 3.17
The Move Guide dialog box.

Working with Snap to Guides

The Snap to Guides feature enables you to automatically snap to, or align, objects to your guides. Choose View, Guides, Snap to Guides to activate this feature. Choose View, Guides, Snap to Guides again to turn off snapping. Doing this removes the check mark in front of the menu command. When it is checked, guide snapping is on; unchecking the feature turns guide snapping off.

Guide Settings

The Guides dialog box allows you to precisely edit your guide's appearance and behavior . Follow these steps to edit guides:

1. Select View, Guides, Edit Guides (see Figure 3.18).

   The Guides dialog box appears.

Figure 3.18   The Guides dialog box.

2. If you want to change the color preference for the guides, select the Color box to open the Color pop-up window and choose a new color. Depending on the art's colors, you might need to change the guide's colors to make them visible.

3. Choose View, Guides, Show Guides to toggle the guides on and off. Choose View, Guides, Snap to Guides to toggle guide snapping on and off.

4. Choose View, Guides, Lock Guides to toggle guide locking on and off.

5. To remove all the guides from a document, simply click Clear All.

After you finish setting your guides, click OK to apply the changes. On a Macintosh, you see the Grids tab in the same panel. You can also set your slice guide colors and visibility in the Edit Guides dialog box.

Working with Document Grids

Sometimes, you might need a grid when you're building objects because it can be helpful in making the objects the correct sizes and proportions. As you might suspect, Fireworks also provides a document grid. Grids work similarly to guides.

You can use the grid to help you align and arrange your document. I tend to view guides and grids on and off throughout my work session. Simply choose View, Grid, Show Grid to view the document grid. Choose View, Grid, Snap to Grid to automatically toggle the snapping feature on and off.

Note

When the Snap to Grid option is on, objects snap to the grid even if the grid itself is not currently visible.

Editing the grid is much like editing the guides:

1. Select View, Grid, Edit Grid to edit your document's grid.

   This opens the Grids and Guides dialog box on a Mac and just the Edit Grid dialog box on Windows (see Figure 3.19).

2. Click the Color box if you want to change your color preference for the grid.

   You can type numbers in or click the arrow to bring up the slider and set the size of your grid.

Figure 3.19
The Edit Grid dialog box.

   Clicking the Snap to Grid check box turns grid snapping on and off.

   Clicking the Show Grid check box hides or shows the document grid.

Magnification: Changing the View of Documents

Sometimes, it's necessary to get close to your artwork to see the small details. It's also necessary to zoom out from the small details to see the bigger picture. Magnification tools allow you to do both of these things.

There are many ways to access the magnification controls that allow you to zoom to a specific magnification:

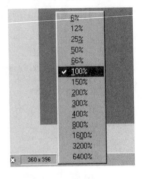

- Click the percentage number that's at the bottom of the document window (to the right of the VCR controls) to access the Set Magnification pop-up box (see Figure 3.20).

- Select View, Magnification, and choose the magnification that you want.

- Select View, Zoom In, or select View, Zoom Out to jump one level up or down in the default zoom settings.

- Select View, Fit Selection to display the object selected in Full View.

Figure 3.20
The Set Magnification pop-up box.

- Select View, Fit All to display the entire document.

- Double-click the Hand tool to view your document at Fit to Window, or double-click the magnifying glass in the Tool panel to view your document at 100 percent.

Of course, you can also use the Zoom tool to set your artwork at a specific magnification (see Figure 3.21).

Using the Zoom Tool

There are even more ways to zoom in and out of your documents, but these methods require you to use the Zoom tool. The *Zoom tool* changes your view to the same increments listed in the Magnification Control menu.

Select the Zoom tool and click the area that you want to zoom in on. You can click repeatedly to zoom in as close as 6,400 percent. You can also click and drag the Zoom tool around the area you want to see; this is similar to creating a rectangle, but when you release the mouse button, Fireworks zooms in on the area that you defined.

Figure 3.21
The Zoom tool.

Alternatively, if you want to zoom out from a magnification, you can press the Option key (on a Macintosh) or the Alt key (for Windows) while using the Zoom tool. When you zoom out, the Zoom tool icon changes from a + sign to a – sign.

Note

You can access the Zoom tool by using the keyboard: press Ctrl-spacebar (for Windows) or Command-spacebar (for the Macintosh). Hold the modifier keys as you click with the Zoom tool (as previously described). Release the modifier keys to return to using your currently selected tool. Add the Option key (Macintosh) or Alt key (Windows) to the key combination to switch to the Zoom tool in zoom-out mode.

Zooming with Command Keys

You can also use command keys to zoom in or out of your artwork. On a Macintosh, hold the Command key while typing + to zoom in and – to zoom out. On the Windows platform, hold the Control key and type a + key to zoom in and a – key to zoom out.

Panning or Using the Hand Tool

After you zoom close in on a document, you might want to see another portion of your art while remaining at the level of magnification you are using. To reposition the document inside of your zoomed-in window, use the Hand tool (see Figure 3.22).

The Hand tool allows you to pan your documents around within a zoomed-in document window. Here's how you do it:

1. Select the Hand tool in the Tools panel.

2. Position the Hand tool inside the document.

3. Click and drag in either direction.

Figure 3.22
The Hand tool.

Note

You can use the spacebar to access the Hand tool without leaving the tool that's currently selected. Just hold the spacebar and the Hand tool appears, which allows you to pan the image within the document window. When you release the spacebar, the tool you were previously using still remains selected.

Working with Layers

After you get deep into working with your documents, you might be adding more objects than you know what to do with at times. To manage all these objects within your document, use the Layers panel (see Figure 3.23).

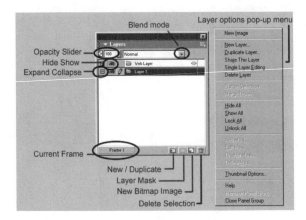

Figure 3.23   The Layers panel and its controls.

The objects that you create live within your layers. You can organize artwork objects based on their image type or by what part of the image the artwork belongs. The Layers system is similar to Windows Explorer or the Finder on a Macintosh in View as List mode in that the +/– (Windows) or arrow (Macintosh) can be clicked to disclose, or hide, the layer's contents. In Fireworks, the Layers panel is similar to the Layers panel in programs such as Macromedia FreeHand, Adobe Illustrator, and Adobe Photoshop. The Layers Panel in Fireworks, however, contains additional information.

Layers are like transparent planes within which your objects are created and placed. Layers allow you to individually control your artwork when building complex or composite images. Different parts of your image can be stored on different layers and selectively turned on or off. In this way, you can view and work on a portion of the artwork that you want to at one time.

Each layer can contain both vector and bitmap objects.

Default Layers

When you create a new document, you automatically have two layers. These default layers are Layer 1 and the web layer. *Layer 1* is a blank layer in which you can create or insert artwork. The *web layer* is where hotspots and slices are stored. These topics are covered in Chapter 4, "Working with Vectors," and Chapter 11, "Working With Behaviors."

Ordering Layers

As previously mentioned, Fireworks places the objects that you create in layers. Each object within a layer is represented by a thumbnail image. Like other graphic programs that you might be familiar with, the last object you create is on top of the first object you create. The first object is positioned at the bottom while the last object is at the top.

You can control the stacking order of each object in the layer by selecting it and choosing Modify, Arrange. The submenu gives you the following stacking options for that object: Bring to Front, Bring Forward, Send to Back, or Send Backwards.

Alternatively, you can use the Layers panel to drag the object to a new position within the layer or move the object to an entirely new layer. You can click and drag an entire layer below or above any other layer in the Layers panel.

Layers help you organize your objects into distinct levels that can be modified as individual units or hidden from view when necessary.

The stacking order on a layer is different from the order of layers. An object can be at the top of the object list and still be beneath an object on a layer that is higher than it.

Sometimes, you might need to move layers themselves. To change the stacking order of layers, click the layer and drag it either above or below another layer within the Layers panel.

Using the Select Behind Tool

A handy tool, called the Select Behind tool, helps you when you work with complex graphics (see Figure 3.24). Sometimes, an image file consists of multiple objects that are stacked on each other. This makes it difficult to select pieces and parts of your artwork that are behind, or underneath, other objects in your artwork. To select items that are stacked behind another item, use the Select Behind tool in the following manner:

1. Click and hold the Pointer tool on the Tools panel to access the flyout that contains the Select Behind tool.

   You can also access the tool by pressing v, which I find very handy. Or you can press the 0 (zero) to switch to the Select Behind tool.

2. Click the tool on the object that you want to select.

   The first click selects the top object; the next click selects the object beneath the top object. The third click selects any object that might be beneath the top and next object, and so on.

   Click as many times as necessary to select the object that you want. Each click selects the next object within the object stack.

Tip

To add objects to your selection, hold down the Shift key as you click. This is a handy tip if you are editing a multiframe document and need to move or transform the same object on various frames. Do this by enabling Onion Skinning and MultiFrame Editing in the Frames panel. See Chapter 12, "Animation," for more information.

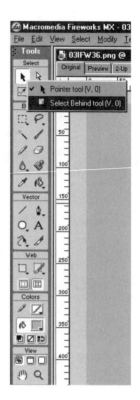

Moving a Graphic Between Layers

To move a graphic between layers, follow these steps:

1. Use the Pointer tool to select the graphic within the layer.

   Notice the blue box that represents the selected object on the Layers panel. This blue box indicates the layer position of the currently selected object.

2. Drag the selection indicator to another layer to drag the graphic to that layer.

3. Click the + (Windows), or triangle (Macintosh) on the layer. You can now see both of the objects within that layer.

Adding Layers

To add (and delete and duplicate) layers, use the Layers panel options pop-up. Follow these steps to add a layer:

Figure 3.24
The Select Behind tool.

1. Click the arrow at the top of the Layers panel to access the Layers panel options pop-up box.

2. Select Add a Layer or use the New Layer button at the bottom of the Layers panel.

3. Type a new name in the New Layer dialog box to name the new layer.

   Here's another way to add a new layer: Click the New/Duplicate Layer button at the bottom right of the Layers panel. You can also duplicate a layer by dragging it to the New/Duplicate Layer button.

Note

The Share Across Frames check box is used in animation. Check out Chapter 12 to learn more about it.

Hiding and Showing Layers

Sometimes, to allow you to focus your attention on the objects on one layer, you might want to show or hide the contents of another layer. Here's how you do this:

1. Click the Eye icon on the Layers panel to turn the layer on and off.

2. Hold down the Alt key (Windows) or the Option key (Macintosh) as you click the Show/Hide button to make all the layers invisible or visible.

3. Click and drag the Eye column to show or hide the objects as your mouse rolls over the Eye icon.

Expanding and Collapsing Objects on a Layer

To either expand or collapse objects on a layer, follow these steps:

1. Click the + or – indicators (Windows) or the arrow icon (Macintosh) on the Layers panel to show or hide the all the objects within a layer. If you want to turn off the thumbnails, choose Thumbnail Options... from the Layers panel's options menu.

2. Hold down Alt key (Windows) or the Option key (Macintosh) as you click the Open Layer button to expand or collapse all layers.

Locking and Unlocking Layers

At times, it might be helpful to lock a layer to prevent you from moving, changing, or selecting it. Here's how to lock or unlock a layer:

1. Click the Lock Column next to a layer on the Layers panel. This is the small box to the left of the Layer name. If the layer is selected and editable, a Pencil icon appears in this column.

    Clicking here locks and unlocks the layer. A lock appears when the layer is locked (see Figure 3.25), which means that its object cannot be moved or deleted.

2. Click the lock to unlock the layer.

3. Hold the Alt key (Windows) or the Option key (Macintosh) and click the Lock Column by Any Layer to lock or unlock all the layers.

You can use the Layers panel's options pop-up menu to lock or unlock all the layers.

Figure 3.25
The Layer Lock.

Single Layer Editing

Single layer editing is another way to use layers. The Single Layer Editing option makes only the currently selected layer accessible for editing. All objects on other layers cannot be selected or edited.

While the Single Layer Editing option allows you to edit objects only on the currently selected layer, other layers in the document act as if they are locked, but they are not. To select objects on the other layers, select their layer in the Layers panel. When you lock a layer, you cannot select or change any objects on that layer until you unlock that layer. This is the inverse, in a sense, from locking layers, and it can be handy when you are working with a complex image that contains multiple layers. Single layer editing is accessible from the Layers panel's options menu.

Naming Layers

To help you keep track of all the layers that you work with, you can name them: just double-click the Layer Name option in the Layers panel. In the Layer Name dialog box that appears (see Figure 3.26), type the new name for your layer.

Note
Do not check Share Across Frames. This option is discussed in Chapter 13 "Optimization."

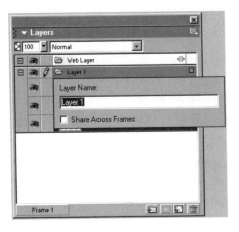

Figure 3.26   The Layer Name dialog box.

Changing the Size of the Layer Thumbnail

You can change the size of the thumbnail displayed in the Layers panel by choosing Thumbnail Options from the Layers panel's options menu. When the Thumbnail Options dialog box appears (see Figure 3.27), choose None to display objects with no thumbnail, or click each of the thumbnail sizes to change the display within the Layers panel.

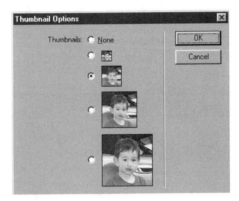

Figure 3.27   The Thumbnail Options dialog box.

Working With the History Panel

The History panel keeps track of every step that you perform as you create your artwork and objects in your Fireworks document (see Figure 3.28). Every time that you use Edit, Undo, you take a step back within the History panel.

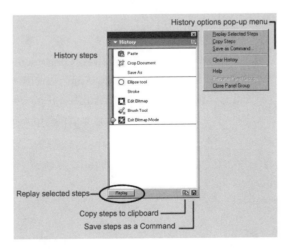

Figure 3.28   The History panel and its controls.

The History panel makes it easy to see your steps and to undo multiple actions. You can also use the History panel to repeat a set of actions. For example, say that you have just performed two actions: You cloned a shape and then rotated it. You can use the History panel to repeat those actions multiple times. Here's how you can do this:

1. Select Window, History to open the History panel. Scroll to the bottom of the list until you see the last two actions.

2. Hold the Shift key and select the last two actions. Click Replay at the bottom left of the History panel.

   A new shape is created at a 45-degree angle from the last shape.

Note

A shape must be selected or Replay does not work.

3. Click Replay again to draw the last shape.

Note

The History panel is *not* available until some initial actions, such as drawing a rectangle and rotating it 45 degrees, have occurred.

The History panel can replay steps, as previously mentioned, and can be used to step back through time, like a magic eraser: Drag the slider on the left up to undo steps, and drag the slider back down to redo steps.

You can also save your steps for actions that you can use again as commands. We create commands in Chapter 15, "Automation."

Summary

Now that you know the basics of working with Fireworks documents and using guides and layers, you're ready to tackle some heavy-duty stuff. Part II, "The Meat of the Matter," delves into working with vectors, fills and strokes, text, effects, and masking. Your Fireworks files are going to make the leap from basic files to real art!

Part II

The Meat of the Matter

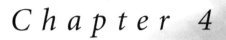

Chapter 4

Working with Vectors

Vector graphics are objects defined by equations, which include information about the object's size, shape, outline, color, and position in space. This makes the graphic resolution independent, which means that the file size remains the same if the graphic is a tiny dot on your screen or a filling a huge area.

Vector objects have much smaller file sizes than other file formats because their code is comprised of mathematical equations, just like those Trigonometry equations that you had to plot in high school math. Remember having to draw parabolas on the board from quadratic equations? You changed one number and the parabola doubled in size.

This is the same math that defines the vector graphics in Fireworks. Simple mathematical changes directly affect the geometric properties of the vector and thereby the shape, size, and dimension of your drawing.

The greatest advantage to working with vector graphics on the web is that their file sizes are very small and "portable." You do not have to wait for insane download times with vector graphics—they load in a jiffy! It is vector graphic technology that makes Flash animation on the web viable. Instead of redrawing a graphic pixel by pixel for each "frame," vector graphics are scaled based on an original equation. (To really understand their power, check out `www.macromedia.com/software/flash/`.)

Note

We discussed vector graphics in Chapter 1, "What's New and Different in Fireworks MX." For a quick history review, refer to that chapter.

Working with Vectors

Vector objects are perfectly suited for many kinds of elements that we create in web design. Building navigation bars, buttons, banners, animations, and working with type are a strong suit of Fireworks.

When you draw using vectors, you create shapes using lines and curves. When you edit a vector image, you manipulate the lines and the curves that describe the shape. You can change the vector object's shape, resize it, move it, change its color, change its position, overlap objects, apply transparency, and still keep the quality of your original artwork.

With the Basic Shape tools, you can draw straight lines, squares, rectangles, circles, ellipses, stars, and polygons (see Figure 4.1).

With the pencil, brush, and pen tools, you can draw free-form vector paths. The pen tool is especially well suited to draw complex curves and shapes in Fireworks, using what are known as Bezier curves.

Figure 4.1   The vector tool bar.

Once drawn, vector objects are flexible. You can edit and manipulate them in Fireworks in several different ways: You can stretch them, skew them, move them, add points to paths, and delete points from paths. You can manipulate the path handles to change the shape of path segments.

Selecting Vector Objects

There are four main tools for selecting vector objects in Fireworks. These tools can also select text blocks, web objects, symbols, and bitmap graphics while in vector mode. Several tools exist for creating and manipulating vector objects in Fireworks. There are also many techniques in which to do this.

When you create or select an object, or when an object is already selected, a blue high-light is displayed (see Figure 4.2). *Highlighting* is feedback from Fireworks. It tells you the selection state of objects on the canvas. The selected line or object is the one you are currently working with and affecting. When you mouse over an object that's not selected, a red highlight is displayed. Don't forget: You can alter these colors from your Preferences panel.

Figure 4.2   The rectangle object is selected.

Two tools are at the top left and the top right of the tool bar. One is a black arrow. The other is white arrow with a black outline.

The black arrow on the left is the regular Pointer tool. This tool can select whole objects and groups of objects. The Pointer tool is actually the first in a group of tools that we refer to as the Pointer tool group (see Figure 4.3). These are the Pointer tool and the Select Behind tool. As you look at the Tools panel, you might notice that some of tools have a small arrow at the lower-right corner of their icon on the Tools panel. This arrow indicates that this tool is part of a group and other tools can be accessed by clicking the tool and holding the mouse button to reveal a pop-up menu. From this pop-up menu, you can select alternate tools in the group.

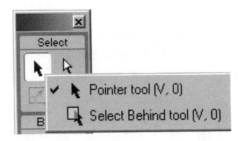

Figure 4.3   The Pointer tool group.

The white arrow on the right is the Subselection tool (see Figure 4.4). It can select points within paths and objects within groups.

Figure 4.4
The Subselection tool.

> ![Note icon] **Note**
> For more information on tool specifics refer to Chapter 2, "Interface, Tools, and Workspace Overview."

Moving Objects

You can move objects in several ways. You can move objects with the regular Pointer tool by

- Clicking and dragging them on the screen
- Cutting them and pasting them
- Using the arrow keys

If you need to be extremely precise, use the arrow keys to move it in 1-pixel increments or hold the Shift key to move it in 10-pixel increments. Or, in the Properties Inspector, you can enter X and Y coordinates for the location of the top-left corner of the selection (see Figure 4.5).

You can also move objects between Fireworks and other applications by using the Clipboard and copying objects and pasting them from the Clipboard or by dragging from the canvas onto the other application's workspace.

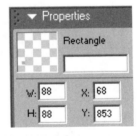

Figure 4.5   Location coordinates on the Property Inspector.

Deleting Objects

If you no longer want an element in your artwork, just delete it. You can delete selected objects from your artwork in several ways:

- You can press Delete or Backspace.
- You can right-click (for Windows) or Control-click (for a Mac) on the object and choose Edit, Cut from the contextual menu. This puts the object on the system's Clipboard, which is handy when you want to mask several objects or use the same object in several masks.
- You can choose Edit, Clear.
- You can choose Edit, Cut.

Duplicating Versus Cloning Objects

In the Edit menu, there are two options: Duplicate and Clone. Both do the same thing (make a copy of your selected object). Duplicate (Edit, Duplicate), however, creates a second object from the original and places it a bit down and to the right of your original element on the existing layer (it's 10 pixels down and 10 pixels to the right.) The Clone option works differently. When you choose Edit, Clone, the clone of the selection is stacked exactly in front of the original and becomes the selected object.

Introducing the Basic Shape Drawing Tools

The basic shape drawing tools, along with the Pen tool, are the building blocks for vector drawing in Fireworks. These tools can quickly create basic shapes, also known as closed paths. The Basic Shape tools include ovals, circles, rectangles, squares, polygons, stars, and rounded rectangles. The tools are located in the Vector Tools section of the Tools panel. When you use any drawing tool to create an object, the tool applies the current fill and stroke to the object. All these are drawings.

Note

When you select any tool in the Vector Tools section of the Tools panel, the program automatically changes to the appropriate drawing mode.

Note

When you select any tool, the options for that tool is available in the Property Inspector.

Creating Ellipses and Circles

If the Ellipse tool is not visible on the Tools panel, click the Basic Shape tool that appears to the left of the Text tool and hold the mouse button. A pop-up menu appears from which you can select the Ellipse tool (see Figure 4.6).

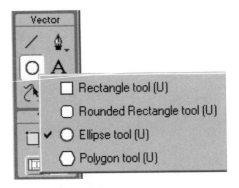

Figure 4.6   The pop-up menu for selecting the Ellipse tool.

Click one part of the canvas and drag to another to draw the shape. Holding the Alt key as you drag draws the ellipse from the center out. Holding the Shift key as you drag the shape with the mouse constrains the ellipse to a perfect circle.

Notice that the shape, size, and position of the ellipse are anchored from the corner where the mouse was first clicked and follow in whatever direction you drag (see Figure 4.7).

Figure 4.7   Ellipse's unique shape and size anchored from the corner.

Note

The basic shapes are drawn from the location where you first click the canvas after you select the tool.

To draw any basic shape out from its center, hold the Alt key (for Windows) or the Option key (for a Macintosh) as you drag.

Creating Rectangles and Squares

The Rectangle tool works differently than the other Basic Shape tools because Fireworks draws rectangles as grouped objects. This grouped behavior allows you to control and redraw the rounded corners using the Property Inspector.

If the Rectangle tool is not visible on the Tools panel, click the Basic Shape tool that appears to the left of the Text tool and hold the mouse button. A pop-up menu appears from which you can select the Rectangle tool (see Figure 4.8).

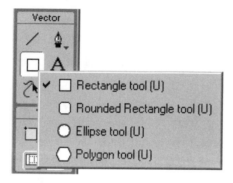

Figure 4.8   Selecting the Rectangle tool.

To create the rectangle, click one part of the canvas and drag to another. Holding the Shift key as you drag the shape with the mouse constrains the rectangle to a perfect square.

Warning

Clicking indiscriminately or making small clicks on your canvas with any shape tools without dragging creates miniscule shapes that you might not see when deselected. These miss-clicks can cause problems later, especially when they are slices on the Web layer.

Creating Curved Corner Rectangles

To create a rectangle with curved corners, select the Rounded Rectangle tool. Notice, on the Property Inspector, the Roundness slider (see Figure 4.9). If the Rounded Rectangle tool is not visible on the Tools panel, click the Basic Shape tool that appears to the left of the Text tool and hold the mouse button. A pop-up menu appears from which you can select the Rectangle tool. Then, click and drag from one part of the canvas to another.

Figure 4.9   The Roundness slider on Rectangle tool Property Inspector.

Note

The Property Inspector also contains settings for stroke position and the fill over stroke check box. These are covered in Chapter 5, "Working with Color Fills and Strokes."

Use the Roundness slider on the Property Inspector to adjust the corner radius of the rectangle interactively from 0 percent to 100 percent, or type a number in the Roundness text field.

You can also adjust the corner radius as you draw by pressing the up or down keys, the left and right arrow keys, or the 1, 2, 3… keys repeatedly. It's fun to watch the corner radius change as you draw it.

Creating Polygons and Stars

Polygons are shapes that have three or more sides. In Fireworks, you can create polygons with up to 360 sides! You can create stars by choosing Star on the Property Inspector (see Figure 4.10 and Figure 4.11). The slider stops at 25, but you can manually type higher numbers. Try typing 999 in the number field beside the slider. You notice that you will still get 360.

Figure 4.10   The Polygon Side slider in the Property Inspector.

Figure 4.11   The Shape selection in the Property Inspector for polygons.

When you draw stars, you can either specify the angle for the star points or have Fireworks assign them automatically by clicking the automatic option. Try playing with the number of points.

Note

Unlike ellipses and rectangles, which drag out from the corner of the shape by default, polygons and stars drag out from the center by default.

To create polygons, complete the following steps:

1. Select the Polygon tool. If the Polygon tool is not visible in the Tools panel, click and hold your mouse on the Basic Shape tool in the Vector area of the Tools panel (just to the left of the Text tool) to reveal the Basic Shape tool group pop-up menu and select the Polygon tool.

2. Slide the Sides slider to the number that you want (or you can manually type the number, up to 360).

Note

Although you can specify up to 25 sides for a polygon, polygons with any more than 10 sides look much like a circle, depending on how big they are. This is not so with stars, with which you can create burst-like graphics when sides are specified to greater amounts.

3. Click and drag on the canvas. The polygon draws out from the center point.

If you hold the Shift key while dragging a polygon or star, it constrains the angles of the polygon or the points of the star.

To create stars, complete the following steps:

1. Select the Polygon tool. If the Polygon tool is not visible in the Tools panel, click and hold your mouse on the Basic Shape tool in the Vector area of the Tools panel (just to the left of the Text tool) to reveal the Basic Shape tool group pop-up menu and select the Polygon tool.

2. Select Star from the Property Inspector.

   The Sides number field with its slider now shows the number of points that will be on the star and the angle controls are added to the Property Inspector.

3. Slide the Sides slider to set the number of points for your star.

   You can set the number of external points from 1 to 360 in the Sides text field. You can also type the number into the field directly.

4. Click the Automatic check box to create stars with parallel-aligned line segments.

   You can also use the slider to set the angle of the points.

5. Click and drag on the canvas. The star draws out from the center point.

Now try this:

1. Select the Polygon tool.

2. In the Properties Inspector, set the shape to Star and the sides to 6, and angle to 20 (see Figure 4.12).

Figure 4.12   Star Property Inspector with Appropriate Settings.

3. Click and drag.

   Now you can see that you have a very pointed six-pointed star.

4. Now, once again, select the Polygon tool.

5. Click the Automatic check box next to angle, and notice that the angle number changes (see Figure 4.13).

   As you drag, you've got more of a six-sided Star of David or the "two triangles overlapping" version of a star. When you click the automatic check box next to angle, Fireworks sets the automatic angle of a 6-pointed star to 57 degrees. Notice that each of the sides of the triangles' arms is parallel-aligned.

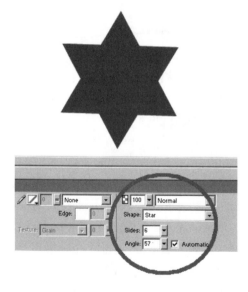

Figure 4.13   Setting the Automatic Angle option.

Warning

Because of the way the Rectangle tool behaves, there is a tendency to think that after you draw a polygon, you should be able to change the number of its sides by changing the sides number in the slider on the Options panel, but you cannot.

Creating Straight-Line Segments

The Line tool creates straight-line segments. To draw straight lines with the Line tool, follow these steps:

1. Select the Line tool from the Tools panel.

2. Position the cursor on the canvas.

3. Click and drag to another location on the canvas.

4. Release the mouse.

As you drag, the line's "direction" follows the path in which you drag the cursor. Also notice that the line is highlighted and that, on either side of the line, there is a single square point. This is the anchor point. The line or line segment between them is referred to as the path. The anchor points are the vectors.

Note

A vector can also be described as any possible point along the path, but that's getting picky. Another way to say it is that a vector is the intersection of an x and y coordinate, not the path between two such intersections. Remember that a vector is actually the equation that determines the direction and shape of a path. Thus, a path exists between two anchor points, or vectors, on a path.

Working with Paths

Two types of paths are available in Fireworks: open paths and closed paths. You create open paths with the Line tool, the Pen tool, and the Brush tool. The Basic Shape tools create closed paths. You can convert open paths to closed paths by cutting them with the Knife tool.

Path Stroke

By default, the path is set to have a stroke of black, one-pixel hardness and is 1-pixel thick. You can also change the stroke attribute by using the Stroke panel. For more information, see Chapter 2 and Chapter 5.

Selecting Paths

You can select path in two ways. Using the regular Selection tool selects the entire path. Using the Subselection tool selects anchor points (or vectors) of paths.

When you click the anchor points of the path (which looks like the end point of the line to you and me), you can drag them around the canvas to reposition the length, width, height, and rotation (see Figure 4.14).

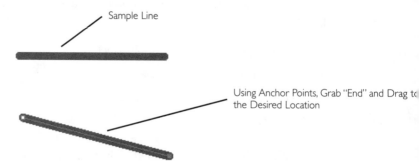

Sample Line

Using Anchor Points, Grab "End" and Drag to the Desired Location

Figure 4.14   The anchor points are selected from a path.

Reshaping and Modifying Paths

After you draw a line, you are not stuck with its position, length, or direction. By using the Subselection tool, you can modify the path infinitely:

1. Select the Subselection tool from the Tools panel.

2. Click the vector path.

    Notice that the path highlights and the anchor points turn white.

3. Directly click one of the points and drag that point around on the canvas to change the vector shape.

4. Click the line and drag it around on the canvas to reposition the line segment without distorting it.

Tip

Interested in mastering the Pen tool? You have to check out the mega drawing lesson on the CD-ROM.

The Pen Tool

The Pen tool creates complex lines, curves, and shapes in Fireworks. You draw complex lines and shapes with the Pen tool using Bezier curves. This tool, when mastered, can turn you into a force to be reckoned with, not only in Fireworks but also in any application that contains Bezier Pen tools. (Macromedia Flash, FreeHand, and Adobe Illustrator and Photoshop all have vector drawing.)

Note

Three types of points exist: corner, curve, and join.

Take a look at the available tool options for the tool that will be displayed on the property Inspector (see Figure 4.15). For example, the Show Pen Preview and Show Solid Points options for the Pen tool can have a drastic affect on how it behaves and how you use the tool.

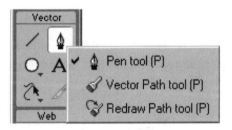

Figure 4.15   The Pen tool options on the Property Inspector.

Drawing Straight Lines

To draw a straight path with the Pen tool, follow these steps:

1. Select the Pen tool from the Tools panel. Position the cursor on the canvas.

   Notice that the Pen cursor displays an X next to it, which indicates the origin point of the path.

2. Click the canvas to create an anchor point.

3. Move the cursor to another location.

4. Click to create a second anchor point. This connects the two points with the vector path.

5. Continue to click in a zigzag fashion around the canvas to created additional line segments (see Figure 4.16).

6. To end the path, click while pressing the Ctrl key in Windows or the Command key on Macintosh.

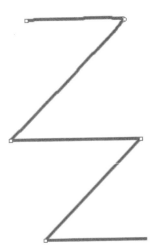

Figure 4.16   Pen tool zigzag.

Drawing a Lightning Bolt

This connect-the-dots style exercise with the Pen tool guides you through creating a complex series of straight-line segments and then closing its path. See Figure 4.17 and follow the visual steps to draw the lightning bolt:

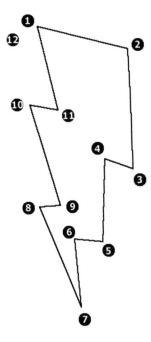

Figure 4.17   Tutorial file `bolt_01.png`.

1. Open the `bolt_01.png` file from the `Exercises/04` folder on the accompanying CD-ROM.

   This file contains a locked layer with the lightning bolt diagram. The layer with the lightning bolt template in it is locked to make tracing it easier.

2. Select the Pen tool from the Tools panel.

3. With the Pen tool, click 1 through 11 in numerical order as you would in a connect-the-dots puzzle.

4. Move the cursor over dot 1. A small circle appears to the right of the pen cursor, which signals that clicking this point closes the path.

5. Click directly on this point to close the path.

6. Save your file as `my_bolt.png`. You use the lightning bolt again in Chapter 6, "Working with Text."

As you can see, it can be simple to create straight-edged shapes.

Drawing Curved Paths

Once you get the hang of working with the Pen tool, you'll discover it's really a blast:

1. Click to select the Pen tool from the Tools panel.

2. Position the cursor on the canvas.

   Notice that the Pen cursor displays an X next to it, which indicates the origin point of the path.

3. Click and drag from the anchor point origin. Release the mouse. This creates Bezier control handles.

4. Move the cursor to another location.

5. Click and drag again to create a curved segment between your two anchor points. Or you can just click to set a corner point for the first anchor point and click-drag for the second. Only one Bezier control handle is necessary to create a curved line between two points.

6. Continue to create curves by clicking and dragging in a zigzag fashion around the canvas. This creates wavy line segments (see Figure 4.18).

7. To end the path, click while pressing the Ctrl key in Windows or the Command key on Macintosh if the Show Pen Preview is on. If it is off, the last click with the tool becomes the endpoint of the path.

Figure 4.18   Using the Pen tool Bezier handles to create wavy lines. (My lines are not artistic, but you get the idea.)

Manipulating Bezier Paths

It is enormously useful to understand what Bezier curves are and, thus, what it means to draw curves with the Pen tool. In my understanding, curves consist of looking at shapes and being able to identify, or break down, the components of their segments and curves.

What exactly is the structure of what you are trying to draw?

Shapes are made up of a series of complex curves. When I examine a shape or think about drawing a shape, I ask myself, "Where does the curve begin and where does it end?"

Shapes are made of different types of points that produce curved and straight vectors. These elements can have different directions and can go for different lengths of space. For this reason, Fireworks provides a few additional aspects of the Pen tool that enable you to alter and create various types of lines.

If you are interested in the Advanced Pen tool tutorial, check out the mega drawing lesson on the accompanying CD-ROM (see Figure 4.19). Working through this exercise gives you a great deal of practice using the full range of drawing tools available in Fireworks.

Figure 4.19   The completed drawing exercise "Mega Drawing," which is available on the CD-ROM.

Look carefully at the image of the butterfly woman. It is made up of a series of complex curves. I created it to help explain point and line types and to give the Pen tool a workout.

Modifying Line Types

This is a great time to discuss line types. In Figure 4.19, notice the number of different line types. For example, the wings are soft, wide, and wavy curves. The fingertips contain curves that change direction. The vest contains elliptical curves joined to straight-line segment.

There are different combinations of clicks and drags that you perform when drawing with the Pen tool. These methods are how you use the tool to get specific results. Here's what I mean:

When you click the left middle of the canvas and then click directly across from it, you create a straight line across the center of the canvas.

When you click and drag up from the left middle of the canvas and then click and drag down directly across from your first click and release, you create a curve that goes up. The direction of the curve follows exactly how you drag.

Initially, when you are dragging, you are setting the Bezier control that determines the direction. Here's the trick to getting your curve segment to fit just right using the Pen tool:

1. Estimate the distance of the curve that you are drawing.

2. Drag approximately one third of the total distance of the curve you are drawing along its axis.

You can further build and fine-tune complex curves by

- Adding points

- Converting corner points to curve points and curve points to corner points

- Changing the direction of straight segments and curves and back again

If you're doing waves or curves, you sometimes need to make tight turns. Sometimes, a turn might be a curve, and other times, a turn might be an angle turning into a curve.

Grouping Path Objects

Grouping makes several path objects into one object, like in the wing of the butterfly woman (refer to Figure 4.19). You use the butterfly warrior artwork to learn more about Color Fills and Stroke in the next chapter.

Note

I've found that using a pressure-sensitive tablet gives my hand and line fluidity. If you have a pressure-sensitive tablet, you might experience the fluidity with which you can draw. I like the feeling of drawing this way because it's more natural and, having studied drawing and sculpting, it allows me to use skills from those disciplines more intuitively.

In the Modify menu, there is an option called Combine Paths (Modify, Combine Paths). Click anywhere on this option to reveal the Combine submenu.

To the Combine submenu's right is a submenu that contains the four combine options: Union, Intersect, Punch, and Crop. The combine option is a cool feature that enables you to create elements from existing closed-vector objects by selecting two or more objects and combining their paths in the four following ways:

- **Union**—Creates one object from two or more overlapping items. The resultant object is a single path.

- **Intersect**—Creates one object from the intersection of two or more objects. *Intersection* means the area that is common to both objects.

- **Punch**—The opposite of Intersect. Intersect leaves you the common area, but Punch only leaves you the area of the bottom object that's *not* common to the overlapping object.

- **Crop**—The reverse of punch. Removes portions of selected paths outside the area defined by an overlapping selected path. Similar to Intersect, but more suited to use with multiple objects. It's similar only in that the common area in the bottom object is left after the operation, but the common area of the top object is not.

Exercise 4.1   Building a Ciber-Training Interface

This exercise guides you through the steps for making a ciber-training interface. Each of these files is available on the CD-ROM: `ciber_combine01.png` through `ciber_combine07.png`. You can try drawing them from scratch in the following steps, or go right to the CD-ROM and inspect the artwork:

1. Choose File, New to create a new file. Make the canvas width 800 pixels and the canvas height 600 pixels. Make the resolution 72 ppi. Set the canvas color to white. Click OK.

   Notice that your file automatically contains two layers in the Layers panel. One is named Layer One and the other is named Web layer.

   By default, every Fireworks document contains these two layers. Layer One always contains artwork elements, and Web layer is a special layer that contains web elements including hotspots and slices.

2. Select the Rounded Rectangle tool from the Tools panel. Set the Stroke to None and the Fill to Light Gray, hexadecimal color number CCCCCC. Using the Property Inspector, set the Rectangle Roundness to 80. (See Figure 4.20.)

Figure 4.20   The Rounded Rectangle tool Property Inspector settings.

3. Dragging from the upper left to the lower right, create a tall, narrow, and rounded rectangle with the width of 163 and the height of 627.

4. Choose the Pointer tool from the Tools panel and position by clicking and dragging the rectangle to move it to the position at x = -17, y = -32, or use the x, y location fields in the Property Inspector to set the location numerically.

5. Deselect the rectangle by clicking away from it in the canvas or by pressing Ctrl-D (for Windows) or Command-D (for a Macintosh).

   Deselecting deactivates vector shapes so that they are not affected by changes.

6. Select the Rounded Rectangle tool from the Tools panel. Set the roundedness setting to 100 in the Property Inspector.

7. Click and drag a wide horizontal rectangle with the width of 780 and the height of 118.

8. Switch to the Pointer tool and position your rectangle at the coordinates of x = -28, y = -56 by clicking and dragging the rectangle, or by using the x and y coordinates in the Property Inspector.

9. Hold the Shift key and click the vertical rectangle; now both rectangles should be selected.

10. Choose Modify, Combine Paths, Union.

11. Switch from the Rounded Rectangle tool to the Rectangle tool.

12. Click and drag a small rectangle with the width of 128 and the height of 94. Switch to the Cursor tool and position this rectangle at x = -44, y = 500.

13. Holding the Shift key, select the unionized shape along with your new rectangle, and choose Modify, Combine Paths, Union (see Figure 4.21).

The resulting shape is used for the background element of the ciber-training user interface.

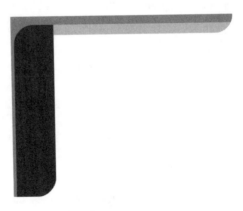

Figure 4.21   Ciber-Training user interface.

Note

It is perfectly acceptable that the vector shapes that you have drawn overlap or bleed out from the canvas into the work area. In Chapter 14, "Exporting," all the areas outside the canvas are not exported.

Adding Layers

Now you add layers into the mix. You work with the single object that you just created out of two other objects:

Note

For a refresher on some of the things that you can do with layers and how to work with them, see the section, "Working with Layers" in Chapter 3, "Setting Up a New Document and Navigating the Workspace."

1. Double-click the object in the Layers panel and change the name to Base Art.

2. Duplicate the single object that you created so far.

   There's only one object in your Base Art layer. The name of this object, by default, is Path.

3. With the Pointer tool, click the Path object to select it.

4. Copy this object, making an exact duplicate of it.

   You can make duplicates of objects in Fireworks in more than one way. Choose one of the following options:

   - **Option #1**—Choose Edit, Clone. You have made an exact duplicate in place of your original.

   - **Option #2**—Select Copy, Control-C (for Windows) or Command-C (for a Macintosh) and Paste, Control-V (for Windows) or Command-V Paste (for a Macintosh).

   - **Option #3**—Choose Edit Menu, Duplicate. (Clone puts your copy in exact registration with your original, whereas Duplicate positions your duplicate cascaded down and 10 pixels to the right of the original object.)

5. Click the cloned object to select it on the Canvas.

6. Use the Fill button. You can just click the Color box on the Property Inspector. It reveals the Color box pop-up menu. Change the color from light gray to medium gray, and choose hexadecimal number color 999999.

7. Click in the Tools panel to select the Rounded Rectangle shape object. Reset the roundedness to 20. Drag a rounded rectangle with a width of 800 and the height of 600.

Hint: At this point, while your rectangle is still selected, it's helpful to change the color. This makes it easier to tell your *cookie cutter* from your *cookie dough*.

8. Using the Pointer tool, reposition your object to x = 11, y = 28.

   Look at the lower left-hand corner of your canvas. You need to make some adjustments to trim the bottom corner to a straight segment.

This piece of artwork is available on the CD-ROM in `ciber_combine04.png` (see Figure 4.22).

Figure 4.22   The tutorial file `ciber_combine04.png`.

Scaling the Rectangle Object

Now you will create a shape to use as a modifier:

1. Click and select the green rectangle object.

2. Switch to the Scale tool in the Tools panel.

   Eight square black rectangles are around the perimeter of the shape and one round circle is in the middle of the shape. The dot at the center represents the center point. The default setting is Center.

   You can reset the center point of an object by clicking and dragging the center point to a different location on the shape. The eight square bullets around the outside edge of your rectangle are its Bezier control handles.

3. Click the lower-right Transform handle of your rectangle while holding the Shift key. Drag your shape's width to an approximate width of 850 and height of 640. Note: The lower left-hand corner edge is now "trimmed" by a straight shape instead of a curved shape (see Figure 4.23).

Notice that the object is not completely "trimmed." The object is partially off the canvas and is not exported with the final image or table. Because it is larger than the canvas, it's not completely trimmed unless you have the preferences set to Delete Objects When Cropping in the Editing section, and if you crop your document before exporting. In this case, objects that are partially off the canvas are trimmed in that only the part on the canvas is exported.

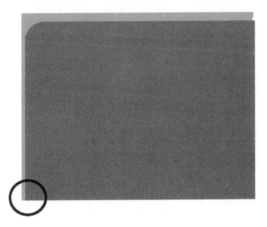

Figure 4.23   The tutorial file `ciber_combine05.png`.

4. Using the Pointer tool, click to select the rectangle (if it is not already selected) and hold the Shift key to select the path object located in the middle position within the stack of three objects on your Base Art layer.

5. With these two objects selected, choose Modify, Combine Paths, Punch.

   The result is a single shape from the original two, creating a bracket around the top and left sides of your user interface object. Because this object was created from a clone of the original, the curved edge at the upper right aligns perfectly with the layer beneath.

Naming Objects

You can organize layers and objects in a document by naming them. This helps you to keep track of the objects in your artwork. Here's the process:

1. Double-click to select the name path on the bottom object of your Base Art layer. Change the name to Bottom.

2. Double-click the word "Path" in the top layer to select the name field. Rename it Top.

3. Click the bottom layer to select it. This automatically selects the object on the bottom layer.

4. Choose Edit, Clone to make an exact duplicate of the bottom layer in exact registration to it.

5. Double-click the name of the newly created layer, which exists directly on top of the bottom layer, and change its name from bottom to middle. See Figure 4.24.

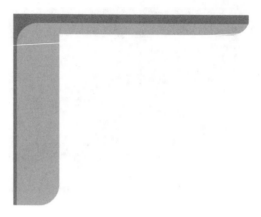

Figure 4.24   The tutorial file `ciber_combine06.png`.

Hiding a Layer

Another of the many ways Fireworks helps you to keep track of and isolate just the right elements you are working with is the hide and show options on the Layers panel. This next part of the exercise gives you some practice using this feature:

1. Click the eyeball of the Top user interface object in the Base Art layer to hide it.

2. With the Pointer tool, click the middle layer, which automatically selects it.

3. Change its color from light gray to dark gray, hexadecimal number color 333333.

4. Select the Regular Rectangle tool from the Tools panel.

5. Click and drag outside the canvas from the upper left down vertically across to the lower right, just trimming at the edge of the vertical area of the interface panel. See Figure 4.25.

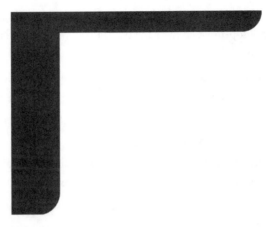

Figure 4.25   Tutorial file `ciber_combine07.png`.

Note

To make your work easier to see, after this rectangle is drawn, change its color to something other than the current color.

Using Guides

Guides are lines that you can drag out from the rulers onto the document canvas. Guides are used as drawing aids to help you place and align objects within your design. You can use them to mark important places of your document, such as the baseline of type elements, a shape's center point, and areas within which you want to work very accurately.

Note

Guides are invisible when your files are exported and are used as design tools only.

To help you align objects precisely, Fireworks lets you snap objects to guides. Guides can be locked and unlocked to allow flexibilty and protection in the workspace:

1. From the View menu, choose Rulers and make sure that they are checked on (Ctrl-Alt (for Windows) or Command-R (for a Macintosh).

   This option allows Fireworks to display rulers at the top and left of your Document window. You can click inside the ruler and drag a guide onto the canvas to aid in positioning your artwork. The cross-hair icon that appears at the intersection of the vertical and horizontal rulers allows you to change the document's origin (0,0), thus repositioning the grid. Double-click this icon to restore the origin to the top-left corner of the canvas.

2. For now, click the eyeball to hide the rectangle layer. The middle layer should appear to be the top-most layer, as the other two layers that are actually above are currently hidden.

3. Under View, Guides, hold your mouse down to display the Guides' submenu. Check to make sure that the Snap-to-Guides option is checked.

4. Click in your vertical ruler at the left and drag into the canvas, allowing your guide to gently snap to the edge of your vector shape.

   Notice that, when Snap-to-Guides is checked on, a slight snapping sensation occurs when your guide picks a vector point or an exact point on the ruler.

5. Align your guide with the right edge of the middle user interface object's vertical segment.

6. Click the eyeball next to the top-most rectangle layer to display it.

7. Using the Pointer tool to select the rectangle, move it to align it perfectly with the new guide that you just set.

   Hint: Use the arrow keys on your keyboard to move vector objects 1 pixel at a time. Holding the Shift key while using the arrow keys move vector objects 10 pixels at a time.

8. After the rectangle is positioned along the right edge of the vertical element on the middle object, select both the rectangle and the middle object.

9. Choose Modify, Combine Paths, Crop. The resulting object is a curved corner vertical panel (see Figure 4.26).

10. Click the eyeball of the top object within the base layer to see the result.

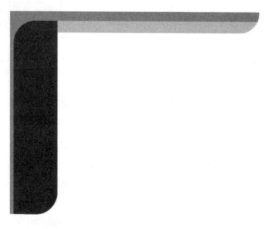

Figure 4.26   The tutorial file `ciber_combine08.png`.

Aligning and Stacking Objects

Under the Modify menu, there are options for Alter Path, Arrange, Align, and Transform. All these options give you additional flexibility and power for manipulating vector objects in Fireworks.

With the align commands, you can align objects to other objects along a vertical or horizontal axis. You can also align selected objects vertically along their left edge, right edge, or center. Additionally, objects can be aligned horizontally along their top, bottom, or center edge. The bounding box (singular), which encloses the entire selection, defines the edges used to align objects. That's why the align commands appear to align to the largest object.

To change the stacking order of a selected object or group within a layer, you can do the following:

- **Modify, Arrange, Bring Forward**—Moves an object up one level in the stack or group

- **Modify, Arrange, Bring to Front**—Moves an object to the very front of the stack or group

- **Modify, Arrange, Send Backward**—Moves the object down one level in the stack or group

- **Modify, Arrange, Send to Back**—Moves the object down to the bottom of the stack or group

Exercise 4.2:   Drawing a Panda Head with Basic Shapes

Drawings in Fireworks are composed of a collection of simple shapes or complex curves drawn with the Basic Shapes tool. For this exercise, you create a panda graphic by using some of the Basic Shape tools (see Figure 4.27).

Figure 4.27   The complete panda graphic.

Along the way, you get some practice using several panels and many of the transform functions, including the following:

Duplicate   Layers Panel

Group   Arrange

Set Fill and Stroke   Align

Scale   Modify

Rotate   Property Inspector

Flip

Drawing the Panda Head

The following sets of steps take you through the process of drawing the elements of a simple but cute looking Panda head.

1. Look at the Tools panel. Make sure that the stroke color is set to black and the fill is set to white.

    Hint: Click the Set Default Brush and Fill Colors buttons on the Tools panel.

2. Choose File, New. Create a new document with the width set to 600 and height set to 400. Make the canvas color white.

    You are making the canvas larger than the panda's head. This means that the object won't fill the canvas completely, allowing space around the outside edges of your canvas, within which you are going to construct the other elements of the panda's head and body.

3. Select the Ellipse tool from the Tools panel.

4. Click and drag on the canvas with the Ellipse tool. Create an ellipse that's approximately 146 pixels wide by 123 pixels tall.

    If you want, you can drag out an ellipse of any size and then, using the Property Inspector, select your ellipse and type 146 in the width selection text field and 123 in the height selection text field.

5. After your ellipse is drawn and sized correctly, look at the attribute of the ellipse known as the stroke.

The Stroke Panel

The default stroke for objects is pencil, one pixel soft, and at one pixel:

1. With the ellipse selected, change the thickness of the stroke from 1 to 6 by using the pop-up slider on the right side of the panel (just above the Amount of Texture pop-up slider). This slider is known as the Tip Size and, like many other panels and fields in Fireworks, you can just type a 6 to replace the stroke of 1 with a stroke of 6.

   After you do this, you see that your circle's outline becomes thicker.

   To get a better idea of what you're creating open the file panda artwork from your Vector folder. It should look like Figure 4.28.

   You need to refer to this image to make sure that you're on the right track. The tutorial file is also available on the CD-ROM.

Figure 4.28 Drawing the panda's head, step by step.

Now you must create the panda's ears (see Figure 4.29). For this, you also use the Ellipse tool, except that you want to actually create a circle.

Figure 4.29   The panda's ear.

  2. Select the Ellipse tool and position your cursor near the upper-left corner.

  3. Click and drag while holding the Shift key to create a circle. I created my circle at 47 wide by 47 wide.

   The attribute of the last item drawn carries over to the next item. The circle is 47 pixels by wide and 47 pixels high and is filled with white and stroked with 6 points of black.

   We are going to need to make the ears black, and we'll do that in the next step. But, we also want a duplicate of this ear shape for the other side of the panda's head. This gives us an opportunity to begin working with guides.

   If your rulers are not showing, choose View, Rulers and make sure that they are checked on. After your rulers are on, you can click in the horizontal and vertical rulers and drag down to pull guides from the ruler.

  4. Create a guide by clicking in the rulers to the horizontal or vertical rulers and drag onto the canvas and drag out. Notice that, as you drag, your guide follows your cursor.

  5. Position your guide at the center of the large oval, which is the panda's head. This is so that you can position the ears on either side of the panda's head symmetrically.

  6. Select the large oval.

  7. Click in the left ruler and drag until you are on top of the ellipse's center point.

  8. When you have your cursor right on top of that center point, release it. Your guide is now aligned to the center of the panda's head.

  9. To make an exact copy of the panda's ear, use the Clone option.

 10. Select the panda's left ear, making sure that the panda's head is not selected.

11. Choose Edit, Clone.

Look in the Layers panel. Notice that another object, called Path, has been created. The clone of the ear sets directly on top of the first ear.

From this point, you want to position the ear on the other side of the panda's head. To do this, use your arrow keys.

12. Tap the right arrow (on the keyboard); notice that the ear that needs to be on the right side begins to move across the screen.

Tip: To get it to move more quickly, hold the Shift key and the right ear moves in 10-pixel increments instead of 1-pixel increments.

13. Tap several times until you position the ear on what looks equidistant from the center line (see Figure 4.30).

Figure 4.30   The panda's ears.

Technical Tip: To be perfectly equal, use this technique: Use the Property Inspector to find the x location of the cloned ellipse and set it's new location to be of equal distance from the center guide that was at 300 pixels. So the second-ear ellipse will be set at 300, plus the difference between 300 and the position of the original ear ellipse. Enter that number in the Property Inspector.

Creating the Left Eye

Now that you have the ears spaced equidistantly on either side of the panda's head, it's time to create the left eye with a series of ellipses (three in total):

1. Click and drag the outer ellipse on the left side of your panda's head and the left side of the guideline.

Use the Property Inspector to help you make it approximately 57 pixels wide by 45 pixels high. With the tip or stroke size set to 6, it makes it difficult to visualize what this eye is going to look like.

2. With the first eye ellipse still selected, change the tip size, or stroke thickness, from 6 to 2 using the Property Inspector (see Figure 4.31). This time, instead of creating a completely new ellipse by clicking and dragging, use the existing ellipse to create the next one inside of it.

Figure 4.31   The panda's eye.

3. Make sure that your ellipse is selected and choose Edit, Clone. This makes an exact copy of your original and places it directly on top of the original. Now, resize the clone.

4. With the ellipse still selected, choose the Scale tool from the Tools panel.

   Notice eight Transform handles around the outside edge of the bounding box—one on each corner and one on each side. In the very center is what is called the center point. Leave that alone for now.

5. Click the upper-left Transform handle and drag the ellipse down toward the right.

6. Scale the ellipse to about 80 percent of the original size. Choose Modify, Transform, Numeric Transform to set the mode of transformation to scale and enter 80 into one of the numeric fields, making sure that Scale Attributes and Constrain Proportions are checked. Click OK.

7. With the second ellipse still selected, select Edit, Clone.

   You just cloned the object and the bounding box appears around the second ellipse.

8. Click and drag the upper-left handle to about 60 percent of the original size (see Figure 4.32).

Figure 4.32   The panda's eye—continued.

Modifying the Three Ellipses

You will now modify these three ellipses to make the panda's eye look like an eye:

  1. With the smallest ellipse still selected, change its attributes of stroke to none.

  2. Click in the Color box to the right of the pencil in the Colors panel.

  3. Move your cursor to the top part of the Color panel where you see a white square with a red line through it.

  4. That item is none. Click it.

  5. Use black for the fill. In the Colors panel, click the Color box to the right of the Paint bucket and choose Black. Now the pupil of the panda's eye is black with no stroke (see Figure 4.33).

Figure 4.33   The panda's eye with a pupil.

  6. Set the fill and stroke for the outermost circle. Select it and choose None for the stroke and Black for the fill.

  7. Reposition the three eyepieces and get them lined up properly.

  8. Click the smallest circle—the one that represents the panda's pupil.

9. Use your arrow keys on your keyboard to nudge the pupil shape over to the left and up a bit.

10. Select the white of the panda's eye with the pupil by holding the Shift key and mouse over it until you see the red highlight.

11. Click the eye shape. Move the eye shape over and up just a bit if necessary (see Figure 4.34).

Figure 4.34   The panda's eye is in position.

Making Additional Adjustments

The panda's eye would look a bit cuter if we make a few tweaks to it:

1. Select the pupil again, and scale it down from the upper left-hand corner to about 94 percent of its original size.

2. Select the outermost black circle of the panda's eye.

3. Make it larger by clicking and dragging the left Transform handle at the top and scaling it to about 108 percent of its original size. This exaggeration creates the "cute" look.

Before you can duplicate the panda's left eye and create the right eye from it, you'll need to group all the three panda eye pieces so that they act as one element. Grouping makes it easier to select graphics that consist of several objects, by making them into one group. The following section shows you how to do this.

Grouping the Eye Objects

1. Select each one of the three parts of the eye and choose Modify, Group.

   Notice that the four points surrounding the group indicate that they are grouped.

   Hint: You can add an object or another group to the original group by selecting both the object (or group) and the original group and then selecting Modify, Group again. This is called nesting a group.

2. To select objects within the group, you do not have to ungroup it. You use the Subselection tool to select objects within a group, or press the Alt key (for Windows) or the Option key (for a Macintosh) while selecting the part of the group with the Pointer tool).

Duplicating the Eye

Now that the panda's left eye is grouped, you can duplicate it to create the right eye:

1. Move and then flip the eye to get it into the correct position.

2. With the eye group selected, choose Edit, Clone. Now the clone of the eye is now selected.

3. Move the clone approximately 70 pixels by holding down the Shift key, and tapping the right arrow seven times.

4. Because we want both eyes looking straight ahead, flip the right eye so that the pupil is pointing towards the left.

5. With the right eye selected, choose Modify, Transform, Flip Horizontal.

The eyes are complete (see Figure 4.35). Yippee!

Figure 4.35   The panda's eyes are finally complete.

Creating the Panda's Nose

The panda's nose is a small triangle that we create by following these steps:

1. Choose the Polygon tool from the Basic Shapes tools in your Tools panel.

2. Make sure that the Tool option is set to Polygon and Side is set to 3 in the Property Inspector.

3. Click and drag on your canvas to create a downward-pointing triangle.

    Because the last item that you created was a black fill with a black stroke, the triangle will be drawn with a black fill and a black stroke.

4. While the triangle is still selected, set the stroke in the Property Inspector to None (see Figure 4.36).

Figure 4.36   The panda's nose.

5. Zoom in on the triangle to get a better look by clicking the Zoom tool in the Tools panel.

6. Move the magnification-glass cursor over the triangle. Click and drag a marquee around the panda nose triangle to zoom in on it.

    You can see that it jumps to the center of your screen and makes your triangle look really big, even though it's really small.

    Look closely. The first thing I noticed when I zoomed in on my triangle was that the top two points, the bar across the top of the triangle, was not level. Yours might be different, but here's what I did to fix mine:

    Because the shape is not quite right, you must understand the reason why and adjust the shape by using the Pen tool and Bezier control handles.

Why not rotate with the Transform tool? You can rotate in 1-degree increments by using the Modify, Transform, Numeric Transform command and then use Edit, Repeat Transform to rotate the triangle to the exact location where you want it to appear.

Using the Zoom Tool

There are two alternate ways to zoom:

- **Option #1**—You can hold down the Ctrl key (for Windows) and type minus or the Command key (for a Macintosh) and type minus to zoom out one increment at a time. You can zoom in and out to get different views of your object and see how it looks at different scaling.

  In this case, although I know the triangle is still too big to be the panda's nose, it is probably be easier to manipulate the corner points to round them with the nose at a larger size.

- **Option #2**—Click to Select the Zoom tool from the Tools panel. Then click and drag around the triangle to zoom in on it. With the triangle still selected, choose the Pen tool. (The Pen tool is the tool that you use to make Bezier curves.) You can create complex shapes with this tool by clicking and dragging in different directions and then joining to make closed paths, also know as complex shapes.

  In this case, you use the Pen tool to modify the points of the nose shape. This method is the way to use the Pen tool to modify points of paths that you have already created from the basic shapes.

Click and drag the right corner-top point of the triangle and begin to drag out just a little bit.

Notice that, if you drag one way, your corner point begins to look like a loop, but if you slowly rotate the cursor around to the top and drag, your corner begins to round.

I want to round the top two corners, but not the bottom of my triangle. To round the top correctly, I move the cursor to the point on the left with the Pen tool. That point becomes selected and, when I begin to drag again, if I drag up I see a loop, and if I drag down, my triangle begins to become round on that corner. I am going to try to match the angles of the way I dragged on the right and have them doing the symmetrically opposite thing.

I release the mouse and I have what looks more like a nose shape than a triangle. Then, I zoom back out to 100 percent.

We talked about other ways of duplicating, such as copy and paste, duplicate and clone. The following trick is another way of copying items:

1. Select the final nose of the three noses, and hold down on it with the Pointer tool and drag over and place this triangle on your panda's face.

2. Release the mouse and then the Alt (or Option) key.

Scaling the Nose

You will now scale the nose by following these steps:

1. Select the Scale tool from the Tools panel.

2. Click and drag from the right corner toward the center until about 70 percent of its original size. Press the Enter key. You can click on the Pointer tool and remove the Transform handles.

   You can then move the nose back into place with the Pointer tool. My panda's nose doesn't look small enough for me, so I want to scale it one more time. I like the width; however, I don't like the height. I am going to zoom in on it again.

3. Using the Subselection tool, select the bottom-most point of the panda's nose by clicking once to select the shape, and then clicking directly on the bottom point. You can tell when the bottom point is selected because it fills in dark blue.

4. Click the point again with the Subselection tool and drag it slowly upward on the center guide, compressing and shortening the nose.

   I moved the bottom point on my triangle six pixels up to flatten out the nose (see Figure 4.37).

Figure 4.37   The panda's nose has now been scaled down.

The Panda's Snout

You will now draw the panda's snout and mouth, or more precisely, make it an indication of the panda's snout and draw its mouth with small lines, using the Line and Pen tools:

1. Select the Line tool from the Tools panel.

2. Click at the base of the triangle of the panda's nose and drag down, holding the Shift key along the guide to drag out the snout. The length of the snout is 14 pixels. The width is 1 pixel.

    I want the panda's mouth to be a curved line, not a straight line, and you can't draw curved lines with the Line tool, so you must use the Pen tool (see Figure 4.38). The Pen tool makes Bezier curves, which are adjustable. Release the mouse button, then move the Pen tool across to the other side of the mouth, and click and drag it up.

Figure 4.38   The panda's snout and mouth.

3. Select the Pen tool from the Tools panel.

4. Click on the left side of the panda's face and drag to the right and slightly down on the canvas. Release the mouse.

5. Move the cursor to the right side of the face.

6. Click and drag up and to the right slightly.

Warning

Be careful when you draw the panda's smile that you don't get too close to the bottom of the panda's snout.

You can make the mouth longer or shorter by using the Subselection tool. To do this, select the end points of your vectors and click and drag them with the arrow tools to change, elongate, or shorten the angle of the mouth.

Adjusting the Ears

To get the size right, the panda's ears originally started out as white circles with black fills, but that's not what they're supposed to look like when the panda's finished:

1. Change the attributes of the two ears at the same time by clicking one and Shift-clicking to select the other, going to the color portion of the Tools Pallet, changing the fill from white to black.

   You now want the ears to go behind the head, but because they were originally drawn after the head's oval, their stacking order puts them in front of the head's oval. The order in which objects appear on a layer or within your artwork depends on the order in which they were drawn. Just like other graphics programs, the first item is underneath the next item, and the last object created is on top of the stack.

2. To change the stacking order of ears, use the Arrange submenu or the Modify menu (Modify, Arrange, Send to Back).

That's it. You have completed the panda's head.

Creating the Panda's Body

In this section of the exercise, you complete the panda's body by using rounded rectangles and choosing Modify Paths, Union:

1. Select the rounded rectangle from the Basic Shape tools set in the Tools panel.

2. Click and drag to create a rounded rectangle with a corner radius of 33, a width of 96, and a height of 120 (see Figure 4.39).

Figure 4.39   The panda's arm is created with a rounded rectangle.

When you draw this rectangle, it will be on the very top of your stacking order of your objects.

3. Send it to the back of your artwork by either clicking the tool bar or choosing Modify, Arrange, Send to Back. You want it sent to the very back so that you know it's behind the head (see Figure 4.40).

Figure 4.40   The panda's arm is sent to the back of the artwork.

4. Create two smaller rectangles for the panda's arms. Continue using the Rounded Rectangle tool.

5. Change the roundness setting to 100 in the Property Inspector and create a rectangle with a width of 76 and a height of 24 at the top left of your panda, so that it looks like your panda's arm is reaching to the left.

6. With this arm selected, click and hold the Shift key and the Alt key (for Windows) or Shift-Option (for a Macintosh).

7. Drag the top arm down to the bottom base of the panda's body.

8. If you need to nudge the arms into position, you can do that with the cursor keys (see Figure 4.41).

Figure 4.41   The panda with two arms.

Although you could make these into a group to make them easier to manage, I think I it is better to make these three objects into one actual object by uniting them into one complex shape (by using Modify, Combine Paths, Union):

1. Click the three component parts: the panda's two arms and body.

2. Select Modify, Combine Paths, Union.

3. The new panda shape acts like its just been drawn and comes to the top of the stacking order.

Creating the Panda's Tail

To create the panda's tail, follow these steps:

1. Select the Ellipse from the Basic Shapes tool in the Tools panel.

2. Move the cursor to the lower end of the panda's back on the right.

3. Holding the Shift key, click and drag from inside the panda's body out toward the outside of the panda's body.

4. Make a circle that overlaps half inside the panda's body and half outside the panda's body. With that shape, this new circle tail is still selected.

5. Hold the Shift key and select the body as well.

6. Choose Modify, Combine, Union, making the panda's arms and legs, body, and tail into one complex shape.

7. Choose Send to Back to push the panda's body to the back of the stacking order.

Adjusting the Panda's Arms

Finally, the panda's arms seem a little long, so adjust them using the Subselection tool in a special way:

1. With the panda deselected, choose the Subselection tool.

2. Click with the cursor outside to the upper left of the panda to deselect all the selected objects. Click down and around just the tips of the panda's paws.

3. Carefully select just the rounded tips of the arms on the top and bottom.

   Just the correct points are selected because they are the ones highlighted in dark blue (if your preferences are set on default).

4. Press the right-arrow key several times until the arms become shorter.

The panda is now complete.

Creating the Tree for the Panda

You must now create the tree by using the Rounded Rectangle tool and the Ellipse tool to create the stem and leaves. This procedure involves converting points:

1. Select the Ellipse tool, set the stroke to none and the fill to light green. I used 99CC00.

2. Drag an ellipse with a width of 13 and height of 41 for the first leaf. You make the rest of the leaves from this original.

3. Zoom in on the ellipse that you just drew, select the Zoom tool, and click and drag a marquee around the leaf to zoom into it (see Figure 4.42).

4. Select the Pen tool.

5. Click the very top point of the ellipse and then on the bottom point of the ellipse to change the round points at the top and bottom to corner points. This creates a pointy leaf.

   Figure 4.42   The leaves that were created from the Ellipse tool.

   Now, you need to rotate the leaf.

6. Use the Rotate tool to rotate the leaf so that it's coming out of the stem.

7. With the leaf selected, choose the Transform tool from the Tools panel.

   When the cursor is set away from the now selected leaf, it displays the rotation pointer. When the cursor is placed on one of the object's corner points, it becomes a double-headed diagonal arrow. When it's on one of the side handles, it becomes either a vertical or a horizontally aligned double-headed arrow.

8. Move the cursor toward the upper left-hand corner from the leaf, but not touching it. When you're about a quarter of an inch away, click and drag down to rotate the top of the leaf down, and the bottom of the leaf up.

9. If you hold the Shift key while rotating, the rotation occurs in 15-degree increments.

10. Rotate the leaf down 45 degrees.

11. Switch back to the Pointer tool and move the leaf over toward the bamboo by clicking and dragging it.

   I left mine just a hair away from the edge of the bamboo leaf (see Figure 4.43).

12. Using Ctrl-minus (for Windows) or Command-minus (for a Macintosh), zoom out from the screen so that you can see the artwork at 100 percent.

Figure 4.43   Bamboo leaves.

13. Click the leaf, hold the Shift key, and drag with the Alt key clicked to duplicate the leaf.

14. Release the mouse and then the keys.

15. Holding the Shift key again, select the top leaf and position it beneath.

16. Select both leaves and choose Clone.

17. Hold down the Shift key, tap the right-pointing arrow 3 times to move the leaves on the right 30 pixels, and hold the Shift key and tap the down arrow 4 times to move them down 40 pixels.

18. With the leaves still selected, Choose Modify, Transform, Flip Vertical to flip them on their vertical axis.

The bamboo stalk is now complete (see Figure 4.44).

Figure 4.44   The completed bamboo stalk.

For the finishing touch on the panda's face, I changed the mouth from a smile to a little circle because it makes him look more panda-like (see Figure 4.45).

Figure 4.45   You now have a complete panda. Way to go!

Summary

Understanding vectors, vector tools, and all the many options is fundamental to working with Fireworks. It's also fun! In this chapter, you learned

- What vectors are
- How to create, copy, duplicate, clone, and move vectors
- The Vector tool basics
- The Vector Tool options
- A great panda tutorial put all of it together

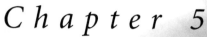

C h a p t e r   5

Working with Color Fills and Strokes

Fireworks offers many ways to color in and outline the objects that you create. The inner part of a vector object's color is known as *fill* and the outline of the vector object is known as *stroke*.

The Property Inspector contains controls for modifying both fills and strokes. Additionally, you can create your own custom strokes by using the Edit Stroke dialog box to change specific stroke characteristics.

In this way, you can manipulate and control a vector object's color in a number of different ways. You can always modify and edit Fireworks objects infinitely because they have been saved in .png format.

If you haven't already, you can find out the details of working with the Fill and Stroke panels in Chapter 2, "Interface, Tools, and Workspace Overview."

Working with Color

Fireworks supplies several color models from which you can select and mix your own colors. The Fireworks Swatches Panels allow you to maintain color standards for

- Web color
- Windows system color
- Macintosh system color

You can create your own groups of swatches that you can reuse, export, and share with other web designers.

You can mix colors using hexadecimal, RGB, CMY, HSB, or grayscale color modes. You can also set the view of your document to express any of these color models.

As many artists and designers can tell you, colors convey a meaning, energy, and mood of images. It's helpful to consider color harmony and contrast, and to think about what colors mean to your audience.

In our communities, we share understanding about the meanings and associations of color. For example, you might associate orange with danger (or The Home Depot) and green for freshness. Many people still associate pink with girls and blue with boys.

Over the past few years of teaching web design, I have taken many surveys on color and have come up with a few common color associations:

- **Red**—Associated with love, hot, stop, passion, danger, warning, and appetite
- **Orange**—Associated with autumn, warning, and Halloween
- **Yellow**—Associated with cheeriness, energy, radiance, and sunshine
- **Green**—Associated with spring and newness

- **Blue**—Associated with calm, cool, peace, water, and sky

- **Purple**—Associated with royalty, impressiveness, and enchantment

- **Brown**—Associated with earth, warmth, home, and chocolate

A few variables affect colors and how they appear; we use a few terms to describe these variables. Although there are no formal rules about color use, many color theories exist. The effects of color on people's moods and emotions have been studied and well documented.

Note

I always found the study of color interesting. Growing up, my parents had a book that influenced me as a young artist. It is called *The Luscher Color Test* by Dr. Max Luscher (edited by Ian A. Scott).

Color Resources

The web offers great information about color. You can find a good basic article, with resources, on color and designing for the web at www.colormatters.com.

Another site, www.colorschemer.com, is great if you are color blind or have no color sense. At this site, you can find many links, and references, on color and vision, color and design, color and the body, and more.

The Color Schemer was designed to make it quick and easy to create harmonious color schemes. You simply select one color (either by entering RGB or hex values, picking from a web-safe palette, or selecting a color from anywhere onscreen), and you are presented with a set of 16 colors that relate to the selected color.

The Pantone system is certainly one of the world's foremost authorities on color. At the web site www.pantone.com, you find yet another plethora of wonderful color tools and resources to use.

One of many neat things that you can do here is click the Digital link at the bottom of the home page. When you click this link, a window pops up that allows you to match a print color to a web color.

Besides what is mentioned here, there are many other resources of interest on trends, and research that can help you on issues from calibration to why color is essential.

Color Terminology

Some terms are worth knowing and understanding when using Fireworks to create or manipulate colors for web images. Here are a few:

- **Hue**—The color part of color, such as red or blue. Technically, hue is the wavelength of a color.

- **Saturation or intensity**—The amount of color in a color. Technically, the absence of white in the color is what designers call *color saturation*.

- **Brightness or value**—The amount of lightness or darkness in a color. The presence of lightness is measured in *lumens*.

- **Neutral colors or monochromatic hues**—Black, white, or gray.

- **Chromatic color**—All colors other than black, white, or gray.

- **Monochromatic color**—Color combinations that use various values of a single hue.

In the corporate world, color equals equity, as in brand equity. I spent a number of years working at Campbell Soup Company in Camden, New Jersey, where I began to understand the meaning of color as equity. Think about all the company logos that depend on a specific color. Here are some examples: The Home Depot (orange), IBM (blue), and CliffsNotes (yellow and black). All those brands, if correctly branded, immediately evoke a response. My family refers to a specific brown as "UPS brown." (Hopefully, you know what color I'm referring to.)

Color recognition is an aspect of marketing. The consumer recognizes specific colors and makes associations to the product with which it associates the color. Working with certain colors on the web requires consideration, especially if you're trying to match a specific color.

Printing is known as reflective art. The color that you see on printed paper is comprised of mixtures of colored ink applied to various types of paper. Every edition of a print is virtually identical to others from the same print run using the same inks and paper.

In the case of web design and graphics, artwork is viewed on any number of given systems on any number of given monitor resolutions that might or might not have been gamma adjusted. Art is also viewed on any number of browsers.

Many factors come together that inhibit computer color from being 100 percent accurate to all viewers. Because computer monitors blend red, green, and blue light together to create what the viewer sees, the color settings of any viewer's particular system or monitor determines how the color looks.

Understanding Gamma

Computer color settings are known as *gamma* and the *gamma value* of monitors can be adjusted with gamma-adjustment software.

Platform differences, meaning differences between the Windows and Macintosh systems, play a role is this dilemma. Each system has its own inherent gamma setting.

Different gamma settings exist for different systems. The Macintosh system has a default setting of 1.8. The Windows system defaults to 2.2, which is the standard for television as well. Macs generally appear brighter or lighter; its lower gamma setting more accurately matches print output. When you create your graphics on a Mac and view them on the Windows platform, however, they generally appear darker. On the other hand, when you create graphics on a Windows machine and view them on a Mac, they appear considerably brighter.

It's extremely important to check your work using both platforms. Find a happy medium that looks good on both systems.

Switching Between Gamma Views

Fortunately, Fireworks provides you with an option to view other gamma settings (see Figure 5.1). Depending on the system that you use, you can switch the view accordingly.

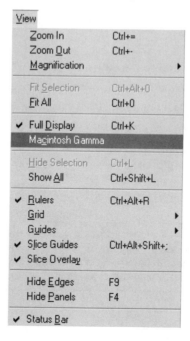

Figure 5.1   The View menu displays the Gamma setting.

Choose View, Macintosh Gamma in Fireworks for Windows to see how your art looks on a Mac. Choose View, Windows Gamma in Fireworks for a Macintosh to view the way your work looks on a Windows machine.

Web-Safe (Browser-Safe) Colors

The colors you see on your monitor are measured in the number of data bits that your video card can render. (This is also known as number of colors.) The least-common denominator user has an 8-bit, or 256-color, capable monitor.

The browser, however, has its own reduced palette of 216 colors, which is known as the *web-safe color palette*. A thorough understanding of color depth and web-safe color is essential when you create art for web pages. Eventually, web-safe color will follow the dinosaurs' fate as more systems support 32-bit color depth, or millions of colors.

Of the 256 colors in the 8-bit minimum system a monitor displays, 40 colors are not common on both Windows and Macintosh systems. These colors are subtracted from the 256, which leaves 216 colors common to both platforms. This allows you to safely use any color from this 216 color palette, insuring that your color looks true when viewed on different platforms using different browsers without any dithering.

To simulate a color that's not represented in the monitor's color spectrum, a computer uses *dithering*. It does this by mixing two or more colors together to create the missing color.

It is especially helpful to use the browser-safe color palette when you want to fill art with flat or solid color. Logos, cartoons, and drawings can be susceptible to ugly dithering when the browser-safe palette is not used. This is becoming less of an issue with the pro-liferation of systems that have 24- and 32-bit capabilities. Although you are welcome to use any colors that your system can handle, browser-safe colors are guaranteed not to dither. If you stick to these 216 colors, they will look the way you want them to (most of the time).

Note

Even browser-safe colors can dither on a 16-bit monitor because some of the web-safe colors are not in the 16-bit gamut. Also, don't forget that America Online (AOL) browsers, when viewing pages through a dialup connection, are set to recompress images on-the-fly and, no matter how "safe" you think it is, AOL might distort the image.

In general, the browser-safe color palette of 216 colors is employed when you are creating anything with flat colors. In the case of photographic images, however, the Export palette needs to be a 24-bit palette, not an 8-bit palette. Usually, photographs are exported using the jpeg format and are dithered by the browser if necessary.

In Fireworks, the web-safe palette can be accessed in a couple of ways:

- By default, the Color box pop-up window that displays when you click any Color Cube in the program is set to the web-safe palette, which contains the web-safe palette and several colors that duplicate web-safe swatches.
- Holding down the Shift key when you select colors using the Eyedropper tool causes the tool to convert colors to web-safe colors as you sample them.

Web Dither

The Fill panel contains a category called *web dither*. With this feature, you can convert any non-web-safe color into a color pattern of web-safe colors that closely matches the desired color.

Sampling Color

You can sample a color from anywhere on your screen, including other Fireworks documents, non-Fireworks documents, and your desktop. You can use the colors that you sample as the colors of your fills and strokes for your current artwork. This process is known as *sampling*.

Note

Your monitor needs to be at 32-bit color depth to get the best, and most accurate, sample. 24-bit is okay, but *not* 16-bit; it just doesn't provide the quality you need.

Applying Color That's Sampled from Your Screen

Sampling enables you to identify and use the exact color that you want. It also enables you to identify a color's hexadecimal value before and after you apply it to selected objects. Here's how to use sampling:

1. Select a stroke or fill Color box on the Tools panel or from any of the other Color boxes in the program. The Color box pop-up window appears (see Figure 5.2). The pointer changes to an eyedropper.

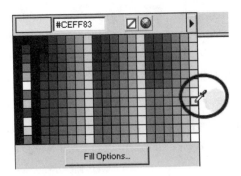

Figure 5.2   The Color box pop-up window with the eyedropper cursor.

2. Move the cursor around the screen. Notice the hexadecimal value that's displayed in the field at the top of the Color box pop-up window.

3. Click anywhere onscreen to select a color. If an object is currently selected, the color is applied to the selected object.

   On a Windows machine, you must click and hold the mouse button and move your cursor over the color that you want to sample. Release the mouse over that color, and it is inserted into the field at the top center and appears as the current color in the Color box.

   Hint: Hold the Shift key to shift colors to web-safe colors as you sample them.

Changing Color Sets

Fireworks enables you to use different color sets from which to create your artwork:

1. Click any of the Color boxes throughout the program. The Color box pop-up window appears.

2. Click the Color box panel's Options pop-up menu in the upper-right corner to display the color sets.

   As you can see in Figure 5.3, the options are Color Cubes, Continuous Tone, Windows System, Macintosh System, and Grayscale.

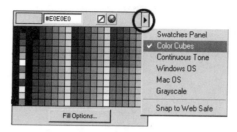

Figure 5.3   The Color options pop-up menu is expanded by using the control circled at the top right of the Color box panel.

You can add, delete, sort, and replace color swatches in the Swatches panel if you so desire. The colors changed automatically updates in the Color box pop-up windows as well.

 Caution

Changes to the Swatches panel cannot be undone by using Edit, Undo.

Working with Swatches

To add a color from a Fireworks document to the Swatches panel by using the Eyedropper tool, follow these steps:

1. Select the Eyedropper tool from the Tools panel.

2. Move the cursor around the screen and click the color that you want to add. To select a color outside of Fireworks on a Windows machine, hold the mouse button as you move the cursor out of the Fireworks program window. Release the mouse button.

   On a Mac, you don't have to hold the mouse button. Just click to sample the color.

3. In the Swatches panel, move the pointer to an open space after the last swatch. The pointer becomes the paint-bucket cursor.

4. Click the empty swatch to dump your color into it.

After you add colors to the Swatches panel, you can save them. To save a selection of your sampled colors, display the Swatches panel, if it's not already showing, and follow these steps:

1. Click the Options pop-up box (use the right-pointing arrow) at the top of the Swatches panel.

2. Choose Save Swatches. The Save As dialog box appears.

3. Give your swatches a name. Fireworks adds the `.act` extension, which saves the color as a swatches file. Click Save.

To delete a swatch from the Swatches panel, simply hold the Ctrl key (for Windows) or the Command key (for a Macintosh) and move your cursor over a swatch. Then, click the swatch to delete it from the Swatches panel.

To clear an entire Swatches panel, click the Options pop-up arrow at the top of the Swatches panel to reveal the swatches options. Then, click Clear Swatches.

To return to the default color swatches, click to reveal the swatches options, and choose Color Cubes. You can sort the swatches by color by choosing Sort By Color from the Swatches panel Options pop-up menu.

If you have saved your own swatches set, you can load your swatches by following these steps:

1. Click the Swatches panel Options pop-up box. Select Add Swatches.

2. Navigate to the Swatches panel that you saved. It is an `.act` file.

3. Select it and click Open to add it to the current swatches.

Working with the Color Table

In the lower portion of the Optimize panel, you can find the Color Table (see Figure 5.4). The Color Table panel gives you information about the status of colors in your document. When you view it in the Preview, 2-Up or 4-Up tabs of the Document window and the image or selected slice is optimized in one of the several 8-bit formats.

The Color Table contains your document's swatches. These swatches can contain different attributes, marked as follows:

● A square in the lower-left corner of a swatch indicates that this color has been altered by the Edit Color button or menu command found under the Options pop-up menu. The edited color will only be included in the palette of the exported index color image, while the Fireworks source PNG will remain unchanged.

- A square in the lower-right corner of a swatch indicates that the color is locked.

  A *locked* color in the Color Table remains in the current image's or slice's palette, no matter what changes you make to the image. Locking a color allows users to force images or slices that use this locked color to maintain the same exact color across many images. This is important when using an adaptive palette, where the same color in a sliced image can be dithered to a color that is close, but not exactly, the same across slices in the image. This can be caused by changes in the elements in the slice that affect other colors within that slice.

- A checkerboard square across the swatch indicates that the color is transparent.

- The diamond configuration in the middle of the swatch indicates that the color is a web-safe color.

- Swatches with more than one indicator mean that the color has multiple attributes.

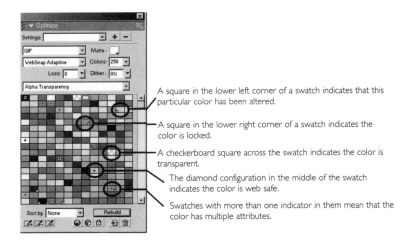

A square in the lower left corner of a swatch indicates that this particular color has been altered.

A square in the lower right corner of a swatch indicates the color is locked.

A checkerboard square across the swatch indicates the color is transparent.

The diamond configuration in the middle of the swatch indicates the color is web safe.

Swatches with more than one indicator in them mean that the color has multiple attributes.

Figure 5.4   The lower portion of the Optimize panel is expanded to reveal the Color Table. Color-attribute indicators give feedback about colors within the document.

Custom Swatch Groups

To create a custom swatch group using the Color Table, follow these steps:

1. Open the Optimize panel if it is not already opened.

2. Create a new file (at 500 × 500 pixels at 72 ppi). Set the canvas to anything you want.

3. In your file, draw a series of different-colored rectangles on the canvas (see Figure 5.5).

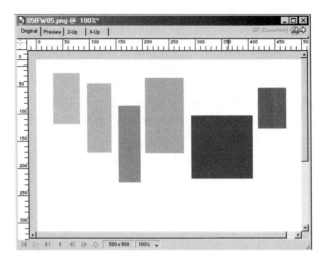

Figure 5.5   Rectangles that have been drawn on the canvas.

4. Expand or tear out the Options panel. Notice the Color Table in the lower half of the panel.

5. Add a new shape with a new color to the canvas.

6. Click the Rebuild button (see Figure 5.6).

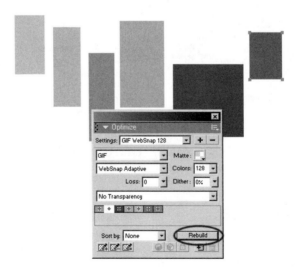

Figure 5.6   The opened Optimize panel with the Color Table.

Notice that the colors in the table update to match the colors on the canvas. The number of colors replaces the Rebuild button (see Figure 5.7).

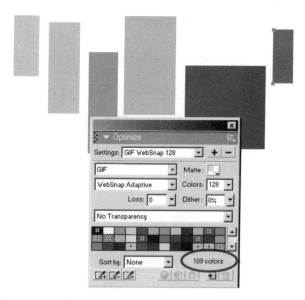

Figure 5.7   The number of colors replaces the Rebuild button.

7. Select the Options pop-up menu.

8. Choose Save Palette. The Save As dialog box appears (see Figure 5.8), which allows you to name and save your palette as an .act (Color Table) file.

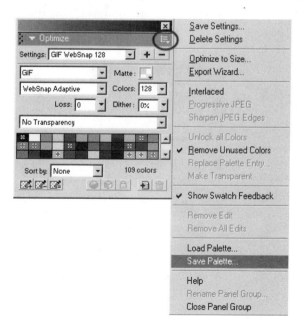

Figure 5.8   The Save Palette option from the Options pop-up menu.

9. Click Save and save your palette in the appropriate folder (see Figure 5.9). I save my palettes with the projects to which they correspond. Some people like to save their palettes inside the Fireworks program folder.

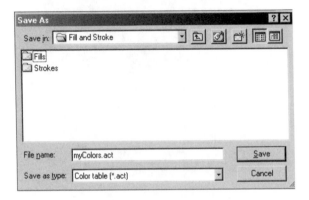

Figure 5.9   Saving a Color Table (`.act`) file in the Save As dialog box.

Load Palette

To use the newly created palette with a new document, follow these steps:

1. Create a new document.

2. Click the Options pop-up arrow from the Optimize panel and choose Load Palette (see Figure 5.10).

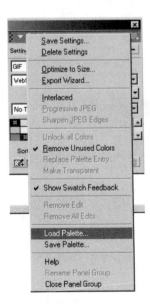

Figure 5.10   The Load Palette option from the Options pop-up menu.

3. Navigate to the `.act` file that you saved and select it (see Figure 5.11). (You can also use a GIF image.)

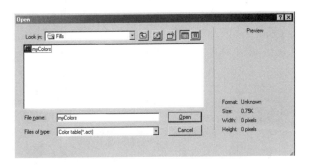

Figure 5.11 The Open dialog box, loading a Color Table (`.act`) file.

4. Double-click it or click Open to load it.

5. The Color Table of your new empty document now contains the swatches from the palette you saved and loaded (see Figure 5.12). To use this palette as your swatches for use in the document, open the Swatches panel, click the Swatches Panel options pop-up arrow, and choose Current Export Palette. Now, all the Color box pop-up windows have only the colors that are in the Color Table. You're all set to control the colors used in the image.

When you open an existing document that already contains many colors, the Color Table panel initially appears empty.

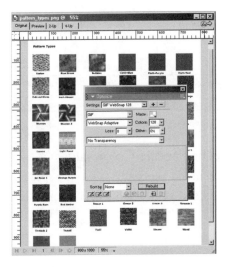

Figure 5.12 The Color Table of an existing document with empty swatches on the Optimize panel.

You can activate the Color Table in the Optimize panel in two ways:

- Click the Preview tab in the Document window (see Figure 5.13). The Color Table builds based on the default setting of GIF Web Snap 128, which places 128 colors in the Color Table. When you click the Original tab, you see that the Color Table stays loaded with this file's swatches.

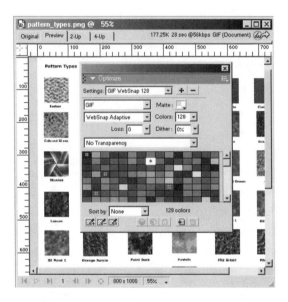

Figure 5.13   You can activate the Color Table by clicking the Preview tab.

- As previously mentioned, you can also use the Rebuild button at the bottom of the Optimize panel.

Note

Refer to Figure 5.6. It shows the opened Optimize panel with Color Table displayed and the Rebuild button circled.

Identifying and Sampling Specific Color Values

Times can arise when you need to know the value of a specific color. By using the Info panel, you can view a color's RGB, hexadecimal, HSB, or CMY values (see Figure 5.14).

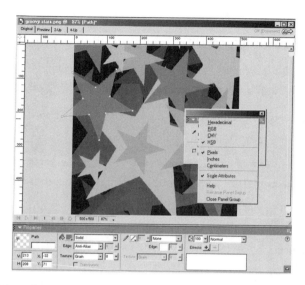

Figure 5.14 The Info panel Option pop-up menu displays the color mode choices.

Use the Info panel Option pop-up menu to set the color mode that you want to display.

Another neat feature about sampling colors is this: Using the Eyedropper tool, you can view the color value of any visible object in any open application in the Color box pop-up window. Another way to do this is to use the Color box pop-up window, or you can use the Color Mixer. If you move the pointer or the eyedropper cursor around your screen, you can examine the color value of objects within your document (see Figure 5.15).

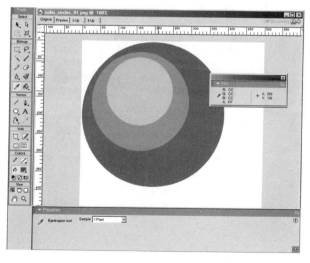

Figure 5.15 The Info panel displays a specific color value.

Within Fireworks, you can view the color value of a selected vector object's stroke and fill colors in the Property Inspector, the Color Mixer, or the Color box.

Let the truth be told: It is the Property Inspector, which is new in Fireworks MX, that is the main command and control center for creating and applying fill and stroke.

By using the Property Inspector, you can infinitely experiment with and apply fills and strokes to your vector objects. Here's the drill:

1. Select the Pointer tool or the Subselection tool from the Tools panel. You want to click the objects that are within groups by using the Subselection tool.

2. Click a vector object within your canvas.

3. Look at the Property Inspector. It shows you the fill and stroke properties of the selected object.

In Figure 5.16, I selected a star that contains a fill of green, with an anti-aliased edge and a 13-point black stroke set to soft, edge 50, and a texture grain of 30 percent. Currently, no effects are applied to the star.

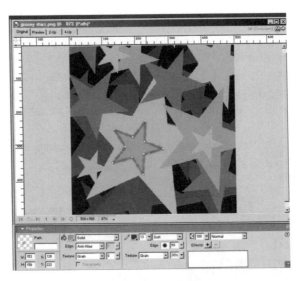

Figure 5.16   The Property Inspector displays the fill and stroke attributes for the selected vector star.

Setting the Fill Color

To set the fill color for any of the basic shape tools using the Property Inspector, follow these steps:

1. Click the Color box in the Property Inspector. The Color Cube pops up.

2. You can choose one of the following:

    - Choose a color from it.

    - Choose no color.

    - Move the cursor over an object on the canvas. The cursor displays the eye-dropper. Position the cursor on top of the object that contains the color you want to use and click.

    - Click the color wheel to choose the system color picker.

It's good to know that you can change the value system that's displayed in the Color Mixer or in the Property Inspector. The default for the Info panel is Hexadecimal. Although the Info panel displays the letters R, G, B, and Alpha, the default color space is actually Hexadecimal. Additionally, the Color Mixer's default is Hexadecimal.

Note

You can also choose the fill settings to use with the Paintbucket tool when filling pixel selections. All the features described in this section are also applicable to the Paintbucket tool's fill options.

Modifying Fills

Of course, after you set the fill of an object, you're going to want to change it, right?

You can control the edges of your fills, specifying hard, anti-alias, and feathered edge options, along with feather distance. You can also set a texture, specifying it's percentage in amount. (A texture works like a grayscale mask.) The Amount field enables you to specify the brightness of the mask, which, in turn, determines the amount of texture applied to the object's fill.

Five basic categories of fills exist (see Figure 5.17). Each category is covered in detail in the following sections.

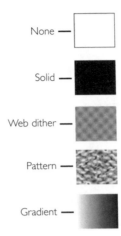

Figure 5.17   The five main fill categories.

Changing the Fill Category

Within web dither, pattern, and gradient, you can specify a number of variances:

1. Select an object to fill by using the Pointer tool from the Tools panel.

2. Click the Fill Category pop-up menu in the Property Inspector (see Figure 5.18).

3. Select one of the five options.

   Obviously, selecting None sets the fill color to no color.

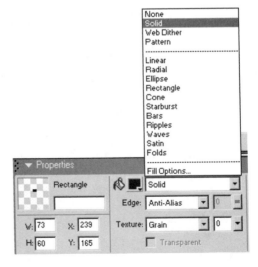

Figure 5.18   The Fill Category pop-up menu in the Property Inspector.

Web Dither

Times might arise when you want to use a color that's not in the 216 web-safe color palette, but you still want the color to look its best and to avoid ugly dithering. This situation calls for the use of web dithering.

Web dither mixes two web-safe palette colors and combines them to simulate a color that's not in the palette. Note that creating a web dither can impact your file size. You can use a web-safe color, a non-web-safe color, and you can also use transparency to create an image that appears translucent to a background color or image when it's placed on a web page—more about this later.

To use web dither, follow these steps:

1. Select an object containing a non-web-safe color by clicking it with the Pointer tool.

2. Select the Web Dither option from the Fill panel's Fill Category pop-up box. The object's current fill displays in the color well to the right of the fill type (see Figure 5.19).

    Notice the four checkerboard Color boxes beneath the sampled color.

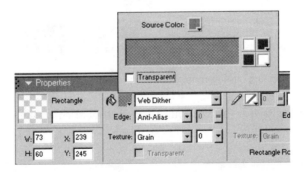

Figure 5.19   The Web Dither Options pop-up box.

These two web-safe colors dither together to simulate the original non-web-safe color. The web dither appears on the object and becomes that object's fill color.

Textures

You can further enhance both your fills and strokes by applying textures to them. Fireworks provides textures from which you can set and apply in various levels of opacity. The default for texture is grain at zero percent. You can add textures to any fill.

Adding Texture to a Fill

Although fill and stroke properties are normally considered exclusive to vector objects, a marquee selection can have a fill applied to it that has the fill, edge, and texture settings:

1. Select an object by using the Pointer tool.

2. Choose a texture from the Texture pop-up menu or use an external texture that you created by choosing Other from the Texture pop-up menu and navigating to a texture file (see Figure 5.20).

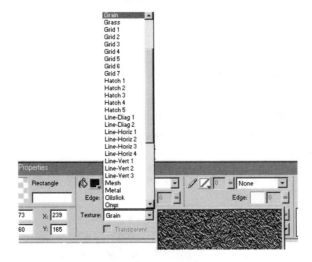

Figure 5.20   The Texture Options pop-up menu.

3. Enter a percentage in the Amount of Texture field or slide the Percentage slider to increase or decrease the percentage of texture intensity (see Figure 5.21).

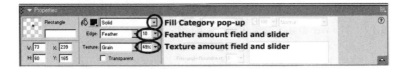

Figure 5.21   Category, Feather, and Texture amount controls.

The texture percentage also controls the degree of texture transparency. Textures modify the brightness of a fill, but do not affect the hue.

Exploring Textures

To examine and tinker with the current set of Fireworks textures, follow these steps:

1. Open the `texture_types.png` file from the `Exercises/05` folder on the accompanying CD-ROM (see Figure 5.22).

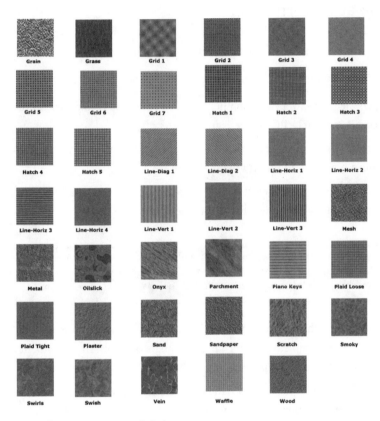

Figure 5.22   The texture types at default percentages.

2. After you open this file, you can see that it contains 41 swatches to which I have applied the various texture types to a gray color chip of hexadecimal value 666666.

3. You can modify and tinker with these texture chips by selecting them and changing their fill color and adjusting the percentage of their texture opacity.

The texture types have been set at their default opacity percentages.

A Look at Pattern Fills

Pattern fills are another option for stylizing your vector or bitmap object's fills in Fireworks. Fireworks ships with 44 different pattern types.

To experiment, explore, and tinker with the pattern types, follow these steps:

1. Open the `pattern_types.png` file from the `Exercises/05` folder on the accompanying CD-ROM (see Figure 5.23).

2. After it is opened, you can click the swatches that I have preapplied the various pattern types to and modify them.

3. With the Pointer tool, select a vector object that contains a pattern. You can notice that handles project out of the tile.

Note

The handles appear only if the Pointer or PaintBucket tools are the currently selected tools. If you apply a pattern or gradient fill to a bitmap, you can change its angle and aspect by clicking and dragging the Paintbucket tool over the pixel selection.

4. You can click the anchor points of the handles and modify how the pattern fills the tile. For example, you can change the angle of a pattern or gradient and the scale or distance of the pattern of gradient.

5. You can also click the "round handle" origin and drag the position of the pattern within the fill of the tile to change its effect.

Warning

Textures and patterns might seem like a clever and quick way to add dimension to your Fireworks art files, and they are. Be careful not to overuse these, however, because your artwork can look canned or very "I've seen this before-ish." The key phrase for designing using pattern and texture types is "less is more," and, if possible, use your own custom patterns and textures.

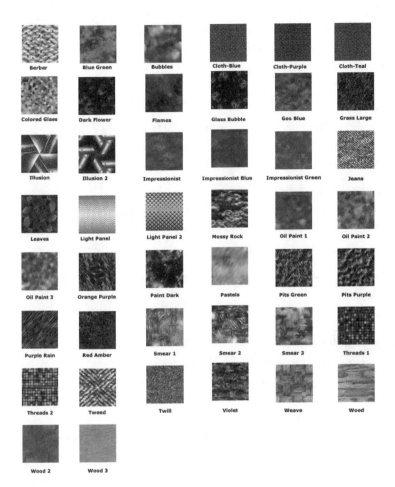

Figure 5.23   Pattern types.

Custom Patterns and Textures

You can create your own patterns and textures by using bitmap files that you created. File formats, including PNG, GIF, JPEG, BMP, TIF, and PICT (for a Mac), all work as pattern and texture file formats.

To add a preexisting texture of your own creation to the Texture pop-up menu in Fireworks, copy the texture file to the `Fireworks MX/Configuration/Textures` folder in your Fireworks MX Application folder.

To use your own external pattern or texture file, follow these steps:

1. In the Fill panel, choose a fill type from the Fill pop-up menu.

2. If you haven't added the texture to the pop-up menu, choose Other from the Texture pop-up menu and navigate to the texture file.

   You can also select the texture from the Texture pop-up menu if you have already added the texture or pattern and restarted Fireworks. You must exit and restart to initialize textures and patterns in Fireworks.

3. Set your percentage preference from 0 to 100.

4. If you want to make the lighter areas of your texture transparent, select Transparent.

Creating Gradient Fills

Gradient fills are fills that blend from one color to another. Fireworks contains 11 gradient fill types. To see these 11 types, open the file Gradient Types from the Fills folder (see Figure 5.24).

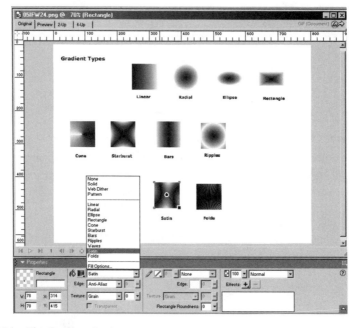

Figure 5.24   The Gradient Options pop-up.

Applying Gradient Fills

Fireworks ships with 13 preset color combinations. The gradient appears in the selected vector object and becomes the active fill for vector objects as you create them:

1. Select the object by using the Pointer tool from the Tools panel.

2. From the Property Inspector, choose a gradient fill from the Fill Category pop-up menu.

3. From the Preset Gradient Color Sets menu, select a color combination.

Editing a Gradient Fill

You can change the colors of gradient fills in the following way:

1. Select an object that contains a gradient fill.

2. Click the Fill Category pop-up button on the Property Inspector.

3. Select the last item in the list, which is Fill Options.

   The Edit Gradient panel displays with the current gradient in the Category field, color name in the color preset field, edge type, texture type and amount, and the Transparent check box (see Figure 5.25).

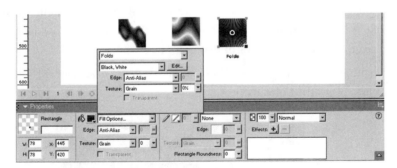

Figure 5.25   The Edit Gradient panel.

4. Click the Edit button to reveal the Gradient Color Ramp and Preview (see Figure 5.26).

   The Color boxes above the Color Ramp control the transparency of your colors. The Color boxes below the Color Ramp control the actual colors that make up the gradient.

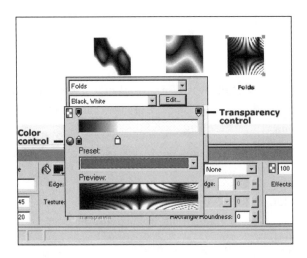

Figure 5.26   The Gradient Color Ramp and Preview.

5. To change the color of an existing gradient, click one of the Color boxes within the Color Ramp area. Choose a color from the Color box pop-up window by clicking a color swatch or selecting the None button, clicking the Color Picker button, or selecting a color from your computer screen using the eyedropper.

6. To add a new color swatch to your gradient, click the area beneath the Color Ramp where the Gradient Color boxes are (see Figure 5.27). Follow the previous procedure to change the color of that Color box.

   To remove a box from your gradient, click the box and drag it away from Color box area below the Color Ramp.

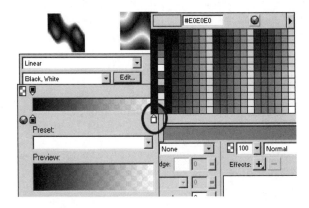

Figure 5.27   The Swatch panel pops up when you double-click to select a Color box on the Gradient Ramp.

7. To control and edit the transparency of your gradient, click one of the Color boxes within the transparency control and adjust the Opacity slider (see Figure 5.28).

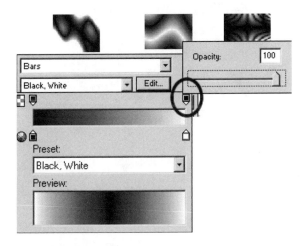

Figure 5.28   The Opacity slider panel pops up when you double-click to select a transparency box on the Gradient Ramp.

Gradient fills, like pattern fills, contain handles that allow you to move, rotate, skew, and change the width of an object's gradient. When you use the Pointer tool to select an object with a gradient fill, handles appear. Click and drag these handles to adjust the position of the gradient fill. Or you can also click the round handle and reposition the starting point of the gradient.

Saving Fills as Styles

After you create a gradient, you might want to save it to use again. You can save your gradient fill settings as a style and use it on objects within any document you create. To do this, follow these steps:

1. Select the object that contains the gradient, pattern, or texture that you set.

2. From the Styles panel Options pop-up menu, select New Style (see Figure 5.29).

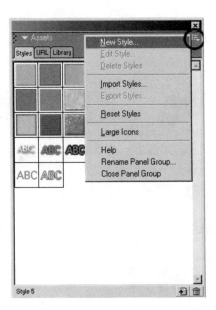

Figure 5.29   The Assets panel with the Styles Options pop-up menu displayed and New Style selected.

3. The New Style dialog box appears, allowing you to name your style and select options for properties, including fill type, fill color, effect, stroke type, and stroke color.

   You can also notice options for text font, text size, and text style. You can choose these when applying stroke, fill, and effect attributes to a text object.

4. Give your style a name and click OK (see Figure 5.30).

   Your style now appears in the Styles panel for any document that you create in Fireworks.

To learn more about saving effects and working with styles, check out Chapter 7, "The Wonderful World of Live Effects."

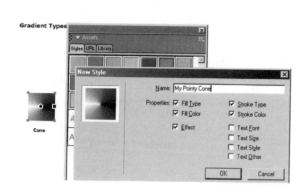

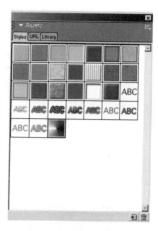

Figure 5.30   Saving a custom gradient as a style.

Setting Transparency Using Layers

You can modify the opacity and transparency of objects in Fireworks in the following way:

1. Choose Window, Layers to open the Layers panel, if it is not already showing.

2. Select an object whose transparency you want to adjust.

3. Look at the Layers panel (see Figure 5.31). You can notice the object is selected within its layer in the Layers panel.

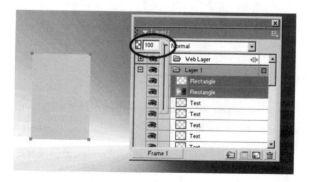

Figure 5.31   The Transparency field and slider in the Layers panel.

4. To adjust the object's transparency, click the Transparency slider at the upper left of the Layers panel.

The default setting for layer transparency is 100 percent.

5. Pull the slider down to decrease the opacity and thereby increase the transparency of objects within layers.

You can also type in the Transparency field to set the transparency to a specific percentage.

Blending Modes

You can further enhance an object's appearance by applying blending modes on the Layers panel (see Figure 5.32). This becomes especially interesting when you overlap various objects in your artwork.

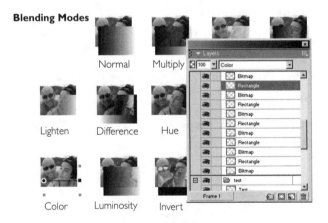

Figure 5.32   The Blending Modes control in the Layers panel.

Blending modes is a way of using an object's color to interact with an underlying object's color in such a way as to produce an effect that's similar to a mask or a filter.

Blending modes is created by the presence of the following attributes:

- The blend color, which is the color that is applied to the blending mode.
- The transparency, or opacity, of the color to which the mode is applied.
- The base color, or the color beneath the blend color.
- The final result color or effect of the blend of the interacting objects.

To get a better idea of blending modes in action, open the `blending_modes.png` file from the `Exercises/05` folder on the accompanying CD-ROM (see Figure 5.33).

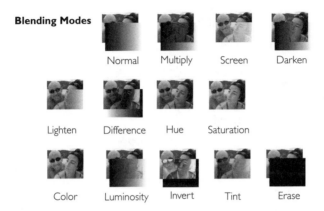

Figure 5.33 The Blending modes.

Notice that a total of 13 blending modes exist:

- **Normal**—Does not apply any blending.
- **Multiply**—Takes the base color and multiplies it with the blend color to yield darker colors.
- **Screen**—Multiplies the opposite, or inverse, of the blend color to give a bleaching effect.
- **Darken**—Uses the darkest shade and lightens all colors lighter than the blend color.
- **Lighten**—Uses the lightest color as the blend color and darkens all the colors darker than it.
- **Difference**—Subtracts the object color from the base color, or the base color from the object color. The color with less brightness is subtracted from the color with greater brightness.
- **Hue**—Uses the hue value of the blend color and the luminance and saturation of the base color to create a result.
- **Saturation**—Mixes the saturation of the blend color with the luminance and hue of the base color to create a result.
- **Color**—Mixes the hue and saturation of the blend color with the luminance of the base color while preserving the gray values. This colorizes, or tints, the image.

- **Luminosity**—Mixes the luminance of the blend color with the hue of the base color to create the result.

- **Invert**—Inverts the base color.

- **Tint**—Adds gray to the base color.

- **Erase**—Erases all the base color pixels.

When you group objects that use different blending modes, the group's blending mode dominates the blending modes of the individual objects. When you ungroup them, the original blending modes are restored.

Edge Control

Fireworks enables you to modify the edge of a filled object. You can set the edge to Hard, Anti-alias, and Feather (see Figure 5.34):

- **Hard**—Sets the edge to a hard, or distinct, edge. Sometimes, this results in jaggy edges.

- **Anti-Alias**—The default edge setting for vector objects. Anti-Aliasing smoothes the jagged edges that occur on diagonal lines and rounded objects so that the colors of the object blend smoothly into the background.

- **Feather**—Creates a faded edge effect Feather creates a fade to transparent that starts with opaque image color at a specific pixel distance inside the selected object's path or selection marquee and extending to an equal pixel distance beyond that path or selection marquee where the image's pixels become transparent.

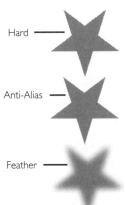

Figure 5.34   Three stars with their edges set to Hard, Anti-Alias, and Feather.

Controlling Object Edges

To control the edge of an object by using the Property Inspector, follow these steps:

1. Display the Fill panel if it is not already showing.

2. Select an object by using the Pointer tool from the Tools panel.

3. In the Fill panel, choose an option from the Edge pop-up menu: Hard, Anti-Alias, or Feather.

4. To set a feathered edge, select the number of pixels on each side of the edge that are to be feathered.

   The default setting for Feather is 10. As you increase the amount, the object's edge becomes increasingly more transparent to the underlying canvas or underlying objects.

Applying and Editing Strokes

Now that you have the details on how to work with fills, it's time to learn the ins and outs of strokes.

Fireworks enables you to set the *stroke*, or the outline, of your vector objects to an incredible assortment of looks and feels. Stroke settings, which reside in the Property Inspector, can be applied to open paths, such as those created with Pencil, Brush, and Line tools. They can also be applied to closed paths, including basic shapes (shapes created with the Pen tool), and to text objects.

You can adjust the size, color, and texture of strokes. You can fine-tune and control strokes of your vector objects in a variety of ways. You can simulate natural media, including brushes, crayons, chalk, pencils, oil paints, air brush, and things that you never conceived of, such as 3-D glow, toxic waste, and fluid splatter.

Fireworks allows for pressure-sensitive input by using a pressure-sensitive drawing tablet that gives you a natural pressure-sensitive look and feel; plus, it lets you simulate a tablet using your mouse.

Eleven stroke categories exist in Fireworks, each with its own set of presets. There are a total of 48 various strokes in all.

Controlling Strokes

The best way to learn about the stroke options is to examine them and try them out:

1. Open the Stroke panel if it is not already showing.

2. Open the `stroke_fun.png` file from the `Exercises/05` folder on the accompanying CD-ROM (see Figure 5.35).

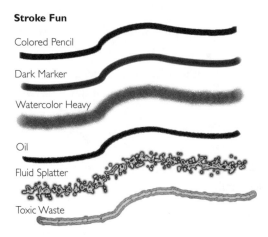

Figure 5.35   You can play with the strokes I made in the `stroke_fun.png` file.

Notice that the file has six strokes of the same basic configuration with different attributes applied to them.

3. Using the Pointer tool from the Tools panel, click each of the strokes one at a time to see their settings reflected in the Stroke panel (see Figure 5.36).

With a stroke selected, you can alter the path's attributes by using the Stroke panel. Just make sure that the stroke you want to modify is selected.

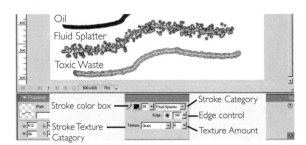

Figure 5.36   The Stroke panel controls in the Property Inspector. These attributes reflect the Fluid Spatter stroke that I applied.

4. You can change the stroke category and the stroke name by using the Stroke list and Category list pop-up menus in the Stroke panel.

5. You can use the Color box on the Stroke panel to change the stroke's color.

6. You can change the softness of the stroke tip by sliding the Edge Softness slider. Sliding the slider up increases the stroke softness, while sliding the slider down makes the stroke appear harder.

7. You can apply texture to a stroke by choosing a texture from the Texture Name pop-up menu and increasing the texture value.

After you create a stroke that you like, you can save it for future use.

Saving Strokes

Strokes can be saved as styles in much the same way as fills:

1. Select the object that contains the stroke you want to save.

2. From the Styles panel Options pop-up menu, select New Style.

   The New Style dialog box appears, which allows you to name your style and select options for properties, including effect, stroke type, and stroke color.

3. Give your stroke style a name and click OK.

   Your style now appears in the Styles panel for any document that you create in Fireworks.

Understanding Pressure Sensitivity

Personally, I was excited when I realized that you can create pressure-sensitive effects in Fireworks to simulate the look and feel of creating with natural media (see Figure 5.37):

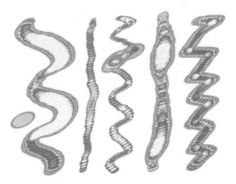

Figure 5.37   My stroke style, Wild Cherry, with pressure sensitivity applied using a Wacom Tablet.

1. If you have never worked with pressure sensitivity, open the `wild_cherry.png` file from the `Exercises/05` folder on the accompanying CD-ROM.

2. Select one of the objects on the page and view the Property Inspector.

   By examining each of the strokes, you can get an idea of what you can do with pressure sensitivity. I created this stroke using a *Wacom Tablet*, which responds to both speed of motion and pressure applied.

3. To save this stroke style to your preset, select one of the paths and follow the previous list's instructions to save it to your presets.

Using Pressure Sensitivity

I find that pressure-sensitive stroke types work best when trying to simulate pressure effects with either the mouse or a tablet:

1. Select the Brush tool from the Tools panel.

2. Use the Property Inspector to set the Stroke category to Airbrush, or Calligraphy, Quill (see Figure 5.38).

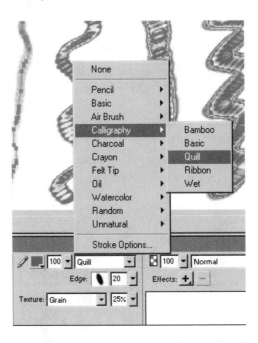

Figure 5.38   The Stroke Category pop-up menu with Calligraphy, Quill selected.

3. Click and drag to create the stroke. If you are using a mouse, pausing while dragging creates a thickening of the stroke simulating pressure. If you are using a tablet, experiment with pressure and speed as you drag.

Refining and Tweaking Your Stroke

After the initial stroke is set, you can continue to modify it. Here's how:

1. Click Stroke Options to further enhance and customize your stroke (see Figure 5.39).

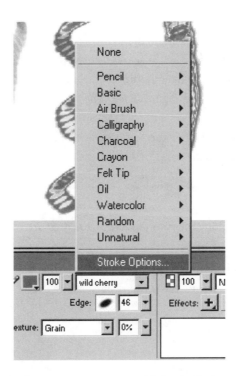

Figure 5.39   The Stroke Category pop-up menu with Stroke Options selected.

2. Make the adjustments that you desire by altering the settings for Category, Edge Softness, Tip, Texture, Location on Path, and Fill over Stroke.

3. If you want, you can make even more precise modifications by clicking the Advance button and launching the Edit Stroke controls (see Figure 5.40).

This panel contains tabs for Options, Shape, and Sensitivity.

The Path Scrubber Tool

I have just one more thing to mention about working with strokes: the Path Scrubber tool.

The Path Scrubber tool, which is found in the Tools panel, helps to further manipulate the pressure-sensitive effects of strokes. It has two variations—the Path Scrubber Additive tool and the Path Scrubber Subtractive tool (see Figure 5.41). The Additive tool increases the thickness, or pressure, of the stroke, and the Subtractive tool decreases the thickness of a stroke, which minimizes the pressure's appearance:

1. With the path still selected, select the Path Scrubber Additive tool.

2. Click and drag it along the path to increase the pressure effect on the path.

3. Switch to the Path Scrubber Subtractive tool and drag it along the path to decrease the pressure effect along the path.

Figure 5.40   The Edit Stroke Options, Shape, and Sensitivity menus.

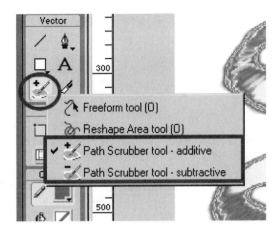

Figure 5.41   The Path Scrubber Additive and Subtractive Tools.

You can use the Alt key (for Windows) or the Option key (for a Macintosh) to switch between the Path Scrubber Additive and Subtractive tools.

Summary

Now, you can see the myriad of possibilities and directions that are open to you when creating fills and strokes in Fireworks MX. The only real limits you have are time and imagination. Go for it!

Chapter 6

Working with Text

So far in Fireworks MX, we have looked at some aspects of the drawing drawing process which, as you now know, is vector-based art. If you are wondering if text is related to vector art, you are right. So much can be done with text and type. Type is an integral part of many web sites, and it is the look and feel of the type design that often sets the character of the entire web site.

In web design, type can act as a vehicle to attract viewers' attention. Key messages, brand identities, and various kinds of information and articles need to be communicated in a compelling way by using type. In order to retain viewer interest, especially where a reasonable amount of reading is required, text needs to offer legibility along with presenting a striking, interesting, and aesthetically pleasing design.

To break this chapter up into digestible bits, we're going to look at the following:

- The Text tool
- Some rules of thumb
- The Basics settings
- Using the Text tool
- Tutorials

If that sounds like a lot, it's because it is. Fireworks has some fun and powerful text features. Let's get into it!

Working with the Text Tool

You create text in Fireworks by using the Text tool (see Figure 6.1) and the Property Inspector (see Figure 6.2). Together, these tools enable you to create and customize text and text objects.

Figure 6.1
The Text tool.

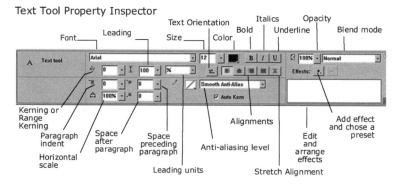

Figure 6.2   The Property Inspector for the Text tool.

Text Fundamentals

Take a look at some definitions for the text settings. Many of these settings are available in the Property Inspector:

- **Alignment**—Type can be set to Left, Center, Right, Justified, or Stretched alignment.

- **Anti-Aliasing**—Used to smooth out the edge of text. (This is a great tool if you're not familiar with it. We discuss this effect a bit later in this chapter.)

- **Baseline Shift**—The adjustable distance between the bottom of text and the invisible baseline on which it sits.

- **Blend Mode**—A live effect of taking two objects and combining them. The object on top is the object that changes. There are multiple settings, including Multiply, Screen, Darken, Lighten, Difference, Hue, Saturation, Color, Luminosity, Invert, Tint, and Erase.

- **Color**—The hue preference setting for letters or words.

- **Fonts**—The style or family of a typeface.

- **Kerning**—Increases or decreases the spacing between certain pairs of letters to alter their appearance. Kerning is measured as a percentage.

Note

What is kerning? *Kerning* is the art of adjusting the space between characters in order to ensure a smooth flow of information from the text to the brain. The eye is extremely good at recognizing breaks in a regular pattern. Upon encountering too much or too little space between characters within a word, a reader's eye stumbles. If you use kerning correctly, a reader's brain interprets a string of letters into a single word.

- **Leading**—The distance between lines in a paragraph. It can be measured in pixels or as a percentage.

Note

From where does the term *leading* come? The term leading (rhymes with netting) originally referred to strips of lead that typesetters placed between lines of type in order to space them out. When you read, the spaces between lines isolate the line you're reading from the lines above and below it. Each row of space guides your eyes from the end of one line to the beginning of the next. If there is too little or too much space, you get lost along the way and have to work hard to absorb the information.

- **Opacity**—A setting making text not transparent or translucent. (In other words, can you see through it?)

- **Orientation**—The direction of text. Text can go left to right, right to left, or vertical or horizontal.

- **Size**—Type size is based in "points," which is the typographical basic unit of measurement equal to about 1/72 of an inch. Twelve points are in a pica. (Thirteen inches are in a foot, 454 grams in a pound, and how many pecks in a bushel?)

- **Spacing**—This basic setting includes space after a paragraph and space preceding a paragraph.

When you use the Fireworks text-editing features in combination with strokes, fills, effects, and styles, you can create some really exciting and original text graphics. These include the ability to manipulate the text as vectors while still maintaining "editablity" (for example, transform, skew, distort, rotate, and attach to path) and still retain your ability to edit!

Rules of Thumb for Choosing Fonts

Often, students learning to create type graphics with fonts ask me, "What is the right font to choose?"

Although choosing fonts is primarily a matter of personal taste and style, an understanding of the fundamentals of typography is a valuable asset when you compose and design with type.

Simply put, the idea when designing with type is to make it readable. Here are some explanations, definitions, and insights that can be applied to font use:

- **Choose fonts appropriately**—Know and understand your design goals. Every client and every job have different parameters and considerations. Think about the audience for which you are designing. Become a chameleon and use fonts that appeal to your particular readers as they communicate your client's message.

- **Less is more**—Limit the number of typefaces used in a document to two or three. You need not rely on different faces to create interest from your audience. Experiment and explore the variations of size, weight, extension, compression, and contrast within a particular type style. In this way, you create a hierarchy of emphasis without creating cacophony of different styles. When you choose typefaces to combine with each other in a document, select fonts that create enough distinction and variation from one and other. If the styles you choose are too similar, the page lacks contrast and interest.

- **Display text and body text**—Display text is designed to be eye catching and is used for setting headlines and subheads. Although used in smaller amounts at larger sizes, display text sets the tone and style of a document. Body text generally carries the bulk of the text of articles. It is designed to be functional, thus lending legibility to larger blocks of text.

- **Type styles simplified**—At the most basic level, type styles can be sorted into three categories: serif, sans-serif, and script (see Figures 6.3, 6.4, and 6.5).

SERIF FONT, serif font

Figure 6.3   An example of the serif font.

SANS SERIF FONT, sans serif font

Figure 6.4   An example of the sans-serif font.

SCRIPT FONT, script font

Figure 6.5   An example of the script font.

- Serif fonts are categorized by the stems, or feet, that extend from their letter-forms. Originally designed to aid reading by leading the eye of the reader from one character to the next, serif fonts are most commonly used as body text. When used in headlines, serif fonts can make the text appear too busy.

- Ornament-free, clean, and elegant lines categorize sans-serif fonts. Generally, the results with the greatest impact are achieved by using sans-serif fonts in head-lines.

- Script is categorized by its cursive and calligraphic style. In general, the wide variety of script fonts lend elegance and classic flow to letterforms. Script fonts are excellent for when a personal touch needs to be emphasized or communicated.

In truth, there are several more subcategories to these. Due to limited space, however, only these three fundamental categories are reviewed.

- **Leading**—Also known as line spacing, leading is the distance between lines of type (see Figure 6.6). This distance is measured from baseline to baseline.

leading @ 100%
leading @ 100%

leading @ 136%
leading @ 136%

Figure 6.6   Leading.

  Tight leading refers to a small amount of leading, or space, between the lines. Loose leading refers to much space between lines. An art director might say, "Loosen up," or "Tighten up the leading," when referring to a design. Solid leading refers to no space between the lines. Auto leading tends to be about 20 percent of the point size. Typically, the standard normal range used for leading is 2 to 6 points. If you set the leading to a negative number, the lines overlap.

- **Size setting**—Setting the size of type for web design is different than setting the type for print publications because the reader is probably going to be reading text on a computer monitor instead of a piece of paper. Because computer monitors have a range of resolutions, you might want to follow certain guidelines for readability, especially concerning body text. A good rule of thumb depending on the line lengths that you are setting is this: Set body text between 8 and 16 points, and set subheads and headlines from 16 points upward.

- **Letterforms**—Let there be air! Like other elements in design, text can benefit from the use of negative space, also known as white space (or air). When letterforms are jammed together with little or no air between them, they become cluttered and difficult to read. This is especially true with small text.

- **Capitalization**—Be careful how and where you choose to apply capitalization. When overused, capitalization can lose its impact and it can be difficult to read individual letterforms in larger blocks of text.

- **Centering**—Centered text has its proper use for specialty settings, such as invitations, menus, and so on. Like capitalization, however, this is not something that you want to do to large text blocks. Type set this way is difficult to read because the eye must find the beginning of the next line, which might start in a different place for each line.

- **You're stepping on my face**—Be careful that, when you distort and manipulate text elements, you don't render them illegible. There is a difference between tweaked and trashed.

- **Color**—Be mindful when applying color to text. Although it's perfectly acceptable to use color to create emphasis and interest within the text, overuse and misuse of color can make your work look unprofessional. For more information about designing with color, visit Chapter 5, "Working with Color Fills and Strokes."

Missing Fonts

When you open a Fireworks document that uses fonts that are not currently installed in your system, you are greeted with the Missing Font dialog box. At this point, you can choose to install the font in your system.

Note

Have you never installed fonts, or are you having problems? Check out tech notes on the Macromedia web site:

www.macromedia.com/go/3648 for Macintosh

www.macromedia.com/go/3649 for Windows

You can change the missing font to another font by selecting an alternative that Fireworks can use:

1. Open the file that doesn't contain a font currently installed in your system.

2. In the Missing Fonts dialog box, click the Change All listing under the Change Missing Fonts heading on the left side of the panel. Or, to change a single font, click the name of that font from the left side of the panel.

3. Choose the font that you want to substitute from the list on the right side of the panel.

4. Click OK to apply the changes.

Dealing with Missing Fonts from Photoshop Files

When you open Photoshop files in Fireworks, Fireworks retains the Photoshop layers and gives you the option to

- Maintain your text as editable text
- Rastorize, or fix, your text

After your text is rastorized, it becomes a bitmap representation of its former vector self. Rastorizing text allows you to maintain the look and feel of your original, although the text is no longer editable as text (it's now an image). You can apply transformations to it as you would any other bitmap object, and it is subject to the kinds of pixel distortions that any other bitmap undergoes when it's stretched, skewed, rotated, and so on. Fireworks makes use of the font's metrics, or outlines, and this makes it different from many other programs. The use of the outlines font allows Fireworks to render its many fill, stroke, and live effects to text, as well as transform and flow text to paths without losing your ability to edit in the least.

Creating Text

Adding text and text effects to your canvas is easy. Simply complete the following steps to create basic text:

1. Select the Text tool from the Tools panel (refer to Figure 6.1).

2. Click the canvas to create an area where you want to set text.

3. The Property Inspector switches to text-editing mode, displaying the many options that are available for settings text attributes.

4. Type your text.

Moving Text Blocks and Auto Size

Like any other object in Fireworks, you can click text blocks and move them anywhere in your document.

As you type on the canvas, the text you create is placed into what is known as a text block. (With standard settings, you see a blue box around the text.) If you remove the text, the text block contracts to fit around the remaining text. To control the width of text or resize the text block, select the text, and click and drag it on a resize handle.

You can also set text to a particular size block by clicking and dragging the size of the block before you enter the text instead of just clicking the canvas. This action creates a text block with a fixed height. If the text you type exceeds the height of the text block, the text block expands to fit the text, but the text block maintains the width that you set by clicking and dragging. If the text characters exceed the width of the block, the text wraps and the box expands its height.

Setting Text Attributes

In the Property Inspector, you can set text to attributes the in the following manner.

To set the font, highlight the text and use the Font pop-up menu. You can also change the font of any given text block with the Pointer tool by selecting the text block and changing the text attributes in the Property Inspector.

To change the point size, use the Point Size slider or type directly into the Point field to change the size of the type.

To modify the text style, click the Bold, Italic, or Underline buttons in the text editor. Text styling, such as bold, underline, or italic, is discarded if the type is converted to paths.

To set text kerning, click between two letters. Slide the Kerning slider or type in the Kerning field. Positive numbers increase the space between the letterforms, while negative numbers decrease the space between the letterforms (see Figure 6.7).

kerning 0%

k e r n i n g   5 0 %

kerning -8%

Figure 6.7   Kerning.

Note

To have Fireworks apply built-in kerning settings from the typeface that you are using, you can click Auto Kern in the Property Inspector. If the check box to the left of the Apply button is checked, the selected changes automatically update the text on the canvas.

To apply *range kerning*, also known as tracking, to your text, with the text highlighted, use the Kerning slider to alter the spacing between letters across an entire word or sentence.

To set the leading, highlight the text on the canvas, choose Window, Property Inspector to open the Property Inspector (if it is not already open). Click the Leading slider and drag the arrow up or down, or type the desired amount of leading into the Leading field just to the right of the slider to increase or decrease leading.

To modify the baseline shift of text, with the text highlighted, the Baseline Shift button appears on the Property Inspector. Slide the Baseline slider or type numbers into the field. Positive numbers raise the text, while negative numbers lower the text from the baseline (see Figure 6.8).

Figure 6.8   The Baseline shift.

You can also modify the compression or extension of letterforms by using the Horizontal Scale slider. When the text is highlighted, slide the Horizontal Scale slider or type numbers directly into the field. When you increase horizontal scaling, your text becomes extended. When you use lower numbers, you compress the letterforms.

You can also set the justification, or horizontal alignment, of text. With the text highlighted, click one of the five alignment settings to change the text's justification.

You can change the direction of text so that it reads from right to left instead of left to right. To change the text direction, with the text highlighted on the canvas, click the Direction button to change from pointing right to reverse, or pointing left. This feature is perfect for foreign languages. See Figure 6.9.

Figure 6.9   Text orientations.

Sometimes, depending on the size and use of a particular text element on your page or button, you might want to have more control over the edges of your text. Fireworks allows you to set anti-aliasing to your text. You can apply four anti-aliasing settings to your text:

- No Anti-Alias
- Crisp Anti-Alias
- Strong Anti-Alias
- Smooth Anti-Alias

Similar to kerning, to see the effect of anti-alias modifications, click the Apply button before you choose OK (unless the check box to the left of the Apply button is already checked.) To toggle the preview of your text on and off, click the Show Font and Show Size check boxes on and off.

Tip

In earlier versions of Fireworks, to see the formatting changes, you had to click Apply and/or click OK to apply the changes and close the text editor. These check boxes are no longer in the Property Inspector in Fireworks MX. Now it just renders wherever changes are made.

Applying Text Fills, Strokes, Styles, and Effects

Like any other object in Fireworks, you can apply fills, strokes, effects, and styles to text. Even after fill, stroke, and effects have been applied to your text, the text remains editable in Fireworks, and the look and feel that you set is updated as the text is edited.

Note

To learn more about fills and strokes, check out Chapter 5, "Working with Color Fills and Strokes." and Chapter 7, "The Wonderful World of Live Effects."

Making Changes After the Fact

After the text is set, you can modify it by double-clicking the text block or highlighting the text block and choosing the text editor:

- With the text selected, you can click and drag the text block handles to rewrap the text.
- You can use the Scale tool to resize the text.

  You can also change the text by choosing Text, Font or by using other options under the Text menu. Choose Text, Size to change the font size, and choose Text, Style to apply bold, italic, underline, or plain attributes.

  You can modify the text alignment, and you can open the text editor by choosing Text, Text Editor.

- You can select multiple blocks of text and apply changes to all of them simultaneously.
- With the text selected, you can change the color of the text block by clicking the Color box from the Color box pop-up menu.
- You can add a stroke to a text by highlighting the text, clicking the Color box for stroke. (See Chapter 5 for more information.)
- You can apply effects to text.

Distorting Text

Along with scaling the text with the Transform tool, you can also distort it in many ways.

If you have distorted the text with more transformations than necessary and would like to return to the non-transformed version of your text, you can do so:

- Choose Modify, Transform, Remove Transformations and the original formatting of your text is restored.
- You can distort text with the Scale tool and the other tools in the Transform tool group that appear in the pop-up menu when you click the tool and hold down the mouse.
- You can also modify text by choosing Modify, Transform and choosing one of the choices in the Transform menu.

Wrapping Text Along Paths

Fireworks gives you the power to wrap text along paths (see Figure 6.10). Instead of just typing in regular rectangular blocks, Fireworks allows you to draw a path and attach text to it. The text flows along the path and remains editable.

Note
The path does not maintain its stroke, fill, or other effects. It serves as the shape and direction for your text.

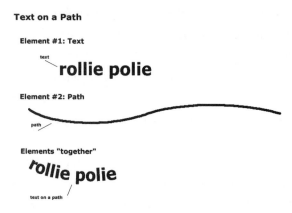

Figure 6.10   The elements for "text on a path."

To wrap text along a path, complete the following steps:

1. From the `Exercises/06` folder, open the file `text_on_path.png`.

2. Select both the text and the path. Do this through drag-select with the Pointer tool, or by selecting the first item and pressing and holding the Shift key while clicking the second item.

3. Choose Text, Attach to Path. The result matches the item labeled "text on a path." You can still edit the text on this path in the Property Inspector.

Note

Avoid using text that has returns in it when you're attaching it to a path. You can get strange and unexpected results. Then again, maybe that's what you're trying for…

To detach text from a path, simply undo the previous step:

1. Select the path and text by selecting the first item and then pressing and holding the Shift key while clicking the second item.

2. Choose Text, Attach to Path.

To adjust the text fffset along its path, follow these steps:

1. Display the Property Inspector.

2. Type in the text offset panel to move the text along the path.

Text alignment on a path behaves in much the same way as alignment of text not on a path. This means that you can align the text left, centered, right, justified, or stretched in relationship to the path.

Text orientation refers to how the text aligns with the path. To adjust the orientation of the text, follow these steps:

1. Make sure the text is selected.

2. Choose Text, Orientation. The Orientation pop-up menu gives you four options:

   • **Rotate Around Path**—Aligns the letters perpendicularly to the path. This is the default option.

   • **Vertical**—Aligns the letters straight, relative to the document as the letters follow the path.

   • **Skew Vertical**—Aligns the letters along the path, but slants them vertically.

   • **Skew Horizontal**—Aligns the letters straight against the path and slants them horizontally, according to the path's curve or angle.

Converting Text to Paths

It is great that the Fireworks text, in text blocks or on paths, is editable text. This allows you to modify and work with aspects of the character of text blocks infinitely. However, sometimes, you want to manipulate text into a logo form or some other unique character based on text. Times might also arise when you want to share your documents with other artists who might not have the fonts that you use in your document.

These situations are good times to use the convert text to paths feature. After text is converted to paths, it is no longer editable as text; however, it is editable in many other interesting ways as path objects.

First, you need to select the text, text block, or text on a path:

1. Choose Text, Convert to Paths.

2. Choose Modify, Ungroup or Alt/Option-click the desired character to reach the paths.

You can now use the Subselection tool to modify and manipulate the paths.

Note

Try using the Join command so that you can make the text path object a single composite path.

Exercise: Adding Text to the Ciber Interface Navigation Bar

In this exercise, you add text for six sections of the Ciber web site:

ABOUT US

CLASSES

REGISTER

BUZZ

DIRECTIONS

CONTACT

1. Open the file `ciber_type_01.png`, as shown in Figure 6.11.

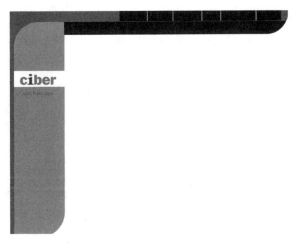

Figure 6.11   The Ciber interface that was created in previous tutorials.

The file contains a version of the Ciber interface that you created in Chapter 4, "Working with Vectors." There are six black rectangles along the top part of the document; each rectangle will house some text for a navigation button.

Two layers are in this file so far—one named "black buttons" and one named "Base Art" (see Figure 6.12). These layers are both currently locked to prevent you from moving or modifying anything that you don't want.

The "black buttons" are not buttons yet. We make them into buttons in future chapters. They will become objects, rollovers, then buttons. Don't let this confuse you.

Figure 6.12   The Layers panel in the Ciber interface.

2. From the Layers panel Options pop-up menu, choose New Layer. Name your new layer Rollover Text White.

3. Select the Text tool from the Tools panel. Click the rectangle at the left end of the row of rectangles at the top of the canvas.

4. In the Property Inspector, make the following settings:

   Font to Verdana

   Size to 10

   Color to white

   Bold

   Left alignment

   Anti-alias to Smooth Anti-Alias

5. In all caps, type **ABOUT US**.

   For now, don't worry about placing or aligning the text on the black rectangle buttons perfectly. We'll use the alignment tools to aid us in this endeavor a bit later.

6. Look at the Layers Panel. Notice that a new object appears in the rollover text white layer. Because it is a text object, it takes the default name "text."

   It is a good work habit to rename objects and check to see if they are in the correct layer as you create them.

7. Double-click the word "text" on the new ABOUT US text object that you created. Name it ABOUT US w. The "w" stands for "white." See Figure 6.13.

Figure 6.13   The ABOUT US object label in the Layers panel.

You will now make the other five items with the first item's text selected (ABOUT US):

8. Click the ABOUT US text object and drag it over to the rectangle just to the right while holding down the ALT key (Windows) or the Option key (Macintosh).

   This creates a duplicate of the original text.

9. Double-click the second ABOUT US type. Click the text object and, when the I-beam cursor appears, highlight the text with the ABOUT US text already selected in the preview window.

10. Start typing **CLASSES** in all caps. Click OK.

11. Follow steps 8 through 10 to create the remaining four text objects (see Figure 6.14):

> REGISTER
>
> BUZZ
>
> DIRECTIONS
>
> CONTACT

It's now time to align the text with their appropriate rectangles.

Note
If you'd like, you can open the file `ciber_type_02.png`.

Figure 6.14   The file `ciber_type_02.png`.

1. Click in the lock column of the Layers panel to unlock the black rollovers layer in your Layers panel.

2. Using the Pointer tool from the Tools panel, click the ABOUT US type and, holding the shift key, click the rectangle immediately behind the text.

3. With both objects selected, choose Modify, Align, Center, Vertical.

4. Choose Modify, Align, Center, Horizontal. Your text is aligned perfectly with its rectangular button.

5. Repeat steps 1–4 for the other five items and their rectangular rollovers to center the text objects with their rectangular buttons. Save your file to your hard drive (see Figure 6.15).

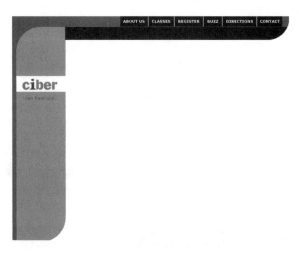

Figure 6.15   The Ciber interface in its final phase.

Note

To save time, you can use the following align key commands:

- To center vertically, use Ctrl-Alt-2 on Windows, and Command-2 on a Macintosh.
- To center horizontally, Ctrl-Alt-5 on Windows, and Command-5 on a Macintosh.

6. When you have aligned all the text in the navigation bar, save your file as ciber_type_03 in your type folder.

Next, you duplicate all six of the text items, give them a new color, offset them slightly, and put them in their own frame for use in Chapter 11, "Working with Behaviors":

1. From the Layers pop-up menu, create a new layer. Name it Button Text Gray.

2. Using the Pointer tool, select all six of the text elements in the Text White layer.

3. From the Edit menu, choose Edit, Clone. This makes six exact duplicates of your original text elements.

Here's a trick: With your elements still selected, hold the Shift key and click the last one in the list, the duplicate of Contact W. This turns it off, thereby deselecting it. Continue to hold down the Shift key and click the item again. Look at the title bar on the Document window, and notice that the number of selected objects is reported there. When the duplicate text objects are all selected, you see `(6 Objects)*`. When the sixth text object is deselected, you see `(5 Objects)#`. This is also displayed in the upper-left area of the Property Inspector. Notice the asterisk (*) after the closing parenthesis. This indicates that the file has been edited and the changes made since the last Save command are not saved. They appear in the History panel.

4. Release the Shift key and drag all six selected objects into the Button Gray layer. Note that, if you inadvertently deselect any of the items, you can still move them into the Text Gray layer one by one.

5. With all the objects that you just created now in the Text Gray layer, change their color all at once by clicking the Fill Color box on the Tools panel and selecting Medium Gray hexadecimal #99999 from the Fills panel Options pop-up menu.

6. Save your finished file as `Ciber .Type` to your layer for future use in Chapter 11.

Exercise: Designing with Text as Outlines

After you convert text to paths, you can do many neat things with it. You can modify the letterforms by using the pen and Subselection tools. You can customize text with the use of path elements and the combine commands. You can use text as a mask and fill it with bitmap and vector artwork.

Phase 1: Overview of the Project

In this first phase, you'll just open the file and take a look at the text that has been converted to paths.

1. Open the file named `custom_text_01.png` (see Figure 6.16).

bIG FUN

FIGURE 6.16   `custom_text_01.png` of Rustproof Body font.

Notice that the file contains a treatment of my logo set in an unique font. The font is called Rustproof Body. It was designed by Ray Larabie (`www.larabiefonts.com`). He designs beautiful typefaces that he generously distributes to the World Wide Web community. He also sells some of his type designs and accepts online donations. Be sure to check out his work.

It is probably likely that you do not have this font currently loaded in your system. The reason why you can see it in all its glory and beauty is because I previously converted this text to paths, so what you see is a vector or path rendition of the original type I set ready for some modifications.

2. In the file you just opened, `custom_text_01.png`, you see that it contains the words "Big Fun" with the text already converted to paths.

3. Zoom in on the word "Big" by using the Zoom tool so that you can see the letterforms for "b," "i," and "g" close up in your canvas.

Phase 2: Working with the Word "Big"

Now you'll add some effects to the letterforms "i" and "g," and you'll use Fireworks guides features to do it.

1. You might want to use the rulers to set some guides. To view the rulers, if they are not already showing, choose View, Rulers. You can drag out from the vertical ruler to create a guide(see Figure 6.17).

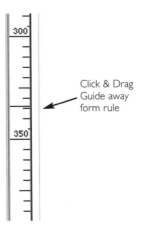

Click & Drag
Guide away
form rule

Figure 6.17   Text converted to paths.

2. Click the ruler and drag it to the edge of the "i". A line appears. That's a guide. It only appears for your use. It doesn't print nor export. You can grab the guide and move it wherever you'd like.

3. Grab another and place it on the other side of the "i."

4. Select the Rectangle tool from the Tools panel.

5. Click and drag a small rectangle to use as the "dot" in the "i." Notice step 2 in your figure. I made my rectangle 26 pixels wide by 10 pixels high.

6. Create another rectangle for the bar of the G. Refer to Figure 6.18. The bar needs to align with the left side of the stem of the "g" and overhang to the right just a bit. I made my bar 26 pixels wide by 15 pixels high.

   I like to make the rectangles that I'm going to combine with the text a different color. This makes them easier to see against the color of the paths. I gave my rectangles a fill of red and a stroke of none.

Figure 6.18   The word "Big" as it should look at this point in the project.

Phase 3: Working with the Word "Fun"

You will now add some additional rectangles to the "u" and "n" letterforms to trim them down:

1. Zoom in on the word "Fun."

2. Place a rectangle at the right side of the letter "u" to use as a rectangular punch that cuts a chunk out of the letter "u," which creates a serif font. I made my rectangle 7 pixels wide by 54 pixels high.

3. Using the Pointer tool and holding down the Alt key (Windows) or the Option key (Macintosh), create an identical rectangle by clicking and dragging from the "u" across the left bottom of the "n." Your figure should look similar to Figure 6.19.

Figure 6.19   The word "Fun" completed in this exercise.

Phase 4: Putting It All Together

Combine the rectangles with the Big Fun letterforms in the following way:

1. By using the Pointer tool, select the Big Fun paths. Select the rectangles for the dot on the letter "i" and the bar on the letter "g."

2. Take the paths (text converted to paths) and ungroup it. Choose Modify, Ungroup.

3. Choose Modify, Combine, Union.

4. With the letterform still selected, Shift-click to select both the remaining rectangles on the "u" and the "n."

5. Choose Modify, Combine, Punch to trim the sides of the "u" and "n" letterforms. Your result needs to match Figure 6.20.

Figure 6.20   "Big Fun" at Phase 4 of the exercise.

Phase 5: Fine Tuning

Phase 5 of this tutorial includes fine tuning using the Pen tool, the Subselection tool, and the arrow keys:

1. Select the Subselection tool from the Tools panel.

2. Using the Subselection tool (and holding down Ctrl (Windows) or Command (Macintosh), click the two left points of the hole in the letter "b" (see Figure 6.21).

3. With the two "b" points selected, use your arrow keys to move them over to the left about eight points.

4. Click the bottom-most points of the letter "b".

5. Move the two bottom points down three points by using the down arrow key on your keyboard.

Figure 6.21   The letter "b" with the two left inside points subselected.

Now modify the letter "g" by opening up the inner space:

1. Using the Subselection tool, select the top two inner points of the beginning inside of the "g."

2. Move these two points up about six pixels.

3. Close up the space at the bottom of the inner portion of the "g" by selecting the bottom-most inner point on the left and the three side points on the right.

4. Move the shaft up three pixels by using the arrow key on your keyboard. Move the left side of the inner space of the "g" to the left by selecting the top and bottom corner pixels and moving them.

Now you must narrow the right stem of the "u" and the left stem of the "n" to match step 4 in the figure:

1. Using the Subselection tool, click the left two points of the right stem of the letter "u" and move the inner space over about 15 pixels to the right by using the arrow keys.

    Refer to the "u" in step 4. Now do essentially the same thing with the left stem of the letter "n."

2. Select the inner-most points on the right side of the left stem with the Subselection tool.

3. Using the left arrow key, move the two selected points to the left.

Next, you must skew the logo text:

1. Select the entire Big Fun text element.

2. Select the Skew tool from the Tools panel.

3. Click the center-top handle and drag your skew approximately 20 pixels along the X-axis to the right.

Tip

Watching the Property Inspector while you drag to skew the text object allows you to set the skew precisely. Choose File, Save As and save your file as Big Fun Logo 01.png.

Here's a preview of Chapter 9, "Masking." Let's try our hand at using text as a mask for vector shapes. Here's another example of using text as a mask. In this case, bitmap artwork is used as the fill for the mask.

Phase 6: Using Text as a Mask for Vector Shapes

1. Open the file `bitmap_text_mask.png` (see Figure 6.22).

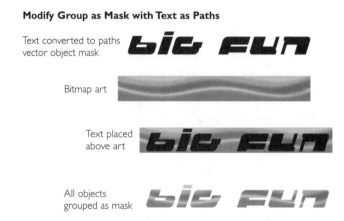

Figure 6.22   The `bitmap_text_mask.png` file.

The first object is identical to the artwork that you created in the first part of this tutorial, the Big Fun logo. Just beneath it is a piece of bitmap artwork that I created using Fireworks.

2. Using the Pointer tool, click the text converted to paths, the Big Fun logo, and drag it on top of the bitmap artwork, matching the figure just beneath it, which is labeled Text Placed Above Art (see Figure 6.23).

Figure 6.23   Text is placed directly on top of bitmap artwork (wavy lines).

Because the text is going to be the shape of the mask, and the bitmap art is going to be the fill inside of it, the text must be above the art.

3. Select both the text and art and choose Modify, Mask, Group As Mask. The result should match the last image on the page, which is labeled All Objects Grouped as Mask.

4. Because the bitmap artwork is a bit larger than the overall size of the Big Fun logo, you can still move the artwork inside the mask because there's a little bit of leeway. By using the Pointer tool, click your masked object.

5. Click and drag the center handle slightly up, down, left, and right to modify where the mask is (see Figure 6.24).

All objects grouped
as mask

Figure 6.24   The text as a mask.

Editing Text in Masks

You can create masks with live text in much the same way and still edit the text that you use in your mask group. To do this, follow these steps:

1. Click the mask thumbnail in the Layers panel.

2. Highlight the text that you want to change on the canvas.

3. Enter the text that you want to use.

Sometimes, it might be necessary to ungroup your text. When you create text using the Text tool, you create editable text that can be modified infinitely. When you convert text to paths, it becomes a vector object, which is as flexible as any other vector object (which you already know if you worked through Chapter 4, "Working with Vectors").

When you convert text to paths, you are left with a group of simple and composite path objects that the vector group's previously text now contains.

Sometimes, it's necessary to dig deeper into the vectors of text to modify them more. This is the case in the of the lightning bolt logo (see Figure 6.25):

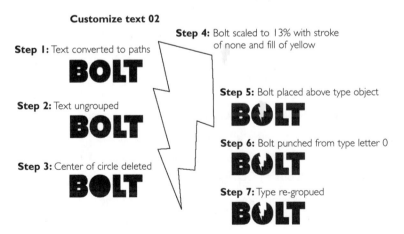

Customize text 02

Step 1: Text converted to paths

Step 4: Bolt scaled to 13% with stroke of none and fill of yellow

Step 2: Text ungrouped

Step 5: Bolt placed above type object

Step 3: Center of circle deleted

Step 6: Bolt punched from type letter 0

Step 7: Type re-gropued

Figure 6.25   The lightning bolt logo.

1. Open the file `custom_text_02.png`, as shown in Figure 6.26.

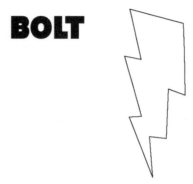

Figure 6.26   The file `custom_text_02.png`.

2. Open the Layers panel if it is not already displaying.

3. Using the Pointer tool from the Tools panel, select the lightning bolt logo text (see Figure 6.27).

Figure 6.27   Text converted to paths.

Look at the Layers panel. Notice that the object is selected in the Layers panel and has the name group "four objects."

I created this text using another one of Ray Larabie's fonts from his web site (`www.larabiefonts.com`). The font is called Strenuous. It's a sans-serif font with a hearty, playful, and vibrant feeling. The text has already been converted to paths.

4. With the text selected, choose Modify, Ungroup or click the Ungroup button on the Windows toolbar (See Figure 6.28).

The layer that was previously labeled Group for Objects has now split into four objects—two are simple paths and two are composite paths.

Figure 6.28   The text is ungrouped.

5. Using the Subselection tool from the Tools panel, click the letter "O" to select it. Notice the inner circle of the "O" contains eight anchor points. Use the Pen tool and double-click the points to delete. The last point might have to be selected and deleted with the Subselection tool.

6. After you delete all eight points, select the "O" and choose Modify, Split. Then use the Select Behind tool to select the inner circle and delete it. This leaves you with a solid black "O" (see Figure 6.29).

Figure 6.29   The center circle of the "O" has been deleted.

As you can see, the file also contains the lightning bolt art that you might recognize from Chapter 4. It's now time to modify the lightning bolt to prepare it for punching from the letter "O":

1. Display the Info panel if it is not already showing.

2. Select the lightning bolt by using the Pointer tool from the Tools panel.

3. Select the Scale tool. Hold down the Shift key. Click and drag the left-top handle of the lightning bolt and drag it down to scale it to 13 percent (use the Property Inspector to verify the percentage).

4. Change the color of the lightning bolt. Change the stroke to none and fill to bright yellow (see Figure 6.30).

   This helps distinguish the shape against the solid black "O" of the text that the lightning bolt will be punching.

Figure 6.30   The bolt is now scaled and filled.

5. Drag the resized yellow lightning bolt on top of the letterform for the solid black letter "O" (see Figure 6.31).

Figure 6.31   The bolt is placed on top of the letter "O".

6. Hold the Shift key and click the "O" shape so that both the "O" and the lightning bolt are selected. Choose Modify, Combine, Punch. The lightning bolt acts as a cookie cutter and the black "O" acts like dough and cuts the shape away, leaving the Lightning Bolt logo (see Figure 6.32).

Figure 6.32   The bolt is punched.

7. Regroup the type by selecting the type and choosing Modify, Group (see Figure 6.33).

Figure 6.33   The type is regrouped.

Summary

Type and text can be amazing tools in your designs. With simple or extreme changes, type can give your web pages the professional edge. Whether it's communicating an emotion or information, text is a powerful tool.

Chapter 7

The Wonderful World of Live Effects

It wasn't too long ago that creating and adding effects to images and artwork was domain inhabited by only a few handfuls of computer graphic-arts wizards. Creating effects, such as drop shadows, glows, bevels, and the like, were a fairly complex and detailed process. If you have been around awhile in the computer graphics and web graphics field, you know what I'm talking about. If you are just coming online recently in this field, you are one of the lucky ones.

These days, creating effects and adding effects to artwork is incredibly streamlined. With Fireworks, you can add effects to both vector and bitmap artwork. Effects enhance, emphasize, and add dimensionality, punch, and pizzazz to your artwork.

Fireworks MX Effects

Currently, there are eight major effect types within Fireworks version 2.1. Within each of these categories are variations on the Adjust Color theme.

Within Adjust Color, you can apply auto levels, brightness/contrast, color fill, curves, hue/saturation, invert, and levels:

- **Bevel and Emboss**—Includes Inner Bevel, Inset Emboss, Outer Bevel, and Raised Emboss
- **Blur**—Includes Blur, Blur More, Gausian Blur
- **Other**—Includes Convert to Alpha and Find Edges
- **Shadow and Glow**—Includes Drop Shadow, Glow, Inner Glow, and Inner Shadow
- **Sharpen**—Includes Sharpen, Sharpen More, and Unsharp Mask
- **Eye Candy 4000 LE**—Includes Bevel Boss, Marble, and Motion Trail

Note

Eye Candy 4000 LE and Alien Skin Splat are filters created by a company called Alien Skin Software. This private company is dedicated to creating easy-to-use plug-ins for designers. It has graciously arranged to let us preview a few of these awesome effects. To learn more about the company and buy some products, check out: www.eyecandy.com/alienskin.html.

Alien Splat—Chock-full of edges options

To find these, select an object on the canvas and click the Effects button on the Property Inspector.

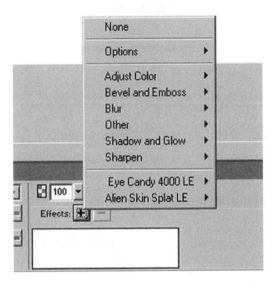

Figure 7.1   Major types of effects.

This is a lot of lists to remember. You might want to dog-ear this page for when you consider effects. Then again, you can always jump right in and try them out.

Applying Effects

To apply an effect to an object or an image, simply select the object, whether it's a bitmap, vector, or text. Then, click the Add Effect button in the Property Inspector. This logs the Effects panel.

Initially, when the Effects panel is launched, it contains no effects and, therefore, appears empty. As effects are added to your objects, they appear in the Effects panel as a list (see Figure 7.2).

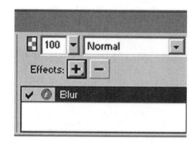

Figure 7.2   Effects are logged in the Effects panel.

Here's how to apply an effect to a vector object:

1. Open the jack.png file from the Effects folder (see Figure 7.3).

2. Select the drawing of the jack.

3. In the Property Inspector, click the Add Effects button to display the Effects panel (see Figure 7.4).

4. Using the Effect pop-up menu, apply the desired effect to the jack artwork.

   After you select your effect, another set of controls are displayed in the Effects panel. Specific aspects of that effect can be controlled with various panels. Continue reading for a discussion of these panels.

5. When you finish tweaking your desired effect, press Enter or click in the Document window to close the Control panel.

   After the effect is applied to the artwork, notice that it appears as a list item within the Effects panel.

Within the Effects panel list, each effect contains an On and Off check box in the left-most column and an Edit Effects icon represented by a blue circle with a white letter "i" in it (see Figure 7.5). Clicking the check box turns the effect on and off. The default of the object is the effect turned off. The "i" is the Info subpanel for that effect. You can adjust the effects properties there.

Figure 7.3   The vector object jack.png from the Effects folder.

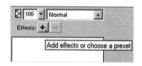

Figure 7.4   The Add Effects button in the Property Inspector.

Figure 7.5   The On and Off check box within the effect's Property Inspector.

Bevel Effects

The Bevel effect transforms an object by applying three-dimensionality effects to them. You can achieve various Bevel effects, such as outer and inner bevels, and effect the size, bevel edge shapes, colors, contrast, softness, and angle of your bevel. Four bevel presets exist: Raised, Highlighted, Inset, and Inverted.

When you apply a Raised Emboss or an Inset Emboss effect, the Emboss effect pushes the shape of one object into another or from out of the background. This effect can look especially interesting when it's applied to a texture or a complex color background.

Obviously, the best way to learn about effects is to tinker with all the effects controls. To get a better understanding of how the Bevel effects work, however, open the file called `bevels.png` from the `Effects` folder (see Figure 7.6). I created this figure to help you get a better idea of how the controls for bevels work:

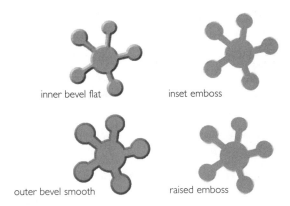

inner bevel flat   inset emboss

outer bevel smooth   raised emboss

Figure 7.6   The tutorial file `bevels.png`.

1. Select the object labeled Inner Bevel Flat.
2. Click the Effect Info icon in the Effects panel to display the settings of this particular effect.

   Notice that the bevel edge shape is set to flat, the width to 6, contrast to 75 percent, softness to 2, angle to 135, and the button preset is set to Raised.
3. Click the pop-up menu for raised and switch it to various choices—Highlighted, Inset, and Inverted.
4. Notice how the look of the effect is altered.
5. When you finish, set it back to Raised.

6. Switch to the Bevel Shape pop-up menu and toggle through the choices—Smooth, Sloped, Frame 1, Frame 2, Ring, and Ruffle—to see how each setting effects the look of the inner bevel flat.

7. Continue to tinker in this way with each of the objects, changing their width, contrast, softness, and angle to really customize your inner bevel look to any number of combinations.

8. Next, experiment with the jack object labeled Inset Emboss, manipulating it in much the same way.

9. Click the object to select it. Click Open Effect Information in the Effects panel.

10. Notice that the first control is the width of the Inset Emboss. I changed this earlier from the default, which is 2, to this setting of 6, to emphasize the pushed-in feeling of the object.

11. Continue to click and slide the Width slider upward. This makes your jack object more exaggerated. As you slide the width's numeric value down, your emboss becomes more subtle.

You now move on to working with the jack object labeled Outer Bevel Smooth:

1. Click the object to select it and click Edit, Arrange Effects icon from the Effects panel.

2. Notice that there is a color other than the color of the object in the color well. It is the default color of red (DF0000).

3. Click the Color box and change it to another color. (I used black.)

4. Continue to edit the width, the bevel edge shape, contrast, softness, angle, and the presets to make the variations of the effect known as Outer Bevel Smooth.

The last object is the jack artwork object labeled Raised Emboss and that effect applied to it.

The effect contains a width of 5 and the default settings for contrast, softness, and angle. There is a different option here than on any of the other bevel type controls: the Show Object check box. When you click to deselect this check box, your object becomes invisible on the existing background of white, which removes its color and displays only the object's beveled edge as shading.

The button presets for the Bevel button allow you to create variations of Raised, Highlighted, Inset, and Inverted. The idea behind this is to allow you to quickly create a set of button choices based on a single original shape. (Raised is the default setting.) This changes the object by applying a three-dimensional look to it. Highlighted is also raised, but additionally, the object receives a 25-percent white tint to it. Inset reverses the lighting to swap, or create, a depressed 3-D effect. Inverted reverses the lighting and lightens the object with tint.

Shadow Effects

Within Fireworks, there are basically four types of Shadow effects (see Figure 7.7):

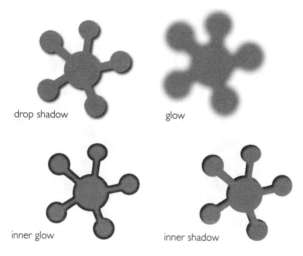

drop shadow   glow

inner glow   inner shadow

Figure 7.7   The tutorial file `shadow effect.png`.

- **Drop Shadow**—When you choose the Drop Shadow effect from the Effect list, you can control the distance of the shadow, the color of the shadow, the opacity of the shadow, the softness, and the angle. You can also convert your object to a knockout, which turns the original object invisible and leaves only the shadow object.

- **Glow**—Controls Halo Offset, Opacity, Softness, and Color. The default color of Glow is red #DF0000.

- **Inner Glow**—When you apply the Inner Glow effect, you can control the Halo Offset, Opacity, and Color. However, the glow appears inside the object instead of outside the object.

- **Drop Shadow**—Inner Shadow effects are the same as those for Drop Shadow. The Inner Shadow, however, makes the object look like a hole instead of a floating element.

Glow Effects

When you apply a Glow effect, you can control the offset of the glow to the object and the offset, or thickness, of the halo or glow itself (see Figure 7.8). The Halo Offset makes the glow appear heavier, or darker and thicker, while the offset control moves the position of the glow itself closer or further away from the object to which you apply it. (Open the figure called `glow offset.png` from the `Effects` folder.)

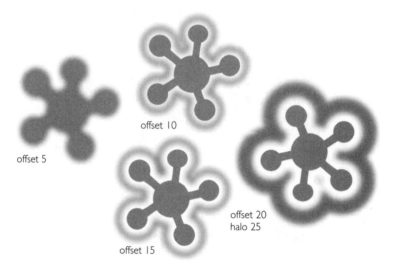

Figure 7.8   The tutorial gile `glow offset halo25.png`.

Notice that it contains the jack width offset with glow applied to it and the offset of 5, 10, 15, and 20 applied to four different versions of the original vector shape. In each of these cases, the glow moves closer or further in to the object, depending on the main offset setting.

Next, try this:

1. Select the object labeled Offset20 and click the Information icon to open the Glow Control Panel (or double-click the effect name) (see Figure 7.9).

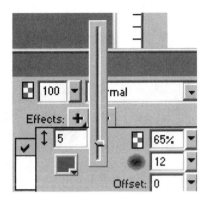

Figure 7.9   The Glow Control Panel in the Property Inspector.

2. Change the Halo Offset from 20 to 25.

   You can now see that the halo, or glow, is thicker.

3. To make the halo darker in color or more prominent, increase the opacity by clicking and dragging the Opacity slider (see Figure 7.10).

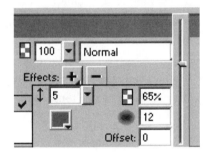

Figure 7.10   The Opacity slider in the Property Inspector.

4. To make the halo lighter or more transparent, decrease the percentage of opacity.

5. To make the glow appear hard-edged, slide the Softness slider to 0.

6. If you want your glow to take on a watercolor appearance, slide the Opacity slider to the 70–100 percent range (see Figure 7.11).

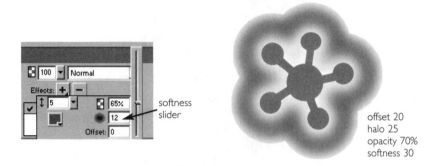

offset 20
halo 25
opacity 70%
softness 30

Figure 7.11   The Opacity slider in the Property Inspector.

The example glowoffsettweaked has the glow set on Offset 20, Halo 25, Opacity 70 percent, and Softness 30, which creates an almost flower-like effect.

Blur and Sharpen Effects

The Blur effect softens the overall look of your objects. These effects can make objects appear to be in the distance or to be less prominent in the image. Although these effects are most effective when used on pixel-based or bitmap images, they do also alter patterns, textures, and gradients that are applied to vector objects. Because the Blur effect works by altering the black and white information in your image into variations of gray, some of the image detail is lost as the contrasting tones in the image soften:

1. Open the file named blureffects.png from the Effects folder (see Figure 7.12).

Figure 7.12   The Blur effects.

2. To apply the Blur effect or Blur More effect, click the original photo of my brother and me and select Blur or Blur More from the Effect Category pop-up list.

3. When you examine this figure, you can see that the difference between Blur and Blur More are subtle.

4. To apply the Gausian Blur effect, select Gausian Blur from the Effect Category pop-up list. The Gausian Blur dialog box appears.

5. You can slide the Blur Radius slider to the right, which increases the blur radius, or to the left to decrease the amount of blur in the image.

6. The Preview check box allows you to disable preview for faster results.

The Sharpen effects work in a similar fashion to Blur effects:

1. Open the file `sharpeneffects.png` from the `Effects` folder and follow along (see Figure 7.13). The original image was photographed from a car, so the result was blurry.

   There are three main sharpening effects: Sharpen, Sharpen More, and Unsharp Mask. When you examine the Sharpen and Sharpen More versions of the effect, you can notice that the difference is subtle. To have a greater control over the sharpening, however, use the Unsharp Mask effect.

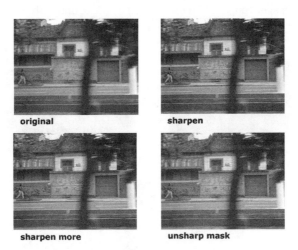

Figure 7.13   The Sharpen effects.

2. You can also stack Sharpen effects so that you are reapplying the Sharpen effect numerous times, which increases the image's sharpness.

3. To use Unsharp Mask, select the image and choose Unsharp Mask from the Effect Category pop-up list. The Unsharp Mask dialog box appears.

4. When you click and drag the Sharpen Amount slider, you alter the contrast that's applied to the image. The higher the number, the greater the sharpening.

5. The Threshold slider allows you to set how different the pixels must be before they are affected by the sharpening. A low number means that the pixels in the image are all sharpened. A higher threshold number means that only those pixels that are very different in brightness will be sharpened.

6. The Pixel Radius slider allows you to control the number of pixels around the edge of the object that have the Sharpen effect applied to them.

We'll now demystify the Unsharp Mask:

1. Click the Unsharp Mask image and then click to select the Unsharp Mask Effect dialog box from the Effects panel.

2. Notice that the Sharpen amount is set to the maximum (500). The Pixel Radius is set to .02 and the Threshold is set to 0. This means that I am using the maximum sharpen amount at a low pixel radius and low threshold. Therefore, all the pixels in the image will be sharpened as much as they can, very close to the edge.

3. To get a better idea of how this Unsharp Mask feature works, open the file called unsharpcompared.png (see Figure 7.14). The file contains three different Unsharp Mask versions of my little cat, Einstein.

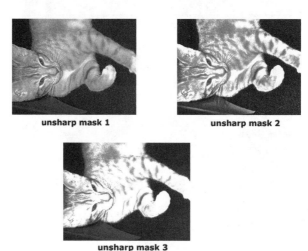

Figure 7.14   The Unsharpen Mask effects.

4. The first item, labeled `unsharpmask1`, contains the Sharpen amount of 162, the Pixel Radius of .09, and the Threshold of 0. This brightens up the highlights of the image, but does not grossly affect it.

5. The next version of the Unsharp Mask, labeled `unsharpmask2`, has a Sharpen amount of 300, the Pixel Radius of 4, and again, a Threshold of 0. In this image, the stripes and markings on Einstein are more pronounced, and the artwork begins to have a polarized and contrasted feeling.

6. Out of the three, the last item, labeled `unsharpmask3`, is the most tweaked. The Sharpen amount in this image is set to 245, the Pixel Radius is set at 80, and again, the Threshold is set at 0, which gives this item the most contrasted and glowing overall look.

7. Experiment by increasing the threshold. This tends to bring in some strange polarizing affects. Each image is going to be different, so while there are certain predictable results, there's always room for a happy accident.

When used strategically, Sharpen can really add interest to your images:

1. Open the `unsharpcomparedto.png` file (see Figure 7.15).

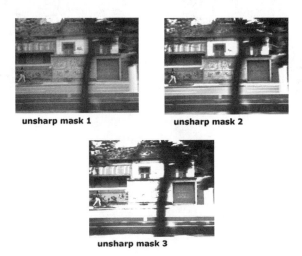

unsharp mask 1   unsharp mask 2

unsharp mask 3

Figure 7.15   A comparison of Unsharpen effects.

2. The first item in this file, labeled `unsharpmask1`, uses the settings from Figure 7.13. Those are Sharpen Amount 500, Pixel Radius .2, and Threshold of 0.

3. The item labeled `unsharpmask2` is set at Sharpen Amount 134, Pixel Radius 20, and Threshold 0.

4. The image marked unsharpmask3 has the Sharpen Amount setting of 500, the Pixel Radius of 250, and the Threshold of 0. In this image, when the Sharpen Amount and Pixel Radius amounts were increased, the image took on the look of a painting with its areas of color increasing in contrast and brightness.

Other Effects

Within the Effects pop-up menu, the category Other contains two effects: Convert to Alpha and Find Edges. The Find Edges effect allows you to change the color of pixels of an image. It uses the image's pixels to etch lines where there are edges in the image. It can be a beautiful, neon-looking effect or an effect that looks more like an etching or engraving:

1. Open the findedges.png file from the Effects folder (see Figure 7.16). This file contains a version of the original photo that I took of some people dancing in my friend Page's nightclub.

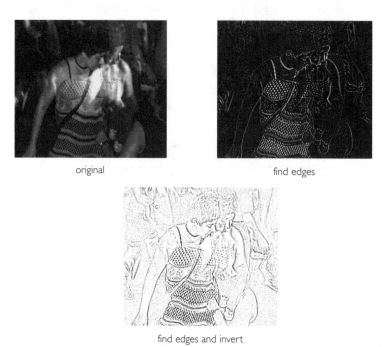

original   find edges

find edges and invert

Figure 7.16   The Find Edges effects.

2. The image on the right, labeled Find Edges, is that same image as the original with the Find Edges filter applied to it.

3. The last image, labeled Find Edges and Invert, is the find edges image with an additional effect applied to it, called Invert Effect. This effect reverses the colors in the image so that while the Find Edges effect created a neon-like version of the original, the Find Edges and Invert looks more like a line drawing or an etching.

This Convert to Alpha effect allows you to convert an object or image into a grayscale channel version of itself. In this way, you can create semitransparent effects based on the colors of an image:

1. Open the `converttoalpha.png` file (see Figure 7.17). The item labeled Original is a photo or bitmap graphic of my brilliant nephew Raphael, along with some vector objects, lightning-bolt shapes, emanating from his hand.

original   lightning bolts with convert to alpha

Figure 7.17   The Convert to Alpha effects.

2. To the right, the image labeled Lightning Bolt with Convert to Alpha is the same bitmap image; however, the lightning bolts have been converted to alpha by the Convert to Alpha effect.

3. Notice how the transparent effect of the objects allows different amounts of the object or photo beneath to be seen. Areas that are lighter in color allow the image underneath to be seen more, whereas areas that had a darker color hide more of the underlying image.

The Convert to Alpha effect looks similar to masking using grayscale values. If you want to check out more information on masking, go to Chapter 9, "Masking."

Adjusting Color Effects

Finally, there are the Adjust Color effects. Fireworks contains various effects that enable you to alter and modify the look of colors in objects and images. These effects allow you to alter aspects of the image, including brightness and contrast, and allow you to adjust the overall tonal relationships between tones in an image. These effects are likened to those that you might find in programs such as Photoshop, where sophisticated adjustments can be made easily.

Auto Levels

The Auto Levels effect applies a preset adjustment of levels to the tones of your object or image:

1. Open the `autolevels.png` file from the `Effects` folder (see Figure 7.18).

original

auto levels

Figure 7.18   The Auto Levels effects.

2. On the left, the image named Original is a photo of my brother and our beautiful niece, Nicole. The photo is washed out and flat.

   To the right, the same image, labeled Auto Levels, appears with the Auto Levels effect applied to it.

   This effect is the quickest and most simple way to modify the light and dark areas within an image. However, because there are no controls, this effect is generally only used as a quick fix, a test, or when an image needs just a bit of tweaking.

Brightness and Contrast

The next Adjust Color effect is Brightness Contrast:

1. Select Brightness and Contrast from the Effects Panel pop-up menu. You are presented with the Brightness/Contrast dialog box (see Figure 7.19), within which you can slide the Brightness slider to increase or decrease the brightness of an image, and the Contrast slider to adjust the overall relationship between the darks and lights.

Figure 7.19   The Brightness/Contrast dialog box.

2. By tweaking these two sliders alternately to the left and right, I zeroed in on the setting that looked best for this image. That is, Brightness is set at –6 and Contrast is set at 32. While the Brightness and Contrast effect is a bit more sophisticated than Auto Levels, it is still less effective than both the Curves and Levels effects adjustments.

3. To use the Curves effect, with your image selected, choose Curves from the Adjust Color menu. The Curves dialog box appears. Make sure that the Channel list is set to RGB so that you alter the red, green, and blue channels all at once. Or you can select a specific channel that you might want to adjust.

4. Click and drag the curve line, creating points and repositioning them within the curve graph.

5. Notice that you can add points and drag them anywhere on the graph line. Once you get the hang of this, it becomes fun. Also notice that when you click and drag points on the curve, you change the input and output amounts for that particular point within the image.

6. When you click and drag from left to right, you change the input levels. When you click and drag up and down, you change the output levels.

Try this:

1. Open the `curves.png` file from the `Effects` folder (see Figure 7.20).

original

adjusted with the curve effects

Figure 7.20   The Curves effect.

On the left, the image of Nicole is washed out and flat. On the right, the image labeled `curvesadjusted` is more vibrant and clear. My procedure for adjusting the tonality with this Curves effect is detailed in the remaining steps.

2. First, I select the image and choose Curve from the Adjust Color pop-up menu. Notice that the curve graph is broken into 16 quadrants.

3. My first step is to click at the very center of the line to anchor a point there.

4. Then, I moved up into the first row, fourth quadrant, and clicked and dragged a point to the left to adjust my image's highlight tones.

5. I clicked in the bottom row and dragged a point into the beginning of the second square, creating a subtle sloping S curve and bringing my shadow detail into focus (see Figure 7.21).

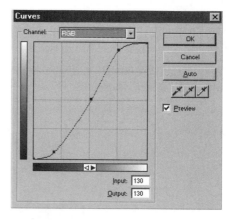

Figure 7.21   The Curves dialog box.

Curves and Levels Effects

Essentially, both the Curves and the Levels effects do the same thing; that is, they allow you precise manipulation over the brightness and contrast of your image's tonal range. They each, however, have their own interfaces and methods for doing this. Here's what I mean.

You can follow along with the curvesandlevels.png file and see if you can get your results to match mine.

1. Open the curvesandlevels.png file (see Figure 7.22).

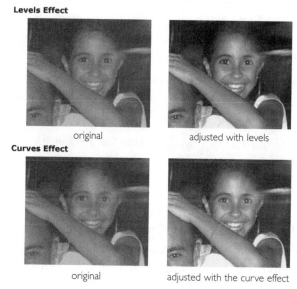

Figure 7.22   Practicing curves and levels.

2. Click to select the close-up of my niece, Nicole, labeled Original. Notice that the item on the right, labeled Adjusted with Levels, has already been adjusted.

3. Click to select the original photo.

4. Click the Add Effect button on the Property Inspector to reveal the Effects panel.

5. Select Adjust Color Levels. The Levels dialog box appears, displaying the Channel pop-up menu, the Input Levels readout, and the Output Levels readout.

6. Look at the top diagram or histogram of the input levels. Notice that most of the data is piled toward the center of the diagram, above the gray arrow or slider. No data is near the white or the black slider. The black slider controls the shadow information, the gray slider controls the mid-tone information, and the white slider represents the highlight information.

7. Click the white slider and drag it to where the data begins; click the black slider and drag it right to where the data begins, and you can see that your image comes into a more balanced contrast level.

   What you have done is distributed all the data across a wider range of tones, which brightened the contrast of the image.

   Now let's switch over to work with curves:

8. Click to select the photo labeled Original in the Curves and Effects portion of the file.

9. Click the Add Effect button in the Property Inspector and launch the Curves effect from the Adjust Color pop-up menu. You are presented with the Curves dialog box, which contains a 4 × 4 grid of 16 squares and a diagonal line that goes from the lower left to the upper right of the document.

   Running along the left side of the grid is a gradient that flows from white to black. Running underneath from left to right is a gradient that flows from black on the left to white on the right.

   Input level changes are made by clicking the line and moving points on the line from the left to the right; output level changes are made by clicking the line and dragging up or down.

   Dragging to the left lightens the image. Dragging to the right darkens the image.

   Dragging down darkens the image. Dragging up lightens the image. By clicking this line and dragging points to new positions, you alter the distribution of grayscale information within the image. You can alter the RGB channels together or separately.

10. Click in the center of the line to anchor the grayscale information.

11. Click in the upper right top-most quadrant on the line in the image and drag it slightly to the left, which lightens the image a hair.

12. Click the line in the lower left-most quadrant of the image and drag the curve line to the right. In a sense, you want to move the highlight information, which is currently very gray, into a lighter range of white tones, and move the shadow information, which is also very flat and gray, over to the dark tones. Doing this redistributes and balances the image. Final input and output intensities are 130-130.

If you compare the two adjusted images, you can see that they are similar, although not quite the same. The Adjusted with Levels image has more contrast than the Adjusted with Curves image.

Hue and Saturation

The Hue and Saturation effect just happens to be my personal favorite. This effect enables you to change the range of colors, or hue, within your images. It also enables you to brighten colors by increasing the saturation, or remove color, in effect turning color images into black and white images by removing all the saturation. Also, you can tone an image by using the Colorize feature. Here's how it works.

Open the hue saturation file from the Effects folder. Notice that it contains four sets of images, one each for Hue, Saturation, Lightness, and Colorize. The images in the left side, all marked Original, are for you to tinker with. The images on the right side are all the images that were adjusted with various versions of the Hue Saturation effect:

1. Starting with the Hue effect, select the photo of the mirror balls labeled Original (see Figure 7.23).

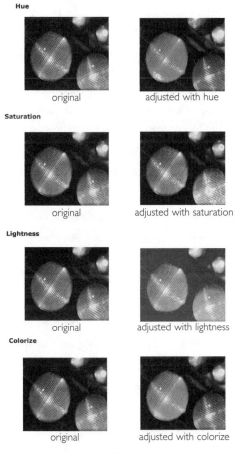

Figure 7.23　Practicing hue and saturation adjustments.

2. Click the Property Inspector to launch the Effects panel and select the Hue Saturation effect from the Adjust Color pop-up menu. The Hue/Saturation dialog box appears. It contains sliders for each of the Hue, Saturation, and Lightness effects, and an additional two check boxes—one for Colorize and one for Preview (see Figure 7.24).

Figure 7.24   The Hue/Saturation dialog box.

3. To alter the hue of the image, click and drag the Hue slider. Clicking and dragging the slider from the center to the right shifts the blue ball from blue into purple ranges, into red ranges, and finally, as you get all the way over to the right, to orange. If you then drag the slider all the way to the far left, as far as it can go, and continue to drag from left to right, you can notice that you have completed a circle around the color wheel. I adjusted my Hue slider to 157, which turns the blue ball reddish orange, the yellow ball blue, the light blue ball red, and the pale purple ball yellow.

    As is true with the hue adjustment, you can type a numeric value for your adjustment and for the saturation and lightness adjustments:

4. Select the image and, using the Hue Saturation effect, slide the Saturation slider.

    Sliding the Saturation slider to the right increases the brightness of the colors within the image, which makes them more vibrant.

    Sliding the Saturation slider to the left decreases the saturation and makes the colors appear more subtle.

    When all saturation is removed, the image appears in black and white. I set my adjustment to 100 percent saturation, beefing up the vibrancy of the colors in the image. (Think of saturation as the amount of color in a color.)

    After you make your hue adjustment, click OK and proceed to work with the Saturation adjustment.

5. Select the original lightness image and the Adjust Color Hue Saturation effect.

6. Slide the Lightness slider to the right to ghost out the image, and to the left to make the image darker and more subdued. I lightened the image to 28, which gives it a bit of a posterized look. Although you can completely lighten and darken images with this feature, you might have better tonal control using the Curves or Levels adjustments.

Finally, we move on to the Colorize effect:

7. Launch the Hue Saturation effect for the final colorize original image. The Hue Saturation panel opens.

8. Click the Colorize check box and slide the Hue slider, Saturation, and Lightness controls to create a monotone colorized version of the mirror balls.

9. To create my sepia-toned mirror-ball image, I adjusted the hue to 31, saturation to 47, and lightness was left at 0.

Invert Effect

The final effect in this batch is the Invert effect:

1. Open the `inverteffect.png` file from the `Effects` folder.

Notice that the image on the right is an inverted version of the image on the left (See Figure 7.25).

original

invert

Figure 7.25   Inverting an image.

2. To invert the image, select it, choose the Adjust Color Invert effect, and that's it.

It's obvious that the use of the Invert effect turns a positive image back into its negative version. You can also create some beautiful effects with color images using this effect.

Now that you have applied some effects to objects and have the hang of that, we are going to review the Effects panel. The Effects panel enables you to alter your effects, enables you to turn them on or off, and also to change the order of the effects. When you change the order of the effects, you actually change the appearance of the effect as well.

Modifying Effects

Click the Information icon in the Effects panel to open the Effect control. If the effect uses a dialog box to manipulate its particulars, that dialog box appears. You can then make the changes that you desire and click the name of the effect again in the panel to apply the new settings and close the controls.

To turn the effect on and off, click the Preview icon check box in the Effect list. This works like a toggle, allowing you to turn the effect on and off.

To delete an effect, select it and use the Delete Effect option in the Effect menu, or click the Delete Effect icon, or drag the effect to the Delete Effect icon.

To apply multiple effects to your artwork, continue to add effects with the object selected.

To change the order of the effect and how it modifies the image, drag it up or down in the Effect list.

After you create an effect that you like, you can save it by following these steps:

1. Create an effect and apply it to an object.

2. Select Save Effect from the Effects panel menu. The Save Effect dialog box appears.

3. Give your effect a name and click OK. Your new effect appears as one of the effect presets. You can use it with any document that you create in Fireworks.

You can also save a selected effect as a style by selecting New from the Style pop-up menu and giving the style a name.

If you so desire, you can also make alterations to the default effects:

1. To change the default effect settings, apply some effects to an artwork.

2. Select Save Defaults from the Effects panel menu. You are prompted with an Alert dialog box that asks you to confirm that you want to save these settings as defaults.

3. Click OK. The next time Use Defaults is selected, these effects are used.

Summary

You are now armed and dangerous. With the knowledge you have in your possession about adding, working with, creating, and saving effects in Fireworks, you are a force to be reckoned with. Go forth and create!

Chapter 8

Working with Bitmaps

Now in Fireworks MX, working with bitmaps images for web pages and web graphics is more fluid and streamlined than ever. There are some fundamental differences between what and how you create bitmap images versus vector images in Fireworks.

Fireworks actually uses two different modes within which you build your objects: bitmap-editing mode and vector-editing mode. When it comes to transitioning between working with bitmap tools and images versus vector tools and images, the mode switching that occurs in Fireworks MX is transparent to the user. You don't see it occurring. In my opinion, this one feature makes Fireworks MX absolutely the best tool to use for creating web, animation, and multimedia graphics on the market today.

My hat is off to the fine and brilliant folks at Macromedia for making this possible. Fireworks MX is pretty flawless! In part, this is because of the changes made to the Tools panel and to the new Fireworks MX seamless mode-switching feature.

Because bitmap images are made up of pixels, when you compose or edit them they are in a certain sense, married to the canvas. Unlike vector artwork, which can be moved or reshaped, bitmap images rely on selecting, painting, erasing, and cloning techniques to create and manipulate the pixels in an image.

Although you work on pixel-based images using the bitmap tools, bitmap images are objects. They can also be selected, scaled, and can have effects applied to them, just like vector images. When you select a bitmap image with the Pointer tool, it resides as though it's in a vector container.

There is a wide range of possible ways that bitmap images can be manipulated. Digital painting has truly become a fine art. It's impossible to cover the awesomeness of this comprehensive topic, but I endeavored to create a chapter that provides you with a strong platform of knowledge from which you can jump into the deep subject of this great art.

It's up to you now to jump in!

Importing Bitmaps

The most likely way that you want to work with bitmap images in Fireworks probably includes scanned images, images from your digital camera, or images from other applications, such as Photoshop or Corel Painter.

Painting and Creating Bitmap Objects Using Fireworks MX

As previously mentioned, this wonderful new upgrade to Fireworks makes switching between bitmap mode and vector mode virtually seamless. Now, all you have to do is choose a vector or a bitmap tool from the Tools panel, and you are automatically editing in the correct mode.

Striped Border No More

In previous versions of Fireworks, a striped border around the canvas indicated that you were working in bitmap mode. If you miss this feature, and want to see the familiar striped border, choose Bitmap, Options, Display Striped Border from the Edit category of the Preferences dialog box.

Creating Your Own Bitmap Artwork in Fireworks

When you create a brand-new bitmap object in Fireworks, the object is added to the current working layer of your document. When the Layers panel is expanded, you see a thumbnail and a name for each bitmap object that you created under the layer on which it lives. In Fireworks, bitmap objects are organized as separate and discreet objects within layers, which allows you to change their stacking order, opacity, blending mode, name, and so on. To learn more about layers, check out Chapter 3, "Setting Up a New Document and Navigating the Workspace."

Bitmap Tools in Brief

Essentially, two main tools are used for painting and drawing bitmaps onto your canvas in Fireworks: the Brush tool and the Pencil tool.

Three main tools are used to make selections of bitmap objects and portions of bitmap images: the Marquee tool, the Lasso tool, and the Magic Wand tool.

Finally, three more tools exist in the bitmap area of the Tools panel. These tools are used to modify and alter aspects of your bitmap creations: the Eraser tool, the Blur tool, and the Rubber Stamp tool.

Bitmap Tool Groups

When you look closely at the Marquee tool, the Lasso tool, or the Brush tool, you can see that they are each accompanied by a small black down-pointing arrow. This indicates that this tool is part of a tool group (see Figure 8.1). Inside these tools are additional tools associated with their function (see Figure 8.2). To access these tools' pop-up functions, click and hold their icons and their tool group pop-up menus appear:

- The rectangular Marquee tool groups include the Oval Marquee tool.
- When you click the Lasso tool, you can see the Polygon Lasso tool, which is also an option.
- The Blur tool contains the Sharpen tool, the Dodge tool, the Burn tool, and the Smudge tool.

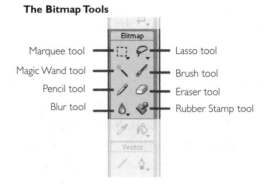

Figure 8.1   The Bitmap tools in the Tools panel.

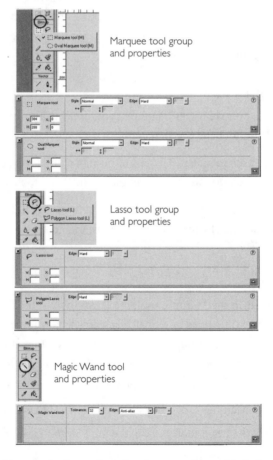

Figure 8.2   The bitmap selection tools and tool groups, along with their corresponding properties in the Property Inspector.

Starting to Paint with Fireworks

If you have arrived at this spot in this book, you are ready to learn how to create your own bitmap objects in Fireworks. As you might or might not know, you can create bitmap graphics in Fireworks in many ways:

- You can use the drawing and painting tools.

- You can cut, copy, and paste pixel selections and other bitmap objects into your creations in a montage fashion.

- You can convert your own vector images into bitmap objects.

- You can make combinations or mixtures of existing bitmaps, bitmaps you have altered, those you have painted or drawn, and vector objects that you might convert and spin into the mix of pixels.

Note

I have always experienced bitmap or painting on a computer as creating a magical painting that's simultaneously always wet and always dry. Here's what I mean: By virtue of the fact that you can continually move, recolor, cut, copy, and paste pixels, you can change the stacking order of your layers and have an infinitely reworkable composition. You can paint on and erase from your pixels at any time, add to and throw away from the document, and always be able to get back to some semblance of the original artwork.

There you have it, a painting that's wet and dry simultaneously.

Creating a New Bitmap Object in Fireworks MX

You can create a brand-new bitmap object in Fireworks MX in two main ways.

Here's the first way:

1. Create a new canvas. Make it white and 500 × 500 pixels per inch (ppi).

2. Select either the Pencil tool or the Brush tool from the bitmap section of the Tools panel.

3. Draw or paint with your tool on the canvas to create a new bitmap object.

   You now see that there is a new bitmap object added into the current layer in the Layers panel.

Here's the second way to create a brand-new bitmap object. This one's a bit different because first, we'll create an empty, or blank, bitmap object and then create inside of that. To create an empty bitmap object, follow these steps:

1. Click the New Bitmap Image button at the lower-right corner in the Layers panel, or select Edit, Insert, Empty Bitmap (see Figures 8.3, 8.4, and 8.5).

2. Build the bitmap inside the new empty object.

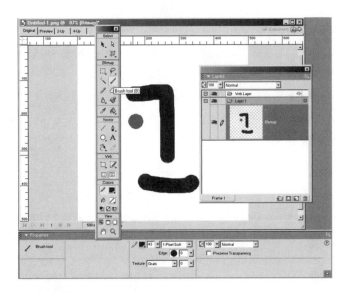

Figure 8.3   The bitmap object is painted into Layer 1 using the Brush tool set at 43, Black.

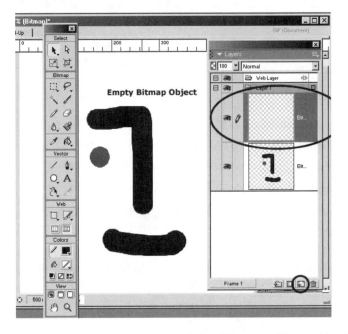

Figure 8.4   The New Bitmap Image button is circled and the empty bitmap object is in the Layers panel.

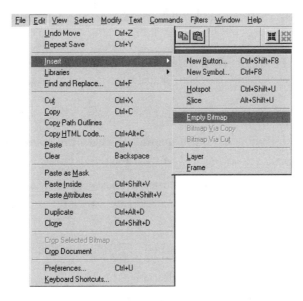

Figure 8.5   Insert the empty bitmap that's selected in the Edit menu.

With an inkling of an idea of how to get your canvas and workspace started in bitmap mode, you need to know the real "nuts and bolts" of working with bitmaps in Fireworks MX.

Selecting: A Complete Overview

Gaining mastery with selections and selection tools is the basis for creating high-quality bitmap objects. That's why this section is all about selecting.

Using the Bitmap Selection Tools

Although you can just pick up one of the bitmap-creation tools, such as the pencil or brush, and start painting directly onto the canvas, there are also times when you need to restrict your *bitmap editing* (also known as *painting*) to a particular area of an image.

This is where the selection tools come in. We review a number of ways to work with selections, including adding, subtracting, and multiplying a selection.

Both the Marquee tool group and the Lasso tool group are used to select pixels or areas of pixels based on shape:

- The Marquee tool selects a rectangular area of pixels within an image. You can constrain it to an exact square by holding the Shift key as you draw.

- The Oval Marquee tool selects elliptical areas in an image. To create perfect circle selections, hold the Shift key while you draw.

- The Lasso tool enables you to select free-form shape areas of pixels within an image. You click it and draw your shape, releasing the mouse, and the selection area closes.

- The Polygon Lasso tool selects a straight-edged, free-form area of pixels in an image by you holding down your mouse and clicking in a series of straight-edge segments, similar to sewing, and creating a selection border for your image.

- The Magic Wand tool allows you to select areas of similarly colored pixels within your image based on color tolerance and edge setting that are selected using the Property Inspector.

So after you define a selection area with one of these tools, you can manipulate, paint, add to, or edit the pixels inside of the selection.

You can also apply filters to these pixels and erase them, all without affecting the pixels outside of the selected area.

Also, you can create what's called a floating selection of pixels that you can edit, cut, copy, or move.

Using the Property Inspector to Display and Modify Bitmap Selection Tool Options

When either the Marquee, Oval Marquee, Lasso, Polygon Lasso, or Magic Wand tools are selected, the Property Inspector displays three edge options for the tools:

- **Hard**—Creates a marquee selection with a non-anti-aliased, or defined, edge.

- **Anti-alias**—Creates transitional pixels, which prevents jagged edges and straightens the marquee selections.

- **Feather**—Softens the edge of a pixel selection by modifying the feather amount. To set the Feather Amount option, you must do so before creating the selection. You can feather existing selections using the Feather option in the Select menu.

Three more options for style are available when the Marquee, Oval Marquee, or Magic Wand tool is selected:

- **Normal**—Creates a marquee in which the height and the width are free and sized independently of each other.

- **Fixed Ratio**—Holds or constrains the height and width to a defined setting that you choose.

- **Fixed Size**—Constrains the height and width to a defined dimension.

Although the Magic Wand tool is a selection tool like the Marquee tools, it uses a tolerance setting to select areas of similar color.

Creating Selections with Marquee

The Marquee, the Oval Marquee, as well as the Lasso tools, enable you to select specifically shaped areas of bitmap images by clicking and dragging the marquee around them.

This section teaches you about using the Marquee and Lasso tools to make selections of and creating bitmap images in Fireworks.

To select a rectangular or elliptical shape of pixels, follow these steps:

1. Open the mushroom.png file from the Bitmaps folder on the CD-ROM.

2. Select the Marquee or the Oval Marquee tool from the Tools panel (see Figure 8.6).

Figure 8.6   The Marquee tool circled in the Tools panel. The mushrooms are selected with the Marquee tools.

3. Set your style and edge options using the Property Inspector.

4. Click and drag the selection marquee around the area that you want it to define.

To create a square or circular marquee, follow these steps:

1. Hold the Shift key as you draw the marquee or the oval marquee.

2. To draw out a marquee from its center point, make sure that nothing is selected, and hold Alt (for Windows) or Option (for a Mac) while you click and draw out the marquee shape from its center.

To create a free-form selection of pixels using the Lasso tool, follow these steps:

1. Make sure that nothing is selected by using Ctrl-D (for Windows) or Command-D (for a Macintosh) to select pixels or, from the Select menu, choose Select, Deselect, or single-click anywhere on the open canvas (see Figure 8.7).

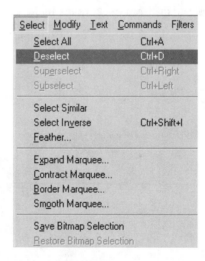

Figure 8.7   The Select menu displays Deselect.

2. Select the Lasso tool from the Tools panel.

3. Set the edge option in the Property Inspector.

4. Click and drag with the Pointer tool around the pixels, creating the shape that you want to select (see Figure 8.8).

Figure 8.8   Make your selection.

On the left side of this image, the Lasso tool was used to select a cloud-like shape around the mushroom. On the right side of the image, the Polygon Lasso tool was used to stitch a controlled, jagged mushroom shape around the mushroom.

The Polygon Lasso tool enables you to click repeatedly around the perimeter of a pixel area that you want to select.

Here's how to plot points to create a marquee selection using the Polygon Lasso tool:

1. Make sure that everything is deselected.
2. Select the Polygon Lasso tool from the Tools panel.
3. Set your edge option in the Property Inspector.
4. Click around the perimeter of the object to plot points around the object until you come to the origin point. Your selection becomes closed.

Note

To constrain the Polygon Lasso tool marquee to 45-degree segments, hold the Shift key while clicking and dragging.

5. Do one of the following to close the polygon: Click at the starting point or double-click in the workspace.

Selecting Pixels and Pixel Areas of Similar Color

Now that you have the basics of marquee selecting, you are ready to move on to learning about selecting areas of pixels with similar color.

Here's how to do it:

1. Open the umbra_f.png file from the Bitmaps folder on your
   CD-ROM.

   Notice that it contains a woman holding an umbrella that has a sky on the inside
   of it. The background she is standing in front of is a gradient from light to
   dark gray.

2. Select the Magic Wand tool in the Tools panel. Set the tolerance in the Property
   Inspector to 32 and the edge to Anti-Alias.

3. Click in the upper left-hand corner of the image to select a range of pixels similar in color (see Figure 8.9).

Note

The tolerance setting allows for control over the range of colors that are touching each
other.

Figure 8.9   A Magic Wand selection applied to the umbrella elf. The pixel tolerance is set to
                32. The upper-left corner area of the background has been clicked on with
                the tool.

Continue to select the background of the image as follows:

4. Hold the Shift key and click in the upper right-hand corner of the image.

5. Continue to hold the Shift key while you click around to select the rest of the image's background (see Figure 8.10).

Figure 8.10   Using the Magic Wand tool and the Shift key to add to the selection, the Magic Wand selection was applied to rest of the umbrella elf's background. The pixel tolerance is set to 32.

6. To select the picture between the ankles and feet on the picture, search to the Zoom tool and zoom in on the portion between the ankles and feet.

7. Switch back to the Magic Wand tool, set the color tolerance to 20, hold the Shift key, and click the small groups of pixels between the ankles and feet (see Figure 8.11).

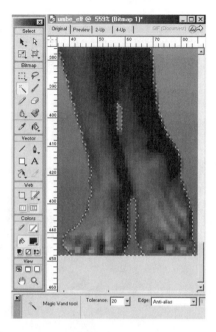

Figure 8.11   The zoomed-in portion of the feet and ankles. The additional unselected pixels are selected using the Magic Wand tool and the Shift key at a tolerance of 20 pixels.

Changing the Magic Wand selection tolerance to lower numbers collects, or selects, fewer pixels. If you set the tolerance to a higher number, you collect, or select, a wider range of colors in the selection.

Here's another way to select similar colors within a document:

1. Select an area of color with the Marquee Lasso tool or the Magic Wand tool.

2. From the Select menu, choose Select Similar. The result is one or more new marquees with selections containing the selected range of pixels that you specified.

Note

You can adjust the tolerance for the Select Similar option by choosing the Magic Wand tool and then changing the tolerance setting in the Property Inspector before using the option.

Adding and Subtracting from Selections Using Modifier Keys

After you create your selection areas, you can adjust and modify the active selections themselves. You can add to or remove from the marquee border without affecting the pixels beneath it. You can also add or delete pixels from the marquee border by using modifier keys:

- You can add to your selection by holding the Shift key while dragging a marquee tool, drawing with one of the Lasso tools, or slicking with the Magic Wand.

- If you hold down the Alt key (for Windows) or Option key (for a Macintosh) and select part of a selected area with one of the selection tools, you can selectively deselect part of the existing marquee.

It's easy to add to your selections creatively. After drawing a selection with any of the selection tools, you can use another selection tool to perfect the shape of your selection.

To add onto an existing selection, follow these steps:

1. Choose any bitmap selection tool.

2. Hold down the Shift key and create your selection with either of the tools.

3. Continue to do this with as many tools as you need to create the perfect complex selection.

Note

When you overlap your selection areas, they join to create one continuous selection area.

Creating a Complex Selection with Multiple Selection Tools

To create a complex selection with two or more selection tools, simply complete the following steps:

1. Open the doorway.png file from the Bitmaps folder on the CD-ROM.

2. Using the Ellipse tool and, if you want, the Info panel, gauge the size of your ellipse (see Figure 8.12).

Note

You might have to drag out the selected ellipse several times before you get the general width and height. Click and drag with the Ellipse tool until you match the top of the arch.

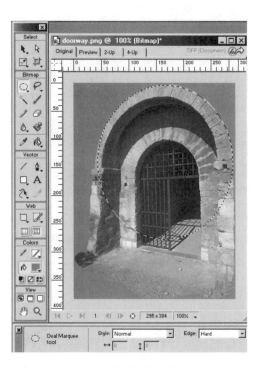

Figure 8.12   The top of the arch is selected with the Elliptical Marquee tool.

The first part of the selection (the top of the arch) is done for now; however, the idea is to select the entire perimeter. Now switch to the Polygon Lasso tool and use it to add to your selection in the following way:

1. With your elliptical selection still selected, choose the Polygon Lasso tool from the Tools panel.

2. Hold down the Shift key, click once, and release the Shift key.

3. Begin to make small clicks around the outside edge of the stone doorway shape. Try to be as precise as possible, which means making as many small one-segment clicks as you need (see Figure 8.13).

4. Click straight across the bottom and work your way up the right side to enclose the entire shape (see Figure 8.14).

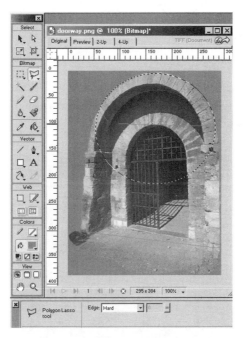

Figure 8.13   The Polygon Lasso selection in progress.

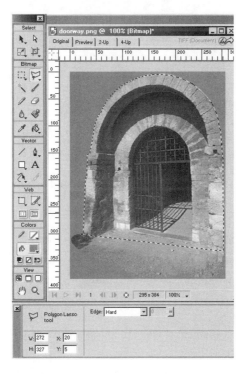

Figure 8.14   The Polygon Lasso selection is added to the ellipse selection.

Finally, we'll use the Polygon Lasso tool to finish up the curved shape at the bottom of the doorway's entrance:

1. Switch from the Polygon Lasso tool to the Lasso tool on the Tools panel.

2. Hold the Shift key and click once with the Lasso tool to set the origin point. Release the Shift key and draw your free-form Lasso tool to follow the gentle curves in front of the door (see Figure 8.15).

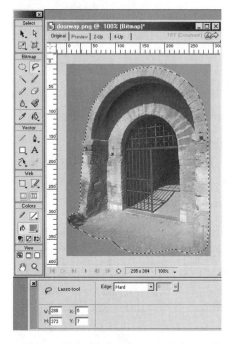

Figure 8.15   The Lasso tool is used to add the selection of the gentle curves in front of the door.

The selection can be complete is it is now, or you can add one more tricky element.

Selectively Deselecting Using Modifier Keys

Now that the main outline of the selection is set, we'll examine how to deselect an inner portion of the selection, in a sense, making a donut. You use modifier keys to do this action using the Lasso tool or any of the selection tools.

Here's how to do it:

1. With the selection still active, select the Polygon Lasso tool from the Tools panel.

2. Hold down the Alt key (for Windows) or the Option key (for a Macintosh), and click within the area that you want to begin deselecting.

   I suggest that you choose the lower left-hand corner of the innermost doorway. The idea here is to remove the gate leaving the hole.

3. Continue clicking to outline the arch shape, double-clicking when you return to the origin point from where you began selecting. This should result in the inner portion of the door or gate being deselected from the doorway image (see Figure 8.16).

Figure 8.16   The Polygon Lasso tool and the modifier key used to deselect part of the selection.

Note

When you hold the Alt key or Option key and place the tool over the selected area, the selection tool displays a minus tool along with its icon. When you place a selection tool over a selected area while holding the Shift key (on either platform), the selection tool displays a plus sign.

Selected areas or marquees can also be moved. To move a marquee, do one of the following:

- Use the arrow keys to nudge the marquee in 1-pixel increments or hold the Shift and arrow keys to nudge the marquee in 10-pixel increments.
- Drag the marquee with a Marquee or Lasso tool or the Magic Wand tool to a new location.

Another nice way to adjust a marquee selection is by using the spacebar. You can easily reposition a selected marquee area as you draw by pressing the spacebar while you draw it.

Here's how to reposition a selection by using the spacebar:

1. Using one of the Marquee selection tools, begin dragging to draw the selection.
2. Continue to hold the mouse button while pressing the spacebar.
3. Drag the marquee to the other location on the canvas.
4. While still holding the mouse button, release the spacebar.
5. Continue drawing the selection in your new location.

Remember that selections are similar to stencils that allow you to protect or select pixel areas of your image for painting, copying, pasting, and a myriad of modifications. Now it's time to learn about just what you can do to bitmap images with selections, as well as without.

Modifying Selections

This section covers some of the finer points of working with and modifying bitmap selections.

Saving Selections

After you go to all the trouble of preparing the perfect size, shape, and location of a selection, you will probably want to save it for later use in your work session.

Here's how to save a marquee selection:

1. From the Select menu, choose Select, Save Bitmap Selection (see Figure 8.17).
2. If you deselect the selection, you can go back to it and restore it.

To restore a marquee selection, from the Select menu, choose Restore Bitmap Selection (see Figure 8.18).

Note
You can only save one selection at a time in a Fireworks file.

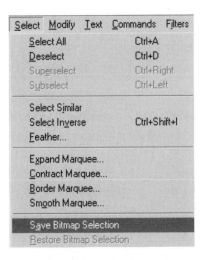

Figure 8.17   The Select menu displays the Save Bitmap Selection option.

Figure 8.18   The Select menu displays the Restore Bitmap Selection option.

Creating and Working with a Floating Pixel Selection

One key technique that's used to manipulate bitmaps is called *floating selection.*

Now that you have some cool images and know how to create selections, you are able to start building, montaging, and painting with bitmap images and the bitmap tools.

When you want to move, edit, cut, or copy a bitmap object, you must first make it into a floating selection.

To make a floating pixel selection, follow these steps:

1. Make sure that something is selected within the bitmap image.
2. Do one of the following: Either choose the Pointer tool and draw the selection to a new location, or hold the Ctrl key (for Windows) or the Command key (for a Macintosh) and draw the selection by using any tool from the bitmap section of the Tools panel.

Next, to move a floating selection, try one of the following:

- If a non-selected bitmap tool is active, hold the Ctrl key (for Windows) or the Command key (for a Mac) and drag the floating selection.
- Use the arrow keys or Shift-arrow keys, or drag the floating selection with the Pointer tool or any bitmap selection tool.

Working with More than One Image at a Time

After you deselect a floating pixel selection or choose any of the vector or web tools from the Tools panel, the floating selection merges into the current bitmap object. Often, bitmap images are collaged, or composited, making multilayered bitmap images by cutting or copying.

Here's how to move a selected bitmap area from one image to another by cutting or pasting:

1. Open the files named umbra_f, mushroom, and doorway from the Bitmaps folder on the CD-ROM.
2. Select the doorway image, as previously described.
3. Copy the archway area of selected pixels.
4. Switch to the mushroom.png file and paste. You are presented with the dialog box for resample (see Figure 8.19).

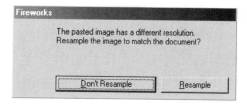

Figure 8.19 The Resample dialog box.

5. Click Don't Resample, and the rather large archway appears as its own object within your Layers panel. The archway is resized later.

6. For now, click the Hide or Eye icon in the Layers panel to hide the archway layer (see Figure 8.20).

Figure 8.20 The bitmap image of the doorway hidden in the Layers panel.

7. Save your file. I named my file `fairy.png` and saved it in the `Bitmaps` folder on the CD-ROM.

Inverting a Pixel Selection

This tutorial shows you how to turn a selection into the opposite, or inverse, of what you have selected.

Here's how to create an inverse of your pixel selection:

1. Use the `umbra_f` file for this exercise.

2. Make a pixel selection of the background by using one of the selection tools.

3. From the Select menu, choose Select Inverse Selection.

Now you can see that all the pixels that were not within the original selection are now the ones selected.

Basic Image Composition

Next, you begin to work with multi-bitmap objects within a single document to create a photo montage:

1. Copy the elf figure and paste it into the `fairy.png` image.

   Look at Figure 8.21. You see a process flow of the pixel selections being copied from the doorway and `umbra_f` files and pasted into the `mushroom` file to create the `fairy03.png` document.

The Mushroom Image

The Doorway Image

The Doorway copied and pasted into the mushroom Image

The umbra_elf image selected via select inverse

The Elf copied and pasted into the Mushroom image that contains the Doorway image.

Figure 8.21   The process flow of pixel selections being copied from file to file to create the `fairy_03.png` document.

2. Save your new composite file as `fairy03.png`. If you want, you can open this file to follow along with the rest of the exercises from this point on.

Modifying Selections Edges

So far, the selections that we created have been relatively straightforward. A few techniques for modifying the edges of selections are good to know about. One of these techniques is called feathering.

Feathering

Feathering creates a somewhat see-through, or softened, effect along the edge of the pixels that you select. Setting the feather amount to various degrees increases and decreases the amount of softness, or feather, along the edge. Feathering can be set before a selection is made with a selection tool, or after a selection is already created with a selection tool.

Here's how to feather selections by setting the feather of a selection with the menu.

To feather a pixel selection with the menu, follow these steps:

1. Open a bitmap image.

2. From the Select menu, choose Feather. The Feather dialog box appears (see Figure 8.22).

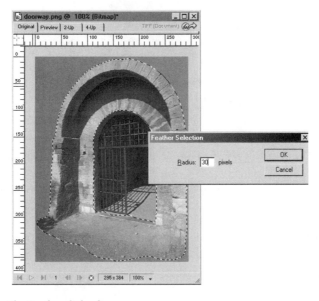

Figure 8.22   The Feather dialog box.

3. Enter the feather amount in the feather dialog box. The selection marquee changes size to reflect the feather amount.

4. Change the number in the Feather dialog box if you want to adjust the feather amount.

5. Click OK.

Voila! You can now examine the appearance of the feathered selection without the surrounding pixels.

To do this, from the Select menu, choose Select Inverse and press Delete. You can then use the History panel, or Undo, to replace the deleted area and, thus, preview your feathered edge.

Look at Figure 8.23, which shows the doorway image cut away from the document after its selection edge was feathered to 30.

Figure 8.23   The image cut away from the document, with a feathered edge of 30.

After you cut away an image that has a feathered edge applied to it, you'll probably want to paste it into an existing document, such as the mushroom file, or into a new document.

In Figure 8.24, the feathered edge doorway has been pasted into a new canvas with a black background. You can see that semi-transparent pixels are along the selection edges. These are the feathered edges.

Figure 8.24   The image with a feathered edge of 30 pasted into a new blank canvas.

Expanding and Contracting a Selection

Now and then, you might need to expand or contract around the drawn edge of the marquee to include more or exclude some of the selection contents.

Here's how to expand or contract a selection marquee:

1. Draw the marquee with any selection tool.
2. Under Select, choose Expand Marquee.
3. Enter the number of pixels by which you want to increase or expand the border.
4. Click OK.

To minimize, or contract, the border of a marquee, follow these steps:

1. Create a pixel selection.
2. From the Select menu, choose Contract Marquee.
3. Enter the number of pixels by which you want to contract the border of your marquee (see Figure 8.25).
4. Click OK.

Expanding a Marquee

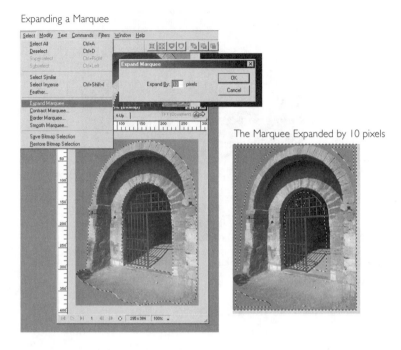

The Marquee Expanded by 10 pixels

Contracting a Marquee

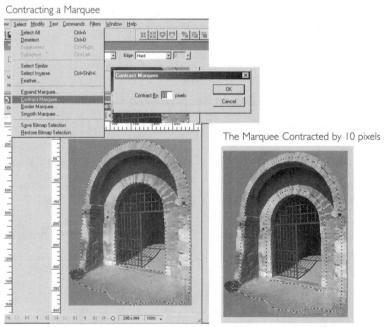

The Marquee Contracted by 10 pixels

Figure 8.25   Expanding (top) and contracting (bottom) selection marquees.

Creating a Frame Selection Around an Existing Selection

Another neat thing that you can do to modify selections is use a selection to make a border, or frame, around an area of the bitmap image.

After this area is selected, you can color it, modify it, paint in it, or apply effects to create an interesting effect. There are still a few more things to know about selections, however.

You can create an additional marquee from an existing marquee by using Border Marquee from the Select menu (see Figure 8.26).

Create a selection

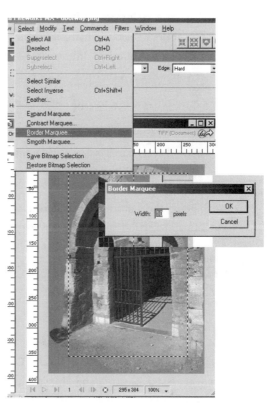

Set width of Border Marquee

Figure 8.26   Creating a border from an existing selection.

Times might arise when you make a selection and the edges of it are a bit jagged. You can smooth and minimize excess pixels along the edges of your selections using the Smooth Marquee option. Smoothing the edges of your selections is especially helpful after you use the Magic Wand tool. Here's how you can smooth the edges of a selection marquee:

1. From the Select menu, choose Select Smooth Marquee.

2. Enter a sample radius to specify the desire amount of smoothing.

3. Click OK.

You might need to do a few tests by smoothing and undoing the marquee until you decide on the desired range of smoothing you need. The creation of each individual selection is slightly different.

Transfering a Selection Marquee

You can transfer a selection marquee from one bitmap image to another or between one bitmap object and another on the same layer or between different layers. You can also transfer your selection marquee to a mask.

Here's how to transfer a marquee selection from one bitmap object to another:

1. Make a selection using the Marquee tool.

2. In the Layers panel, select a different bitmap object on the same layer or an object from a different layer.

At this point, the marquee is transferred to that object. You can also transfer it by using Save Bitmap Selection and Restore Bitmap Selection from the Select menu.

Note

Fireworks MX treats masks and masked objects as separate objects. To learn more about masks, see Chapter 9, "Masking."

Editing Your Selected Objects

After you master selecting and are working with selected objects, you're ready to move on to some of the transformations or modifications that you can do to selected objects. As you have started to experience, Fireworks provides you with various ways to edit selected objects. You can move objects on the canvas or from one application to another, you can clone and duplicate selected objects, and you can delete or remove objects from your project altogether.

Bitmap objects and vector objects behave virtually the same when it comes to transforming them. Some of the same commands and procedures for transforming and distorting selected objects are also found in Chapter 4, "Working with Vectors."

Selections can be moved. To reposition a selection marquee, you can do one of the following:

- Drag it with the pointer Subselection or Select Behind tool. This cuts the image and moves it, but using the Marquee tool moves the marquee selection only, and does not affect the underlying image.
- You can press any arrow key to move the selection object in 1-pixel increments.
- You can hold the Shift key while pressing an arrow key to move your selection in 10-pixel increments.
- You can enter the object's X and Y coordinates in the bottom section of the Info panel.
- You can enter the X and Y coordinates for the location of the top-left corner of the selection in the Property Inspector.

To move or copy selected objects by pasting, you can do any of the following:

- Choose Edit, Cut, or Copy.
- Choose Edit, Paste.
- To duplicate selected objects, choose Edit, Duplicate. If you repeat the Duplicate option, the duplicates of the selected object appear in a staggered, cascading arrangement 10 pixels lower and 10 pixels to the right of the previous duplicate.
- You can clone, or make an exact duplicate, that's placed precisely in front of the original by choosing Edit, Clone.

You can also duplicate a selection by doing one of the following:

- You can drag the pixel selection using the Subselection tool.
- You can use the Pointer tool to click the selection and then Alt-drag (for Windows) or Option-drag (for a Macintosh).

Deleting Selected Objects

If you decide to delete a selected object, you can do one of the following:

- Press Delete or Backspace.
- Choose Edit, Clear.
- Choose Edit, Cut.
- Right-click (for Windows) or Ctrl-click (for a Macintosh) on the object and choose Edit, Cut.

If you decide that you want to delete a selection or cancel it, you can do one of the following:

- Choose Select, Deselect or click anywhere in the image outside of the selected area.
- If you are using the Marquee, Oval Marquee, or Lasso tool, you can press Escape. This makes you lose the tool and revert to the Arrow tool. But, if you want to retain the tool (for example, Marquee), follow step 1.

Transforming and Manipulating Selected Objects and Selections

After you create your selections or select an object or a group of pixel selections, you can transform them by using the Scale, Skew, and Distort tools, as well as the Menu options (see Figure 8.27).

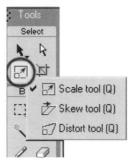

Figure 8.27 The Scale tool group including Scale, Skew, and Distort tool group.

When an object is selected, choosing any of the transformation tools or Transform Menu options displays the Transform handles around the selected objects (see Figure 8.28).

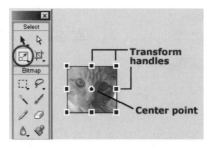

Figure 8.28 The Transform handles and the center point.

To transform a selected object using the Transform handles, follow these steps:

1. Using the Pointer tool, select the object that you want to transform.

2. Select a Transformation tool from the Tools panel. As you move your pointer on or near the selection handles, the pointer changes to indicate that you can perform transformation.

   Do one of the following to transform the object:

   - Click and drag on a Transform handle to transform according to the active Transformation tool.

   - Place the pointer near a corner point and click and drag to rotate the object.

   - Double-click inside the window or press Enter to apply your transformation or Esc to cancel the action and revert back to the original state.

The Modify Menu

A great selection of Transform tools is under the Modify menu with which you might want to experiment (see Figure 8.29).

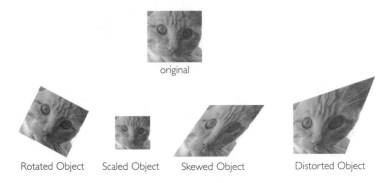

original

Rotated Object   Scaled Object   Skewed Object   Distorted Object

Figure 8.29   The Transformation tools are applied to an object.

Some of these options, such as Free Transform, Scale, Skew, and Distort work in the same way as their corresponding tools on the Tools panel:

- Rotate 180, Rotate 90 degrees, Clockwise, and Counterclockwise let you make fast work of rotating your objects to a precise increment.

- Flip Horizontal and Flip Vertical allow you to quickly manipulate the orientation of your image.

- Numeric Transform, however, is the real star of the Transform menu items.

Transforming Items Using Numeric Transform

Numeric Transform allows you to enter specific values for your transformations instead of dragging to scale, resize, or rotate the object. This results in a more precise result.

Here's how to resize selected objects using Numeric Transform:

1. Select the object that you want to modify.

2. Select Modify, Transform, Numeric Transform (see Figure 8.30). The Numeric Transform dialog box appears (see Figure 8.31).

Figure 8.30   The Modify menu with Transform selected and the Transform options pop-up menu.

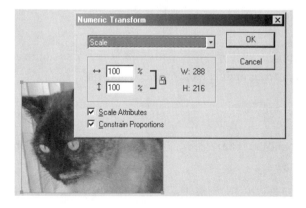

Figure 8.31   The Numeric Transform dialog box.

3. From the pop-up menu, select the transformation type that you want to perform on your selection.

4. Select Constrain Proportions to maintain the horizontal and vertical aspect ratio when scaling or resizing.

5. Select Scale Attributes to transform the fill, stroke, and effects along with the object as you transform it.

6. Deselect Scale Attributes to transform only the path of the object.

7. Type the numeric values to transform the selection.

8. Click OK.

Painting (Retouching Bitmaps)

Now that you have made it through all the information about creating selections and transforming selected objects, it's time to talk about my favorite subject: painting (otherwise known as retouching bitmaps). Fireworks MX provides you with an amazing array of tools that enable you to retouch and manipulate the pixels of your bitmaps objects. You can alter an image's size, reduce or increase its sharpness or focus, and clone its pixels to another part of the image or object itself.

This section gives a rundown of the Fireworks retouching tools.

The Rubber Stamp Tool

The *Rubber Stamp tool* enables you to clone, or copy, one area of a pixel or bitmap image to another and paint it, or stamp it, to another location within the image (see Figure 8.32). Cloning is useful for retouching images, such as fixing a deteriorated or scratched photograph. It's also great for cleaning up dust from images and for creating or extending one part of an image's texture into another area of an image. It's also fun to use it to duplicate an element within an image somewhere else in that image.

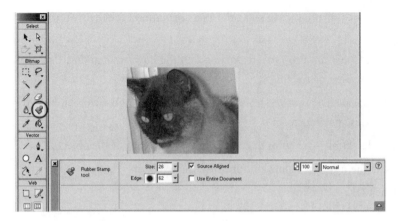

Figure 8.32   The Rubber Stamp tool is circled in the Tools panel along with the Property Inspector displaying the Rubber Stamp tool options.

Cloning Part of an Image

You can use the Rubber Stamp tool to clone portions of a bitmap image:

1. Select the Rubber Stamp tool from the Tools Panel.

2. Click one area of the image to define it as the origin point of the area that you want to clone. Notice that the sampling pointer changes to a crosshair pointer.

   To define a different area of pixels with which to clone, Alt-click (for Windows) or Option-click (for a Macintosh) in a different location of your image to change the definition of the origin point.

3. Move your cursor to another location within the image.

4. Click and drag to paint, or stamp, your pixels from the source of the cloning to this destination, or painting, point.

Setting Rubber Stamp Tool Options

You can change the brush preferences so that the painting tip of the rubber stamp looks like a crosshair or a blue circle:

1. Select the Rubber Stamp tool from the Tools panel.

2. Using the Property Inspector, you can set the following options:

   - **Size**—Sets the size of the stamper tip.
   - **Edge**—Sets the softness of the stroke you are painting.
   - **Source Aligned**—When Source Aligned is selected, the sampling pointer is restricted to move vertically and horizontally in alignment with the destination of the painting tip.

When Source Aligned is deselected, the origin of the sample is fixed so that you continue to paint from one specific spot within the image over and over again.

- **Use Entire Document Samples From All Objects on All Layers of the Document**—When this option is deselected, only the active object's pixels are sampled.

- **Opacity**—Enables you to set how much of the background can be seen through the new cloned pixels.

- **Blend Mode**—Affects how the cloned image interacts with its background.

After you get the hang of it, you find that the Rubber Stamp tool is magical and powerful.

The Blur Tool Group

The *Blur tool group* contains the Blur, Sharpen, Dodge Burn, and Smudge tools (see Figure 8.33). Each tool has controls that you can set in the Property Inspector.

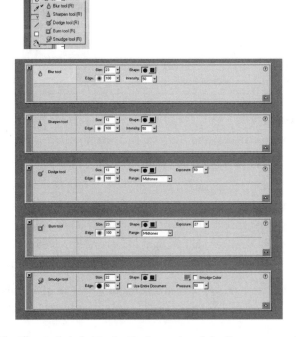

Figure 8.33   The Blur tool circled in the Tools panel, and the five corresponding Property Inspectors are displaying their tool options.

Blurring and Sharpening Pixels

The Blur and Sharpen tools are, in a sense, two sides of the same coin. They both affect the sharpness or blurriness of an image.

Depending on the image to which you apply it, the Blur and Sharpen tools can create the appearance of an image becoming more or less in focus. The Blur tool enables you to emphasize or de-emphasize parts or pixels in an image. Their names, Blur and Sharpen, tell you exactly what they do.

Blurring or Sharpening an Image

Now that you know what the tools do, here's the info on how to use them:

1. Select the Blur or Sharpen tool from the Blur tools group of the Tools panel.

2. Set your brush options settings in the Property Inspector:
   - **Size**—Enables you to set the size of the brush tip.
   - **Edge**—Specifies the softness of the brush tip.
   - **Shape**—Enables you to set a round or a square brush tip.
   - **Intensity**—Varies the amount of the blurring or the sharpening that's applied to the image or selection.

3. Click and drag the tool over the pixels that you want to blur or sharpen.

Tip

The Alt key (for Windows) or Option key (for a Macintosh) enables you to toggle between Blur and Sharpen tool behaviors.

Dodge and Burn Tools

It's now time to use the Dodge and Burn tools. These tools are a pair of tools, like the Blur and Sharpen tools, that produce the opposite effect of each other.

In traditional darkroom photography, the *Dodge tool* is a piece of paper or cardboard stuck on a stick that allows the photographer to underexpose portions of an image during the paper-exposure process. The *Burn tool* is usually a large piece of cardboard with a hole in it. The hole in the board allows light to be concentrated on one specific spot of the paper (adding to the exposure time) during the image-making process.

The Dodge tool lets you lighten pixels in an area of a bitmap image, and the Burn tool enables you to darken pixels of a bitmap image.

The Smudge Tool

The last tool in the Blur tool group is the *Smudge tool*. The Smudge tool works by picking up colors and pushing them in the direction that you click and drag within a bitmap image. It's kind of like finger painting.

To smudge the colors in an image, follow these steps:

1. Select the Smudge tool from the Blur tool group.

2. Set the Tool options in the Property Inspector:

   - **Size**, **Shape**, and **Edge**—These are all the same for the Smudge tool as they are for the Blur tool.

   - **The Pressure setting**—Enables you to set the intensity of the smudging.

   - **Smudge Color**—Enables you to smudge using a specific color at the beginning of each stroke. If this option is deselected, the tool uses the colors directly under the pointer where you are smudging.

   - **Use Entire Document**—Enables you to smudge color data from all the objects on all the layers at once. When this option is deselected, the Smudge tool only uses colors from the active object on the active layer.

3. Click and drag the Smudge tool over the pixels to smudge them.

The tools in the Blur tool group are great for distorting pixels in your bitmap images, but they're not the only way to affect them.

Filters

You can manipulate and adjust the colors and tones within bitmap images using color and tone adjustment filters. *Filters* enable you to improve and enhance the colors in your bitmap images in several different ways. You can manipulate the contrast and brightness, the range of tones, the color, hue, and the saturation of colors within your images. Adjustment filters give you the power to correct, enhance, and control the image's color and pixel data. You apply adjustment filters to pixel selections and selected bitmap objects.

Within filters, you can add your own Photoshop plug-ins to Fireworks and use them to create effects. You can also apply Fireworks effects to your bitmap objects, but not to selected pixels as such, with the effects in the Property Inspector. You can, however, define an area of a bitmap, create a separate bitmap object from it, and apply a live effect to it. If you apply a filter to a selected vector object using the Filters menu, the vector object is converted into a bitmap.

You can also apply filters in an irreversible and permanent manner. You do this by choosing them from the Filters menu. It is recommended, however, that you use filters as Fireworks live effects whenever possible.

Applying Live Effects

To apply a live effect to an area of a bitmap that's selected with a marquee, follow these steps:

1. Select a bitmap selection tool and create a selection marquee.

2. Choose Edit, Copy.

3. Choose Edit, Paste. Your selection is now pasted in exact registration with the original pixels that you copied or cut and pasted. The selection, however, is now a separate and different bitmap object.

4. Click the thumbnail of the new bitmap object in the Layers panel to select the new bitmap object.

5. Apply a live effect from the Property Inspector. The live effect is now applied only to the new bitmap object, simulating the application of a filter to a pixel selection.

Figure 8.34   The Filters menus.

Applying Adjustments Using the Adjust Filters

You can apply a number of adjustments to your bitmap images by using the Adjust Color filters, which are located in the Filters menu.

The Adjust Color filters include the following:

- Auto Levels
- Brightness
- Contrast
- Curves
- Hue/Saturation
- Invert
- Levels

Both the Levels and the Curves features adjust a bitmap's tonal range.

With Levels, you can shift the concentration of pixels in the highlight, midtone, and shadow ranges. You do this by sliding the appropriate slider, which reassigns pixels of one color value to have a different value (either lighter or darker).

For minor-level tweaks, instead of setting the adjustment by hand, you can use Auto Levels and let Fireworks make the adjustment for you. The results of Auto Levels varies depending on the severity of the required adjustment. Images with severe tonal-range issues do not adjust as well with this method as those with minor problems.

The Curves filter enables you to adjust colors along the tonal range of your image without affecting other colors in the image. In this way, the Curves adjustments give you precise control over your image's tonal range.

Using Levels to Adjust Bitmap Images

In theory, a bitmap image with a full tonal range must have an even number of pixels in all areas. You use the Levels filter to correct and modify pixels where they appear in high concentration within your image. Adjusting image levels is one of those things that you need to try in order to understand.

To adjust highlights, midtones, and shadow values using Levels, follow these steps:

1. Select a bitmap image.
2. Open the Levels dialog box (see Figure 8.35) by either choosing Filters, Adjust Color Levels, or, in the Property Inspector, click the Add Effects button and then select Adjust Color Levels from the Effects pop-up menu.

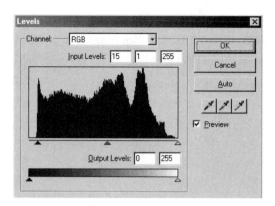

Figure 8.35   The Levels dialog box.

3. Using the Channel pop-up menu, select whether you want to modify individual color channels red, blue, or green, or make adjustments to all color channels (RGB).

4. Drag the input sliders under the histogram to adjust the shadow, midtone, and highlight information (see Figure 8.36).

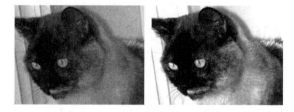

Figure 8.36   Levels used to adjust the image balance. The original image is shown on the left.

The black slider on the left controls the shadow information.

The gray slider in the center is the controls midtone range.

The white slider on the right controls the highlight values.

As you move the sliders, the values are updated in the input levels boxes.

5. Drag the output level sliders to adjust contrast values within your image.

As you move these sliders, their values are automatically updated in the output levels boxes.

> **Note**
>
> Applying filters from the Filters menu is destructive to your images. This means they cannot be undone except when Edit, Undo is available in the Edit menu.
>
> As previously mentioned, this is why many users prefer using live effects. Live effects maintain the ability to adjust, turn off, or remove filters from images created with Fireworks MX infinitely.

Using the Auto Levels Filter

Sometimes, it's quick and easy to let Fireworks make the tonal-range adjustment of an image for you. Here's how:

1. Select the image that you want to adjust.

2. To select Auto Levels, do one of the following:

   - Choose Filters, Adjust Color, Auto Levels.
   - In the Property Inspector, click the Add Effects button and then select Adjust Color Auto Levels from the Effects pop-up menu.

Using the Curves Filter

In principle, the Curves and Levels adjustments mean the same thing. Curves, however, provides precise control over the tonal range of your images.

Levels uses highlights, shadows, and midtones to correct and adjust the tonal range of images, whereas Curves lets you selectively adjust any color along the tonal range of your image, not just one of the three variables. It does this without affecting other colors along the range. Here's how it works.

The grid in the Curves dialog box contains two brightness values:

- **Vertical axis**—Represents the new brightness values shown in the output box.
- **Horizontal axis**—Represents the original brightness of the pixels shown in the input box.

When you first open the Curves dialog box, the diagonal line indicates that no change has been made to the image's values so far and that the input and output values are the same for all the pixels.

To adjust a specific point in the image's tonal range, follow these steps:

1. Select an image.

2. To open the Curves dialog box (see Figure 8.37), do one of the following:

   • Choose Filters Adjust Color Curves.

   • In the Property Inspector, click the Add Effects button and then select Adjust Color Curves from Effects pop-up menu.

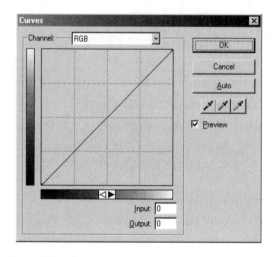

Figure 8.37   The Curves dialog box.

3. In the Channel pop-up menu, select either an individual color channel or RGB (for all colors).

4. Click to create a point on the grid's diagonal line and drag it to a new location to adjust the curve.

Each point on the curve has its own output and input values. When you drag the point, the output and input values are updated automatically. The curve displays the brightness values of 0–255, with 0 representing the shadows.

To delete a point along the curve, click the point and drag it outside the grid. You can add multiple points along the curve to adjust it. Clicking and dragging those points up, down, left, and right changes their values to the new location that you select.

The beginning and end points of the curve can also be moved up, down, left, and right to adjust the 0 and 255 value points. They cannot be deleted off of the curve, however.

Brightness and Contrast

The Brightness and Contrast adjustment feature enables you to quickly correct images that are either too light or too dark, or make images dramatically darker or lighter.

Adjusting the brightness or contrast of an image is done by using the Brightness/Contrast dialog box:

1. Select an image.

2. Open the Brightness/Contrast dialog box (see Figure 8.38) by either:
   - Choosing Filters, Adjust Color, Brightness Contrast.
   - In the Property Inspector, click the Add Effects button and then select Adjust Color, Brightness/Contrast from the Effects pop-up menu.

3. Click and drag the Brightness and Contrast sliders to modify the settings. Values range from –100 to 100. To set the adjustment, click OK.

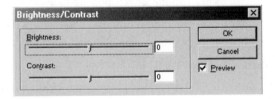

Figure 8.38   The Brightness/Contrast dialog box.

Hue/Saturation

If I had to vote for my favorite filter or adjustment option, I would choose the Hue/Saturation adjustment. It is just so much fun!

You can use Hue/Saturation to adjust the color, hue, intensity of color, the color saturation, and the lightness or darkness of color in an image. You can also colorize an image, changing it to a monochromatic style, such as a sepia tone or a blueprint.

The Hue/Saturation dialog box gives you four ways to adjust your images (see Figure 8.39). You can control the following:

- The hue (or color)
- The saturation (or amount of color)
- The lightness of images
- You can click the Colorize checkbox, which creates monochromatic images that can then be adjusted using Hue/Saturation and Lightness

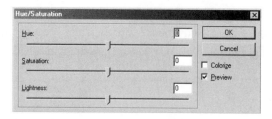

Figure 8.39   The Hue/Saturation dialog box.

To adjust the hue or saturation of an image, follow these steps:

1. Select an image.

2. To open the Hue/Saturation dialog box, do one of the following:
   - Select Filters, Adjust Color, Hue Saturation.
   - In the Property Inspector, click the Add Effects button. Then, select Adjust Color, Hue/Saturation from the Effects pop-up menu.

3. Drag the Hue slider to change and modify the colors within the image. Color values range from −180 to 180.

4. Drag the Saturation slider to adjust the intensity, or purity, of colors. Dragging the Saturation slider to −100 decreases all the color within the color. Dragging the slider to 100 maximizes the brightness or saturation of the color within the color.

5. Drag the lightness slider to modify the lightness or darkness of the colors within the image. Values also range from −100 to 100.

6. If you click the Colorize button in the Hue/Saturation dialog box, you can change a full color or RGB image into a two-tone image. Then, you can change the Hue and Saturation sliders to colorize your two-tone image.

7. When you're finished with your adjustment playtime, click OK to set the changes.

Invert

The next option is Invert. It is used to invert an image's color values. This means that you can change the colors of an image to their inverted values on the color wheel, making a negative, and sometimes very psychedelic, effect (see Figure 8.40).

To invert a bitmap image's colors, select an image and do one of the following:

- Choose Filters, Adjust Color, Invert.
- From the Property Inspector, click the Add Effects button and then choose Adjust Color, Invert from the Effects pop-up menu.

Figure 8.40   The original cat image (left) and the inverted image (right).

The Blur and Sharpening Options

Similar to the other adjustments, you can set blurring and sharpening options that you can apply as live effects or as irreversible and permanent filters.

Blurring softens the look of bitmap images, which in a sense, pushes them out of focus. You can choose from three main blurring options in Fireworks:

- **Blur**—Softens the focus of selected pixels. It is the smallest amount of softening available.
- **Blur More**—Blurs approximately three times as much as Blur alone.

  Sometimes, Blur More is helpful to use multiple times to achieve the effect that you desire.
- **Gausian Blur**—Applies a weighted average of blur to the pixels within an image to produce a fuzzy effect.

To blur an image, select an image and do one of the following:

- Choose Filters, Blur, Blur More.
- Click the Add Effects button in the Property Inspector and choose Blur or Blur More from the Effects pop-up menu.

Remember that applying a filter from the Filters menu is permanent except when Edit, Undo is available. To maintain the ability to adjust, turn off, remove, or modify this effect, apply it as a live effect using the Add Effects button.

To blur an image using Gausian Blur (see Figure 8.41), follow these steps:

1. Select an image.

2. Open the Gausian Blur dialog box by doing one of the following:

   - Choose Filters, Blur, Gausian Blur.
   - Click the Add Effects button in the Property Inspector and then choose Blur, Gausian Blur from the Effects pop-up menu.

3. Drag the Blur radius slider to adjust the amount of blur that's applied to the image.

4. You can set values that range from .1 to 250. Increasing the Blur radius results in a stronger, more pronounced blur effect.

5. When you finish setting the blur, click OK.

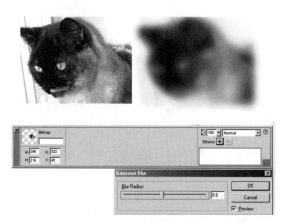

Figure 8.41   The original cat image (left) and the blurred image (right).

The Find Edges Effect

The Find Edges effect converts a bitmap to an image that looks like a line drawing. It does this by identifying the color transitions within an image and changing them into lines.

Here's how to apply the Find Edges effect to a bitmap (see Figure 8.42):

1. Select a bitmap image using the Pointer tool.

2. Select Filters, Other, Find Edges, or click the Add Effects button in the Property Inspector, and then choose Other, Find Edges from the Effects pop-up menu.

Note

The Find Edges effect generally looks better when it's applied to a high-contrast image.

Figure 8.42   The original cat image (left) and the image with the Find Edges effect
applied (right).

Sharpen Images

Sharpen does the opposite of the Blur feature. Fireworks contains three options for
sharpening images:

- **Sharpen**—Adjusts the overall focus of blurred images or blurred areas of an
  image by increasing the contrast of adjacent pixels.

- **Sharpen More**—Increases the contrast of adjacent pixels approximately three
  times more than Sharpen does.

- **Unsharp Mask**—Usually, the best option for sharpening an image. This is
  because Unsharp Mask sharpens an image by adjusting the contrast of the pixel
  edges within the image. Unsharp Mask gives you the most control.

To use Sharpen, select an image, choose a sharpen option, and do one of the following:

- Select Filters, Sharpen, Sharpen or Sharpen More.

- Click the Add Effects button in the Property Inspector and then choose Sharpen,
  Sharpen or Sharpen More from the Effects pop-up menu.

To use Unsharp Mask to sharpen, follow these steps:

1. Select an image and open the Unsharp Mask dialog box and do one of the
   following:
   - Choose Filters, Sharpen, Unsharp Mask.
   - Click the Add Effects button in the Property Inspector and then select
     Sharpen, Unsharp Mask from the Effects pop-up menu.

2. Drag the slider to adjust the sharpen amount from 1 percent to 500 percent.

3. Drag the Pixel radius slider to set the radius from .1 to 250.

   Increasing the radius results in a larger area of sharp contrast surrounding each pixel edge.

4. Click and drag the Threshold slider to select the pixel threshold from 0 to 255.

Note

Value ranges between 2 and 25 are most commonly used. Increasing the threshold sharpens only those pixels that have a higher contrast in an image. Decreasing the threshold affects pixels of a lower contrast. Setting the threshold to 0 sharpens all the pixels within the image.

5. When you have arrived at the desired sharpen settings, click OK.

Now that we covered the adjustment features for modifying bitmap images, you need to know just a couple more items.

There are times when you might want to isolate or crop out a single bitmap image within a larger Fireworks document. The Crop tool comes in handy in cases like these.

Cropping a Portion of a Bitmap Image

You can crop a bitmap image without affecting other objects within the document. Here's how:

1. Select a bitmap object by clicking it with the Pointer tool or by clicking its thumbnail in the Layers panel. Or, you can draw a selection marquee around it by using a bitmap selection tool.

2. Select Edit, Crop Selected Bitmap (see Figure 8.43). You'll see crop handles appear around the entire selected bitmap or around the selection marquee, if you drew one.

3. Adjust the crop handles by clicking and dragging until the bounding box encloses the area of the bitmap that you want to keep.

4. Double-click or press Enter to crop the selection. The pixels in the selected bitmap outside the bounding box are removed, but the other objects in the document remain.

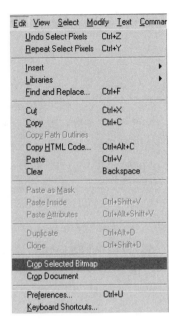

Figure 8.43   The Crop Selected Bitmap menu option.

Fun with Bitmaps

It's time to have some fun with bitmaps. I created four lessons that will try your skills at working with bitmap images in Fireworks MX. These hands-on exercises teach you techniques through the process of making a new creation.

I think that people learn best from hands-on exercises. Therefore, I suggest that, during the process, you take your time and let yourself feel free by learning through experimenting and having happy accidents. When you try different things, such as different variations on a theme, you begin to have a context in which to contrast and compare results and, thus, in the future, choose the right procedure, technique, or direction for making your work look the way you want.

Exercise 8.1 covers retouching and colorizing a black-and-white image. You get familiar with using levels, the Burn and Dodge tools, Rubber Stamp tools, and modifying techniques, including working with hue, saturation, and colorize. Also, you workout the selection tools and make something cool out of a nasty-looking original photograph.

Exercise 8.1   Balancing Tonal Range, Retouching, and Colorizing a Black-and-White Photo

If you want, you can look at the finished version of the file by opening `j&a_final` from the `Lesson_01` folder:

1. Open the scanned image `j&a_01.psd`.

   This is a Polaroid picture that was scanned on a flatbed scanner at 300 ppi, 100 percent size, and 256 levels of gray.

   Notice that the image is of poor quality. Not only is it dark and muddy, but it's covered with dust and scratches. The first thing that this image needs is the overall tonality adjusted so that it is not so dark and oversaturated in the shadows.

2. Using the Pointer tool, click to select the image.

3. With the object selected, click the Add Effect button in the Property Inspector and select Adjust Color, Levels (see Figure 8.44). The Levels dialog box appears. At this point, you can either

   - Click the Auto button and see what happens.
   - You can start playing with the sliders.

Figure 8.44   Open your image and use the Property Inspector to open the Levels dialog box.

Adding a Live Effect

Adding a live effect from the Property Inspector is the preferred way to add effects to bitmap images. This method keeps your effects adjustments infinitely modifiable.

4. To optimize range of tones throughout the image, adjust the sliders (see Figure 8.45):

- Shadow Left
- Midtone Center
- Highlight Right

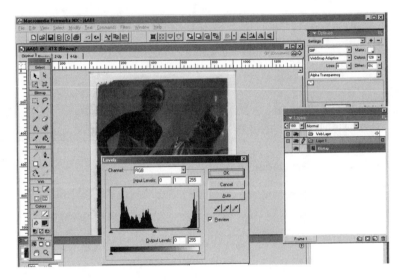

Figure 8.45   Use Levels to adjust the midtones and highlight areas.

This image needs lightening in the midtones and highlight areas because the data is so heavy in the shadow area.

I adjusted my Input Levels to 25, 1.68, 152 (see Figure 8.46).

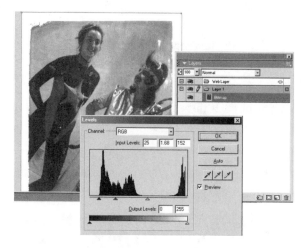

Figure 8.46   Results of the Levels adjustments.

Note

Additionally, you can modify the overall lightness or darkness of an image, or an area of an image, by adjusting the Output Levels.

Lightening Pixels with the Dodge Tool

Now that the image is adjusted overall, it looks like the faces are too dark. The next step is to lighten exposure on the faces by using the Dodge tool.

5. Zoom in on the faces so that they both fit in the screen.

6. Select the Dodge tool from the Tools panel (see Figure 8.47).

Figure 8.47   Select the Dodge tool.

7. Using the Property Inspector, set the brush size so that it is appropriate to the size of the faces (see Figure 8.48).

Figure 8.48   Set the Dodge tool options in the Property Inspector and position the tool over the face.

8. Adjust the opacity, or strength, of the Dodge brush to about 50 percent so that the dodge looks gradual, not ghost-like. Save the image as `j&a02.png` on your hard drive.

Cloning Pixels with the Rubber Stamp Tool

Now, you remove the dust and scratches by retouching the image using the Rubber Stamp tool to clone pixels from one area of the image to another. This example uses non-aligned cloning.

Aligned cloning works best when you want to move an entire image or texture within an image to another place in the image.

Non-aligned cloning is better for cleaning up an image with many scratch marks and dust. Aligned maintains a constant distance between the sample point and the painting tip. Non-aligned enables you to repeatedly sample from the same spot each time, while moving the paint tip around the image.

9. Select the Rubber Stamp tool from the Tools panel. Set the Rubber Stamp properties using the Property Inspector. Make sure that you have the aligned check box deselected.

10. After the settings are adjusted in the Property Inspector, hold the Option key (for a Macintosh) or the Alt key (for Windows) and make a sample in a non-scratchy part of the image.

Obviously, you need to paint dark pixels to patch dark scratches, light pixels to fill in where you need light pixels, and so on. You will also want to sample and resample areas multiple times as you go around the image and clean up the dust spots, changing the tool size, its opacity, and so on.

11. Continue to take samples and paint all around the image to clean up dust and scratches. Save the image when you're satisfied with it (see Figure 8.49).

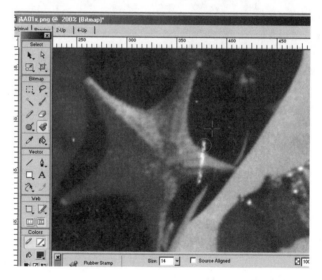

Figure 8.49   Setting the sample position.

Note

Here are some handy shortcuts:

- Hold the spacebar to activate the Hand tool and drag to reposition your image in the window.

- To select the Zoom tool from the keyboard, hold the spacebar-Command (for a Macintosh) or spacebar-Ctrl (for Windows). Zoom in on the desired area and then release the keys.

- To select the Zoom-Out tool from the keyboard, hold spacebar-Command-Option (for a Macintosh), or spacebar-Ctrl-Alt (for Windows). Click the desired area to reduce the view of the image and then release the keys.

Now that the image is all balanced and cleaned up, it's time to learn how to turn a black-and-white image into a toned image.

Toning the Image

Here, you tone an image with the Hue/Saturation effect:

12. Using the Pointer tool, select the image.

13. From the Property Inspector, click the Add Effects button and select Adjust Color, Hue/Saturation.

The Hue/Saturation dialog box appears.

14. Click the Colorize check box to select it.

15. Using the Hue slider, adjust the image color to a sepia or brown tone.

I set my file to a value of approximately 20.

16. Click OK and save the file (see Figure 8.50).

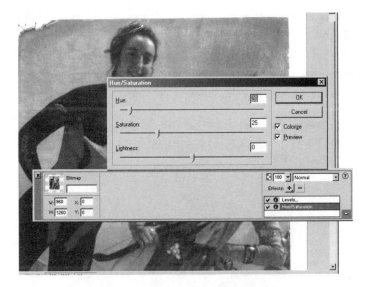

Figure 8.50   Toning an image with the Hue/Saturation effect.

Now, you will select and modify areas of the image using the filter set and the selection tools to create a colorized and hand-painted effect.

Coloring the Vest

17. Select the Polygon tool from the Tools panel and click and drag around the warrior's shiny vest to select it on either side of the bow that she is holding (see Figure 8.51).

Figure 8.51   Selecting the left side of the vest using the Polygon Lasso tool.

18. Using the Polygon tool, surround all the pixels on the left side of the bow.

19. After that is selected with a marquee (see Figure 8.52), press the Shift key and select the areas of the vest on the right side of the bow (see Figure 8.53). Remember to hold the Option key (for a Macintosh) or the Alt key (for Windows) while you begin the selection of the vest's right side. A plus (+) next to your polygon cursor should appear as you select it.

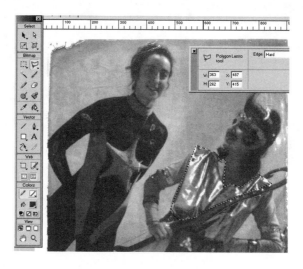

Figure 8.52   The left side of the vest selected and the Lasso tool is in the process of selecting the right side of the vest.

Figure 8.53   The vest is now completely selected.

Changing the Color of the Vest

20. From the Filter menu, select Adjust Color, Hue/Saturation (see Figure 8.54). The Hue/Saturation dialog box appears. You might want to reposition the panel so that you can see the adjustment you're about to make.

21. Check that the Colorize button is selected and then slide the Hue slider to change the color of the vest (see Figure 8.54).

Figure 8.54   Using Adjust Color from the Filters menu to change the vest's color.

22. Finish by continuing to select additional areas of the photo and colorize it as you see fit.

Exercise 8.2   Working with Multiple Objects to Make a Simple Composite

This exercise consists of taking two photographs and blending them to look like one photograph. If you'd like to see the final version of this file, open surfs_up from the Lesson_02 folder (see Figure 8.55).

Figure 8.55   The completed surfs_up image.

In this exercise, you practice using the Feathered Edge commands and the Eraser tool to blend two images together (see Figures 8.56 and 8.57):

Figure 8.56   The left side of the surfs_up image.

Figure 8.57   The right side of the surfs_up image.

1. Open the files right_01.png and left_01.png from the Lesson_02 folder.

2. Select the bitmap object in left_01 with the Pointer tool; copy it.

3. Switch to the image right_01 and use Edit, Paste to paste left_01 into the right_01 image. left_01 contains an image of a surfer on the left side of a wave and right_01 contains an image of a surfer on the right side of a wave.

4. With both objects now in the right_01 image, you can close the left_01 image without saving any changes (see Figure 8.58).

   Now both images are in the same document.

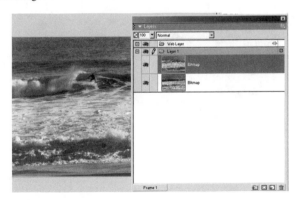

Figure 8.58   The Layers panel displays both objects now in the same document.

5. Select the Marquee tool from the bitmap area of the Tools panel.

6. Click and drag a selection marquee over the right side of the top portion of the cresting wave.

7. From the Select menu, choose Feather. Set the Feather radius to 15 pixels and click OK (see Figure 8.59).

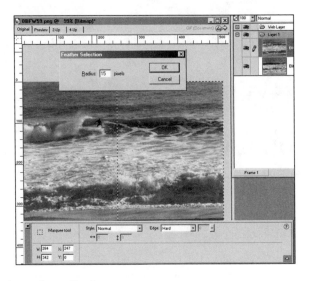

Figure 8.59   The Feather radius is set to 15.

8. Press the Delete key on the keyboard to delete the empty wave, revealing the surfer on the wave beneath it. Deselect the marquee by clicking outside of the marquee, or choosing Select, Deselect (see Figure 8.60).

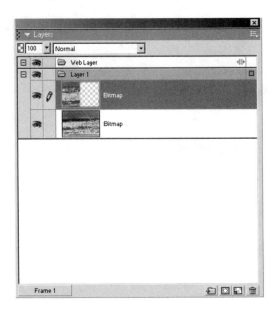

Figure 8.60   The Layers panel displays the right side of the left surfer image deleted with a Feathered Edge of 15.

9. Choose the Eraser tool from the Tools panel.

10. Click to erase additional portions of the left image to make it look like it's blending into the right image more realistically (see Figure 8.61).

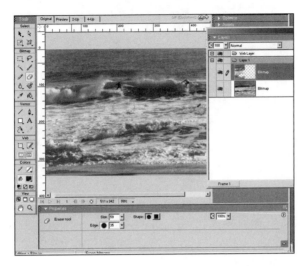

Figure 8.61   Erasing additional portions of the left image makes it look like it's blending into the right image more realistically.

You can play with different opacity settings of the Eraser tool to vary the amount of pixel material removed and reveal the churning water and wave from the image beneath.

11. Save your file.

Merging Two Objects Into One

After you complete removing the portions of the top image to reveal the portions of the bottom image to your liking, you probably want to make this a single object.

12. Click to activate the left surfer on the top-most stack of the objects and from the Layer tools options pop-up menu.

13. Choose Merge Down (see Figure 8.62).

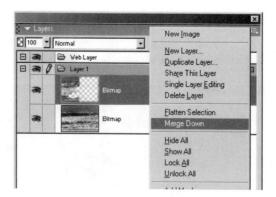

Figure 8.62   Using Merge Down from the Layers tools pop-up menu to make the document into a single bitmap object.

14. Save your file.

That's all there is to it. You have made a seamless composite of two images into one. The feathering and erasing techniques that you just practiced will take you a long way with editing bitmap images. Ready to learn more?

Exercise 8.3   Complex Color Correction

Again, we are faced with a bad photograph to contend with. This image of my dear friend, David, contains an overall pink cast because tungsten film was used in a daylight situation. The purpose of this lesson is to show you how to adjust an image that seems impossible to fix and instill it with sharpness and brightness.

To look at the final result that you hope to achieve, open the `dave_Final` file from the `Lesson_03` folder (see Figure 8.63).

Figure 8.63   Dave is looking good.

Using the Levels Adjustment Effect

1. From the Lesson_03 folder, open the dave_01 file.

2. Select the image using the Pointer tool.

3. From the Property Inspector, click Add Effect and select Adjust Color, Levels.

4. The first step is to bring highlights back into the image. When you look at the Level dialog box, you can see that there is no data above the Lightness slider, which means that there is no highlight information.

5. Click and drag the Highlight slider to the left, where the data heap begins.

6. Select the Highlight Sample tool and click in the pink background to remove the pink and reset its value to white.

7. When you have done these two adjustments, click OK.

   The level's adjustment is applied to the image. Although the image looks better, it is not correct yet.

Fine-Tuning the Levels Adjustment Effect

Some images require more than just one modification to their data points to correctly and fully adjust their tonality. With the range of tones in this image shifted somewhat, you need to use the Levels effect to readjust the adjustment.

8. Double-click the Levels effect to open the Levels panel again.

   The midtone range of data is too dark.

9. To open up and lighten some of the midtone colors, slide the Midtone slider to the left, increasing the distance between the highlight and midtone slider.

10. Click OK when you complete the adjustment to your liking.

    I dragged mine to approximately 1, 2.73, 221. That looks better; however, the image lacks contrast.

    Now, increase the image contrast by adding the Brightness/Contrast live effect:

11. Click the Add Effects button on the Property Inspector and select Adjust Color, Brightness/Contrast. The Brightness/Contrast dialog box appears.

12. Slide the Contrast slider to the right to increase the contrast.

13. Slide the Brightness slider to the right to slightly increase the brightness.

    I set my brightness and contrast settings to a brightness of 9, and a contrast of 16.

14. Click OK.

Balancing the Color Using Levels

Although the overall brightness and sharpness of the image has been enhanced, the skin tone still looks magenta. At this point, color theory and color photography theory come in handy. Let's explore.

Because I want to decrease the magenta tint in the image, I use its opposite color, which is green. By adjusting inverse level of green, I affect the magenta in the image.

15. Click the Add Effects button.

16. Select Adjust Colors, Level.

17. When the Levels dialog box appears, change the channel from RBG to green.

18. Slide the Midtone slider to the left, which decreases the magenta and increases the green.

Alternately, you can slide the Highlight slider toward the left and adjust the Midtone slider left and right.

I set my green Input Levels to 0, 1.12, 226.

The picture looks much better (see Figure 8.64).

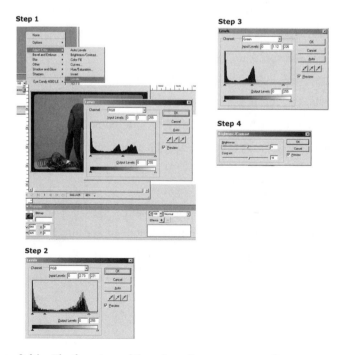

Figure 8.64   The four steps of the color-adjustment process flow.

There you have it. Fireworks MX live effects enable you to infinitely adjust and readjust a bitmap image without ever compromising its quality.

Exercise 8.4   Image Composition

This exercise teaches you the serious fundamentals of photo composition with Fireworks MX through building this multi-image graphic.

This exercise teaches you how to build and collage an image starting from scratch. This process touches on a variety of techniques, features, tools, and ideas commonly used in bitmap-image design.

You are going to use low-resolution images to create an image whose resolution is suitable for multimedia and web work. Because the images are at screen resolution (72ppi) your file manipulations should not require a huge amount of memory. These images will look great onscreen, but would not be considered print quality.

To get an idea of what the final outcome of this exercise is, open the `fun_with_layers` file from the `Lesson_04` folder (see Figure 8.65):

Figure 8.65 Fun with layers finale.

1. Open the `fun_with_layers` file from the `Lesson_04` folder.

   The image contains five layers, starting from the bottom:

   - **Background layer**—Contains a bitmap image of clouds.
   - **Rainbow layer**—A bitmap image of a sky with a rainbow masked with a vector mask.
   - **clouds_blu layer**—A bitmap image of clouds masked with a vector mask.
   - **Floor layer**—A floor tile.
   - **The top-most layer**—A bitmap image of a flower.

   These different elements, when composited together into one collage, make a result that is greater than their individual parts—an image that is a digital painting.

2. Save the file as `my_fun_with_layers.png`.

   This is the file that all the other pieces are composited into.

3. From the `lessons_04` folder, open the `yellow_flower` file.

4. Select the Magic Wand tool from the Tools panel. Set the tolerance to 100.

   This isolates the yellow flower from the background of green leaves.

5. Begin by clicking one of the yellow petals of the flower.

6. Hold the Shift key and continue clicking through each of the petals and then at the red-and-dark maroon center area of the flower (see Figure 8.66).

Figure 8.66   The yellow flower petals are all selected.

7. With the yellow flower all selected, choose Select, Feather from the Select menu.

8. Set the Feather radius to 5 pixels and click OK. This makes the edge pixels around the flower softer and helps them blend into the composite image better (see Figure 8.67).

Figure 8.67   The Feather radius is set to 5 pixels.

9. Copy the yellow flower.

10. Paste the yellow flower into the my_fun_with_layers file.

   Upon pasting, the Resample dialog box appears, asking you whether you want to resample this image or not (see Figure 8.68). Because the original yellow_flower file was a higher resolution than the my_fun_with_layers file, you want the flower to fit proportionately in the new image.

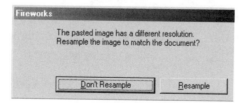

Figure 8.68   The Resample dialog box.

11. Click Resample. The yellow flower is now in the my_fun_with_layers document and appears as the default name bitmap object in Layer 1.

12. Change the default name bitmap to yellow flower by double-clicking in the Name field on the yellow flower object and name it `Yellow Flower` (see Figure 8.69).

Figure 8.69   The yellow flower is now in the `my_fun_with_layers` document and named `Yellow Flower` in the Layers panel.

13. Save your file.

14. Close the original `yellow_flower` file and do *not* save the changes.

Creating the Persian Rug Floor

15. Open the `fabric` file from the `Lesson_04` folder. The object in the file is a Persian rug-type floor tile.

16. Select the object.

17. Copy the object.

18. Switch to `my_fun_with_layers` and paste the object.

    You are presented with the Resample dialog box. In this case, you do not want to resample the image because you want it as large as you can get it.

19. Click Don't Resample. The floor tile image pastes into the `my_fun_with_layers` file and seems to hide the yellow flower (see Figure 8.70).

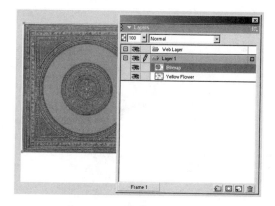

Figure 8.70   The floor tile image is pasted into the my_fun_with_layers document.

20. In the Layers panel, move the new bitmap image, the floor tile, below the yellow flower object (see Figure 8.71).

    After you move the new bitmap object, the floor tile, below the yellow flower object, change its name to Floor Tile in the Layers panel.

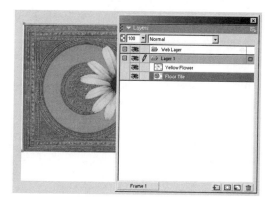

Figure 8.71   The floor tile moved below the yellow flower object, and is named floortile.

Distorting the Floor Tile for Perspective

21. Select the floor tile with the Pointer tool and move it to the bottom-middle of the document (see Figure 8.72).

Figure 8.72   The floor tile is selected with the Pointer tool and moved to the bottom-middle of the document.

22. Select the Distort tool from the Tools panel.

23. Click and drag the lower-left corner point of the floor tile all the way over until it reaches the far-left corner of the document.

24. Click the bottom-right distort handle and drag it until it reaches the far right-lower corner of the document.

25. Click the top-center point distort handle and drag the top of the tile down to approximately the horizontal middle of your document.

Tip

You can gauge where you are in the document by watching the tic mark in the ruler as you drag.

26. Save the file (see Figure 8.73).

Figure 8.73   The floor tile is modified to create a perspective effect.

Changing the Tile's Colors

The colors in the yellow flower and the Persian rug tile look too similar, so you need to change them using live effects on the Property Inspector.

27. Make sure that the floor tile object is still selected.

28. Click the plus on the Effects area of the Property Inspector and select Adjust Color, Hue/Saturation (see Figure 8.74).

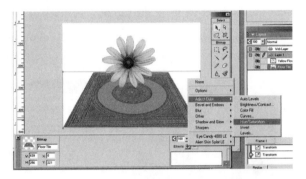

Figure 8.74   The floor tile object is selected with the Hue/Saturation dialog box displayed.

29. When the Hue/Saturation dialog box appears, adjust the hue to 153 and the saturation to –10.

Now the tile looks more in the range of cyan and teal, which is complementary to the yellow flower and makes it stand out (see Figure 8.75).

Figure 8.75   The Hue/Saturation dialog box with Hue set to 153 and Saturation set to –10.

30. Click OK to accept the effect. Save your file. Close the original fabric file and do not save the changes.

Building the Sky Background

31. Open pinkclouds_02 from the Lesson_04 folder.

32. Select it with the Pointer tool; copy it.

33. Switch to my_fun_with_layers and paste.

    The very Pink Clouds object pastes at the top of your stack of objects in Layer 1.

34. Select the pinkclouds_01 bitmap and drag it to the bottom of the stack of objects in Layer 1. Name the object pink_clouds in the Layers Panel.

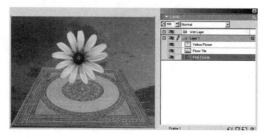

Figure 8.76   The pinkclouds_01 bitmap object at the bottom of the stack of the my_fun_with_layers.

35. Close the pinkclouds_02 image and do not save any changes.

Preparing the Second Part of the Sky Image Before Placing It

36. Open the pinkclouds_01 file from the Lesson_04 folder.

37. Choose Modify, Canvas, Image Size to open the Image Size dialog box.

38. Make sure that Constrain Proportions is checked off and Resample Image is checked on. Change the resolution from 180 to 72. Change the pixel width from 360 to 640, and change the pixel dimension height from 288 to 480. Make sure that the sample method is selected as Bicubic for the smoothest resample of your image (see Figure 8.77).

39. Click OK.

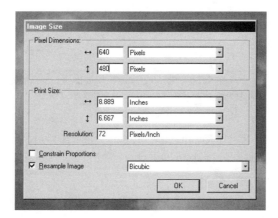

Figure 8.77   The Image Size dialog box with the pixel dimensions changed from a width of 360 to 640 and the pixel height changed from 288 to 480.

Creating a Mirrored Effect

To create an inkblot effect or mirror effect with the clouds image, you must select the left side of the image, copy it, paste it, and flip it onto the right side of the image. Then, you can merge the image so that it is one object.

40. Select the Marquee tool from the Tools panel. Click and drag over the left side of the `pinkclouds_01` image (see Figure 8.78).

Figure 8.78   The left side of the `pinkclouds_01` image selected with the Marquee tool.

41. Copy the selected portion of the image. Deselect the marquee selection of half of the image, and paste.

Note

If you do not deselect the selected portion of the image, the copy pastes right into that selection and does not create the new bitmap object that you need.

42. With the Pointer tool, select the new bitmap image, the half of the original picture that you copied and pasted, and choose Modify, Transform, Flip Horizontal from the Modify menu.

43. With the Pointer tool, click and drag the flipped-over portion of the image while holding the Shift key.

44. Drag to place it on the right side of the image. Now you have two clouds that are reflected across the center (see Figure 8.79).

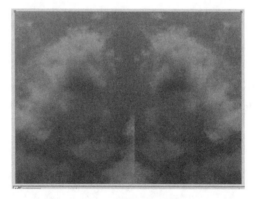

Figure 8.79   Two clouds are reflected across the center of the image.

45. Click the top bitmap object in the layer and, from the Layers Option pop-up menu, choose Merge Down.

The image becomes one object instead of two objects.

Brightening the Image

46. Select Filters, Adjust Color, Levels. Click Auto to see what happens. It looks good, so click OK.

This is a permanent effect that is not removed when you move this object from this file to the `my_fun_with_layers` file.

47. Make sure that the object is selected and copy it. Using the Window menu, switch to `my_fun_with_layers` and paste (see Figure 8.80).

Tip

If you select the Pink Cloud layer before pasting, the new image pastes above it.

Figure 8.80   The new Blue Clouds bitmap image pasted above the Pink Clouds object in the stack.

48. Select the new bitmap in the Layers panel and rename it `bluesky`.

Adding a Mask to `bluesky`

Now, you need to add a mask to the `bluesky` object so that you can see the Pink Clouds peeking out from underneath it. You do this by using a bitmap mask.

49. Make sure that the `bluesky` object is selected in the Layers panel.

50. Click the Add Mask button at the bottom of the Layers panel.

51. Select the Brush tool from the Tools panel and set the size of the brush to 300 by typing in the Brush Size field.

52. Set the brush opacity to 50 percent. Move the brush out into the canvas.

Remember that you are painting on the mask, not on the original image.

53. Begin clicking to paint large dabs of black into the mask at the bottom left and right corners, hiding the `bluesky` image and revealing the Pink Clouds image underneath.

Continue to click and put mask material into the Blue Sky mask around the edges and the top of the Blue Sky mask so that the blue pixels from the Blue Sky and the pink pixels from the Pink Clouds mix together to create a purple-like halo effect (see Figure 8.81).

Figure 8.81   The mask painted to reveal the Pink Clouds image and blend the two sky images together.

54. Close the original `pinkclouds_01` file and do *not* save the changes.

Adding the Rainbow

For a finishing touch, add a rainbow to the image. This lends a sense of transition and, at the same time, ties the top and bottom portions of the image together.

55. Open the `rainbow` file from the `Lesson_04` folder. Select it with the Pointer tool; copy it. Switch to the `my_fun_with_layers` file.

56. Select the Blue Sky layer and paste. The bitmap appears to cover both the Blue Sky and the Pink Clouds. You'll now add a vector mask to the Rainbow bitmap image so that the top portion of the Blue Sky and the bottom portion of the Pink Clouds image are revealed.

57. Change the name of the Rainbow bitmap objects to `rainbow` in the Layers panel (see Figure 8.82).

Figure 8.82   The Rainbow image added above the clouds objects.

Making the Bitmap Mask for the Rainbow Object

58. Make sure that the Rainbow object is selected in the Layers panel.

59. Click Add Mask to add a bitmap mask to the rainbow.

60. With the Brush tool, paint in the upper-right and then lower-left corner of the Rainbow image to reveal the portions of the Blue Sky and the Pink Cloud objects from beneath it.

I set my brush options to size 200 and opacity to 60 to remove the portions of the Rainbow image that I didn't want.

Now all you have to do is save your file, and you're done (see Figure 8.83).

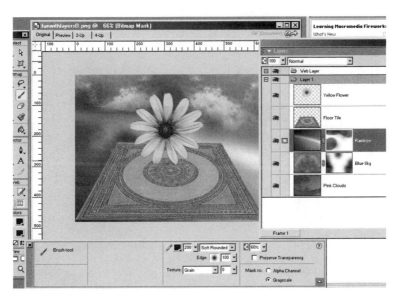

Figure 8.83   The final file with the Rainbow image masked.

Summary

Congratulations! If you followed this chapter all the way through from the beginning, you have learned a lot about how to work with, create, and edit bitmap images. I tried to turn you on to some of the many techniques that I like to use when creating and working with bitmap images. Continue to experiment with variations on these processes and use your own images to come up with all kinds of unique and interesting designs. Mastering selections, painting, effects, masks, and image composition is now within your grasp. Go for it!

Chapter 9

Masking

Understanding the basics of working with vector and bitmap images is essential. Getting a handle on layers lets you leverage vector and bitmap objects. Now it's time to really cook. Masking is one of the great tools that let us make some hot graphics.

What Are Masks?

Masks are objects that change the shape and/or opacity of other objects. Simply put, masks are a way to selectively show and hide content. Here's an analogy: Masking is like holding a card with holes in it in front of my face. When you look at me, you might see an eye and my lips, but the card masks my nose and middle of my face. If I move the card up a little, you can see my nose but not my eyes. In this simple example, the card acts as a mask that allows only certain parts of my face to be visible.

Both vector and bitmap objects can be used as the mask object. The mask object is the one doing the masking. The masked object is the object that is being masked. Therefore, you have the mask and the "maskee."

There are essentially four different types of masks. Each type is a way of making objects interact with each other to create a specific effect. Each of these interactions has it's own distinct properties. You can use masks to create combinations of objects that are, in a sense, blended objects. You can also change the behavior of a mask with the click of a button. For now, let's talk about the four main types of masking techniques:

- A vector masking a vector
- A vector masking a bitmap
- A bitmap masking a vector
- A bitmap masking a bitmap

Vector Masks

Vector masks are sometimes known as clipping paths or paste insides. The path of a vector mask object acts as a cookie cutter and crops the underlying object(s) to its own shape. Sound confusing? It's not, really. Just try the following example and it might make more sense.

Vector Masking a Vector

One way to mask vector artwork with a vector mask is to use a method called paste inside:

1. Open the file `vector_vector.png` from the `Exercises_09` folder on the accompanying CD-ROM (see Figure 9.1).

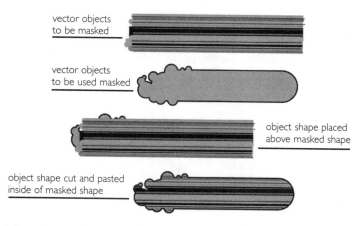

Figure 9.1   The four steps of the vector masking a vector process.

In this file, you see four images: stripes, a bubble shape, the stripes on top of the bubble shape, and the bubble shape masking the stripes.

The top-most object in the file, labeled "stripes," is a bunch of different colored strokes of varying thickness grouped together.

2. With the Pointer tool, drag the stripes on top of the bubble shape (see Figure 9.2).

Figure 9.2   A group of stripes placed on top of the bubble shape.

3. With the vector object that you want masked (stripes) placed on top of the object that will be its mask (the bubble shape), cut the stripes object by choosing Edit, Cut.

4. Select the bubble shape and choose Edit, Paste Inside. The result matches Figure 9.3.

Figure 9.3   A group of shapes masked by a bubble shape.

Positioning the object that you want masked on top of the object that is going to be the mask makes it easier to get your desired results. If you do not position the object to be masked properly, you can still reposition it after the mask has been made. To do this, click the masked object to select it. Then, drag the move handle to move the object inside of the mask (see Figure 9.4).

Figure 9.4   The selected move handle.

Using Type as a Mask

People always want to know how to get a cool-looking fill inside their type elements. Well, another great option within the vector mask category is using type as the vector mask object. The best part about this is the "editability." You don't have to redo all the steps if you made a spelling error or want to add a word. Just change the type by selecting it with the Text tool and typing the new text. Voila!

Here, the process is basically the same as the previous steps, except the object for your mask is text:

1. Type a word in a font that you like.

2. Create or find some vector or bitmap art that you like.

3. Position the objects on top of each other.

4. Cut the art to be masked.

5. Select the type and choose Edit, Paste Inside.

6. Select the text with the Text tool and change it.

Tip

To get a more integrated edge, use one of the colors from your maskee for your type so that, when the type masks the vector art, its edge looks smooth.

Paste Inside Text Mask

Big Fun Typed using Verdana Bold (42 points)

BIG FUN

Typed placed over vector art

Vector art cut and pasted inside of type

BIG FUN

Edited text still masks art!

Lori Rocks

Figure 9.5 The process flow of editable type as a mask.

Vector Masking a Bitmap

Now, you'll use the Paste as Mask command. In this example, you use a vector object with a feathered edge as the mask and a bitmap image for the object as the maskee:

1. Open the file vector_bitmap.png from the Exercises_09 folder on the accompanying CD-ROM (see Figure 9.6).

Vector Bitmap

wave path with
feathered edge applied

bitmap image

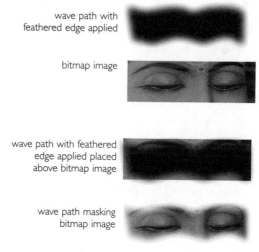

wave path with feathered
edge applied placed
above bitmap image

wave path masking
bitmap image

Figure 9.6 The process flow of vector masking of a bitmap object.

2. Using the Pointer tool, select the object "wavy shape" (see Figure 9.7).

Figure 9.7   The wavy vector shape with a feathered edge of 12.

3. Drag it on top of the bitmap image of eyes (see Figure 9.8).

Figure 9.8   The wavy vector shape is placed on top of the bitmap image of eyes.

4. With the wavy shape still selected on top of the bitmap object, choose Edit, Cut.

5. Select the eyes with the Pointer tool and choose Edit, Paste As Mask.

   Your result matches the result shown in Figure 9.9.

Figure 9.9   The wavy vector bitmap masking bitmap eyes.

Cool, huh? But, there's still more that you can do! After this mask is completed, you can still alter the vector path into which the bitmap image is masked:

1. Select the Subselection tool from the Tools panel.

2. Click the mask thumbnail in the Layers panel.

   Notice the path highlights displaying the control points and outline of the path (see Figure 9.10).

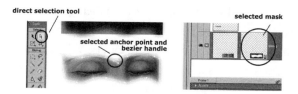

Figure 9.10   The Image Subselection tool, Bezier Handles, and the selected mask.

3. Click and drag the vector points and Bezier control handles, or use the Freeform or Reshape Area tools to alter the shape and, thus, your mask's look.

   After a vector mask is created, a Pen icon appears at the bottom right of the mask thumbnail within the Layers panel (see Figure 9.11).

Figure 9.11   The Pen icon/masked object.

The Pen icon lets you know that you have created a vector type mask. Also, when the Mask icon is selected in the Layers panel, the Property Inspector displays information about how the mask is applied.

Remember when we mentioned the second method of controlling masks earlier in this chapter? Well, here's more detail to help you understand how to alter the behavior of masks.

Look at the Property Inspector. Notice that either the Path Outline or Grayscale Appearance is selected (see Figure 9.12).

Figure 9.12   Grayscale Appearance is selected in the Property Inspector.

Each of these options has distinct characteristics. When your mask is set to Grayscale Appearance, the opposite value of the image's pixels determines the percentage at which you will see the masked object. For example, if you use a dark gray shape of 70 percent opacity for your grayscale mask, your masked content shows through at 30 percent opacity.

When your mask is set to Path Outline, the mask does just what it sounds like: It uses the outline of the mask to alter the shape of the object being masked without affecting the opacity of the object inside the mask.

You can use these options to change the way a mask works and radically modify your images. Play with it. You'll begin to feel the amazing power of manipulating masks.

Bitmap Masks

The second category of masks is *bitmap masks.* As previously mentioned, there are two types:

- A bitmap masking a bitmap
- A bitmap masking a vector

Bitmap Masking A Bitmap

The following example uses a bitmap of clouds as a mask for a bitmapped image of eyes:

1. Open the file `bitmap_bitmap.png` from the `Exercises_09` folder on the accompanying CD-ROM (see Figure 9.13).

Figure 9.13   The process flow for masking bitmapped images with bitmap masks.

Notice that there are four images. The first is the bitmap that's to be used as the mask. The second image, eyes, is the bitmap that's going to be masked. The last two images are of the masking process. Let's try it!

2. Using the Pointer tool, select the object "bitmap image to be used as mask" (clouds). (See Figure 9.14.)

Figure 9.14   A bitmapped image of clouds to be used as mask.

3. Drag it on top of the bitmapped image of eyes (see Figure 9.15).

Figure 9.15   The bitmapped image of clouds placed on top of the bitmap of eyes.

4. With both objects selected, choose Modify, Mask, Group As Mask.

    If you look at where the cloud image was black in the mask, the eyes image shows through as 0 percent opacity. Where the areas of the mask were white, there is no effect on the masked image at all, and its opacity is 100 percent. In this type of masking, the grayscale value of the cloud's bitmapped image filters the bitmap image of eyes. (See Figure 9.16).

Figure 9.16   The bitmapped image of clouds masking the bitmapped image of eyes.

Bitmap Masking a Vector

Now we're going to make a bitmap object mask a vector object (see Figure 9.17). In this example, we use a negative photo bitmap of an eye as the mask. Along with it, there are three different colored rectangles (grouped) as the vector object to be masked:

Bitmap Vector

eye (bitmap)

rectangle (vectors)

rectangles on
top of eyes

rectangles and eye
grouped as mask

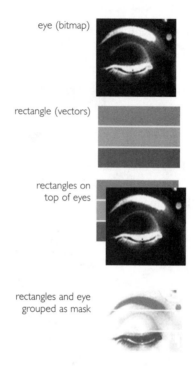

Figure 9.17   The process for a bitmap object masking a vector object.

1. Open the file `bitmap_vector.png` from the `Exercises_09` folder on the accompanying CD-ROM.

   Notice the first image is the bitmap object, and the second is the vector object.

2. Place the bitmap object (eyes) on top of the vector object (colored rectangles). (See Figure 9.18.)

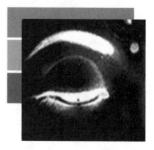

Figure 9.18   The bitmap object of eyes is placed on top of the vector object of colored rectangles.

3. With both selected, choose Modify, Mask, Group As Mask (see Figure 9.19).

Figure 9.19   The bitmap object of eyes is masking the vector object of colored rectangles.

Groovy! The color from the vector filters through the grayscale appearance of the negative photo bitmap. Remember that the grayscale appearance filters through the mask.

Notice how much color filters through in certain areas. Look at the eyebrow, for example. Because the bitmap image we used as a mask has a no color in the eyebrow, we get tons of color filtering through from the underlying vector image. In a nutshell, where the negative is black, none of the underlying image shows through. Where the negative is white, all of the underlying image shows through. Where the negative is gray, some of the underlying image shows through.

Note

This is the opposite behavior from masks in previous versions of Fireworks.

Bitmap Masks from Scratch

In addition to making interesting masks, bitmap masks have a few unique qualities. Both types of bitmap masks have certain features. When you use a bitmap, the pixels of the mask object affect the visibility of the underlying objects.

Bitmap masks can be applied in two different ways. One is to use an existing bitmap object to mask other bitmap or vector objects. This method is similar to the way that vector masks are applied.

The other is by creating what is known as an *empty mask*. Empty masks start out as either totally transparent or totally opaque. A *transparent* (or white) mask shows the entire masked object, and an *opaque* (or black) mask hides the entire masked object. You can use the bitmap tools to draw onto or modify the mask object, revealing or hiding the underlying masked objects. Let's try an example:

1. Open the file `paint_mask_01.png` from the `Exercises_09` folder on the accompanying CD-ROM. Look at the Layers panel (see Figure 9.20).

   Two objects are in the Surfers layer. The first one is labeled "left" and the one below it is labeled "right."

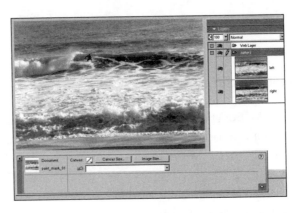

Figure 9.20   The Layers panel with the surfers bitmap photo.

2. Select the layer labeled "left" and click the Add Mask button at the bottom of the Layers panel to add an empty mask to the bitmap object (see Figure 9.21).

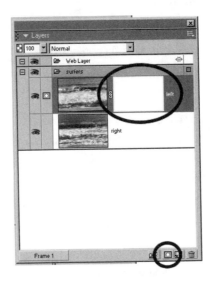

Figure 9.21   The Layers panel with the Add Mask icon and the newly created empty mask.

3. Select the Brush tool. Using the Property Inspector, set the brush tip size to 70 with a stroke category of soft rounded. Begin painting.

   You might notice as you paint on the mask (hiding the water on the top image) that the image beneath is revealed (see Figure 9.22). Wherever the paint is applied, the ocean and surfers from the image beneath filter through the mask.

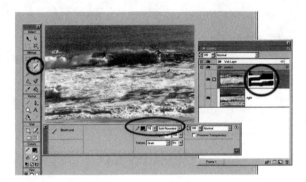

Figure 9.22   The Brush tool is selected. The Property Inspector with the Brush tool settings and the mask in the Layers panel are shown.

Experiment with it, and you'll eventually get it. Try painting with black and dark gray on the mask so that all the surfers from the bottom image are revealed. To bring back parts of the top image that you have hidden, paint in white on the mask.

Paste Mask

You can use just about anything to make a mask with. This fun example uses a felt pen drawing as the mask and a rectangle with a spectrum radial gradient applied to it as the object being masked. It creates an effect that's similar to a wax crayon scratchboard that kids make in school:

1. Open the file paste_mask_01.png from the Exercises_09 folder on the accompanying CD-ROM.

   This file contains a rectangle to which a radial gradient with a spectrum fill has been applied.

2. Open the file love_rules.png from the Exercises_09 folder on the accompanying CD-ROM (see Figure 9.23).

3. This felt-pen drawing that we scanned and then inverted by choosing Filter, Adjust Color, Invert serves as the mask.

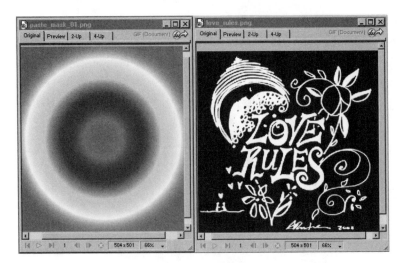

Figure 9.23   Both images are to be used in Paste Mask.

3. Using the Pointer tool, select the `love_rules.png` bitmap object and copy it.

4. Switch to `paste_mask_01.png`.

5. Click the Add Mask button at the bottom of the Layers panel to add a mask to the rectangle with the cool colors in it.

6. Choose Edit, Paste. The drawing becomes the mask.

7. In the Layers panel, click back on the masked object (colored rectangle). By using its handles, you can now reposition the center of the gradient as desired. We centered our gradient in the middle of the "o" in "love." It looks fine!

8. Open `paste_mask_02.png` from the `Exercises_09` folder on the accompanying CD-ROM to see the final version and compare yours to it.

Figure 9.24   The Paste Mask fantastic final result.

Summary

Masks are a way to amplify your creativity. No longer are you confined to just bitmaps or vectors. You can create effects that look like silk screens, rubber stamps, air-brush, wood cut, and textile swatches by making your masks out of anything and everything that you can think of. You can use your digital photos as textures for both your mask and masked objects. Anything that you can digitize can be folded into the mix. You can take your bitmaps and vector art to a new level by using masks.

Part III

Making It Move and Getting It Out There

Chapter 10

Image Maps

Technically, an *image map* is a map of screen coordinates that define regions, or hotspots, of a browser window. They are assigned to functions or links. An image map usually overlays a graphical image to give the user clues about the associated actions. (Actually, many people refer to the graphic itself as the image map.) Image maps are often used as navigational tools, as links to other sites or pages, or to draw attention to a particular concept of a web site.

An image map can be server-side, which means that it resides on the server and is downloaded as needed; or client-side, which means that it's part of the web page's HTML. Early versions of HTML supported only server-side image maps. Now, server-side is used only in certain cases for when control is required. Client-side image maps relieve some of the load on the server. In addition, because they are part of the web page, client-side image maps still work when browsing offline.

The challenge in preparing an image map is defining which parts of the image are linked to which URLs or functions. Determining and typing all the coordinates of all the points that are needed to define hotspots is definitely cumbersome. Luckily, Fireworks helps you through this process. It enables you to load your image and draw the hotspots, and then Fireworks writes the appropriate HTML to implement the image map. This chapter covers the basics of creating image maps in Fireworks.

Creating Image Maps

To create an image map, you need to do three things:

1. Build a graphic that serves as the background for the image map.
2. Decide what areas are the hotspots.
3. Link the hotspots to the URLs or functions that are associated with them.

In Fireworks, hotspots are created or defined by using the Hotspot tool or by converting an object into a hotspot. The Hotspot tool enables you to make three basic hotspot shapes: rectangles, circles, and polygons (see Figure 10.1).

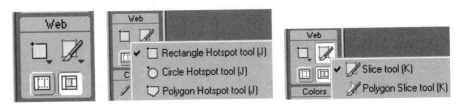

Figure 10.1   The Web section of the Tools panel contains the Hotspot tool, the Slice tool, and buttons that show or hide slices and hotspots.

After you draw the hotspot, it appears as a translucent shape that overlays your graphic. The default display color for the hotspot overlay is light blue; however, you can assign the color of your choice by clicking the Color box in the Property Inspector when a hotspot is selected.

Hotspot Properties

The Property Inspector sets the properties for your hotspot (see Figure 10.2):

- **Navigator box**—The position of the hotspot is shown in the navigator box on the left side, and the coordinates are shown underneath the navigator box. Fireworks outputs these coordinates into an HTML file while you're exporting, if you choose to do so.
- **Shape menu**—Sets the shape of the hotspot to Rectangle, Circle, or Polygon.
- **Link text box**—Indicates what happens when the hotspot is clicked. It can be either a URL or a link. The Link pop-up menu shows the URLs that are in the current URL library.
- **Alt text box**—Corresponds to the alternate image HTML tag. The text name or explanation entered here appears when the mouse is held over the area. It is a requirement for web sites that are going to be section 508-compliant.
- **Target text box**—Normally used with HTML framesets to define where the linked web page appears. Five choices can be accessed through the Target pop-up menu:
    - **None**—This allows you to type a window name, which can be helpful for opening HTML files in named (by JavaScript) windows.
    - **_blank**—Opens the linked file in a new window without closing the browser's current window.
    - **_self**—Opens the linked file into the current frame and replaces the current page. This is the default setting.
    - **_parent**—Opens the linked file into the parent frameset of the current frame, if there is one.
    - **_top**—Opens the linked file in the outside frameset of the current web page, replacing all the existing frames.

Figure 10.2   The Hotspot properties in the Property Inspector.

Modifying Image Maps

Because hotspots are vector-based in Fireworks, you can go back and modify them any time you want. You can move them and even change their shape.

You can move a hotspot by clicking it with the Pointer tool and dragging it to a new position. You can also use the arrow keys to nudge a hotspot by 1-pixel increments in the direction of the arrow. (With the Shift key, the nudge becomes 10-pixel increments.)

You can also change hotspot shapes by selecting different shape types from the Shape pop-up menu in the Property Inspector. To do this, make the hotspot that you want to change active by clicking it with the Pointer tool. Then, choose the new shape from the Shape pop-up menu.

When you change a hotspot shape from one to another (for example, a square to a circle), it does not return to the original size if you change it back. It assumes a default size.

Exporting Image Maps

Fireworks not only supports optimizing and exporting the image used by the image map (see Chapter 13, "Optimization" for more information), but it also generates the necessary HTML code into a file that can be used as a standalone web page or formatted for your favorite web-authoring tool.

To export the image and the HTML file, choose File, Export (see Figure 10.3). Make sure that you choose the optimization settings you want for the image before you choose File, Export.

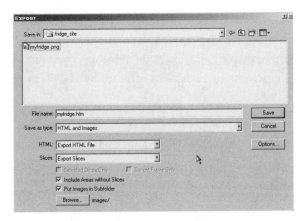

Figure 10.3   The Export dialog box with the image map choices set.

The HTML export options are set by clicking the Options button on the right side or by choosing File, HTML Setup (see Figure 10.4). Click the General tab. You can choose from four standard HTML styles within Fireworks:

- **Dreamweaver HTML**—Codes are styled for Macromedia Dreamweaver. In the case of image maps, generic and Dreamweaver codes are the same.

- **FrontPage HTML**—Because FrontPage relies on webbots to format its code, Fireworks builds the proper code for an image map webbot. Fireworks also creates comments within the code that provide directions for proper insertion of your Fireworks code into FrontPage.

- **Generic HTML**—Generates basic code that is standard for most web-authoring tools and hand-coding.

- **GoLive HTML**—Codes are optimized for use with the Adobe GoLive editor.

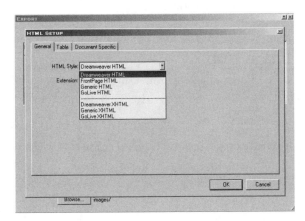

Figure 10.4   The HTML Set Up dialog box enables you to define how the HTML file is output.

Understanding the Code Behind the Image Map

Although Fireworks automatically generates all the coordinates and HTML tags that you need to get your image map running on your web page, you must understand what's going on behind the scenes. There are two parts to the HTML image map code: the <IMG> tag and the <MAP> tag.

The <MAP> element defines a map that associates locations on an image with a destination URL or another function, such as a JavaScript command. Each hotspot is defined by an <AREA> tag:

```
<map name="m_00000001">
<area shape="poly"
coords="174,468,184,438,174,404,168,396,178,362,190,272,196,222,156,230,
➥146,202,142,184,138,174,152,158,160,178,168,212,188,192,212,176,222,150
➥,244,136,260,146,272,170,266,186,276,208,282,226,322,230,328,214,332,22
➥8,348,216,352,240,330,250,292,248,258,228,254,284,260,306,242,352,222,4
➥10,214,442,204,462,192,468,174,468" href="amanda.htm" target="_blank"
➥title="Amanda" alt="Amanda" >
<area shape="rect" coords="127,38,208,77" href="somewhere.htm"
➥title="hotspot line" alt="Hotspot Link" >
</map>
```

The <IMG> element defines the various image parameters. It is bound to the map by the USEMAP attribute, which is set to the name of the map:

```
<img name="n00000001" src="00000001.jpg" width="896" height="592"
➥border="0" usemap="#m_00000001" alt="the picture">
```

Note

The name defined in the USEMAP attribute of the <IMG> element matches the name attribute in the <MAP> tag.

Now, aren't you glad you have Fireworks?

Building an Image Map

In this exercise, you create an image map by using an image that the art department designed. The department kindly marked where the hotspots must be and what shapes they must take:

1. Open the file called fridge.png from the Exercises/10 folder on the CD-ROM and save it to your hard drive as myfridge.png (see Figure 10.5).

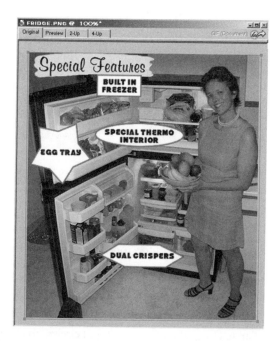

Figure 10.5   The areas that need hotspots are already identified in the `fridge.png` file.

2. Display the Layers panel if it is not already showing (choose Window, Layers or click the Layers icon in the mini-launcher).

Note the three layers within this file:

- **Web layer**—Where the hotspot objects reside.

- **Button Labels layer**—Holds the objects that show where the hotspots are to be placed and their text descriptions.

- **Main Image layer**—Currently locked. It contains the bitmap refrigerator image and the headline "Special Features."

3. Select the Rectangle Hotspot tool from the Tools panel. Click and drag around the words "Built-In Freezer" to create a rectangular hotspot.

Hotspots live on the Web layer and are automatically placed there even if the Web layer is not selected. The Web layer is shared across frames; if you put a hotspot on an animated GIF, that hotspot can be found on every frame of the animated GIF.

If you need to reposition the hotspot, select it with the Pointer tool and drag it into position. The arrow keys are an excellent way to nudge your shape into position.

4. If the Property Inspector isn't showing, choose Window, Properties. If it isn't fully open, click the small arrow on the bottom-right corner. Select the Link text box and type `freezer.htm` (see Figure 10.6). Press Enter/Return to confirm what you've typed.

Figure 10.6   Type the URL where this hotspot links to in the Link text box.

5. Click in the Alt text box and type `Built-In Freezer`. Leave the Target text box blank.

6. Click and hold the Hotspot tool in the Tools panel to reveal the Hotspot tool group menu. Select the Circle Hotspot tool.

7. Click and drag by the "Special Thermo Interior" oval to create a round hotspot. Hold down the Alt key while dragging to draw a circle from the center point.

   By default, the Circle Hotspot tool creates round circles. To change the circle shape into an ellipse, click the Scale tool in the Tools panel. Using the control handles, click and drag to reshape your circle to fit the elliptical navigation button (see Figure 10.7). Notice that the Property Inspector's Shape setting reports that the hotspot is a polygon.

Figure 10.7   The Scale tool in the Tools panel sets up control handles that you can click and drag to reshape the circular hotspot into an ellipse.

8. In the Link text box in the Property Inspector, type `thermo.htm`. In the Alt text box, type `Special Thermo Interior`. Leave the Target text box blank.

   As you can see, the shape is no longer a circle, but a polygon. By scaling the circle with the Scale tool, you transformed it into a polygon.

9. Click the current Hotspot tool in the Tools panel and hold the mouse button to reveal the Hotspot tool group. Choose the Polygon Hotspot tool.

10. The Polygon Hotspot tool works like the Polygon tool. Click each of the seven points of the "Dual Crispers" polygon in order. As you click each point, Fireworks builds the path, which creates an oblong diamond shape.

    You can use the Subselection tool to modify a polygon hotspot by clicking and dragging the individual points on the hotspot's path.

11. In the Link text box in the Property Inspector, type **crisp.htm**. In the Alt text box, type **Dual Crispers**. Again, leave the Target text box blank.

12. Select the Pointer tool from the Tools panel and click the star shape surrounding the Egg Tray label.

13. Choose Edit, Insert, Hotspot. Fireworks uses the star object to generate a hotspot that's exactly the right size and shape.

14. In the Link text box, type **egg.htm**. In the Alt text box, type **Egg Tray**. Leave the Target text box blank. Save your file (by choosing File, Save).

You can also convert multiple paths into one or multiple hotspots (see Figure 10.8). To do this, Shift-select the paths to be converted. Then choose Edit, Insert, Hotspot. You must choose how to create the hotspot(s). Click the Single button to create a single hotspot that overlays all the selected objects, or click the Multiple button to create individual hotspots for each selected object.

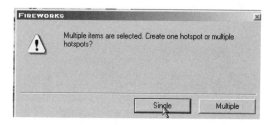

Figure 10.8   You can convert multiple objects into either a single or multiple hotspot(s).

Exporting the myfridge.png File

Now that all the hotspots are defined (see Figure 10.9), the links and Alt tags entered, it's time to export the image and the associated HTML file so that it can be used on your web page:

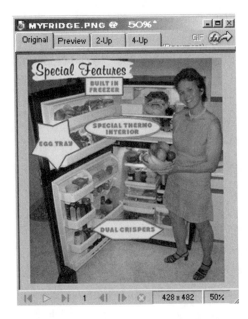

Figure 10.9   The myfridge.png file with all the hotpots defined.

1. Open the Optimize panel if it isn't visible by choosing Window, Optimize or by clicking the Optimize icon in the mini-launcher at the bottom right of the Document window.

2. From the Settings pop-up menu, choose JPEG–Smaller File (see Figure 10.10). Click the Preview tab in the Document window to see how the image looks as a compressed JPEG.

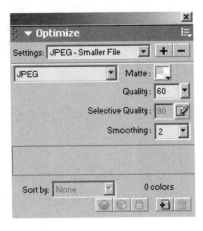

Figure 10.10   The Optimize panel with the JPEG–Smaller File setting selected.

3. Because your export preferences were set in Chapter 13, you can export without
   worrying about resetting them. Click the Quick Export button in the top-right
   corner of the Document window. Choose Dreamweaver from the Quick Export
   pop-up menu, and choose Export HTML from the Dreamweaver pop-up menu
   (see Figure 10.11).

Figure 10.11   Use the Quick Export feature to output the `myfridge.jpg` image and the
`myfridge.htm` file.

Summary

Now you know how to take advantage of some very interesting and helpful techniques
for creating, designing, and assigning interactivity to you graphics for your web pages.
Isn't this stuff great?!

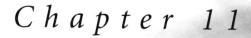

Chapter 11

Working with Behaviors

One of the quickest ways to create a good impression on your visitors is to present your content in a sophisticated layout with attractive graphics and subtle, yet intuitive, interactions. For years, the main technique for creating sophisticated and professional-looking layouts has been the use of HTML tables with merged cell regions, nested tables, and complex JavaScript interactions. Although this approach is sufficient to produce professional layouts, it can be difficult to maintain.

Today, because more applications and dynamic data are used on the web, code is more complex than ever. With DHTML, JavaScript functions usually appeared between the <head> tags, whereas the content between the <body> tags was mostly static HTML. Now, the content between the <body> tags can be more complex, with ASP or ColdFusion placeholders and sometimes hidden HTML form elements. Also, instead of relying exclusively on nested tables, many sites now use Cascading Style Sheets (CSS) to format and position elements.

As a result of the increased complexity of web-page code, especially between the <body> tags, maintaining graphics with their attached behaviors or updating web sites with graphics has a new layer of complexity. You can't just blithely automate image updates without running the risk of adding errors into your code.

Fortunately, Dreamweaver and Fireworks integration is, and has always been, strong. Chances are that you can accomplish your graphic layout, behavior creation, and maintenance objectives with one tool or another of Fireworks and Dreamweaver integration. No single workflow is best in every situation, however. This chapter discusses creating useful, manageable, and easy-to-implement behaviors within Fireworks MX, with an eye toward maintenance.

What Is a Behavior?

A *behavior* is composed of three elements: an event, an event trigger, and a resulting action (see Figure 11.1). An *event* is generally a user-based interaction with an HTML object that initiates the action, such as the double-click of a mouse or the loading of the page. A *trigger* is the web object (slice, hotspot, or button) that is acted on by the event to cause the desired action. Common *resulting actions* include the swapping of one image for another, the opening of another window, or the replacement of a current document with another document.

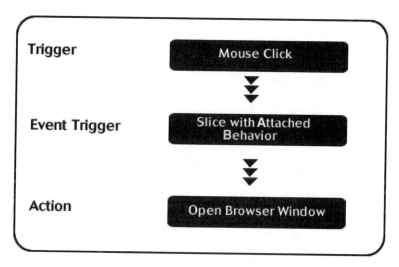

Figure 11.1   The anatomy of a behavior.

Event triggers aren't just confined to JavaScript-based behaviors that you can assign within Fireworks or Dreamweaver MX. You can create a degree of interaction based purely on standard HTML navigation actions. Assigning links to the image or buttons you create within Fireworks MX allows for quick and easy creation of navigational systems or interface components, which you can later build on to create more complex interactions by assigning JavaScript behaviors within Fireworks or Dreamweaver MX.

Links

The simplest type of interaction that you can allocate to an element within Fireworks is a standard HTML navigation *link*. When clicking the mouse (event) on a specified image (trigger), a new document loads in the current window (action). Linking behavior is so commonplace and basic, however, that it has been incorporated directly into standard HTML. In other words, you do not need to use JavaScript to make a link work. For this reason, in Fireworks, a link is not referred to as a behavior. A behavior in Fireworks is always a JavaScript-enabled action.

About URLs

Although you don't use the Behavior panel to add links to your page, you might (you don't *have* to) need to specify the link to page action. You can do this through the URL field in the Property Inspector or the URL panel. You can select multiple types of link actions by choosing the format of the URL that you enter.

Absolute URLs

To load a page from another web site into the main window, enter a full site location (`http://www.sitename.com/filename.html`), and do not select a target. Figure 11.2 shows an absolute relative URL.

Figure 11.2   Setting a link that opens an absolute relative URL in a new window.

Document-Relative URLs

To send users to another page within your web site, use a simple document-relative URL link by entering the desired destination folder path (if needed) and filename without selecting a target. Figure 11.3 shows an example of a document-relative URL.

Figure 11.3   The Link field displays an example of a document-relative URL.

Document-relative paths provide a method of linking the page where the link is contained to the destination file. Using document-relative URLs, you can link to files in the same directory. For example:

```
filename.html
```

Linking to a file contained within a subdirectory of the current directory looks like this:

```
foldername/filename.html
```

Linking to a directory that's above the current directory looks like this:

```
../filename.html
```

Sending an Email

To open a blank email from the user's email program, enter **mailto:** followed by the email address, with no space between the two (see Figure 11.4). The email that opens has the desired email address already filled in.

Note

You can add a subject to your email link by adding `?subject=Your Subject` after the email address. If you do this, the final email address looks like the following:

`mailto:someone@somwhere.com?subject=Your Subject`

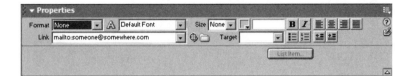

Figure 11.4   Setting an email link.

Opening New Windows

To load either an internal or external page into another window or frame, select the target `_blank`, or enter a desired window name in the Target field (for example, `_new` to open the link into the particular frame). This option is usually used to load pages from an external web site into a new window instead of writing the content of the site into the same window, which keeps the users within your site while still displaying the external data. This method of loading pages is especially useful when creating links to PDFs and having them open in a new window.

Assigning a URL to a Slice

To assign a URL to a selected slice using the Property Inspector, follow these steps:

1. Choose Window, Properties to open the Property Inspector (if it's not already open).

2. Enter a URL in the Link field.

3. Enter information into the Alt field. Although this is optional, entering alternative text for your images is important for aiding visually impaired users as they navigate your site with audio editors, or for providing information to users with images turned off in their browser preferences.

4. Enter a target window or frame in the Target pop-up menu. If you are making a simple link, there's no need to add anything here.

To assign a URL to a slice using the URL panel (see Figure 11.5), follow these steps:

1. Select the slice.

2. Type the URL in the Link field, or select the desired URL from the URL pop-up menu.

3. Click the plus (+) button if you want to add the link to the link list.

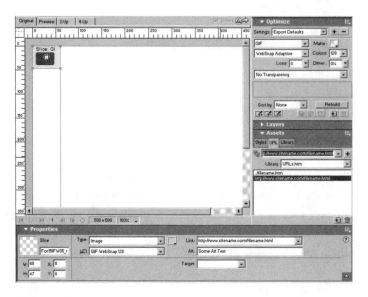

Figure 11.5   Creating a link using the URL panel.

Understanding Triggers

As previously described, triggers are made from web objects, including slices, hotspots, and buttons. These objects are defined using the Fireworks Web layer.

Note

Button slices do not appear in the Web layer until you open them in the Button editor.

A Quick Slicing Review

Although the process of creating slices in your Fireworks document was covered in Chapter 13, "Optimization," it's essential that you understand what slices are and how they are rendered before you attempt to add interactivity to your project.

After a web page's design is complete, a process called *slicing* is used to cut web documents into smaller and more manageable pieces. This is done for a several reasons:

- Slicing a larger parent image into smaller child images helps reduce the overall download time of images by removing redundant pixel information.

- Users see the progressive download of the page structure and component images, which helps keep their attention.

- Slicing images allows for greater flexibility and design control when the final design enters the HTML-authoring environment.

- Slicing a parent design enables you to assign individual optimization methods for each individual slice within the design. This has the benefit of assigning the most effective compression method to the content of the slice (for example, JPEG for photos, GIF 89a for line art/solid color blocks).

Perhaps the most important feature becomes available when you slice designs that are created in Fireworks MX: You can assign behaviors and extended interactivity to your web pages, as you see a bit later in this chapter.

Web Layer Overview

The Fireworks Web layer is a particularly powerful application feature because it enables you to assign interactivity and HTML information to document slices.

In some ways, the Web layer functions like other layers. The Web layer, and the slice objects and hotspots it contains, can be viewed or hidden, locked or unlocked.

In most aspects, however, the Web layer behaves differently from other layers in a Fireworks document. Whereas you might have multiple basic layers, adding and deleting as you go, one Web layer is always shared across all frames in a Fireworks PNG. This layer contains only hotspot and slice information, which is exported as image maps and sliced images with links and JavaScript behaviors within the Fireworks table structure (see Chapter 14, "Exporting").

Creating slices, optimization, and compression issues are covered in Chapter 13, and hotspots are explained in Chapter 10, "Image Maps." This chapter builds on these lessons by covering the process of setting links and behaviors using objects on the Web layer (see Figure 11.6).

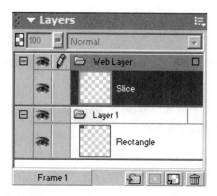

Figure 11.6   The Layers panel, showing the Web layer.

Designing Entire Pages in Fireworks

One of the best, and often overlooked, uses of Fireworks is to create entire page designs with it. Fireworks' always-editable vector graphics make the trial-and-error process, which is so important to the creative process, painless. You can move items around, resize them, or change their color if you don't like them. You can create a design and multiple variations by simply copying and pasting objects. Because Fireworks designs don't rest on HTML like Dreamweaver designs do, you can redo entire structures using drag and drop instead of fussing with tables, merged areas, and cellpadding.

The wall that many users run up against, however, is how to seamlessly get their designs out of Fireworks and into Dreamweaver. Sooner or later, you must deal with HTML tables (or another HTML-positioning strategy, such as CSS or layers). You can make the transition in many ways, each with their own advantages and disadvantages. For simplicity, the ways can be divided into two main categories:

- Exporting Fireworks page designs using Fireworks HTML
- Reconstructing a Fireworks table manually in Dreamweaver, and exporting individual pieces from Fireworks and placing them in the Dreamweaver design

A common variation is to use a bit of both categories, building an entire page design in Fireworks, reconstructing that design in Dreamweaver, but exporting multiple Fireworks slices at once, and inserting them as nested tables in Dreamweaver.

Creating HTML Layouts Using Fireworks Slicing

Regardless of the method that you use to get Fireworks' assets into Dreamweaver, the most important step is to divide your Fireworks graphics into pieces that are distinguished by function, such as a rollover or image map, and/or by optimization, such as a JPEG and/or a GIF. This is done by slicing the image within Fireworks using the Slice tool.

If you export a Fireworks file using the HTML and Images setting in the Export dialog box, Fireworks generates an HTML table that replicates the design, which means that each slice is replicated as a table cell, using the <td> tag, in the exported HTML file. Then, Fireworks inserts each of the sliced graphics into these table cells, which gives the holistic impression that the HTML page is a single, large image.

Although HTML tables are the most common output type for Fireworks slices, you can also output slices to CSS layers or Dreamweaver Library files. Both of these options can be found in the Save as Type menu of the Export dialog box. Those who design pages in Dreamweaver with layers and convert the layers to HTML tables at the end of the process can appreciate the CSS layers output option. If you created a Fireworks graphic element, such as a navigation bar, that you intend to use on multiple pages, it's recommended that you export it as a Dreamweaver Library (`*.lbi`) file. It is important to note that the .LBI export does not support the Fireworks pop-up menu feature.

Hotspots and Slices

Slicing a document creates individual images when you export your document. Fireworks also allows for the creation of areas within a single slice to which you can attach behaviors. These areas of interactivity are called hotspots. An image map does not have to be multiple hotspots on one slice image. It can be generated from a single hotspot on a single image, or a single hotspot on a single slice, multiple hotspots on either a single image, or a single slice define multiple image maps.

There are many advantages to working with hotspots. Because a hotspot works as a trigger the same way a slice does, you can use it for rollover effects, links, and pop-up menus. Also, each slice requires a chunk of code to display it properly; multiple slices take longer to download than one image with multiple hotspots. Unlike slices, however, a hotspot cannot act as the object of an action. You cannot swap images within a defined hotspot. To decide between using slices and hotspots, consider the following:

1. Is the area going to be the object of an action? If so, you must use slices. If not, go to question 2.

2. Is there much white space? White space, as part of an image, takes time to download. If the answer is yes, choose slices. If not, go to question 3.

3. Is there font or non-graphical content in the area? If so, uses slices. If not, go to question 4.

4. Do you want to compress different portions of the area using varying options? For example, is part of the area a photograph and best optimized as a JPEG, while the rest is text and renders best as a GIF? (For more details, see Chapter 13.) If so, use slices. If not, the best answer is to use hotspots on one slice.

Naming Slices

Every time you draw a slice, Fireworks automatically gives it a name. The name is typically something along the lines of Untitled-1_r2_c3. The slice name names the graphics within the slices upon export. Imagine how hard it would be to work with the HTML code of a document filled with images called Untitled-1_r2_c3, Untitled-1_r1_c2, and Untitled-1_r4_c1_f2. One way to improve the readability—and therefore maintainability—of your HTML documents that have been exported from Fireworks is to name each of your slices something meaningful, such as navbtn_home, navbtn_about_us, and navbtn_contact.

To name a slice in Fireworks, you first must select it. In the Property Inspector, enter a new name in the Edit the Object Name dialog box. Alternatively, you can double-click the slice name on the Web layer when its view is expanded to show the web objects on the layer (they are not sublayers; they are objects) in the Layers panel (choose Window, Layers).

Note

You cannot use spaces or certain illegal characters, such as a question mark or slash, when you name slices.

Actions

As previously mentioned, a behavior is an *event* occurring to a specific *trigger*, resulting in an *action*. This action acts on the action's *target*. In Fireworks, possible targets include the trigger slice, a different slice, the browser window (if you are referring to targeting a window, that's not a behavior function), or the status bar. Possible actions are swapping one image for another, replacing one document with another (either in the main window or a new one), and defining the content of the status bar. When actions build on each other, you create more complex behaviors, such as four-state buttons, pop-up menus, or navigation bars (commonly referred to as *nav bars*).

Using Behaviors in Your Fireworks Document

There are two basic approaches to adding behaviors to slices and hotspots.

The first method of attaching behaviors involves the Behaviors panel (see Figure 11.7). The Behaviors panel enables you to create complex interactivity and contains a set of interactive behaviors that you can attach to slices, hotspots, and buttons. You can attach multiple behaviors to a single slice, hotspot, or button to create eye-catching effects. Once you get more comfortable with the Behaviors panel, you can use it to create your own custom interactions by editing the existing behaviors.

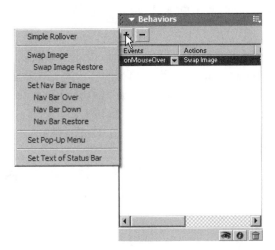

Figure 11.7   The Behaviors panel.

The second method is the *drag-and-drop rollover method*. This is the easiest way to apply interactivity to sliced objects in Fireworks. The drag-and-drop rollover method enables you to simply drag and drop a slice's behavior handle onto a target slice and then quickly set some simple interactivity.

Note

Because Fireworks MX and Dreamweaver MX behaviors are fully compatible, you can export the behavior-enabled hotspot or slice to Dreamweaver and then edit that behavior in the Dreamweaver Behaviors panel, which will be maintained within the round-trip environment.

Using the Behaviors Panel

The Behaviors panel makes assigning interactivity to slices and hotspots easy, allowing you to assign or modify an event, action, and/or target. (You can learn about working with hotspots in Chapter 10, "Image Maps.")

Assigning Interactivity with the Behaviors Panel

The behaviors that are contained within the Behaviors panel are grouped according to their associated action. For example, a simple rollover behavior consists of a Swap Image with a Swap Image Restore behavior and can be targeted only to the slice to which the behavior is applied:

- **Simple Rollover**—To add a Simple Rollover effect to a slice, use Simple Rollover, which is a behavior group comprised of Swap Image and Swap Image Restore. Define Frame 1 as the Up state and Frame 2 as the Over state. Using the selected slice (Web layer objects are shared across all frames), create an image in the second frame for the Up state. For more about this behavior, see the section "Creating a Simple Rollover."

- **Swap Image**—To replace one image with another, use Swap Image. The image under the specified target slice can be replaced with the contents of another frame under the same slice or the contents of an external file.

- **Swap Image Restore**—To restore a swap image to its default appearance in the relevant frame, use Swap Image Restore. This setting is a subbehavior in the Swap Image Behavior dialog box and enables you to specify different mouse events to the behavior instead of the standard OnMouseOver.

- **Set Nav Bar Image**—This behavior has subbehaviors to include Nav Bar Down, Nav Bar Over, and Nav Bar Restore options. These subbehaviors can be added individually to a Swap Image behavior, or selected from the Set Nav Bar Image behavior.

- **Set Pop-Up Menu**—To attach a pop-up menu to a slice, button, or hotspot, use Set Pop-Up Menu. When you use the Pop-Up Menu Editor, this behavior is automatically set. For more about this behavior, see the section "Adding Pop-Up Menus to Your Designs" later in this chapter.

- **Set Text of Status Bar**—To define text for display in the status bar at the bottom of most browser windows, use Set Text of Status Bar.

To create an image change in a different location than the trigger slice, use a Disjointed Rollover. Generally, this behavior uses a trigger slice or hotspot and a target slice that swaps when the user's mouse rolls over or clicks the trigger image or image map that you defined. For this method, you place the image that will appear when the behavior is triggered in a separate frame. For more information about this behavior, see the section "Creating Disjointed Rollovers" later in this chapter.

Attaching a Behavior to a Selected Slice or Hotspot Using the Behaviors Panel
To attach a behavior to a selected slice or hotspot, follow these steps (see Figure 11.8):

1. Click the Add Behavior (+) button within the Behaviors panel.
2. Select a behavior from the pop-up menu.

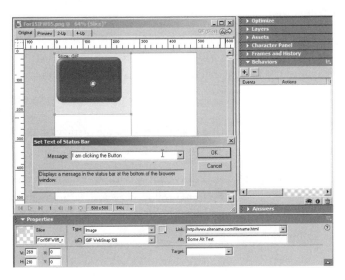

Figure 11.8 Attaching a simple behavior to a slice from the Behaviors panel.

Editing a Behavior

The Behaviors panel provides you with the ability to edit existing behaviors, or behaviors that you have just applied to a slice or hotspot. This means that you can specify the type of event (such as clicking) that triggers the behavior.

Note

You cannot change the event for Simple Rollover and Set Nav Bar Image behaviors. The subbehaviors associated with these are locked. To see all the behaviors associated with one of these, click the Options pop-up icon at the top right of the Behaviors panel and choose Show All from the menu that appears.

To edit a behavior, follow these steps:

1. Select the slice or hotspot that contains the behavior you want to modify. You can see the behaviors associated with that web object displayed in the Behaviors panel.

2. Select the behavior that you want to edit, and click the arrow between the event and action to choose a different event to trigger the action.

Note

By selecting Show All from the Behavior panel's Options pop-up menu, you can view all the events associated with the slice (for example, a Simple Rollover behavior consists of Swap Image and Swamp Image Restore behaviors).

Samples of Behaviors

Let's get started applying behaviors to slices. The most common use of behaviors on the web involves swapping one image with another. When an image swap is caused by the user's mouse passing over the trigger object, the behavior is called a *rollover*.

Rollovers

Rollovers all work the same way. One graphic triggers the display of another when the pointer rolls over it. The trigger is always a web object—a slice, hotspot, or button.

The simplest rollover swaps an image in Frame 1 with an image directly below it (in Frame 2). You can build more complicated rollovers as well. Swap Image behaviors can swap an image from any frame; disjoint rollovers display an image in a slice other than the trigger slice or hotspot.

In Fireworks, when you select a slice, hotspot, or button, any rollover or swap image behaviors attached to that object are indicated by blue behavior lines that extend from the slice's behavior handle to the top-left corner of one or more slices in the document.

Creating a Simple Rollover

A simple rollover swaps an image with another image on a frame under the same slice. A simple rollover involves only one slice, and possibly a hotspot but usually just a slice, as both trigger and target (when using hotspots, the hotspot is the trigger, and the entire slice that contains the hotspot is the target).

The Simple Rollover behavior is used when you want to quickly swap an object under a slice in Frame 2 out for another object under the same slice in Frame 1.

To create a simple rollover, follow these steps:

1. Open the file named `simple_rollover_example.png` from the `behaviors_01` folder.

   The file contains two frames with objects that are shared across both frames within a shared layer. This helps reduce confusion and clutter within the workspace.

2. Select the slice and choose Window, Behaviors to open the Behaviors panel.

3. Select Simple Rollover from the Add Behavior (+) pop-up menu. The Behaviors panel displays a mouse event and an action. Click the Hide Slices and Hotspots button on the Tools panel to hide the objects on the Web layer.

4. Click the Preview tab on the Document window and move your mouse over the icon and the simple rollover is triggered.

Creating Disjointed Rollovers

A disjointed rollover uses a slice, hotspot, or button as a trigger and another slice as a target to swap the image in the target slice when the user's mouse rolls over the web object. The web object that's rolled over is considered the trigger; the slice that receives the action is considered as the target.

As with simple rollovers that use just one slice, you first must set up the trigger and target web objects and the frame in which the swap image resides. Then, you can link the trigger to the target slice by either adding the behavior, as you did the simple rollover, or by dragging the behavior handle from the trigger slice to the target slice (see Figure 11.9). Again, The trigger can be a slice, hotspot, or button.

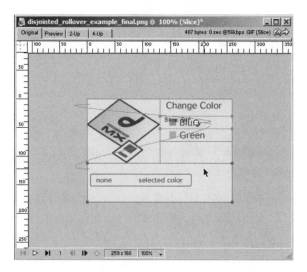

Figure 11.9   Trigger objects and targets.

To create a disjointed rollover, follow these steps:

Note

Alternatively, you can open `disjointed_rollover_example_final.png` and click the Preview tab at the top of the Document window to view the final results.

1. Open `disjointed_rollover_example.png` from the `behaviors_01` folder.

   Notice that all the relevant graphics have been placed within the appropriate frames, ready to apply the behaviors. Study the location of the graphics within the frames and understand how these fit into the creation of the disjointed rollover.

2. Select the Blue_Trigger slice from the Web layer or the active canvas. Drag the behavior handle from the this slice to the upper-left edge of the Icon slice and select Frame 3 as the source of where to swap the image from (see Figure 11.10).

   This creates a disjointed rollover, changing the Big Doc object in Frame 1 to a blue version that is present on Frame 3.

3. Select the Green_Trigger slice from the Web layer or the active canvas. Drag the behavior handle from this slice to the upper-left edge of the Icon slice and select Frame 4 as the source of where to swap the image from.

4. Save this file to a working directory of your choice.

This creates a disjointed rollover for the Green_Trigger slice swapping the Big Doc object on Frame 1 for a green version that's present on Frame 4.

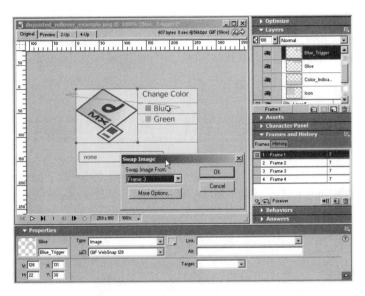

Figure 11.10   Applying disjointed rollovers to multiple slices.

> **Note**
>
> If you accidentally add a behavior, remove it by clicking the blue behavior line for the behavior that you want to remove. A window appears and asks, "Do you want to delete this <behavior type> behavior?" Click OK.

Summarizing steps 1-3, you can see that you have created two disjointed rollovers: rolling over the blue slice in preview mode changes the background to blue, and the green slice changes the background to green. What is easy to do is to apply multiple disjointed rollovers to multiple slices to achieve a satisfying effect.

Applying Multiple Disjointed Rollovers to a Slice

Fireworks MX enables you to drag more than one behavior handle from a single slice to create multiple rollover interactions, or add multiple behaviors from the Behaviors panel. By using this method, you can trigger many disjoint rollovers from the same web object.

To apply more than one rollover to a selected slice, follow these steps:

1. Open the file that you saved from the previous steps, where you created a disjointed rollover.

2. Select the Blue_Trigger slice from the Web layer, and drag a behavior handle to the top left of the Color_Selector slice, selecting Frame 3. Repeat the process for the Green_Trigger slice, but select Frame 4 as the source of where to swap the image from.

3. Select the Preview tab from the top of the Document window to view the results (see Figure 11.11).

You can now see that each slice contains two disjointed rollovers, and moving your mouse over the blue text changes both the selected color box at the bottom of the canvas to blue, and the background of the icon to blue, with the same behavior set occurring for the green text.

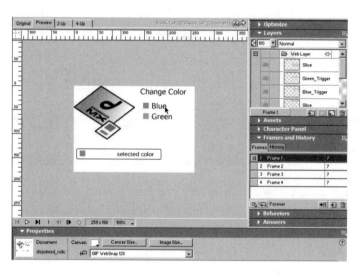

Figure 11.11   Applying multiple disjointed rollovers to multiple slices.

Using External Image Files for Rollover States

You can use an image outside of the current Fireworks document as the source image for a rollover state. You can use GIFs, animated GIFs, JPEGs, or PNGs. When you choose an external file as the image source, that file is swapped with the image under the target slice when the rollover is triggered in a web browser. To preserve image quality, make sure that the external image has the same dimensions as the target slice.

To choose an external image file as the source for a rollover state, follow these steps:

1. While in the Swap Image, Nav Bar Over, or Nav Bar Down dialog box, choose Image File, and click the Folder icon. If you don't see this option in the Swap Image dialog box, choose More Options and perform this step again.

2. Locate the desired file and click Open.

3. If the external file is an animated GIF, deselect Preload Images, because pre-caching can interrupt the display of animated GIFs as rollover states.

Understanding Fireworks Buttons

Many sites today, in addition to a liberal sprinkling of graphics in the banner and in the body, have graphic navigation systems. Navigation systems have become more elaborate as sites have evolved from six-page brochure-like entities to full-fledged multimedia sites with multiple web applications.

Coinciding with the shift in online content is a shift in the metaphor used for designing web graphics. Less and less do we see ourselves designing *pages*; instead, we now find ourselves designing *interfaces*. The shift is an important one because new concepts, such as usability and accessibility, come into play.

Designers and developers must find ways to create graphics that support the goals of the project as a whole. Although it is beyond the scope of this book to delve into usability and accessibility, the following tips can help you use graphics effectively in your web pages (or interfaces):

- When you create buttons or other interface components, they need to be proportional in importance to the function that they are required to carry out.

- Don't confuse the end user by including too many buttons.

- If you use navigation elements and/or buttons frequently (such as Print or Logout buttons), the user expects to find them in the same place on each screen. Don't confuse the user by moving these items to different places on each screen.

- Icons are not just a picture that you create because they look more interesting than text. They are a special class of buttons that representatively depict their purpose. If they do not communicate that purpose intuitively to all users, they fail to have a purpose.

- Keep icons simple. It's easy to get carried away developing beautiful and complex icons, but meaningfulness counts more than appearances.

A button is basically a rollover that has been made into a symbol for repeated use. Using Fireworks buttons and the Button editor, you can assign two, three, or four states to your button that can aid the visual impact of your creations.

Additionally, using the Button editor, you can create and customize buttons by drawing shapes, importing graphic images, or dragging objects from the Document window. The Button editor then guides you through the process for setting up and controlling the button's behavior.

Creating Button Symbols

Buttons are navigation elements for a web page. Buttons created in the Button editor have the following characteristics:

- You can make almost any graphic or text object into a button.

- You can create a button from scratch, convert an existing object into a button, or import already created buttons.

- A button is a special type of symbol. You can drag instances of it from the Library panel into your document.

- You can edit the text, URL, and target for one button instance without affecting other instances of the same button, and without breaking the symbol-instance relationship.

- A button instance is encapsulated. Dragging the button instance in the document moves all the components and states associated with it, so there's no need for complicated multiframe editing.

- A button is easy to edit. Double-click the instance on the canvas, and you can change its attributes in the Button editor or the Property Inspector.

Note

Like other symbols, buttons have a registration point. The *registration point* is a center point that helps you align text and the different button states while in the Button editor.

Inserting Buttons from the Library

To minimize the number of steps necessary to create multiple rollover buttons, create button symbols. After you create a button symbol, you can drag instances of the symbol from the library to the canvas. You can then modify the text for the other instances without affecting the original symbol's integrity.

To insert buttons from the library, follow these steps:

1. In the Library panel, select your button and drag the button instance onto the canvas.

2. Drag two more instances of the button and place them next to each other on the canvas. With the second instance selected, within the Property Inspector, change the button text by double-clicking the Text field and typing some new text to replace the current button text.

3. Repeat step 2 with the last button, until all edits are in place.

4. You can view the final effect by using the Preview tab to view your rollover buttons. After you finish, return to the Original tab to make any alterations that you might need (see Figure 11.12).

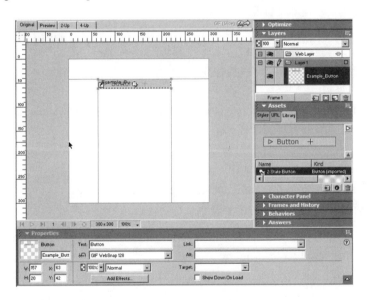

Figure 11.12   Inserting buttons from the Library panel.

Using the Button Editor

The Button editor is where you set up the actions for the button that will be exported as JavaScript and HTML. The tabs along the top of the Button editor correspond to the four button states and the active area. The tips on each option in the Button editor help you make design decisions for all four-button states. Notice that, when the Button editor is open, the Web layer in the Layers panel shows that a slice is present. If you look at the Frames panel, you can see that four frames are in the button, and each frame corresponds to a button state: Up, Over, Down, and Over While Down, respectively (see Figure 11.13).

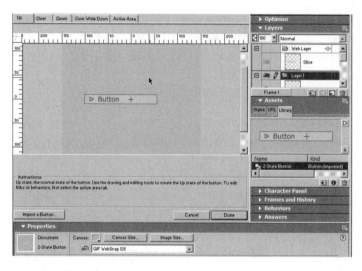

Figure 11.13   The Button editor interface within Fireworks MX, with a sample button from the standard library.

About Button States

A button can have up to four different states. Each state represents the button's appearance in response to a mouse event:

- **Up state**—The default or at-rest appearance of the button. This is what you see when the page first loads in the browser.

- **Over state**—The way the button appears when the pointer is moved over it. This state alerts the user that clicking the mouse is likely to result in an action.

- **Down state**—Often is a depressed image of the button that represents the button after it is clicked. This button state typically represents the current web page on multibutton navigation bars.

- **Over While Down state**—The appearance when the user moves the pointer over a button that is already in the Down state. This button state typically shows that the pointer is over the button for the current web page on multibutton navigation bars.

With the Button editor, you can create all these different button states.

Creating a Two-State Button

To create a button that has a Simple Rollover behavior, you must create a button with two states—an Up state and an Over state.

Here's the method for creating an Up state for a button:

1. Create a new document (by choosing File, New) and select a width of 400, a height of 400, and a resolution of 72.

2. Choose Edit, Insert, New Button. The Button editor opens to the Up State tab.

Note

To use an image already created for your Up state, drag and drop, copy and paste, or import the image into the canvas of the Button editor.

3. To create an image for your Up state, use the drawing tools to create a graphic or copy from your active documents resources (canvas or library).

Here's the method for creating an Over state for a button:

1. With the Button editor open, click the Over tab.

2. To edit the Over state button, click the Copy Up Graphic button. This places a copy of the Up state into the Over state of the Button editor. Make changes to the objects that appear in the Over tab.

3. To use another image, drag and drop, copy and paste, import, or draw a graphic into the Over State window.

4. Click Done to insert the button that you created onto your active canvas. Select the Preview tab from the top of the Document window to preview your button (see Figure 11.14).

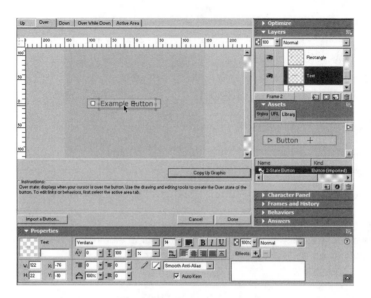

Figure 11.14   Creating a two-state button in Fireworks MX.

Creating a Three- or Four-State Button

In addition to Up and Over states, buttons can have Down and Over While Down states. While three- and four state buttons are not necessary for creating a navigational bar, using them allows you to take advantage of the built-in Nav Bar behaviors in Fireworks. Try opening some of the example three and four button state buttons from the Button Library (Edit > Libraries > Buttons).

To create a Down state, follow these steps:

1. With a two-state button open in the Button editor, click the Down tab.

2. Click the Copy Over Graphic button to place a copy of the Over state button into the Down window, and edit it to change its appearance.

3. Drag and drop, copy and paste, import, or draw a graphic and edit the graphic to your liking. Make sure that the Include Nav Bar Down State check box is checked. (It's located at the top left of the Button Editor window.) See Figure 11.15.

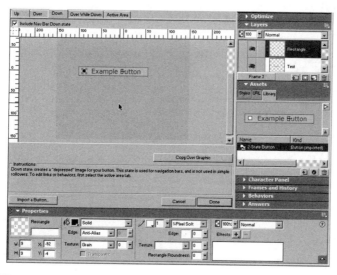

Figure 11.15 Creating the Down state for a four-state button.

To create an Over While Down state, follow these steps:

1. With a three-state button open in the Button editor, click the Over While Down tab.

2. Click the Copy Down Graphic button to place a copy of the Down state graphic into the Over While Down window of the Button editor, and edit it to change its appearance. Making sure that the Include Nav Bar Over While Down state is checked (see Figure 11.16).

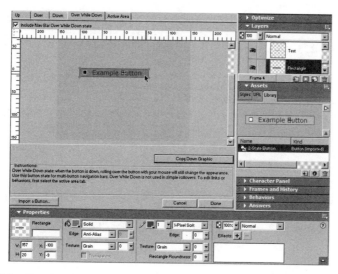

Figure 11.16 Creating the Over While Down state for a four-state button.

Modifying the Active Area of a Button Symbol

The active area of a button symbol is an embedded slice that triggers interactivity when a user moves the pointer over it or clicks it within a web browser. The active area of a button is a symbol-level property and is unique to button symbols.

When a button symbol is created, Fireworks automatically creates a slice that's large enough to enclose all the states of a button. You can edit a button slice only in the Active Area tab of the Button editor and each button can only have one slice. If you draw a slice using a Slice tool in the active area, the previous slice is replaced by the newly drawn slice.

Note

You can draw hotspot objects in the Active Area tab within the Button editor, but you can only edit those hotspots from within the Button editor, not from within the root of the main canvas.

To edit a slice or hotspot in a button symbol's active area, follow these steps:

1. Double-click a button instance on the canvas or double-click the button preview symbol in the Library panel to open the button, and click the Active Area tab.

2. Using the Pointer tool or any of the Slice or Hotspot tools, move, reshape the slice, move a slice guide, or draw a new active area (see Figure 11.17).

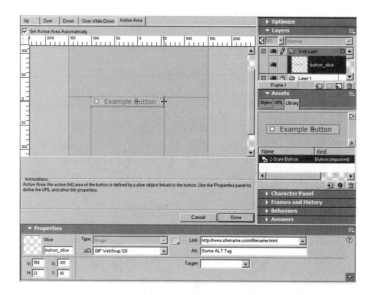

Figure 11.17   Editing a button's active area from within the Button editor.

Creating Navigation Bars

A navigation bar is a group of buttons that provides a navigation mechanism to different areas of your web site. It generally remains consistent throughout the site, providing a constant method of navigation, no matter where the user is within the site. The nav bar looks the same from web page to web page but, in some cases, the links might be specific to the function of each page.

In Fireworks, you make a nav bar by creating a button symbol in the Button editor and then placing instances of that symbol on the canvas.

To create a basic nav bar, follow these steps:

1. Create a button symbol.

2. Drag an instance of the symbol from the Library panel to the workspace.

3. Do one of the following to make a copy of the button instance within your workspace:

    - Select the button instance and choose Edit, Clone.
    - Click and then Alt-drag (for Windows) or Option-drag (for a Macintosh) the button instance on the active canvas to a new location.

4. Hold the Shift key as you press an arrow key repeatedly to position the cloned button, which moves your selection in 10-pixel increments. For more precise control, use the arrow keys without holding the Shift key to move 1 pixel at a time. If you used the Alt-drag or Option-drag method to create your second button, and if the second button is exactly where you want it to be, press Ctrl-Y (for Windows) or Command-Y (for a Macintosh) to repeat the duplication process and create a series of equally spaced buttons.

5. Repeat steps 3 and 4 to create additional button instances.

6. Select each instance and assign it unique text, a URL, and other properties by using the Property Inspector (see Figure 11.18).

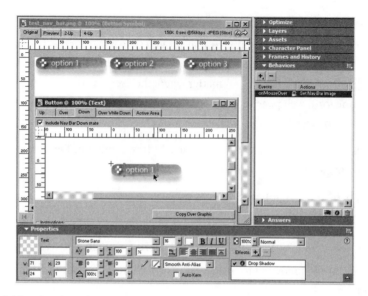

Figure 11.18   Creating a basic nav bar in Fireworks MX.

Adding Pop-Up Menus to Your Designs

The next area of behaviors that we will dive into are the powerful and configurable pop-up menus. The ability to build pop-up menus in Fireworks showed up in the last version of Fireworks—Fireworks 4. Now, with MX, creating pop-up menus has become even better. Fireworks MX pop-up menu enhancements include greater control when creating pop-up menus, and are native within Fireworks MX and Dreamweaver MX. Using a new set of advanced controls, you can now create both horizontal and vertical pop-up menus. The improved code means that now these DHTML menus can dynamically relocate themselves when the trigger is relatively positioned within the document.

Creating and Editing Pop-Up Menus

Pop-up menus appear when the user's cursor is placed over a trigger image that resides on a web page. When the mouse moves over the desired menu item, a list of items that link to other pages or submenu items, which is common in PC and Mac software applications, are displayed.

Designing pop-up menus using Fireworks MX is a multistage process. You create pop-up menus by using the Pop-Up Menu editor, which is accessible after you create a slice or hotspot. The first step is to input your data or list items. Then, you customize the appearance and general settings of the pop-up menu by using the Appearance tab of the

Pop-Up Menu editor. To set advanced characteristics for your pop-up menus, use the Advanced tab in the Pop-Up Menu editor for editing cell width and border width. Finally, the Position tab within the Pop-Up Menu editor enables you to position parent menus and child menu elements precisely by setting their X and Y coordinates. Let's create a simple pop-up menu together:

1. Start by opening the file pop-up_menu.png from the Exercises/11 folder on the CD-ROM. This forms the basis for a download interface.

2. Three slices are arranged horizontally at the top of the document for new, recent, and archived downloads with appropriately named slices. Using the Pointer tool, click to select the "new" slice.

3. Select Add pop-Up Menu by clicking the behavior handle of the "new" slice (see Figure 11.19).

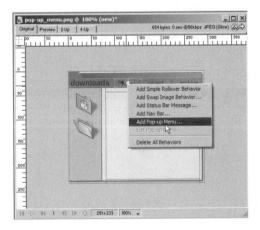

Figure 11.19   Assigning the Pop-Up Menu behavior to slices in Fireworks MX.

4. The Content tab of the Pop-Up Menu editor is ready for your content to be entered. Begin by adding the top level (parent) values for the pop-up menu by clicking the Add Menu button to add entries. Type **IT** in the first menu item to start a new line and tab across to create a new entry, adding **Corporate**, **HR**, and **R&D** for subsequent rows.

Note

If you type something incorrectly and want to delete a menu item, select it and click the Delete Menu Item button from within the Content tab of the Pop-Up Menu editor.

Note

You can navigate between one cell and another by pressing the Tab key to move between the cells. You can also use the up and down arrow keys to scroll through the list vertically.

The text item specifies the text for your menu item. The link item enables you to set your menu item's URL. You can type a link right in the field, or you can select one from the link pop-up menu, if any are available. URLs that have been entered in the document or URL panel's currently selected URL library will be the ones listed in the link pop-up menu. The target item enables you to set a target for frames navigation or to open a new browser window. You can type in the Target field to enter a custom target, or you can select a preset from the Target pop-up menu (see Figure 11.20).

Figure 11.20   Creating the drop-down values for the pop-up menu.

5. Select the Appearance tab to start the process of styling the pop-up menu within the editor and apply the following settings (see Figure 11.21):
    - **Menu Type**—Vertical Menu
    - **Cells**—HTML
    - **Font**—Verdana, Arial, Helvetica, sans-serif
    - **Size**—10

- **Up State**
- **Text**—White
- **Cell**—#666666
- **Over State**
- **Text**—White
- **Cell**—#ff6600

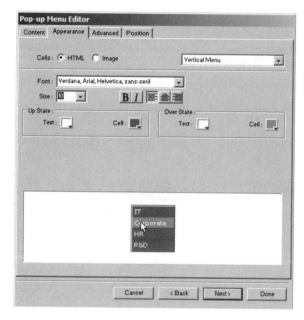

Figure 11.21   Assigning HTML options to the pop-up menu.

Note

While we use HTML tables and cells here for the menu display, experiment with the Image types of pop-up menus. Create and assign new styles from the Styles panel to your pop-up menus.

Warning

Be aware that, when using Image instead of HTML for pop-up menu creation, although you have more freedom in creating and assigning styles to your pop-up menus, download times increase as a result.

6. Click to the Advanced panel to configure additional options for the menu's table properties and table cells. Set the cell width to 187 pixels by clicking the down arrow, selecting Pixels, and typing the value:

- **Cell Height**—Automatic

- **Cell Padding**—3

- **Cell Spacing**—0

- **Text Indent and Delay**—Default

- **Pop-Up Borders**—Checked

- **Set Border Width to 0**

- **Set Border Color to #666666 (gray)**

- **Set both Shadow and Highlight to #ffffff (white)**

7. Click Done to apply the Pop-Up Menu behavior to the slice and return to your workspace.

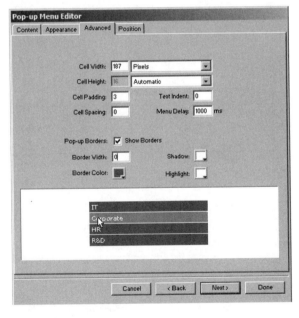

Figure 11.22   Assigning advanced options to the pop-up menu in the Pop-Up Menu editor.

Note

To edit the settings that you just created for the pop-up menu, select the "new" slice again and click the behavior handle. Choose Edit, Pop-Up Menu from the contextual menu that appears. The Pop-Up Menu editor reopens.

You can use one more tab to affect the appearance of pop-up menus—the Position tab. The Position tab enables you to set your parent menu X and Y coordinates and enables you to set child menu positions in X and Y coordinates. The Place in Same Position check box sets all submenus for the menu that you are editing to appear in the same location that's relative to the initial menu item rather than relative to the menu item associated with the submenu item:

1. Select the "new" slice again and click the behavior handle. Choose Edit, Pop-Up Menu from the contextual menu that appears (see Figure 11.23) and select the Position tab. Enter a value of 19 for Y offset and click Done.

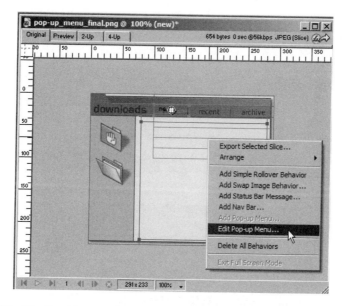

Figure 11.23   The Pop-Up Menu behavior is attached to a slice.

2. Repeat steps 3–7 for the "recent" and "archive" slices to complete the pop-up menus for the interface.

After we cover a few more items, we will be finished with creating pop-up menus. The Indent Menu and Outdent Menu buttons on the Content tab of the Pop-Up Menu editor enable you to create submenus for your pop-up menus. Submenus appear when your pointer moves over or clicks one of the pop-up menu parent items. You can create as many levels of submenus as your design can effectively hold using Fireworks MX.

To create a pop-up submenu, follow these steps:

1. In the Content tab of the Pop-Up Menu editor, create both menu and submenu items, placing the submenu directly beneath the appropriate parent item on the Pop-Up Menu item list. Click to highlight a pop-up menu item that you want to make a submenu item.

2. To set an item as the submenu object of the menu item that's directly above it (parent menu), click the Indent Menu button.

3. To add the next item to the submenu, highlight it and click the Indent Menu button. All items that are indented at the same level become a submenu (or child menu). Click Next to move to the Appearance tab or choose another tab to continue building the pop-up menu. Click Done to close the Pop-Up Menu editor.

Note

You can continue indenting to create submenus within submenus for as many levels as your design can comfortably hold without looking cluttered.

4. To promote a menu item within the parent-child hierarchy, simply highlight the menu item in the Content tab of the Pop-Up Menu editor and click the Outdent Menu button (see Figure 11.24).

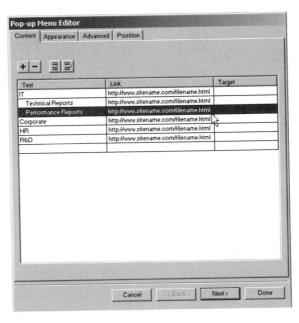

Figure 11.24   Creating child menus within the Pop-Up Menu editor.

Editing Your Fireworks Pop-Up Menus

The Pop-Up Menu Editor enables you to edit or update the content of a pop-up menu, rearrange the menu items, or change other properties on any of the four tabs at any time.

To edit a pop-up menu in the Pop-Up Menu editor, follow these steps:

1. Either click the Show Slices and Hotspots button in the Tools panel or click the Show/Hide Layer column by the Web layer in the Layers panel.

2. Select the slice onto which the pop-up menu is to be attached.

3. Double-click the pop-up menu's blue outline in the workspace. The Pop-Up Menu editor opens with the pop-up menu entries displayed.

4. Make your desired changes on all four tabs; click Done.

To move an entry in the pop-up menu, follow these steps:

1. Double-click the desired pop-up menu and click the Contents tab.

2. Drag the menu item to the desired placement in the list.

Note

Dragging an indented item to the top of the list outdents it to the top level.

3. Click Done.

Adding Pop-Up Menu Styles

Cell styles add graphic treatment to pop-up menus. These features are added by using the Pop-Up Menu editor. Custom cell styles are available along with the preset choices on the Appearance tab when you choose the Image option as the cell type.

To add a custom cell style to the cell style choices on the Pop-Up Menu editor's Appearance tab, follow these steps:

1. Using the Styles panel, apply any combination of stroke, fill, texture, and live effects to an object and save it as a style.

2. Select the new style in the Styles panel and choose Export Style from the Styles panel's Options menu.

3. Navigate to the Nav Menu folder, enter a filename, and click Save. When you return to the Appearance tab of the Pop-Up Menu editor and choose the Image Cell Background option, the new style is available, along with the preset styles for the Up and Over states of the pop-up menu cells.

The `Nav Menu` folder location depends on your operating system (OS). On Windows 98, it's inside the `Configuration` folder under the `Fireworks MX` folder.

In Windows NT, 2000, and XP, it's in the `C:\Documents and Settings\ <username>\Application Data\Macromedia\Fireworks MX\Nav Menu`.

On Mac OS 9.x, it's in `Macintosh HD:System Folder:Application Support:Macromedia:Fireworks MX:Nav Menu`.

On Mac OS X, it's at `Macintosh HD:Users:<Username>:Library:Application Support:Macromedia:Fireworks MX:Nav Menu`.

Summary

The ability to assign behaviors to the images that you create in Fireworks enables you to create full web sites rather than images alone. On export (see Chapter 14), you generate all the HTML, JavaScript, and compressed images you need for a fully functional web page. At this point, all you need to do is upload and you're done. If you want, the tight round-trip integration between Fireworks MX and Dreamweaver MX allows for easy refinement and maintenance of your generated code. This makes Fireworks MX the ideal tool for both web site design and production.

Chapter 12

Animation

The animation that you create in Fireworks is GIF animation. *GIF animation* is similar to flip-book animation. In a flipbook, art is created and placed in slightly different positions on successive pages of a book. When the pages of the book are turned quickly, the artwork appears to move.

GIF Animation Pros and Cons

Before we get into building GIF animations, let's take a quick look at some of the advantanges and disadvantages of working with them.

Let's start with the advantages of animated GIFs:

- The GIF file format supports transparency.

- You can control the number of colors in the palette (2, 4, 8, 16, 32, 64, 128, and 256) for optimum size and compression.

- GIFs are supported by nearly every browser, even older versions, such as Netscape 2.0. No plug-ins are required.

- There's no need to access your provider's web server, Server-Side Includes (SSI), or CGI/Perl scripting. The animation is done at the client level.

- Animations can be looped and reused.

- Animations download once for all and loops occurrences of the animation. This makes it much faster than server-reliant methods.

- Animated GIFs work like any other GIF. They're included on your page in an IMG tag.

- Animations that you find on the web can be saved to your hard drive and dismantled in Fireworks (for learning purposes).

Unfortunately, animated GIFs also have some disadvantages:

- GIF animations have the same limitations as static GIFs. You are limited to a maximum of 256 colors.

- Animations can be slowed down or interrupted by other images being downloaded and other animations playing.

- Animated GIFs can be "borrowed" from your site as easily as any other GIF.

- Creating and controlling animation in Fireworks requires the use of both the Layers and the Frames panels.

- You create your artwork in layers and then use the Frames panel to create animation frames. The Frames panel lets you specify animation options including frame delay and looping.

- To preview your animation, you use the frame controls that are located at the bottom of the Document window.

Building an Animated GIF

You can take three basic approaches to create and assemble animations in Fireworks. You can mix and match, overlap, and combine these techniques to create a your animations:

- *Graphic symbols* are special objects created in Fireworks that can be copied throughout a document as updateable instances and controlled by the parent symbol. When the original symbol is altered, the instances are updated automatically. When you use graphic symbols, frames can be generated by "tweening" between two instances.

- *Animation symbols are the third method.* These are, in a sense, advanced graphic symbols. They allow you create animation by assigning properties such as frames, movement, direction, scale, opacity, and rotation to objects.

- *The frame-by-frame approach* is where you build and design an animation in what I call the "by-hand" method. In this method, you draw, paint, or compose the artwork to be animated on each frame.

Previewing an Animation in Fireworks

Fireworks offers extensive controls for previewing the animations that you build. You don't have to exit the program to see the results of your work. The preview uses the Document window. You can either preview the original artwork or use the Preview tab.

To preview animations within the Document window, use the controls located at the lower part of the Document window. Previewing the animation in the original Document window displays the full-resolution source graphic, not the optimized 8-bit preview that's used for the exported animated GIF. To view the animation with the preview activated, make sure that the Optimize panel is set to Animated GIF.

While you work on an animation, you can preview it to view and test it. Use the frame controls located at the bottom of the Document window to preview an animation in the workspace (see Figure 12.1).

Figure 12.1   The frame controls for previewing a GIF animation are located at the bottom left of the Document window.

Frame and Previous Frame move the animation back and forth one frame at a time. First Frame or Last Frame jump to the beginning or the end of your animation. Play plays the animation. Stop stops the animation.

You can also preview an animation with the onscreen Preview panel after applying optimization settings to see how the exported Animated GIF will look when it's finished (see Figure 12.2).

Figure 12.2   Previewing the animation using the Preview tab in the Document window. The Optimize panel is set to Animated GIF.

Upon exporting, you can set the optimization and the frame properties by selecting File, Export Preview, selecting the Animated GIF format, and clicking the Animation tab (see Figure 12.3).

Figure 12.3 Previewing the animation using the Export Preview dialog box.

Previewing an Animation in a Web Browser

To preview an animation in a web browser, choose File, Preview in Browser, and select a browser from the Preview in Browser pop-up menu.

Note

Previewing animations in 2-Up or 4-Up view is not recommended, especially on machines with limited RAM.

Examining Frame-by-Frame Animation

This hands-on method of creating animation can be painstaking, but when carefully designed, colored, and optimized, it yields surprising results. You might use this method to build an animation that needed effects that Fireworks doesn't offer, or if you want complete control over the progress of the animation.

Exercise 12.1 Completing a Hands-On Animation

The Flying Saucer animation included in the Exercises/12 folder on the CD-ROM shows an example of a hands-on animation. Each individual object is carefully tweaked to create the illusion of flying. You deconstruct it here in these steps:

1. Open the flying_saucer_art.png file from the Exercises/12 folder on the accompanying CD-ROM.

2. Display the Layers panel and the Frames panel if they aren't showing (choose Window, Layers and Window, Frames).

   Notice that it contains the Web layer plus two other layers. One is named Lights and the other is named Ship Parts. Also notice that it contains one frame.

3. Open the `flying_saucer_ani.png` file from the `Exercises/12` folder and click the Play/Stop button in the Document window to watch the animation.

4. Watch the animation for a few moments. Click the Play/Stop button to stop the animation from playing.

5. Click Frame 1 to select it (see Figure 12.4).

Figure 12.4   Note the differences of each frame.

6. With the Layers and Frames panels side by side, click through the five frames of the animation and compare the changes in the Ship Parts and Lights layers.

Notice that the shape and position of the green and purple lights shift as you click through the frames one by one. The red and purple paths alternate their color, length, and position. At the same time, the objects in the Ship layer also change from frame to frame. Both the Dome and Hood gradient fills have been repositioned manually so that they appear to rotate clockwise.

Because I was aware that I wanted the animation to compress well, I chose my colors from the web-safe color palette. I also tweaked the gradients carefully so that they contain the fewest colors possible and actually look okay if they are not dithered. Although dithering sometimes improves the look of colors, it tends to add to the file size and download time.

7. Open the Optimize panel if it's not already showing (choose Window, Optimize or click the Optimize button in the mini-launcher).

8. Click the Preview tab to see the settings that I assigned in the Optimize panel applied to the artwork (see Figure 12.5).

Figure 12.5   The settings of the Optimize panel for the Flying Saucer animation.

Creating Frame-by-Frame Animation

In general, the steps required to create a frame-by-frame animation are as follows:

1. Create the artwork for your animation in one frame.

2. Add a new frame or duplicate the existing frame by using the Frames panel pop-up menu.

3. Create or alter the artwork on the new frame.

4. Continue to do this until the animation is complete.

Distribute to Frames

A variation of frame-by-frame animation is to use the Distribute to Frames option.

Create your artwork in a single frame, understanding that the order in which you create your objects is the order in which they appear in the Layers panel and the order in which their frames are created. (It's a good idea to group objects where their design renders them intricate or complex, like in the case of the flying saucer.)

After you create all your objects to be animated, choose Edit, Select All and choose Distribute to Frames from the Frames panel. You can also use the Distribute to Frames icon, which is located at the bottom of the Frames panel (see Figure 12.6).

Figure 12.6   The Frames panel pop-up menu and the Distribute to Frames button on the Frames panel.

Your new frames appear with each of the objects in its own frame. The number of artwork objects or groups will determine the number of frames in your animation.

Creating Animation Using Distribute to Frames

I've used the flying_saucer_art.png file as the basis for creating five grouped objects that will illustrate the Distribute to Frames operation.

Exercise 12.2   Working with Distribute to Frames

1. Open the flying_saucer_2dist.png file from the Exercises/12 folder on the CD-ROM.

   You can see that the file contains one frame with one layer in it. The layer is named Saucers and the layer contains five groups of objects or five objects that are made up of various parts that have been grouped.

2. Select all the objects in the Saucer layer (choose Edit, Select All).Open the Frames panel pop-up menu by clicking in the upper-right hand corner of the panel. Select Distribute to Frames.

3. Click the Play button to see the flying saucer animate up the screen as it spins. If you want, save your file as `flying_saucer_ani2a` (choose File, Save As).

Finessing the Frames or Frame Controls

Because animation relies on a principle called *persistence of vision*, working with frames can require some adjusting and tweaking to create the optimal visual experience. This is done by setting the frame delay and by adding and subtracting frames.

The frame delay setting allows you to determine how long each frame is displayed. The setting is specified in hundredths of seconds:

- A setting of 100/100 a second displays the frame for 1 full second.
- A setting of 50 displays the frame for half a second.
- A setting of 10 displays the frame at 1/10 a second.
- A setting of 200 displays the frame for 2 full seconds.

To access the Frame Properties box, select Properties from the Frames panel pop-up menu. You can also double-click in the Frame Delay column of the Frames panel (see Figure 12.7).

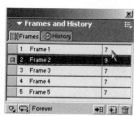 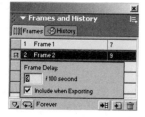

Figure 12.7 The Frames panel pop-up menu shows the Properties choice, the Frame Delay column on the Frames panel, and the Frame Delay text field.

To change the default Frame Delay of 7/100 seconds, enter a number in the Frame Delay text field. The greater the number, the longer the frame is visible. Press Return to apply the changes and close the Frame Properties box.

Alternatively, you can set the frame timing in the Export Preview panel. Choose File, Export Preview, and click the Animation tab to display the frame list (see Figure 12.8). Click a frame to select it, then enter a number in the Frame Delay text box at the top of the panel. Notice that the bottom of the Animation area displays the animation's total runtime.

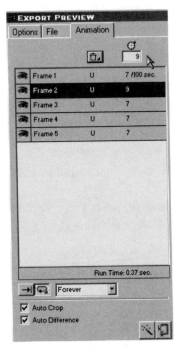

Figure 12.8   The Animation tab in the Export Preview panel. You can change the frame delay by selecting a frame and entering a new number in the Frame Delay box, identified by a small clock.

You can set the frame delay of one or more frames at a time. To select a continuous range of frames, Shift-click the first and the last frames, and all the frames in between are also selected.

To select a noncontinuous range of frames, hold the Ctrl key (for Windows) or the Command key (for a Macintosh) and click each of the frame's name.

Working with Frames

Each document contains a minimum of one frame. You can add more frames to your document in a few different ways. Each frame of the document becomes an image of the animation.

To add a new blank or empty frame, click the New/Duplicate icon in the Frames panel. A new frame appears. This type of frame is a blank frame and doesn't contain any artwork.

To add more than one frame at a time, follow these steps:

1. Select Add Frames from the Frames panel. The Add Frames dialog box appears (see Figure 12.9).

2. Set the number of frames by typing in the field or clicking and dragging the Number slider.

3. Place the new frame(s) in a specific place within the animation stack by clicking one of the four radio buttons that specify the beginning, before, after, and end.

4. Click OK. The new frames now reside in the Frames panel.

Figure 12.9
The Add/Duplicate Frames dialog box, which can be accessed by choosing Add Frames or Duplicate Frames from the Frames panel pop-up menu.

Duplicating Frames

You can make duplicate frames by opening the Frames panel pop-up menu and selecting Duplicate Frames. This is especially helpful when you create frame-by-frame animation:

1. Click to select the frame(s) you want to duplicate.

2. Drag the frames onto the New/Duplicate Frame button. Or you can select the frame for duplication and select Duplicate Frame from the Frames panel pop-up menu. The Duplicate Frame dialog box appears (see Figure 12.9), allowing you to specify where the new frame(s) will be inserted.

Deleting Frames

Sometimes, you need to throw away a frame. To delete frames, simply follow these steps:

1. Click the frame that you want to delete.

2. You can hold the Shift key to click additional frames or the Ctrl key (for Windows), Command key (for a Mac), and click individual frames.

3. Click the Delete icon, which is the trash can, in the Frames panel, or select Delete Frame from the Frames Panel menu.

Naming Frames

Frames are created with the Fireworks default names for frames: Frame 1, Frame 2, and so on. In keeping with good work habits, you might want to name your frames similar to naming layers.

To rename a frame, follow these steps:

1. Double-click to select the name of the frame.

2. Type the new name of your frame in the text field.

3. Press Return or Enter to set the new name.

When using default names for frames, which are based on numbers, frame names will reorder if the position of frames is altered. However, when using custom names, frame names do not change if, and when, you change the order of your frames within your animation.

Changing the Stacking Order of the Frames

To change the stacking order of frames, follow these steps:

1. Click the frame and drag it to a new position within the stack.

2. Release the mouse and the frame appears in the new position.

Working with Onion Skinning

Onion skinning is the name for a technique that comes from the days of film animation. Vellum sheets were stacked to create the hand-drawn frames of the animation in reference to the entire piece.

The onion skinning feature allows you to look at multiple frames at the same time, switch between frames, and make edits to the selected frame while the other frames currently displayed are viewed at a lower opacity. To activate onion skinning, follow these steps:

1. Open the onion skinning controls by clicking the Onion Skinning button on the lower-left corner of the Frames panel (see Figure 12.10).

Figure 12.10   Clicking the Onion Skinning button on the Frames panel to open the Display Options menu.

2. Select the option of your choice:

- Show Next Frame displays the frame after the currently selected frame.
- Before and After shows the frames before and after the currently selected frame.
- Show All Frames displays all the frames in the artwork at once.

Onion skinning can be used in the Document window and the symbol editor. If you turn onion skinning on in the Document window, however, you still need to turn it on separately in the symbol editor.

Onion skinning also enables you to see the individual steps of automatic animation symbols (see Figure 12.11).

Figure 12.11   The flying_saucer_2dist.png file with onion skinning and Show All Layers turned on.

You can also customize the onion skinning feature in the following way:

1. Select Custom from the Onion Skinning Controls menu. The Onion Skinning dialog box appears (see Figure 12.12).

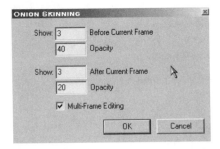

Figure 12.12   The Onion Skinning dialog box, where you can customize how onion skinning works with your file.

2. Change the number of frames that you want to be visible at a time.

3. Change the opacity setting for the visible frames.

Editing Multiple Frames Using Onion Skinning

Times might arise when you want to work with multiple objects that reside on different frames. Multi-Frame Editing allows you to do this:

1. Display onion skinning by clicking the Onion Skinning button in the Frames panel. Make sure that Multi-Frame Editing is checked.

2. Modify the objects on the frames with the tools or commands.

When working with Multi-Frame Editing, the frames available for editing are limited to those visible through onion skinning at a given moment.

Graphic Symbols and Tweening Instances

Tweening is a traditional animation term that refers to how the animation process works. In the traditional animation process, a lead animator draws the key, or main, frames and assistants or "in-betweeners" draw the frames in between.

To automate this process, Fireworks uses a technology called graphic symbols. *Graphic symbols* blend or tween two or more instances of the same symbol. Tweening creates additional instances of the first two symbols that can then be distributed to frames.

Fireworks recognizes many attributes when tweening instances, including the location, transformation, opacity, and live effects. It allows some variation across a number of frames, although each of the frames is more closely related to each other and can be somewhat limited as compared to the flexibility found in frame-by-frame animation.

Here's a brief description of the process.

First, do either of the following:

- Create a graphic symbol by selecting an object and choosing Modify, Symbol, Convert to Symbol. Then, in the Symbol Properties dialog box that appears, give your symbol a name and select a type of graphic.

- Choose Edit, Insert, New Symbol and, after following the previous steps, create your graphic directly in the symbol editor (see Figure 12.13).

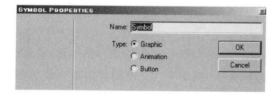

Figure 12.13   The Symbol Properties dialog box lets you name your symbol and choose its type.

Secondly, do the following:

1. Select two or more instances of the same symbol.

2. Choose Modify, Symbol, Tween Instances.

3. Enter the number of tween steps to be inserted between the original pair in the Tween Instances dialog box.

4. To distribute the tweened objects to separate frames, choose Distribute to Frames and click OK.

If you choose not to distribute the objects to separate frames, you can do it later by selecting all the instances and clicking the Distribute to Frames button at the bottom of the Frames panel.

Creating and Tweening Graphic Symbols

To get the feel of it, try out Exercise 12.3.

Exercise 12.3   Working with Graphic Symbols

1. Open the `flying_saucer.png` file from the `Exercises/12` folder on the CD-ROM.

2. Make sure that the Layers panel and Frames panel are showing. If they aren't, choose Window, Layers and/or Window, Frames.

3. Using the Pointer tool from the Tools panel, select the saucer object in the first layer named Flying Saucer.

4. Choose Modify, Symbol, Convert to Symbol.

5. Click Graphic for the type and name the symbol "saucer." It's okay that the object name from the Flying Saucer layer and your graphic symbol are the same. Click OK.

6. Choose Window, Library. Notice that your library now contains an object named "saucer" with the kind set as graphic and the flying saucer displays in the Library Preview panel. You might also notice that the flying saucer art on your canvas has a small square with a black arrow inside of it. This indicates that the object has been converted into a graphic symbol.

   The symbol is animated using tween instances.

7. With the saucer graphic still selected, duplicate, clone, or copy it so that you have two versions of the symbol on your canvas (see Figure 12.14).

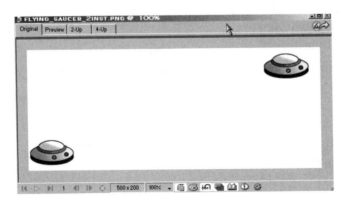

Figure 12.14   Place a second instance of the saucer symbol at the opposite end of the document.

8. With both instances selected, choose Modify, Symbol, Tween Instances. The Tween Instances dialog box appears (see Figure 12.15).

Figure 12.15   The Tween Instances dialog box allows you to set the number of steps for your tween and allows you to distribute (or not distribute) the frames of the instances.

9. Type **5**, but do not check Distribute to Frames. Click OK (see Figure 12.16).

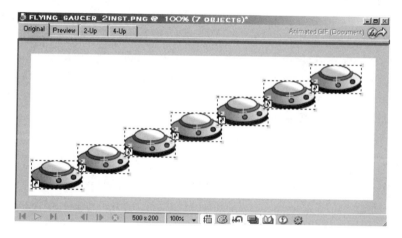

Figure 12.16   There are now seven flying saucers in total, going from the lower left to the lower right of the screen.

10. Choose Ctrl-Z or Edit, Undo Tween Instances to revert to the original two flying saucers (before you tweened them).

11. Deselect the flying saucer in the lower left and scale the flying saucer in the upper right to about twice its original size. Select the smaller saucer, the one on the left, and scale it down so that it is about half of its original size. It should look like Figure 12.17.

Figure 12.17   The flying saucer on the right is twice as big as the original, and the saucer on the left is half of the size of the original.

Because the flying saucer artwork is vector-based artwork, the large flying saucer still looks good, smooth, sharp, and clean when you scale it.

12. After the objects are both scaled, select them and choose Modify, Symbol, Tween Instances.

13. Choose 5 Steps again and click the Distribute to Frames check box. Click OK.

Take a look at the Frames panel. There are now a total of seven frames. You can click each frame one at a time to display it. You can click in the Onion Skinning column on Frame 7 to extend the view of the onion skinning so that you can see all the frames at the same time.

14. Click the Play button in the Document window to play the animation. Notice that the saucer flies from left to right, getting larger at the same time.

15. Save this file (choose File, Save As) as `flying_saucer_ani2a.png`.

To continue with this exercise, you need to set up the symbols to share across all frames.

16. Open the `flying_saucer_share.png` file from the `Exercises/12` folder on the CD-ROM. Notice that it has a total of seven frames.

17. Make sure that Frame 1 is selected. Within the first frame, there is a layer called Background. This layer contains a blue rectangle for the night-sky object and a number of small circles and star polygons on the stars group object. If you examine the Background layer on Frame 2 through Frame 7, you can notice that, actually, nothing is inside the Background layer, and that only on Frame 1 do the contents for the star group and the night-sky objects exist.

18. With the Background layer selected in Frame 1, click the Layers panel pop-up menu and select the Share This Layer option. You are presented with the warning "Sharing layer background will delete any objects on that layer in frames other than the current frame," and the question, "OK to proceed?" Because no other objects are in the Background layer on the other frames, it is okay to proceed. Click OK.

Notice that the Background layer on the frames all contain the star group and night-sky objects. The Background layer has the Share Across All Frames icon, which indicates that this one layer has been set to share across all frames.

19. Click the Play button in the Document window to see the flying saucer zoom across the night sky.

20. You can save your file (File, Save As) as `flying_saucer_ani3.png`.

Modifying Symbols

The power behind graphic symbols is this: When you work with graphic symbols, you can make a change or an update to the original symbol and all the instances are automatically updated throughout the animation.

Exercise 12.4   Adding Effects to Symbols

In this exercise, you add an effect to the flying saucer symbol. This effect is reflected in instances of that symbol:

1. Open the `flying_saucer_ani3.png` file from the `Exercises/12` folder in the CD-ROM. Select Frame 1 and double-click the flying-saucer object. This opens the Symbol window, which allows you to edit the saucer symbol.

2. Choose Edit, Select All to select all the saucer parts in the Symbol window.

3. Use the Effects option in the Property Inspector to add an effect to the selected parts of the saucer object artwork. Click the plus sign, then choose Adjust Color, Hue/Saturation from the Effects pop-up menu.

4. Slide the Hue slider to 105 to change the saucer's color to green. Click OK.

5. Click the Close box to close the saucer symbol.

6. If you look at the Preview window in the Library panel, you might notice that the saucer symbol has been changed and, if you click through the frames of the animation, you can notice that your animated flying saucer has the green hue effect on all seven frames.

7. Save your file as `flying_saucer_ani3green.png`.

Modifying Animation Settings

When you create an animated symbol, you can re-edit the settings for your animation by selecting the instance on the first frame and choosing Modify, Animation, Animate Selection or right-clicking to see the context-sensitive pop-up menu and choosing Animation, Animate Selection. When the Animate Settings dialog box appears, you can change the number of frames, motion, direction, scale, opacity, and rotation.

Adding to the Animation

Sometimes during the animation process, when you have already tweened some instances and built an animation that you want to modify and add to, you might want to create a new object and be able to copy it onto your existing frames. This is different from tweening or sharing across all frames because each object is editable only on the frame where it appears. If you want to know what I mean, try Exercise 12.5.

Exercise 12.5   Copying New Objects to Existing Frames

In this exercise, you add to the Flying Saucer animation:

1. Open the `flying_saucer_ani3.png` file from the `Exercises/12` folder on the CD-ROM. Display the Layers, Frames, and Swatches panels.

2. Click Frame 1 to target that frame. In the Layers panel, insert a new layer between the Background and Flying Saucer layers and name it Planet. To do this, click the New/Duplicate Layer button at the bottom of the Layers panel. Double-click the new layer to open the Layer Name dialog box and type **planet**. Click OK.

3. With the Planet layer selected, choose the Ellipse tool from the Tools panel and draw an ellipse at the bottom of the animation, thus creating a horizon line. The stroke should be set to None. Set the fill to blue (#0066FF). It should look like Figure 12.18.

Figure 12.18   A horizon is added to the Flying Saucer animation. The Layers panel shows the new path.

4. With the elliptical path or planet you created selected, choose Copy to Frames from the Frames panel pop-up menu. In this case, choose All Frames in the Copy to Frames dialog box, thus creating a copy of this object on all frames. Click OK. Then, click through all the frames and you can see the Planet layer.

   You can also choose to copy the selection to the previous frame, next frame, or a range of frames.

5. Modify the location of the planet. Starting on the second frame, move the planet down 10 pixels. (Click the down arrow 10 times.)

6. Select Frame 3. Select the planet object and move it down 20 pixels.

7. Click Frame 4 and move the planet object down 30 pixels, and so on until the planet object has been moved down on Frames 2 through 7. Now when you preview the animation, the saucer blasts off as the earth moves out of view.

8. Save your file as `flying_saucer_copy_obj_fin.png`.

Exercise 12.6   Breaking Apart Tweened Instances

Although the tween instance feature is powerful, there are still some limitations to it that you might want to overcome. Although you can tween size, position, and fade when using animation symbols, you cannot tween color. After an animation is tweened, it can be further tweaked by doing what is called *breaking apart the tween*. Here's how:

1. Use the file that you created in the last exercise, or open the `flying_saucer_copy_obj.png` file from the `Exercises/12` folder on the CD-ROM.

2. Select the earth object in the Planet layer. Choose Modify, Symbol, Convert to Symbol. Name the symbol "earth" and choose the type of graphic. Click OK.

3. With the newly created earth symbol still selected, click Edit, Duplicate to create a new symbol toward the bottom of the Frame 1 panel.

4. With the duplicated symbol still selected, click and drag the Opacity slider in the Layers panel, decreasing the opacity of the lower object to 20 percent.

5. Using the Pointer tool, Shift-click to select the original earth graphic symbol along with the duplicated symbol.

6. With both objects selected, choose Modify, Symbol, Tween Instances. Because there are already seven frames to this animation, I want to tween the instances in five steps and distribute to frames.

7. Click through the frames; you can see the earth move down and become transparent.

But wait, there's more: I want to add an alternating glowing effect to the planet frames as they fade out. If I add the Glow effect to the graphic symbol, the Glow effect will be the same and even as it fades out from Frame 1 to Frame 7. That's not what I want. I want something more custom. So what I need to do is shown in Exercise 12.7.

Exercise 12.7   Adding Live Effects

In this exercise, you further customize the animation by adding live effects:

1. Select the graphic symbol earth on Frame 1 and choose Modify, Symbol, Break Apart.

   Now the relationship between the symbol that was created in the Library and the objects on these frames is broken. You can change this instance of the symbol without affecting any of the others.

2. Select the planet object on Frame 1.

3. In the Property Inspector, click the Effects plus sign button to open the Effects pop-up menu. Choose Shadow and Glow, Glow. Click the color well in the Glow Properties box and choose a bright yellow.

4. With that first glow set, add another effect by clicking the Effects plus sign and choosing Shadow and Glow, Glow and apply the default red glow.

   This creates a neat, stacked glowing effect. Save the effect by choosing Options, Save Style As from the Effects pop-up menu and naming the effect "glowstack." To get the skinny on all you can do with effects, check out Chapter 7, "The Wonderful World of Live Effects."

5. Click to select Frame 2 and click to select the graphic symbol in the Planet layer.

6. Using the Modify menu, choose Symbol, Break Apart. Notice that your symbol changes its object label from graphic symbol to group one object in the Layers panel. With this object selected, apply the Glowstack effect from the Effects pop-up menu.

7. Alter the glow's effect slightly by double-clicking the bottom or red glow object to open its properties box and changing its color to a reddish purple. (I used #660066.)

8. Continue through the remaining frames, selecting the graphic symbol and breaking it apart. Apply the Glowstack effect and alter it with increasing subtlety.

In this way, each instance of the formerly tweened earth symbol retains its opacity while being further customized. Altering the look of the applied Glowstack effect on the various frames in no way changes the original saved Glowstack effect. Each time it's applied, it defaults to the original settings. You can add other settings to your broken-apart frames besides the glow idea that's described.

Animation Symbols

The symbols you've been working with so far have been graphic symbols. Now you're going to work with animation symbols. These contain an entire animation as a symbol that can be reused. With animation symbols, you can insert multiple animations, such as rollovers, into your documents.

Exercise 12.8   Working with Animation Symbols

In this exercise, you convert the flying-saucer object into an animation symbol:

1. Open the `flying_saucer_ani_symb.png` file from the `Exercises/12` folder on the CD-ROM.

    Notice that the file contains one layer for the flying saucer and another layer for the background. The Background layer is already sharing across all frames, even though, as you can notice, only one frame is in this document.

2. Select the flying-saucer object.

3. Choose Modify, Symbol, Convert to Symbol.

4. Name your symbol saucer and click the type of animation. Click OK. The Animate dialog box appears (see Figure 12.19), allowing you to specify the number of frames, motion, direction, scale, opacity, and rotation:

    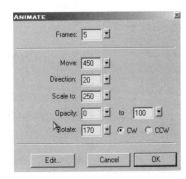

    Figure 12.19   The settings in the Animate dialog box for the flying saucer symbol.

    - For the Frames option, choose 5.

    - For the Motion option, drag the slider up to the very top. Notice that it only allows you to drag up to 250 pixels distance. Because the width of the animation file is 500 pixels, type **450** in the Move text field.

- Set the direction to 20 by clicking the Direction pop-up menu and moving the wheel or by typing directly in the Direction text field.
- Set the scale by dragging up to 250, scaling the saucer to two and a half times its original size.
- Set the opacity to go from 0 at the beginning to 100 at the end of the animation and set the rotate amount to 170, leaving the rotation CW for clockwise as the checked option.
- Click OK.

You should see nothing in Frame 1 because you set the fade from 0 opacity to 100.

5. Click in Frame 5 to see your upside down, large, fully opaque flying saucer.

6. Click the Play button in the Document window to see your flying saucer fade in and spin out of the frame.

7. Save your file as `flying_saucer_ani4.png`.

More About Animation Symbols

After you create an animation symbol, you can edit it in a couple of different ways:

- You can right-click it (Windows) or Command-click it (Macintosh) to modify the animation settings.
- You can change the length and direction of an animation symbol by clicking and dragging the motion path of the animation symbol within the Document window (see Figure 12.20). An animation symbol has a start point, which is represented by a green dot, and an end point, which is represented by a red dot.

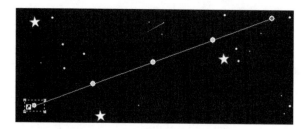

Figure 12.20   The motion path for the flying saucer.

- To modify an animation symbol's motion path, click the green dot of the motion path to reposition the start of the animation.
- Click and drag on the red dot to reposition the end point of the animation.

Sometimes, you might notice that there seems to be no motion path on an animation symbol; you can only see a green dot. If so, you need to add frames to the object by using the Frames panel or by selecting the animation symbol and choosing Modify, Animation, Settings which opens the Animate dialog box.

This next way of working with animation symbols can be a bit tricky at first, but after you understand it, you have mastered the power of animation symbols.

Exercise 12.9   Combining a Frame-by-Frame Animation into an Animation Symbol

An animation can be converted into a symbol even if it already has frames. You would do this, for example, whenever you found that the animation was going to be used more than once. You use the flying saucer file that you examined earlier.

Here's how it works:

1. Open the `frame_ani_symb_combo.png` file.

   Notice that the file contains two layers and one frame. The bottom layer is named Background. It contains the night sky and stars group artwork objects. Also notice that it is displaying the Share Across All Frames icon, which indicates that whatever frames are occurring in this animation will have this background.

   The other layer is named Saucer and is currently empty. This is where you create the saucer animation.

2. Click the Saucer layer to select it.

3. Open `flying_saucer_2dist.png` from the `Exercises/12` folder on the CD-ROM.

4. Choose Select, Select All and then Edit, Copy.

5. Switch back to the combo file. Make sure that you have the Saucer layer selected.

6. Choose Edit, Insert, Insert New Symbol.

7. Give your symbol the name of "saucers." Select animation for the symbol type and click OK. An empty symbol editor window appears.

8. Paste the five saucers into the symbol editor.

   Notice that, with the symbol editor open, the symbol itself can contain frames.

9. With all the saucers still selected, click the Distribute to Frames button at the bottom of the Frames panel. Each of the five flying saucers is moved to its own frame within the animation symbol.

10. Close the symbol editor window.

11. Now you can see that there is an object named Animation Symbol in the Saucer layer. You can also see the animated symbol for saucer in your Document window.

Although the Flying Saucer animation itself has five frame-by-frame frames inherent in it, the document still only contains one frame.

You need to animate the animated symbol by adding frames to the document. You control the frames added to the document by using the animation symbol.

12. Select the animation symbol. Choose Modify, Animation, Settings. Set the Animation to 5 frames, the Move to 63, direction to 16, and leave Scale, Opacity, and Rotate at their default settings.

13. You now have five animated frames animating over five frames. You receive the Fireworks dialog box warning you, "The animation of this symbol extends beyond the last frame of the document," and the question, "Automatically add new frames?" Click OK to add the frames to your animation.

14. You now notice that you are still in Frame 1, there are five frames in your document, and the animation symbol is displaying the animation symbol motion path. Now edit the position and length of the path. Click and drag the symbol to the lower-right corner. Then, expand the distance and angle between the red and green dots by moving the red dot to the upper left. You can continue to modify this animation symbol or add additional symbols by dragging this symbol from the Library panel and adding it to your document.

Caution: It is important to be aware of what point in your animation you are adding an animated symbol. Because an animation symbol has frames in it inherently, it needs those frames to play the entire animation symbol properly. You want to make sure that you target the correct frame for the specific animation symbol and its number of frames that you are adding.

15. Save the file as `flying_saucer_ani6.png`.

Understanding Symbols

After you get the hang of creating symbols, you'll also want to edit them:

- You can alter the name of a symbol or convert it to a different type of symbol by opening the Symbol Properties dialog box. (Select the Library tab in the Assets panel group. Then, open the Library panel pop-up menu and choose Properties or double-click the listing of the symbol.) See Figure 12.21.

- You can tweak and edit the artwork or frames of a symbol by opening it in the symbol editor. Double-clicking a graphic or animation symbol opens the symbol editor, or you can choose Edit Symbol from the Library panel pop-up menu.

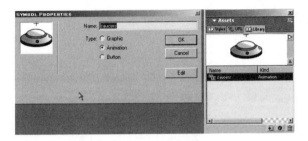

Figure 12.21   Double-clicking the saucers listing in the Library panel of the Assets panel group opens the Symbol Properties dialog box.

- After you create a symbol, you can use it again in another document and you can also share symbols with other artists by using Export and Import Symbol from the Library panel.

- Symbols can be duplicated and altered, changing their appearance and acting as various cast members.

- Button symbols, graphic symbols, and animation symbols can all be managed in the Library panel in the same way.

To export a symbol, do the following:

1. Choose Export Symbol from the Library panel pop-up menu.

2. Click the symbol(s) you want to select for export and click the Export button. Your symbol is now exported to the location of your choice.

To import a symbol, do the following:

1. Choose Import Symbols from the Library panel pop-up menu.

2. Browse for and import the symbol.

The Library panel displays and controls symbols in your document, which allows you to play animated and button symbols and view graphic symbols.

To create a blank symbol, select New Symbol from the Library panel pop-up menu or click the New Symbol icon in the Library panel.

To duplicate a symbol, do either of the following:

- Drag the symbol name onto the New Symbol icon at the bottom of the Library panel.
- With the symbol selected, select Duplicate from the Library panel pop-up menu.

To delete symbols, do any of the following:

- Select the symbol(s) and click the Delete button (the trash can) at the bottom of the Library panel.
- Drag the symbols onto the Delete button.
- Choose Delete from the Library panel pop-up menu.

Note

If you delete a symbol that's currently in use in your document, you see a dialog box alerting you that, "This symbol will be deleted and any instances of the symbol in the document will also be deleted."

Note

Work habit tip: You might want to use the Select Unused Items option in the Library panel to clean up your files and delete symbols that are not currently in use.

Optimization Considerations

On one hand, you might be tempted to create really colorful, outrageous-looking animations that have lots of detail, gradients, effects, and so on, but you must beware: You also want to create animations that optimize well and download in a reasonable amount of time on your users' web browser. A poorly designed and optimized animation makes for a low-grade and low-performing result.

Although I have created the animation methods examples to be interesting, colorful, and fun, they also serve as a helpful and cautionary example of the limitations and pitfalls that you are likely to encounter when optimizing your animations.

Optimizing Your Animations

After you complete creating the animation, you can use the Optimize panel or the Export Preview panel to set the compression settings and to export your file. To set the animated GIF export options, follow these steps:

1. Open the Optimize panel or select File, Export Preview and open the Export Preview window.

2. Select Animated GIF from the Format list.

3. Set the GIF color and, if need be, the transparency options.

Exporting an Animation

Use the Export options to export a file. If you want to compare and contrast compression settings between two different files, I included two files for you to play with.

Open the `flying_saucer_ani5.png` and `flying_saucer_line.png` files from the `Exercises/12` folder on the CD-ROM.

Notice that these files vary greatly in complexity. While `flying_saucer_ani5.png` is rich with colors and effects, `flying_saucer_line.png` uses an economy of colors and effects. Both make for an interesting animation, but you will soon see that if you experiment with the compression settings, `flying_saucer_line` yields a better-performing animation. To enhance your knowledge on optimizing using Fireworks, see Chapter 13, "Optimization."

Looping

To set your animation to play a certain number of times, use looping control in the Document window. The loop controls are at the bottom of the Document window.

These setting include the following:

- Play Once
- Loop
- Number of Repetition pop-up menu
- Numbers (specifies how many times the animation repeats)
- Forever (plays the animation infinitely)

To set looping, follow these steps:

1. Choose one of the previous options.

2. Press Enter or Return to apply your setting.

    The animation's loop time does not include the first time the animation plays.

3. If you want the animation to play three times, set the loop number to 2. You can also set looping in the Export Preview panel.

To further control the play of frames, you can use a technique called frame disposal. *Frame disposal* controls the transition of pixels on one animation frame to that of the next frame or to the background. Frame disposal is also a way of speeding up the download of your GIF animations. You set the disposal of frames by selecting the frame in the Animation Options panel within the Export Preview function. Use the disposal list to choose one of the four options that behave in the following ways:

- **Unspecified**—Allows Fireworks to choose the most efficient disposal method.
- **None**—Leaves pixels that are not covered by the next frame visible. This is a way of building up areas of frames.
- **Restore to Background**—Select this when transparency is turned on so that each frame changes from one to the next.
- **Revert to Background**—Used when objects appear over a frame created earlier in the process. Revert to Background is not supported by all browsers.

Because Fireworks automatically chooses the most effective disposal method for each animation type, in most cases, you do not have to worry about setting the disposal settings. Fireworks recognizes when the background of an animation is transparent and automatically selects the correct disposal method, which is Restore to Background.

In most cases, you do not need to change the disposal setting, as Unspecified is actually automatically chosen as the right disposal method.

Auto Crop and Auto Difference

Auto Crop and Auto Difference are ways of controlling the file size of the animation. These options are on by default to give you the smallest possible files. If you export animations to other applications, however, such as Director and Flash, you might need to turn off these settings.

To set Auto Crop and Auto Difference, follow these steps:

1. Select the Animation tab of the Export Preview dialog box and notice the Auto Crop and Auto Different settings at the bottom of the Animation panel.
2. Check Auto Crop to allow Fireworks to automatically crop the image instead of sending or saving the same information over and over again within the file.
3. Check to select Auto Difference to use a transparency to make the file size more compressed.

Sometimes when you export an animation, you do not want the final animation to contain all the original frames. You do not have to export them all if you do not want.

To set the frames to export in the Frames panel, follow these steps:

1. Open the Frames properties for the frame that you want to omit.

2. Click to deselect Include When Exporting.

3. Close the control and a red X appears next to the frame, indicating the frame will not export as part of your animation.

   You can set the frames to export in the Export Preview by choosing File, Export, and selecting the Animation tab to display the frame list.

4. Click the Hide/Show icon in the Animation tab. When the Hide/Show icon is visible, the frame exports. If the icon is not visible, the frame does not export.

Summary

Whew! You covered a lot in this chapter, starting with the building of animated GIFs. As you worked through the flying saucer exercise, you learned how to work with frames and symbols in animations, including working with onion skinning and tweening. Finally, when it comes down to optimizing the animation without a speedy download and playback, would anyone really take the time to watch it?

Chapter 13

Optimization

Optimization is the process that allows you to set and control the file format and size of your graphics. After you have spent hours creating and building your beautiful web design project, you need to export it from its Fireworks PNG source format to either GIF, JPEG, or web PNG format for use on the web.

In a sense, this is the moment of truth because the decisions you make when setting optimization preferences are a fine balance. On one hand, you want to reduce the file size of your images, but at the same time, you want to maintain as much of the original quality of the image as possible.

Remember that the images you see on the web are not the original files. They are copies of the original files saved in a web-browser compatible file format with optimization settings applied. The file format you choose determines the kind of optimization techniques used to render the images.

Because Fireworks was designed specifically to be a tool that creates files for web graphics, it contains the best tool set for controlling image optimization, also known as *compression*. Optimizing images in Fireworks is a two-part process.

Note

Although the focus is on web graphics, Fireworks can be used for other kinds of screen graphics, such as multimedia and video. Fireworks has excellent ties into Flash and Director, and at least one person I know uses Fireworks graphics for video graphics.

The Optimization Process

In my mind, the best way to learn about optimization is by doing it and seeing the results. First, you need to determine and select the best file format. Different file formats use different methods to compress color information in graphics. Selecting the correct format for certain types of graphics is key in reducing file size.

You also need to understand how and when to use the format-specific options. Each file format contains its own set of options for controlling image compression. GIF file format contains a setting for dithering, number of colors, and transparency. JPEG compression contains matte, quality, selective quality, and smoothing.

Let's start with a brief explanation of the compression settings that are available for optimization.

Selecting File Formats

If you've been surfing the web and interested in graphics for a while, you have probably noticed that GIF and JPEG are the most common graphic file formats used on web pages. This is because these formats compress well, are platform-independent, and are completely browser-compatible. Although the PNG file format is sometimes used, it is not as common because few web browsers support it.

Compression is what enables artwork files to transfer quickly across the Internet. Depending on the content of the artwork in your graphic, its appearance can vary depending on the method of compression that is applied to it. It is helpful to select your file format based on the content and design of your graphic.

The GIF File Format

A Graphic Interchange Format (GIF) graphic can contain a maximum of 256 colors. GIF compression is called *index compression* because no matter how many colors were in a graphic originally, when this compression type is applied, the graphics colors are mapped to the colors in the index, meaning 256-color index (8 bit color). This format offers excellent compression because of its ability to contain exactly as few or as many colors as you set (up to 256). If you compress an image that contains more than 256 colors, the output quality of the image is reduced. GIFs also contain a couple of neat features; they can have transparency assigned to a color (which means that the selected color will be transparent in the graphic), and can use multiple frames for animation.

GIF is considered *lossless compression* and normally loses no image quality because it compresses by scanning horizontally across a row of pixels, seeking out solid areas of color, and abbreviating identical areas of pixels in the graphic. GIFs are only lossless if they contain flat, non-shaded areas of color (see Figure 13.1). GIF images are ideal for use with images that contain solid colors, such as buttons, logos, and line art. GIFs can also be made to appear to be non-rectangular by using their transparency setting. GIF animation works best when vector objects with limited color palettes are used.

Figure 13.1   The GIF file format works best with images that contain flat, non-shaded areas of color, such as line art and buttons.

The JPEG File Format

JPEG is the choice to use when compressing photos or other continuous-tone artwork (see Figure 13.2). The Joint Photographic Experts Group developed the JPEG format specifically for compressing photographic imagery. Unlike GIFs, which contain 8-bit (or 256) colors, JPEGs can contain millions of colors (24-bit). This means that JPEGs produce a higher-quality image for photographs.

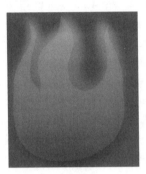 

Figure 13.2   The JPEG file format is best used for compressing continuous-tone artwork, such as pictures or graphics containing gradients and fades.

JPEG is considered a lossy format. This means that when you compress JPEGs using their lower-quality compression settings, the JPEG file format discards data. There are times when data can be eliminated without distorting image quality. If you set JPEG quality settings too low, you can distort image quality, which results in a blocky effect called *noise* or artifacts.

When you optimize a JPEG, you use the quality pop-up slider in the Optimize panel to adjust how much quality will be maintained or lost when compressing the file:

- A high-percentage setting maintains your image quality, but results in a larger file size.

- A low-percentage setting creates a smaller file, but can impact image quality.

You can use the 2-Up and 4-Up previews in the workspace to examine the appearance and estimated file size using different export settings for an exported GIF or JPEG (see Figure 13.3).

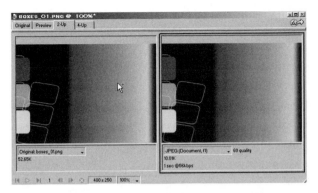

Figure 13.3   The 2-Up preview shows the results of different quality settings, which makes it easy to choose the most efficient optimization setting.

The PNG File Format

Unfortunately, Portable Network Graphic (PNG), which is a versatile file format, is underused because, to date, not all browsers can handle all the PNG characteristics without requiring plug-ins. PNG supports up to 32-bit color, can contain transparency or alpha channels, and can be set to load progressively.

PNG compression is also lossless at high-color depths, which makes it great for compressing photos. Its compression is very effective because, even better than GIF, it not only compresses across rows but it compresses across columns of pixels as well.

Fireworks employs the PNG format as its native file format because it is great for creating transparency, high-color graphics, and well-compressed low-color graphics. The Fireworks PNG file format contains additional source information where proprietary data chunks can be stored. When you save a Fireworks PNG file, the entire Fireworks database for that file is saved in those proprietary chunks. This is why a Fireworks PNG is much larger than the same file exported as a PNG. Because the PNG format is supported in both Flash and Director, Fireworks integrates perfectly into the workflow of those products as well.

Optimization Methods

Fireworks MX provides two ways to set up your optimization and get your artwork ready for the web:

- Specify your settings within the workspace by using the Preview, 2-Up, and 4-Up tabs of the Document window with the Optimize panel and Color Table.

- Define the optimization settings on export by choosing File, Export Preview. Export Preview was used in earlier versions of Fireworks to optimize and export graphics as a separate step in the workflow.

Optimization in the Workspace

In Fireworks, you can preview and choose the optimization settings during the work process by using the Optimize panel and Color Table along with the Preview, 2-Up, and 4-Up tabs in the Document window.

To optimize artwork in the workspace, you use the following:

- **The Optimize panel**—Contains key controls for optimizing (see Figure 13.4).

Figure 13.4   The Optimize panel contains the optimization choices that you want to apply to the image in the active Document window.

- **The Color Table**—Provides feedback by displaying the current colors in your export palette (see Figure 13.5). It also allows you to lock colors, set them to transparent, edit colors, and load palettes for exporting. The Color Table applies only to GIF files (8-bit images).
- **The Preview tab** of the Document window displays how the exported artwork will look (see Figure 13.6). The 2-Up and 4-Up tabs display either two or four panes, each of which can have a different export option.

Figure 13.5   The Optimize panel showing the default Color Table for an image. The Eyedropper icons at the bottom left change the Color Table.

Preset Optimization Settings

Fireworks provides a bevy of common optimization settings (see Figure 13.7), which allows you to quickly set a file format and to apply several format-specific settings. This means that you can start with a preset and adjust it from there to your liking. You can also save your own custom optimization settings by using the Optimize panel and use them later in batch-processing operations.

Figure 13.6
The Preview, 2-Up, and 4-Up tables in the Document window display your image as it will look with various export options.

Figure 13.7   The predefined optimization settings are accessed through the Optimize panel's Settings pop-up menu.

To use a preset optimization, choose a setting from the Optimize panel's Settings pop-up menu:

- **GIF Web 216**—Shifts all colors to web-safe colors within the 216 color palette (the number of web-safe colors common to both Windows and Macs).

- **GIF WebSnap 256**—Converts non-web safe colors to their closest web-safe color and contains a maximum of 256 colors.

- **GIF WebSnap 128**—Converts non-web safe colors to their closest web-safe color, up to a maximum of 128 colors.

- **GIF Adaptive 256**—This palette does not shift colors, but actually uses the exact colors from the graphic, up to 256 colors.

- **JPEG – Better Quality**—Sets the quality to 80 and the smoothing to 0, which creates a high quality, but larger, file.

- **JPEG – Smaller File**—Sets quality to 60 and smoothing to 2, which creates a graphic that's half the size of Better Quality, but with reduced sharpness.

Optimizing and Exporting to GIF

In this example, you optimize and export a Fireworks PNG file using the GIF file format:

1. Open the file called `bee_button.png` from the `Exercises/13` folder on the CD-ROM, and save it to your hard drive. Click the Preview tab.

   The artwork contains components that make up a simple button, and vector objects including rectangles, paths, groups, and text. Because the artwork employs flat color areas and no shading or gradients, it is best optimized using GIF compression.

2. Display the Optimize panel if it is not already showing (choose Window, Optimize, or click the Show Optimize icon in the mini-launcher).

3. Click the Zoom tool in the Tools panel, and click on the bee graphic to magnify the preview.

   Use Alt/option, click to zoom out. You can pan the preview area by selecting the Hand tool and clicking and dragging in the preview, or you can hold down the space bar and click and drag in the preview.

4. Click the 4-Up tab.

   Each of the panes in the Document window can be set as the active panel by clicking inside it. Click inside one of the panels. A black line appears around the pane, which indicates that it is active.

Notice that all previews are magnified to the same amount. When you pan, all previews pan simultaneously, displaying the same portion of the image. This allows you to compare optimization settings in the two or four panels.

5. In the Optimize panel, click in the Settings box to display the Presets pop-up menu and select WebSnap Adaptive 128.

The Color box displays 128, which is the maximum number of colors that can be used in this palette. Below the Color Table and to the right is the number 116. That number represents the actual colors from the graphic that are used in the palette.

Also, the readout below the Preview panel indicates that the file size is 1.28K and the download time is negligible.

6. Click another pane, then click in the Settings box to get the pop-up menu, and select GIF Web 216.

The maximum number of colors indicates 216 and the actual number is 37. The file size has changed to 914 bytes, which is a minor decrease.

7. Click the third pane. Change the maximum colors to 16.

The graphic still looks good and the file size is now 708 bytes. While two-tenths of a kilobyte might not seem like much, little numbers like this multiplied across all the graphics within a page really add up.

8. Choose another pane, and click the Dither check box on and off.

This shaves a hair off the file size. In this case, the dithering option doesn't enhance the graphic.

9. Click the pane with 16 Colors and no dithering to make this pane active.

At this point, you completed the optimization process. You can choose to save your settings for future use, or just click Export and give your file a name to save it to the hard drive.

Saving Export Settings

To save your GIF export settings, complete the following steps:

1. Click the plus sign to the right of the Settings box at the top right of the Preview panel to display the Preset Name dialog box.

2. Name your preset 16_bee_colors and click OK (see Figure 13.8).

The settings are saved and will appear in the Fireworks Presets pop-up menu from now on.

Figure 13.8   Enter the name for your preset in the Preset Name dialog box.

3. To export the file, click Export. Name the file `bee_butt.gif` (see Figure 13.9).

   You might notice the lower half of the Export panel contains options for Save As, HTML, and Slices. Leave the Save as (Macintosh) or Save as Type (Windows) set to Images Only.

4. Click Save.

Figure 13.9   Save the optimized graphic.

Optimizing and Exporting to JPEG

Now you will use the Export Preview facility to optimize an image as a JPEG. The procedure is more or less the same as it is with the GIF. Export Preview was used in previous versions of Fireworks to simultaneously optimize and export graphics. You can open the Export Preview through the Export Wizard or by choosing File, Export Preview:

1. Open the file called `fire_bkg.png` from the `Exercises/13` folder on the accompanying CD-ROM.

   I created this artwork to use as a background tile for a training company web site.

2. Choose File, Export Preview.

The Export Preview dialog box appears. The format defaults to GIF and the palette defaults to Web Adaptive.

Leave this file open because you need it for the following section.

Using Export Preview

When you create artwork in Fireworks, times might arise when you want to export your file by using the Export Preview, optimizing as part of the export process.

When you select File, Export Preview, the Export Preview panel appears (see Figure 13.10). The left side of the panel has tabs for Export options, File-Specific options, and Animation. On the right is the preview area and information on the file size, estimated download time, and a preview of the graphic as it will look when exported according to the current settings. The right side also has settings for zoom, crop, 2-Up or 4-Up previews, and animation controls.

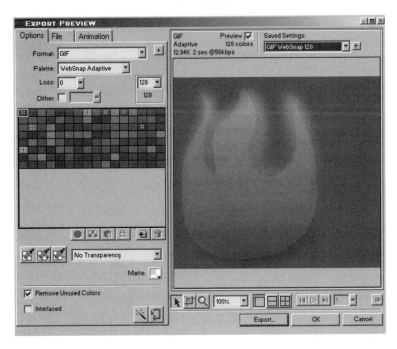

Figure 13.10   The Export Preview panel lets you set your optimization options and do the export in the same step.

At the bottom of the left side are two buttons. The wand activates the Export Wizard, which offers suggestions on the best ways to optimize your image. The icon that looks like a C-clamp activates the Optimize to Size Wizard. With it, you can constrain the graphic to a specific file size:

1. Continue where you left off in the previous section's numbered list. As you change the various optimization settings, the preview image changes to reflect the new choices. You can turn off the preview by clicking to deselect the Preview check box at the upper right. You can bail out of redrawing the preview altogether by pressing Esc (Escape). Because the most important part of this artwork is the flames, you want to set the optimization to suit their gradient content. Pan the image in the preview window so that you can see the flame motif (see Figure 13.11).

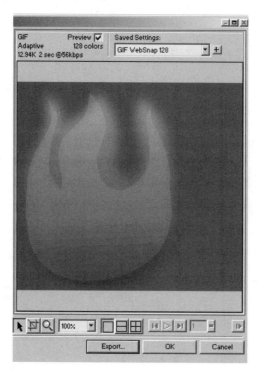

Figure 13.11   Make sure that the flames show in the preview window.

Notice that the gradient appears to be striped. This appearance, called *banding*, is what results when you use the GIF format to optimize a gradient. Also, notice that the file size is a whopping 12.94K. The download time at 56Kbps is 2 seconds.

2. Now click the Format pop-up menu and select JPEG.

   Notice the quality setting defaults to 80 percent. The file size has dropped to 9.44K, and the download is estimated at only 1 second.

3. Click the quality slider and slide the percentage down to 60 percent. The file size trims down to 6.83K and the download time remains at 1 second.

   Feel free to continue to experiment with the quality slider. Adjusting the smoothing value can be a tradeoff. Increasing smoothing can trim the file size a bit but also tends to blur images. Depending on your image content, this might or might not be a problem. The progressive option allows your graphic to display at low resolution and then increase its quality as it continues to download. This is similar to the interlacing option for GIFs.

4. When you are satisfied with the look of the optimized graphic, you can save your setting as you did in the previous example, or you can export the graphic directly to your hard drive.

5. To finish, click the pane with the settings you want to use. Click the Export button and name your file fire_bkg.jpg.

Optimizing Files in the Workspace

In this example, you see the effects of various settings on a graphic that contains a mixture of solid color and continuous-tone sections:

1. Open the file boxes_01.png from the Exercises/13 folder on the accompanying CD-ROM and save it to your hard drive (see Figure 13.12).

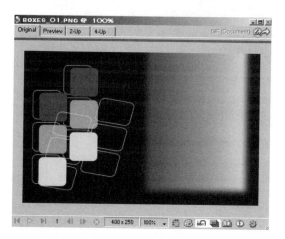

Figure 13.12   You can optimize the boxes_01.png file by using the workspace Preview method.

2. Click each of the Preview, 2-Up, and 4-Up tabs to see the effect of these options. Use the zoom, pan, and magnification controls to reposition the preview. Leave your window at the 4-Up setting for now.

    2-Up and 4-Up previews show the original in the left and top-left preview panes of the tab. You can edit the graphics in this view or set these panes to display optimized graphics using the Preview options pop-up menu at the lower left of each pane.

3. To use the Optimize panel to change the settings for each of the individual panes, you must first make the pane active. Click in the upper-left pane to make the pane active. Then, click the small downward-pointing arrow after the words original: boxes_01.png in the lower-left corner to open the pop-up menu. Change this view from Original to Export Preview. Notice the default settings of GIF 128, Adaptive, 0% dither.

4. Click to select the top-right preview pane. Set it to GIF, Web 216, 100% dither.

5. Click the lower-left preview pane. Set it to JPEG, Better Quality (80).

6. Click the lower-right pane. Set it to JPEG, Smaller File (60).

7. Now, compare and contrast these settings (see Figure 13.13):

    • The upper-left pane downloads in 2 seconds at 56kbps. GIF 128 Adaptive makes the boxes and thin lines look great, but there are gradient bands in the rectangle.

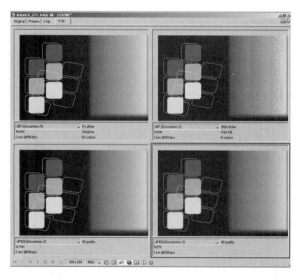

Figure 13.13   The 4-Up preview in the Document window shows four different settings that can optimize and export the boxes_01.png image. It also shows the approximate size and download times of each version.

- The upper-right pane downloads in 1 second at 56kbps, GIF Web 216 makes the solid parts of the boxes look fine, but the thin lines are breaking up and the gradient looks horrible. It is completely dithered because the file only contains 37 colors. To learn about dithering and the web-safe palette, check out Chapter 5, "Working with Color Fills and Strokes."

- The pane on the lower left downloads in 2 seconds at 56kbps. Set to JPEG 80 Quality, the background becomes a bit splotchy around the thin lines, while the solid boxes and gradient look good.

- The lower-right pane downloads in 1 second at 56kbps. The solid areas and thin lines are splotchy, but the gradient still looks good.

The best choice seems to be the JPEG at 80 with no smoothing. The file size, however, is nearly double that of the JPEG at 60. If your page is "heavy" (it already has many downloadable graphics), you might sacrifice some quality for the smaller file size.

8. Click in the pane that you want to export, click Export, and save your file as boxes.jpg.

As you can see, it can be difficult to select the correct optimization setting when images contain both types of design content, solid colors and continuous tone. You can deal with this in a couple of ways. One is slicing. The other way is selective JPEG compression.

Slicing

Slicing can be an important tool in optimizing your graphics. It allows you to chop up a Fireworks document into different pieces and export each part to a separate file, each containing its own individual settings for downloading. Slice properties are fivefold:

- Optimizing an image's file size.

- Assigning a URL to a slice.

- Applying interactivity to a slice.

- Replacing a part of an image with HTML text for import of your file into Dreamweaver.

- Swapping out part of an image, such as a subhead, button, or page motif.

Note

You can find more information about working with slices in Chapter 11, "Working with Behaviors," and Chapter 16, "Integrating Fireworks and Dreamweaver."

You can create slices in different ways:

- You can automatically insert a rectangular slice over your objects.

- You can draw a slice by using the Slice tool from the Tools panel.

- You can make an entire object interactive by selecting the object, inserting a slice on top of it, and assigning a behavior to it.

  When you do this, a rectangular slice encloses the entire object, regardless of the object's original shape. Hotspots can be converted to slices by selecting the slice and choosing Edit, Insert, Slice.

- Polygon hotspots can be generated by selecting closed paths and choosing Edit, Insert, Hotspot. You can then convert the polygon hotspot to a polygon Slice by choosing Edit, Insert, Slice while the hotspot is selected. This is a handy way to generate slices that fit perfectly to vector paths.

Working with Slices

In Fireworks MX, you work with a slice layout by using the Tools panel, dragging, reshaping, and deleting a slice as if it were an object. When you drag a slice guide to resize a slice, all adjacent rectangular slices automatically resize as well.

Slices are reflected in the Web layer of the Layers panel. To view a particular slice, click it in the Layers panel.

Viewing slices (and hotspots) is controlled by the Show Slices and Hotspots and the Hide Slices and Hotspots icons in the Tools panel. You can also use the Web layer to turn visibility of a slice or slices on and off.

Creating Slices

The following example illustrates the process of creating slices for the purpose of optimizing a graphic image. It is also a good way to get around the problem that occurs when images contain both types of design content, solid colors and continuous tone:

1. Open the file boxes_01.png from the Exercises/13 folder on the CD-ROM and save it to your hard drive, or use the file that you saved in the previous examples.

2. Display the Layers panel if it is not already showing. (Choose Windows, Layers, or click the Layers icon in the mini-launcher at the bottom of the Document window.)

3. Select the Slice tool from the Tools panel. Manually create a slice by clicking and dragging a rectangle surrounding the boxes and lines on the left side. Don't include the green gradient.

Red guides appear (see Figure 13.14) that define how Fireworks will automatically divide the image when the slices are exported. As additional slices are added, the slice guide configuration changes.

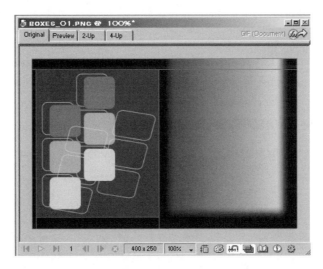

Figure 13.14 When you create a slice, red guides appear that show how the image will be sliced when it is exported.

4. To automatically create a slice for the gradient object, select the rectangle layer by using the Layers panel and choosing Edit, Insert, Slice.

Fireworks automatically inserted a slice with the same dimensions as the rectangle you chose.

You can select several objects using Shift with the Pointer tool to automatically create one or multiple slices. A dialog box allows you to choose either Single to create a single slice object that covers all the selected objects, or Multiple to create one slice object for each of the selected objects (see Figure 13.15).

Figure 13.15   Click Multiple to create one slice for each object, or click Single to create one
slice that surrounds all objects.

5. You can modify the slices that you created by using the Pointer tool and dragging
    the slice guides to reposition them. The `boxes_01` graphic contains some unnec-
    essary slices, so you need to fix that. Click the Pointer tool and position the
    pointer over the top-left slice guide (see Figure 13.16).

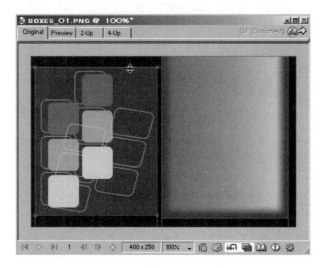

Figure 13.16   After you select the Pointer tool and place it over a slice guide, the drag
indicator appears, and you can move the guide.

6. Click and drag that slice guide off the top of the Document window. Drag the
    left vertical guide off the window (see Figure 13.17).

7. Select the left-vertical guide in the middle (on the boxes side) and move it on
    top of the other middle guide. Finally, align the bottom guide on the left side
    with the bottom guide on the right side (see Figure 13.17).

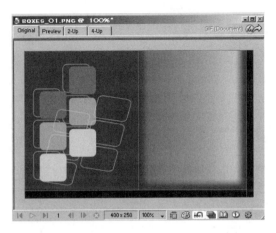

Figure 13.17   The graphic with the slices reduced. This configuration results in two slices.

Note

It's good practice to avoid overlapping slices. This produces complex table layouts and, if you don't know which slice is on top, you can loose an interaction. Remember that, if you do this, the topmost slice retains the interaction.

Specifying Optimization Settings

Now that you created individual slices of your image, you can optimize each of them separately:

1. Display the Optimize panel if it is not already showing (choose Window, Optimize).

2. You optimize the left slice first, so click it to make it active. (You can also activate the slice by clicking its icon in the Web layer of the Layers panel.) Then, click the Preview tab. If you want to compare settings, click the 2-Up or 4-Up tab.

3. To better see the results of the optimization, click the Hide Slices and Hotspots tool in the Tools panel. This removes the overlay color that indicates the presence of a slice or hotspot.

4. Choose your optimization settings from the Optimize panel. Select GIF, Adaptive and 8 colors. You can test other settings by using the 2-Up or 4-Up previews.

5. Activate the right panel (the green gradient) by clicking the icon in the Web layer. Hold down the spacebar and click and drag to pan the window to that slice.

6. Select JPEG – Better Quality for one pane and JPEG – Smaller File for the other. Experiment with the Smoothing slider to get the best image at the smaller file size.

7. When you are satisfied, choose File, Export and save your work (see Figure 13.18).

Figure 13.18   The Export dialog box. You can have Fireworks export the HTML code that's required to build the table for this graphic on the web page and export the slices as separate images.

Overlapping Slices

Times might arise when you draw slices with the Slice tool where you create them in such a way that they accidentally overlap each other. In general, you do not want to do this. It is best to redraw or resize slices so that they don't overlap. In Fireworks MX, the slice guides are draggable, so you can move and combine slice guides easily. If you don't fix this problem, Fireworks considers the top-most slice the dominant slice within the overlapping area when it exports these pieces. In this way, the program minimizes the number of extraneous slices that it would otherwise export, but you might get unexpected behaviors.

Setting Selective JPEG Compression

Selective JPEG compression in Fireworks allows you to set different areas of a single JPEG graphic to a different compression setting. Some areas of an image might require more detail to be held and can be set at a high level of compression, while areas of less significance can be compressed at a lower level. This technique helps reduce the overall size and allows quality to be maintained where needed.

Selective JPEG compression is another technique that can optimize images that contain both solid-color and continuous-tone areas. The boxes_01.png file will be optimized with this method. Then, you can compare and see which method gives the best result:

1. Open the boxes_01.png file from the Exercises/13 folder and save it to your hard drive, or, if you completed the previous exercises, you can open the file that you saved to your hard drive.

2. The boxes_01.png graphic must first be converted from vectors to bitmaps. Select all the objects by pressing Cmd-Ctrl-A or Select, Select All. Then, flatten the image by choosing Modify, Flatten Selection.

3. Using the Marquee tool, click and drag a rectangle over the green gradient for compression (see Figure 13.19).

   You can also use any of the other bitmap selection tools, such as the Lasso tool. You can have only one selection, but this selection does not have to be contiguous. You can use the Shift key to add to your selection, and you can use the Alt/Option key to remove pixels from your selection.

4. Choose Modify, Selective JPEG, Save Selection as JPEG Mask.

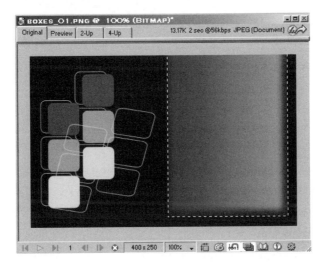

Figure 13.19   The Marquee selection enclosed the green gradient. The pink overlay
highlights the masked area.

5. Choose a JPEG format from the Settings pop-up menu in the Optimize panel.

6. Click the Edit Selective Quality Options button in the Optimize panel to display the JPEG settings dialog box (see Figure 13.20).

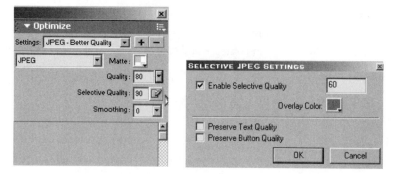

Figure 13.20   Clicking the Edit Selective Quality button displays the Selective JPEG Settings dialog box.

7. Make sure that Enable Selective Quality is checked and type 60 in the field (see Figure 13.20).

   This compresses the selected area to a setting of **60**. The rest of the graphic is compressed at another setting. (Low values mean more compression and high-value settings compress less.)

8. Select an overlay color to highlight the area to be compressed. This does not display in the web browser or affect your graphic.

9. Deselect Preserve Text Quality. No text is in this image.

   This setting automatically sets the compression of text objects to a higher level, overriding the selective quality value. Selective compression is still used for the JPEG mask.

10. Deselect Preserve Button Quality and click OK. There are no button symbols in this image.

    Selecting Preserve Button Quality sets a higher level of compression for button symbols in your artwork. (To learn more about button symbols, check out Chapter 11, "Working with Behaviors").

11. Set the matte color to black (#000000) to match the image's background.

12. Adjust the Quality slider to the compression setting for the rest of the image.

13. When you are satisfied, choose File, Export to export your image.

Compare the results of the selective JPEG compression with the results of slicing this image to see which is best.

Transparency

Now and then, you might want to create a GIF file that appears to be non-rectangular in shape and perhaps shows the pattern of your background tile around it. This is when you use *index transparency*.

The default with index transparency is to make the background transparent upon export. You can also set specific colors to be transparent by using the eyedropper icons on the botton left of the Optimize panel.

> **Note**
>
> When you create an image with a transparent canvas, the canvas behind the image or object appears transparent in Original view. You must choose Index Transparency before export to have the background in the GIF appear transparent.

Setting Transparency with the Optimize Panel

You might want to have a different color be the transparency color, or have multiple colors be viewed as transparent. In this section, we show you how to do just that:

1. Open the file named `star_01.png` from the `Exercises/13` folder of the accompanying CD-ROM and save it to your hard drive.

2. Display the Optimize panel if it is not already showing (choose Windows, Optimize). Click the Preview tab in the Document window so that you can see the effect of the optimize settings (see Figure 13.21).

3. Set the Transparency pop-up menu on the Optimize panel to Index Transparency (see Figure 13.21). The red background disappears. The default transparency color is the canvas color.

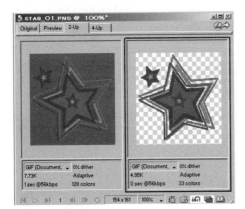

Figure 13.21   The `star_01.png` graphic using the 2-Up preview. This shows the original file and the result if it were exported with the current settings.

To add or remove colors from the transparency, you must use the three buttons on the lower left of the Optimize panel (see Figure 13.22). To make a color appear transparent in a web browser, click the Add Color to Transparency button and click any other color in the document or any swatch in the Color Table to add more colors to the set of transparent index colors for this slice or file.

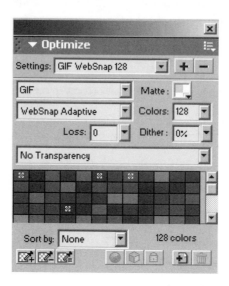

Figure 13.22   The Optimize panel with the transparency icons marked.

4. To make the purple fill in the center star be transparent in addition to the background, click the Add Color to Transparency button and then click in the purple color in the star (see Figure 13.23).

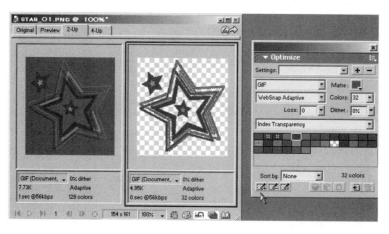

Figure 13.23   The purple fill of the center star is added to the colors that appear transparent.

5. Click the Remove Color from Transparency button in the Optimize panel and click the area in the canvas that contains the color to be restored or on a transparent swatch to remove that color from the transparency. The color appears opaque in the image.

6. To restore the background color so that it appears opaque in the web browser, click the Subtract Color from Transparency button and then click in the red background in the star (see Figure 13.24).

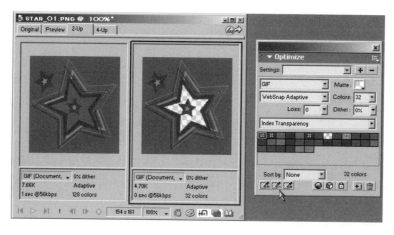

Figure 13.24   The red background is restored to the image. It will be opaque in the exported GIF, but the purple fill of the center star will remain transparent.

Summary

In this chapter, you learned all about optimizing your Fireworks images. Remember that the GIF format is best for line art and illustrations, and the JPEG format is best saved for photographs and other continuous-tone images. In addition to saving images as GIFs and JPEGs, you can optimize images that contain both types of art by optimizing slices. Regardless of the compression methods you end up using, however, the end goal remains the same: speedy graphics.

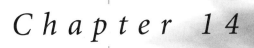

Chapter 14

Exporting

After you apply compression, transparency, matte, link, and interaction settings using the Property Inspector and/or the Export Preview box, you are ready to export your document.

During export, you select which parts of your project to process and in what file format, choose what accompanying code to generate, and/or prepare your file for further development in other applications.

While exporting creates files of many types, your source file remains the original PNG. Remember always to save your source PNG so that you can return to it to make modifications, export into another format, and so on.

The Export Preview and Export Dialog Windows

The first screen in the Export Preview box displays optimization, transparency, and file format information in addition to the document, as it will be rendered using these options. After these properties are set, the document is exported using the Export dialog box. If you already set these options using the Property Inspector, you can skip this step by going directly to the Export dialog box from the File menu.

To export using Export Preview, follow these steps:

1. Choose File, Export Preview to open the Export Preview window (see Figure 14.1).

2. Select optimization, transparency, matte, and file format properties to achieve the desired result. (See Chapter 13, " Optimization.")

3. Click Export when you finish selecting the optimization settings to open the Export dialog box.

4. In the Export dialog box, choose a location to save the exported image to, enter a filename, and set any other applicable options.

5. Click Save.

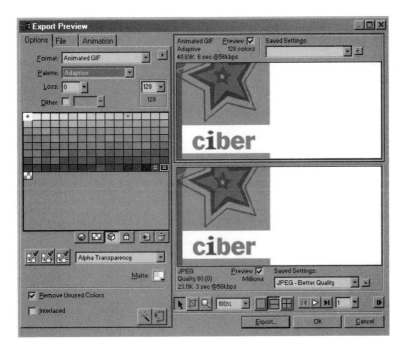

Figure 14.1   The Export Preview window.

To export using the Export dialog box, follow these steps:

1. Choose File, Export to open the Export dialog box (see Figure 14.2).

2. Choose a location to save export the image to, enter a filename, and set any other applicable options.

3. Click Save.

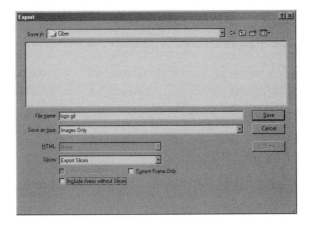

Figure 14.2   The Export dialog box.

Shortcuts to Exporting

Fireworks MX offers two shortcuts for exporting your document: the Export Wizard and Quick Export. The Export Wizard is particularly useful if you are new to compressing and optimizing images, while Quick Export is ideal for preparing to work in additional applications, such as Flash or Director.

The Export Wizard

The Export Wizard guides you through the optimization and export process, and provides recommendations for optimal compression, based on your answers to questions about the file destination and intended use (for more about optimization, refer to Chapter 13). If you prefer to optimize to a target file size, the Export Wizard optimizes the exported file to fit within that size constraint.

While the Export Wizard is a useful shortcut for exporting graphics without prior experience of optimizing and exporting images, it is less efficient for those with a greater understanding of the process. For these users, the Optimize panel and the Preview tab are more convenient than the Export Wizard and offer greater control over optimization.

To use the Export Wizard, follow these steps:

1. Choose File, Export Wizard.

2. Answer the questions in the dialog box and click Continue in each panel (see Figure 14.3).

   To focus optimization on a specific file size, in the first screen, check the Target Export File Size check box and fill in the desired file size (see Figure 14.3).

   The smaller the target size, the greater the compression. As you increase compression, you might be decreasing the quality of your graphic. To learn more about balancing file size and image quality, experiment with this feature of the Wizard, or read more in optimization in Chapter 13.

   Fireworks makes recommendations about file formats.

3. Click Exit. Upon exiting, the Export Preview window opens, displaying your optimization, transparency, and file type settings.

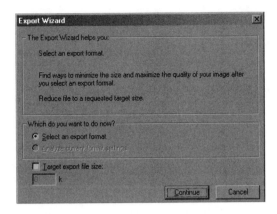

Figure 14.3   The Export Wizard.

Quick Export

The second shortcut to export is the Quick Export pop-up menu, which is located in the upper-right corner of the Document window (see Figure 14.4). This feature is particularly useful for easy export of Fireworks files to other applications. By using the Quick Export button, you can export to a variety of formats, including Macromedia applications and other applications, such as Microsoft FrontPage and Adobe GoLive.

Figure 14.4
Finding the Quick Export feature.

The Quick Export button provides easy access to the more common features used to export a Fireworks file for use in other applications. These features can also be found elsewhere in Fireworks, such as the Export dialog box and the Edit menu. For more information on exporting to each format, refer to the section, "Exporting Files for Work in Another Application" in this chapter.

The Quick Export button can also launch other applications, and preview Fireworks documents in a preferred browser.

Note

The Quick Export button exports graphics and slices according to the specification provided in the Optimize box, so be sure that you have optimized your graphic before you export with the Quick Export button.

To Use Quick Export, follow these steps:

1. Click the Quick Export button to view the pop-up menu and select an export option.

2. The appropriate options automatically are set for you in the Export dialog box. Make changes to the options if you desire.

3. Choose a location to store the exported files, type a filename, and click Save.

To launch another Macromedia application, such as Flash or Freehand, using the Quick Export button, follow these steps:

1. Click the Quick Export button to view the pop-up menu.

2. Scroll over the desired application name to see the submenu.

3. Select Launch from the submenu.

Exporting Entire Documents as a Single Image

To export your work as a single graphic, use the Export dialog box after you finish optimizing the file in the workspace.

To export a Fireworks document as a single image, follow these steps:

1. Select File, Export.

2. Navigate to the desired destination for your image.

3. Enter a filename for your image. You do not need to specify the file extension (`.gif` or `.jpg`, for example). Fireworks adds the appropriate extension for your file format upon export.

4. Select Images Only from the Save As Type menu.

5. Click Save.

Exporting Documents as Animated GIFs

After you create and optimize an animation, you can export it as an Animated GIF, a Flash SWF file, or as multiple files. Let's start with exporting to the GIF format.

If your document contains multiple animations, see the section, "Exporting Multiple Animations from a Single Fireworks Document." To export as a Flash file, see "Exporting Files for Work in Another Application." If you want to save the animation as multiple files, follow the directions in the section, "Exporting Frames and Layers."

To export a Fireworks document as an animated GIF, follow these steps:

1. Select Animated GIF from the file format pop-up menu in the Optimize panel (see Figure 14.5).

2. Choose File, Export.

3. In the Export dialog box, select a destination for the animated GIF and type a name.

4. Click Save.

Note

To preview your animation before exporting, select the Preview tab or press F12 to preview in your browser.

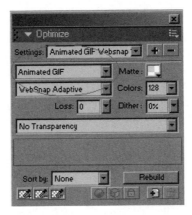

Figure 14.5   Finding the file format menu on the Optimize panel.

Exporting Documents with Slices

By default, Fireworks exports sliced documents with an HTML file for viewing the images in a browser window according to the layout of your png source file, or for editing in another application. To learn more about these features, see the sections, "Exporting to Generate Code" and "Exporting Files for Work in Another Application" in this chapter.

To export a sliced Fireworks document, follow these steps:

1. Select File, Export.

2. Navigate to the desired destination for your images. For web graphics, the best location is typically an images folder within your local web site.

3. Select Images Only from the Save As Type menu.

4. Select Export Slices from the Slices menu.

5. Click Save.

Rather than exporting the entire Fireworks document, you can export selected slices alone. To export selected slices, follow these steps:

1. For a single slice, right-click (for Windows) or Control-click (for a Macintosh) on the slice and choose Export Selected Slice from the context menu. For multiple slices, select all the desired slices by holding down the Shift key while clicking the individual slices until all the desired slices are selected. Then, select File, Export.

2. The Export dialog box now is open. Choose a location for your exported slices.

3. Name your file. If you are exporting multiple files, select a root name for all slices not already named in the Layers panel or Property Inspector. Fireworks generates distinct filenames for each unnamed slice using this root name.

4. Choose Export Slices from the Slices pop-up menu.

5. Check the Selected Slices Only check box if it's not already checked. The Include Areas Without Slices check box should *not* be checked.

6. Click Save.

Updating a Slice

If you have already exported a sliced document, and have made changes to the Fireworks document since exporting, you can update just the slice that changed, without re-exporting the entire document. This is particularly helpful with documents that were rendered in HTML. However, pay attention to the sliced area because changes to the size affects the HTML document (see the section, "Exporting to Generate Code").

To update a single slice from a sliced Fireworks document, follow these steps:

1. Hide the slice definition by clicking the Show/Hide icon (the eye) on the Web layer.

2. Edit the area under the slice definition.

3. Show the slice definition by clicking the Show/Hide icon on the Web layer.

4. Select File, Export.

5. Do not change the filename.

6. Choose Selected Slices Only.

7. Click Save. The exported slice is saved to the same folder with the same name as the original slice.

8. You are prompted with an alert box stating that the file exists, and asking whether you want to overwrite the existing file. Click OK.

Exporting Multiple Animations from a Single Fireworks Document

If your Fireworks document contains more than one animation, you can export each with its own animations settings (for example, looping and frame delay), by inserting slices on top of each other.

To export multiple animations from the same Fireworks document, follow these steps:

1. Select every animation by holding down the Shift key while clicking each animation until all the desired animations are selected.

2. Select Edit, Insert, Slice.

3. You see a message box that asks if you want to insert one slice or multiple slices. Click Multiple.

4. Select an individual animation and choose animation settings using the Frames panel. (To learn about animation, refer to Chapter 12.)

5. Repeat step 4 for each animation.

6. When you finish defining animation settings, make sure that you no longer have any objects or slices selected by choosing Edit, Deselect.

7. In the Optimize panel, select Animated GIF as the file format.

8. Export each animation as an individual slice: Right-click (for Windows) or Control-click (for a Macintosh) each slice and choose Export Selected Slice from the context menu. In the Export dialog box, enter a distinct name for each animation, choose the destination, and click Save.

Exporting a Select Area in Your File

To export an area within your Fireworks document, use the Export Area tool. To export a select portion of a Fireworks document, follow these steps:

1. Choose the Export Area tool from the Tools panel. The Export Area tool can be found in the Crop tool submenu. To access it, click and hold over the arrow in the Crop tool icon (see Figure 14.6).

Figure 14.6   Finding the Export Area tool on the Tools panel.

2. Drag the marquee to encompass the area that you want to export.

3. If you want to adjust the placement of the marquee while still drawing it, hold the mouse button and spacebar to drag the marquee to the desired position. If you release the spacebar, you return to drawing the marquee. If you already released the mouse, and want to adjust your placement, simply click the marquee and drag to the desired position.

4. Adjust the size of the selected area by doing any of the following:
   - Drag a side handle to adjust width, a top or bottom handle to adjust height, or a corner handle to adjust both at once
   - Shift-drag a handle to resize the export area proportionally
   - Alt-drag (for Windows) or Option-drag (for a Macintosh) a handle to resize from the center
   - Alt-Shift-drag (for Windows) or Option-Shift-drag (for a Macintosh) a handle to constrain the proportions and resize from the center

5. Double-click inside the export area marquee to go to Export Preview.

6. Adjust the settings in the Export Preview.

7. Click Export.

8. In the Export dialog box, choose a destination folder and type a filename.

9. Select Images Only from the Save As pop-up menu.

10. Click Save.

Note

You can cancel this process without exporting by double-clicking outside the selected area, pressing Esc, or choosing another tool.

Exporting Frames and Layers

Fireworks can export each layer or frame in a document as an independent image file, using the optimization settings defined in the Optimize panel. The exported file is given the same name as the layer or frame from which it came.

To export frames or layers as multiple files, follow these steps:

1. Choose File, Export.

2. Select a destination folder and enter a filename.

3. In the Save As Type pop-up menu, choose one of the following:

   • To export frames, select Frames to Files.

   • To export layers, select Layers to Files.

4. To crop exported images to fit the objects in each frame, use Trim Images. To export images that remain the same size as the source document, deselect Trim Images.

5. Click Save.

Exporting Symbols

If you have used graphic, animation, and/or button symbols, you can save them as a .png file for future use in other documents. You can export and import these symbols using the Library panel Options menu. To export symbols, follow these steps:

1. Choose Export Symbols from the Library panel Options menu.

2. Select the symbols that you want to export.

3. Click Export.

4. Select a destination folder and enter a filename.

5. Click Save. Your symbols are saved in a single PNG file.

Updating Exported Symbols and Instances Across Multiple Documents

When you create and use a symbol, the original symbol maintains its link to all exported symbols in other documents. This feature allows you to change symbol and instance properties in all documents simply by editing the symbol in the original source document.

To update all exported symbols and instances, follow these steps:

1. Open the original source document, double-click an instance to open the appropriate symbol editor, modify the symbol, and close the editor.

2. Save the file.

3. In the document to which the symbol was exported, select the symbol in the Library panel.

4. Select Update from the Library panel Options menu.

 Note

You can update all exported symbols simultaneously by selecting them all in the Library panel and choosing Update.

Breaking the Link Between Original and Exported Symbols

You can automatically break the link between the exported symbol and the original document by editing the symbol in the current document. Breaking the link lets you edit the exported symbol independently from the original symbol. You are not warned when breaking the link, so be sure that you are working in the correct file when altering a symbol that appears in multiple files.

To break the link between an exported symbol and the original symbol, follow these steps:

1. Open the document in which you want to have the unlinked symbol, double-click an instance of the symbol to open the appropriate symbol editor, modify the symbol, and close the symbol editor.

2. The link between the symbol in the current document and the original symbol is now broken.

3. Save your work to preserve changes.

Exporting and Importing Styles

Styles are useful for maintaining consistency across documents and for continuing work on other computers. To share styles, export your styles as a file.

To export styles, follow these steps:

1. Choose Window, Styles to make the Styles panel visible in your workspace.

2. Select the desired style in the Styles panel.

3. Shift-click to select multiple styles. Ctrl-click (for Windows) or Command-click (for a Macintosh) to select multiple noncontiguous styles.

4. Click the Options pop-up menu in the upper-right corner of the Styles panel.

5. Select Export Styles.

6. Enter a name and location for the exported document.

7. Click Save.

To import styles, follow these steps:

1. Select Window, Styles to make the Styles panel visible in your workspace.

2. Click the Options pop-up menu in the upper-right corner of the Styles panel (see Figure 14.7).

3. Select Import Styles.

4. Choose a styles document to import.

5. All styles in the styles document are imported and placed directly after the selected style in the Styles panel.

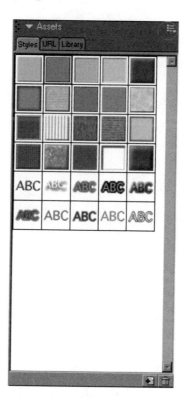

Figure 14.7   Finding the Options pop-up menu on the Styles panel.

Exporting to Generate Code

The default export method in Fireworks generates an HTML file that displays your images according to the layout in your source document and contains JavaScript to make your interactive behaviors work. You do not need to understand HTML and how to write it in order to export a fully functioning web page in Fireworks. After an HTML file is generated, there is no need to change it to make it work, as long as you do not rename or move files.

Note

For more advanced coding, Fireworks also supports Cascading Style Sheet (CSS) layers, UTF-8 encoding, and XHTML.

Hypertext Markup Language (HTML) is currently the standard method of displaying images and data on the Internet. Originally developed as a means of presenting data, HTML is based on a table structure, which means that all content is organized into rows, columns, and individual cells. This is why all slices in Fireworks are square or rectangular—they must fit into the grid a table creates if you are planning to present your document on the Web.

When you export a Fireworks document with slices and HTML, you generate an HTML document that arranges your work into a table, with each slice in its own cell (the intersection between a row and a column).

Fireworks allows you to choose how to format this table. These options are particularly important if your document requires a complex grid.

To define Fireworks HTML tables, follow these steps:

1. Choose File, HTML Setup, or click the Options button in the Export dialog box.

2. Click the Table tab.

3. Choose a spacing option from the Space With pop-up menu:

    - To choose spacing using nested tables select Nested Tables. With this option, a new table is generated inside a specific cell to create optimal alignment. Use this option if you have content that you want to align at the top of a very tall cell.

    - No Spacers creates a single table with no spacers. This option provides no means of controlling alignment within the table, and is only advisable if you plan to edit the HTML in another program (see the section, "Exporting Files for Work in Another Application").

- The optimal means of controlling alignment of your slices in the table is *1-Pixel Transparent Spacer*. A 1-Pixel Transparent Spacer is a transparent GIF that is 1 pixel × 1 pixel in size and named `spacer.gif`. With this option, Fireworks creates an empty row that's 1-pixel high, and an empty column that's 1-pixel wide to define the sizes of these elements throughout the table.

4. Choose a cell color for HTML slices:

   - Select Use Canvas Color to make the individual cells of your table the same color as the document.

   - Use Canvas Color and choose a color from the Color pop-up window if you want your table cells to have a different background color than the document as a whole.

5. Choose what to place in empty cells from the Contents pop-up menu. This option is only necessary if you are exporting unsliced areas of your document (see the following section, "Exporting HTML"):

   - None causes empty cells to remain blank. This option is not advisable because the cells' background color won't show through in some browsers and the spacing within the table might be inconsistent.

   - Spacer Image uses the small transparent image called `spacer.gif` (previously described) in empty cells. Using a spacer GIF to fill in empty table cells is the most effective method of defining table structure across multiple browsers. You do not need to worry about making this image or altering the HTML to include it in all empty cells; selecting this option means that Fireworks will automatically do this for you upon export.

   - Non-breaking space places an HTML space tag in empty cells. Although this is effective for larger cells, a non-breaking space is actually an invisible-typed character. This means that it might stretch your column or row to fit the size of the character. If you look at the spacing between words in this paragraph, you get a good sense of the size of a non-breaking space.

6. Click OK.

Exporting HTML

In Fireworks, you can export HTML using four different methods:

- Export an HTML file. On export, this file is ready to upload and use on the Internet. It can also be opened later in an HTML editor if you want to make modifications.

- Copy HTML code to the Clipboard in Fireworks and then paste that code directly into an existing HTML document.

- Export an HTML file, open it in an HTML editor, manually copy sections of code from the file, and paste that code into another HTML document.

- Use the Update HTML command to make changes to an HTML file that you previously created.

Before you export the document, however, you need to first set the HTML export preferences using the HTML Setup dialog box. These settings can be document specific or used as your default settings for all HTML that Fireworks exports:

1. Choose File, HTML Setup.

   The HTML Setup dialog box appears (see Figure 14.8). The options that you set in this dialog box affects all future Fireworks documents that you create, except the options on the Document Specific tab.

2. On the General tab, choose an HTML style. If you use an HTML editor, such as Macromedia Dreamweaver or Microsoft FrontPage, choose it from this pop-up menu. Doing so allows you to easily open and edit the exported file in that HTML editor. If you don't use an HTML editor or you use one that's not in this list, choose Generic HTML.

3. Choose .htm or .html as the file extension. If you are integrating this code with other HTML documents, select the file extension in those filenames. Generally, it doesn't matter which one you choose, as long as you consistently use the same file extension across files in the same project.

4. Click the Table tab.

   The Table tab allows you to change HTML table properties.

5. In the Space With pop-up menu, choose 1-Pixel Transparent Spacer. A 1-Pixel Transparent Spacer is a transparent GIF that is 1 pixel × 1 pixel in size and named spacer.gif. Using a spacer GIF to fill in empty table cells is the most effective method of defining tables across multiple browsers. You do not need to worry about making this image or altering the HTML to include it in all empty cells; selecting this option means that Fireworks automatically does this for you upon export (see step 3).

6. Click the Document Specific tab.

The Document Specific tab allows you to choose a variety of document-specific preferences, including a customized naming convention for your exported files. Remember that the options you set here apply only to the current Fireworks document unless you make them the default by clicking the Set Defaults button.

7. Click OK.

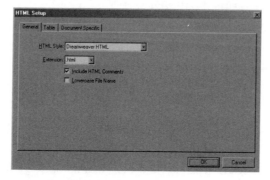

Figure 14.8   The HTML Setup dialog box.

To export Fireworks HTML, follow these steps:

1. Do one of the following to open the Export dialog box:
   - Choose File, Export.
   - Click the Quick Export button at the upper-right corner of the Document window, then choose an export option from the destination application's pop-up menu. Fireworks automatically fills in the text boxes of the Export dialog box with the appropriate settings for the selected application. Note that non-Macromedia applications are found in the Quick Export, Other submenu.

2. Navigate to the desired location.

3. Select HTML and Images from the Save As Type pop-up menu.

4. Click the Options button on the right. The HTML Setup dialog box appears. Ensure that you are on the General tab, and choose your HTML editor from the HTML Style pop-up menu. Select Generic if you code HTML by hand or your desired editor is not listed. (If you do not select your HTML editor as the HTML style, your interactive elements, such as buttons and rollovers, might not function correctly when imported into your HTML editor.)

5. Click OK to return to the Export dialog box.

6. Enter a filename.

7. Choose Export HTML file from the HTML pop-up menu. This setting generates an HTML file and the associated image files in the location that you specify.

8. Choose Export Slices from the Slices pop-up menu if your document contains slices.

9. Choose the Include HTML Comments option if you want Fireworks to include comment tags in the HTML file. These comments are helpful for finding your way around the HTML file, but are not necessary for the function of the page. If you won't be editing the HTML document, you do not need comment tags and need to leave this option unchecked.

10. Choose Put Images in Subfolder if you want images stored in a separate folder. You can choose a specific folder or use the Fireworks default, which is a folder named images.

11. Click Save.

12. After export, you can see the files Fireworks exported on your hard drive. Images and an HTML file are generated in the location that you specified in the Export dialog box.

Copying HTML Code

A fast way to export Fireworks-generated HTML is to copy it to the Clipboard by using the Copy HTML Code option or selecting Copy to Clipboard as an option in the Export dialog box. The latter copies the Fireworks HTML to the Clipboard and generates the associated image files in the location that you specify. You can then paste this HTML into a document in your preferred HTML editor.

Although copying and pasting HTML can be an efficient means of bringing Fireworks HTML into other applications, you need to consider the following when choosing between full export and copying to the Clipboard. When copying,

- You don't have the option to save images in a subfolder. They must reside in the same folder as the HTML file where you paste the copied HTML. An exception is HTML copied to Macromedia Dreamweaver.

- Any links or paths used in Fireworks pop-up menus will map to your hard drive instead of to the relative location of the files in the folder. HTML copied to Dreamweaver is an exception.

- If you use an HTML editor other than Dreamweaver or Microsoft FrontPage, JavaScript code associated with buttons, behaviors, and rollover images is copied, but might not function correctly.

If these issues pose a problem for you, use the Export HTML option instead of copying HTML to the Clipboard.

Begin copying by performing one of the following:

1. Choose Edit, Copy HTML Code;, or click the Quick Export button and choose Copy HTML Code from the pop-up menu.

2. Follow the wizard as it guides you through the settings for exporting your HTML and images, including choosing an HTML style, selecting a base name for your images and navigating to the desired destination folder for the exported images (see Figure 14.9). This must be the location where your HTML file will reside. Note that, if you plan to paste the HTML code into Macromedia Dreamweaver, it does not matter where you export the images as long as they reside in the same Dreamweaver site as the HTML file into which you will paste your code.

3. Click Finish. The wizard exports the images to the specified destination and copies the HTML code to the Clipboard.

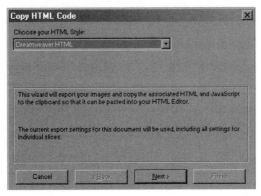

Figure 14.9   Copying to the Clipboard.

To copy Fireworks HTML using the Export dialog box, follow these steps:

1. Choose File, Export. Note: Optionally, if you are exporting to Dreamweaver, click the Quick Export button and choose Copy HTML to Clipboard from the Dreamweaver submenu.

2. In the Export dialog box, specify a destination folder for the exported images. This must be the folder that will contain your HTML document. Note: If you plan to paste the HTML code into Macromedia Dreamweaver, it does not matter where you export the images as long as they reside in the same Dreamweaver site as the HTML file into which you will paste your code.

3. Choose HTML and Images from the Save as Type pop-up menu.

4. Choose Copy to Clipboard from the HTML pop-up menu.

5. Choose Export Slices from the Slices pop-up menu if your document contains slices.

6. Click the Options button, choose your HTML editor from the HTML Setup dialog box, and click OK to return to the Export dialog box.

7. Click Save.

Updating Exported HTML

The Update HTML command allows you to make changes to a Fireworks HTML document that you previously exported. This feature is useful if you want to update only a portion of a document. You can choose to replace just the images that changed, or overwrite all code and images. If you choose to replace only the images that changed, any changes you made to the HTML file outside of Fireworks will be preserved.

To update HTML using the Update HTML command, follow these steps:

1. Initiate the update by doing on of the following:
   * Choose File, Update HTML.
   * Click the Quick Export button and choose Update HTML from the pop-up menu.

2. Select the file to update in the Locate HTML File dialog box (see Figure 14.10).

3. Click Open.

4. If no Fireworks-generated HTML is found, click OK to insert new HTML at the end of the document.

5. If Fireworks-generated HTML is found, choose one of the following and click OK:
   * To replace the HTML previously generated, select Replace Images and Their HTML.
   * To replace only the images, select Update Images Only.

6. If the Select Images Folder dialog box appears, choose a folder and click Open.

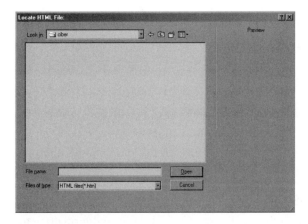

Figure 14.10   Updating exported HTML.

Exporting Files with UTF-8 Encoding

Fireworks allows you to export HTML with UTF-8 encoding. UTF-8, which stands for Universal Character Set Transformation Format-8, is a text encoding method that allows web browsers to display different character sets on the same HTML page.

To export documents with UTF-8 encoding, choose File, HTML Setup. Select Use UTF-8 Encoding on the Document Specific tab and Click OK (see Figure 14.11).

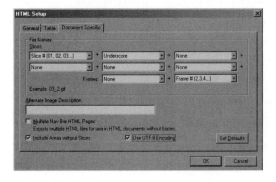

Figure 14.11   Exporting files with UTF-8 encoding.

Exporting XHTML

XHTML is a combination of HTML, the current standard for formatting and displaying web pages, and eXtensible Markup Language (XML). XHTML contains the elements of HTML while adhering to the more strict syntax rules of XML and is viewable by current web browsers, PDAs, mobile phones, and other devices that display XML content.

To export XHTML from Fireworks, follow these steps:

1. Choose File, HTML Setup.

2. On the General tab, select an XHTML style from the HTML Style pop-up menu.

3. Click OK.

4. Export your document by using any of the methods available for exporting or copying HTML. For more information about the various ways you can export and copy HTML from Fireworks, refer to the section "Exporting HTML."

Exporting CSS Layers

HTML constrains web-page layout to a single layer, and formatting to individual documents. However, exporting code by using Cascading Style Sheets (CSS) allows you to layer content on a page and format the appearance of text across pages.

To export a graphic in CSS layers, follow these steps:

1. Choose File, Export.

2. Select a destination folder and enter a filename (see Figure 14.12).

3. Choose CSS Layers from the Save As Type pop-up menu.

4. In the Source pop-up menu, choose one of the following:
    - To export all Fireworks layers as CSS layers, select Fireworks Layers.
    - To export all Fireworks frames as CSS layers, select Fireworks Frames.
    - To export the slices in your Fireworks document as CSS layers, select Fireworks Slices.

5. To automatically crop the exported images and layers to fit the objects, select Trim Images.

6. To choose a folder for images, select Put Images in Subfolder.

7. Click Save.

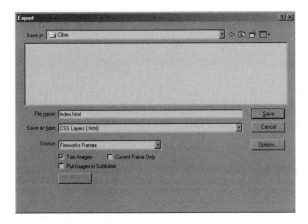

Figure 14.12   Exporting files with CSS layers.

Exporting Files for Work in Another Application

As a program that exports both images and HTML code, Fireworks is an excellent resource for creating web pages. Because the pages generated are fully functional at export, you can choose to finish there. However, you might also want to refine and extend the HTML and JavaScript that's generated by Fireworks. You can do this by using additional applications, such as Dreamweaver and HomeSite, in conjunction with Fireworks. While the process for saving files for use across multiple applications is similar, some differences exist. Whether you choose to export for a given program, or copy using the Clipboard, it is important to know the editor that you intend to use *before* exporting your HTML and JavaScript.

Working with Macromedia Dreamweaver

Because of the extensive integration between Dreamweaver and Fireworks, both exporting and copying Fireworks HTML for use in Dreamweaver are identical to exporting and copying HTML in general (see the section, "Exporting HTML"). The key to successful integration with a Dreamweaver file is selecting the appropriate HTML type in the HTML Setup dialog box.

Additionally, the Fireworks HTML can be exported as a Dreamweaver Library.

To export or copy Fireworks HTML for use in Dreamweaver, follow these steps:

1. Initiate export of copy using File, Export or Quick Export, Copy HTML Code (see the sections, "Exporting HTML" and "Copying HTML Code" for clarification). (When using the copy method, images must reside in the same folder as the exported HTML.)

2. When prompted to select an HTML style (use the Options button when using Export), select Dreamweaver HTML.

3. Finish the export or copy process as usual.

Updating Fireworks HTML Exported to Dreamweaver

The Update HTML option in Fireworks enables you to change an HTML document that you previously exported to Dreamweaver by editing a source PNG image in Fireworks, whether or not Dreamweaver is currently running. For this property to work, however, you must have selected Dreamweaver as the HTML type prior to updating the HTML. When updating, if Fireworks cannot find matching HTML code to update, it gives you the option of inserting new HTML code into a Dreamweaver document. Fireworks places the JavaScript section of the new code at the beginning of the document and the HTML at the end of the document.

Note

While Update HTML is a useful feature, Round-trip HTML is more powerful. For more information, see Chapter 16, "Integrating Fireworks and Dreamweaver."

To update Fireworks HTML placed in Dreamweaver, follow these steps:

1. Edit the source PNG document in Fireworks.

2. Choose File, Update HTML or Quick Export, Dreamweaver, Update HTML.

3. Navigate to the Dreamweaver file that contains the HTML you want to update. Click Open.

4. Navigate to the destination folder for your new images and click Open.

Exporting Fireworks Files to Dreamweaver Libraries

A Dreamweaver Library item is a portion of an HTML file located in a folder named Library at your root site that might then be used in any page of that site.

Dreamweaver Library items are much like Fireworks symbols; changes to the master Library (LBI) document are reflected in all Library instances across your site. You cannot edit a Library item directly in the Dreamweaver document in which it appears unless you want to break the link; you can edit only the master Library item. After you have edited, you are given the option of updating the Library item instances site-wide.

To export a Fireworks document as a Dreamweaver Library item, follow these steps:

1. Choose File, Export.

2. Choose Dreamweaver Library from the Save as Type pop-up menu (see Figure 14.13).

3. Choose the Library folder in your Dreamweaver site as the destination folder. If this folder does not exist, use the Select Folder dialog box to create or locate the folder. The folder must be named Library; the case is important, because Dreamweaver is case-sensitive, and Library items are only recognized within the Library folder.

4. Enter a filename.

5. If your image contains slices, choose the desired slicing options. For more information, see the section "Exporting a Sliced Document."

6. Select Put Images in Subfolder to choose a separate folder for saving images.

7. Click Save.

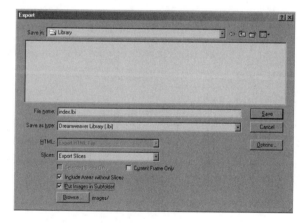

Figure 14.13   Exporting as a Dreamweaver Library item.

Working with Macromedia HomeSite

Both Fireworks HTML and images are easy to introduce into HomeSite files. You can bring Fireworks HTML into HomeSite using all the exporting and copying approaches described in Exporting Fireworks HTML. Unlike Dreamweaver, HomeSite is not an option in defining HTML style in the HTML Setup menu. To work with Fireworks HTML in HomeSite, export using generic HTML.

To export or copy Fireworks HTML for use in HomeSite, follow these steps:

1. Initiate export of copy using File, Export or Quick Export, Copy HTML Code (see the sections, "Exporting HTML" and "Copying HTML Code" for clarification). (When using the copy method, images must reside in the same folder as the exported HTML.)

2. When prompted to select an HTML style (use the Options button when using Export), select Generic HTML.

3. Finish the export or copy process.

The Update HTML command allows you to make changes to a Fireworks HTML document that you previously exported to HomeSite.

To update Fireworks HTML exported to HomeSite, follow these steps:

1. Edit the source PNG document in Fireworks.

2. Ensure that you have Generic HTML selected in the HTML Setup dialog box.

3. Choose File, Update HTML.

4. Navigate to the HTML document that you want to update. Click Open.

5. Navigate to the destination folder for your new images, and click Open.

Working with Microsoft FrontPage

Due to the extensive integration between FrontPage and Fireworks, both exporting and copying Fireworks HTML for use in FrontPage are identical to exporting and copying HTML in general (see the section, "Exporting HTML"). The key to successful integration with a FrontPage file is selecting the appropriate HTML type in the HTML Setup dialog box.

To export or copy Fireworks HTML for use in FrontPage, follow these steps:

1. Initiate export of copy by using File, Export or Quick Export, Copy HTML Code (see the section "Exporting HTML" and "Copying HTML Code" for clarification). (When using the copy method, images must reside in the same folder as the exported HTML.)

2. When prompted to select an HTML Style (use the Options button when using Export), select FrontPage HTML.

3. Finish the export or copy process.

The Update HTML option enables you to make changes to a Fireworks HTML document that you previously exported to FrontPage.

To update Fireworks HTML exported to HomeSite, follow these steps:

1. Edit the source PNG document in Fireworks.

2. Ensure that you have FrontPage HTML selected in the HTML Setup dialog box.

3. Choose File, Update HTML.

4. Navigate to the HTML document that you want to update. Click Open.

5. Navigate to the destination folder for your new images, and click Open.

Working with Adobe GoLive

You can use Fireworks and Adobe GoLive together to create and edit web pages. You can export and copy Fireworks HTML to Adobe GoLive in the same way that you can with most other HTML editors. The only exception is that you must choose GoLive HTML as your HTML style before you export or copy HTML from Fireworks.

Note

The Adobe GoLive HTML style does not support pop-up menu code. If your Fireworks document contains pop-up menus, you must choose Generic HTML as the HTML style before exporting.

To export or copy Fireworks HTML for use in Adobe GoLive, follow these steps:

1. Initiate export of copy by using File, Export or Quick Export, Copy HTML Code (see the sections "Exporting HTML" and "Copying HTML Code" for clarification). (When using the copy method, images must reside in the same folder as the exported HTML.)

2. When prompted to select an HTML style (use the Options button when using Export), select Adobe GoLive HTML.

3. Finish the export or copy process.

Working with Flash

Although you can bring your Fireworks project into Flash in many ways, the best is to import a Fireworks PNG file. This method gives you the most control over how graphics and animations are imported into Flash. However, although PNG is the native file format for Fireworks, PNG graphic files exported from Fireworks are different from the source PNG files that you save in Fireworks. Exported PNG files are similar to GIFs or JPEGs because they only contain image data and not slicing, layers, interactivity, live effects, or other editable content.

You can export Fireworks graphics as JPEGs, GIFs, and PNGs, and import them into Flash using the usual export methods described in the section "Exporting Graphics with Transparency."

While offering you less control than importing Fireworks PNGs, you can also import or copy and paste JPEGs, GIFs, and SWFs that have been exported from Fireworks.

Exporting PNGs with Transparency

The PNG format allows for transparency with 32-bit color images. The Fireworks PNG, the source file format for Fireworks, also supports transparency with 32-bit color images. You can import Fireworks PNG source files directly into Flash.

You can also create transparency with an 8-bit PNG. You can export Fireworks 8-bit PNG graphics with transparency for insertion into Flash.

To export an 8-bit PNG with transparency, follow these steps:

1. In Fireworks, choose Window, Optimize to open the Optimize panel if it isn't already open.
2. Choose PNG 8 as the Export file format.
3. Select Alpha Transparency from the Transparency pop-up menu.
4. Choose File, Export.
5. Select Images Only from the Save as Type pop-up menu.
6. Enter a filename.
7. Click Save.

Importing Exported Fireworks Graphics and Animations into Flash

To import into Flash the graphics and animations exported from Fireworks, use Flash's Import option.

Copying and Pasting Fireworks Graphics into Flash

A quick way to place Fireworks graphics into Flash is to copy and paste them. When Fireworks graphics are copied and pasted into Flash, some attributes are lost, such as live effects and textures. In addition, Flash supports only solid fills, gradient fills, and basic strokes. You might have to ungroup the objects by using Modify, Ungroup so that they can be editable as separate vector objects in Flash.

Note

To copy graphics into previous versions of Flash, you must choose Edit, Copy Path Outlines.

To copy and paste graphics in Flash, follow these steps:

1. Select the object(s) to copy.

2. Choose Edit, Copy or Quick Export, Macromedia Flash, Copy.

3. In Flash, create a new document.

4. Select Edit, Paste.

Exporting Fireworks Graphics and Animations as SWF Files

Fireworks graphics and animations can be exported as Flash SWF files. You can make several choices about how objects are exported.

Unless you choose Maintain Appearance in the Flash SWF Export Options dialog box, you lose some formatting. Although stroke size and color are maintained, formatting lost during export to SWF format includes the following:

- Live effects.

- Fill and stroke categories, textures, and feathered edges.

- Anti-aliasing on objects. The Flash Player applies anti-aliasing at the document level, so anti-aliasing is applied to the document when you export.

- Opacity and blending modes. Objects with opacity become symbols with an alpha channel.

- Layers.

- Masks.

- Slice objects, image maps, and behaviors.

- Some text formatting options, such as kerning and bitmap strokes.

To export a Fireworks graphic or animation as a SWF file, follow these steps:

1. Choose File, Export or Quick Export, Macromedia Flash, Export SWF.

2. Select a destination folder.

3. Enter a filename.

4. Choose Macromedia Flash SWF from the Save As pop-up menu.

5. Click the Options button.

   The Flash SWF Export Options dialog box appears (see Figure 14.14).

6. In the Objects section, choose one of the following:

   • To maintain path editability, select Maintain Paths. However, you lose effects and formatting.

   • To convert vector objects to bitmap objects and preserve the appearance of applied strokes and fills, select Maintain Appearance. Editability is lost.

7. In the Text section, choose one of the following:

   • To maintain text editability, select Maintain Editability. Effects and formatting are lost.

   • To convert text to paths, preserving any custom kerning or spacing you entered in Fireworks, select Convert to Paths. Editability as text is lost.

8. Set the quality of JPEG images using the JPEG Quality pop-up slider.

9. Select the frames to be exported and the frame rate in seconds.

10. Click OK.

11. Click Save in the Export dialog box.

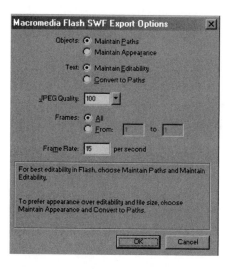

Figure 14.14   Exporting for Macromedia Flash.

Working with Macromedia Director

The Fireworks export process preserves the behaviors and slices of graphics so that you can safely export sliced images with rollovers and layered images for use in Macromedia Director. This lets Director users take advantage of the optimization and graphic design tools of Fireworks without compromising quality. If you are using Director version 8.0 or earlier, you need to download and install the free Fireworks Import Xtra for Director at www.director.com.

Director can import flattened images from Fireworks, such as JPEGs, GIFs, and 32-bit PNG images with transparency. For sliced, interactive, and animated content, Director can import Fireworks HTML.

Exporting Graphics with Transparency

In Director, transparency can be achieved by importing 32-bit PNG images. You can export 32-bit PNG graphics with transparency from Fireworks.

To export a 32-bit PNG with transparency, follow these steps:

1. In Fireworks, choose Window, Optimize.

2. Select PNG 32 in the Export file format.

3. Set Matte to transparent.

4. Choose File, Export.

5. Select Images Only from the Save As Type pop-up menu.

6. Enter a filename.

7. Click Save.

Exporting Layered and Sliced Content to Director

By exporting Fireworks slices to Director, you can export sliced and interactive content, such as buttons and rollover images. By exporting Fireworks layers to Director, you can export layered content, such as animations.

To export Fireworks files to Director, follow these steps:

1. In Fireworks, choose File, Export or Quick Export, Director, Choose Source as Layers (for exporting an animation) or Source as Slices (for exporting interactive content such as buttons) (see Figure 14.15).

2. Select a destination folder.

3. Enter a filename.

4. Choose Director from the Save As pop-up menu.

5. Choose an option from the Source pop-up menu:

   • If you are exporting layered content or an animation, select Fireworks Layers.

   • If you are exporting sliced or interactive content, such as rollover images and buttons, select Fireworks Slices.

6. Select Trim Images to automatically crop the exported images to fit the objects on each frame.

7. Select Put Images in Subfolder to choose a folder for images.

8. Click Save.

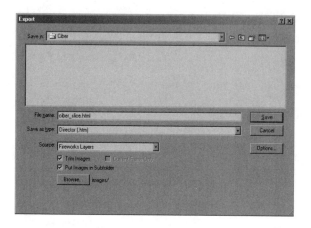

Figure 14.15   Exporting for Macromedia Director.

Exporting to FreeHand and Illustrator

Fireworks creates vector-based images that enable you to export vector paths and copy and paste graphics from Fireworks to vector-based graphics programs, such as Adobe Illustrator and Macromedia FreeHand. Because Fireworks and other vector graphic editors do not always share the same features, however, the appearance of objects differ between applications.

Most other vector-graphic editors, including Macromedia FreeHand, do not support the following Fireworks features:

- Live effects
- Blending modes
- Texture, pattern, web dither fills, and gradient fills
- Slice objects and image maps
- Many text-formatting options
- Guides, grids, and canvas color
- Bitmap images
- Some strokes

To export a vector graphic, follow these steps:

1. In Fireworks, choose File, Export or Quick Export, FreeHand, Export to FreeHand.
2. In the Export dialog box, type a filename and choose a destination folder.
3. Choose Illustrator 7 from the Save As pop-up menu. Illustrator 7 is the graphics file format that you use when exporting from Fireworks to any other vector-based graphics program, including Macromedia FreeHand.
4. Click the Options button.
5. In the Illustrator Export Options dialog box, choose one of the following:
   - To preserve layer names and export only the current frame, select Export Current Frame Only.
   - To export each Fireworks frame as a layer, select Convert Frames to Layers.
6. Choose FreeHand Compatible to export the file for use in FreeHand. This method omits bitmaps and converts gradient fills to solid fills.
7. Click OK.
8. Click Save in the Export dialog box.
9. Switch to an open document in your desired graphics program.
10. Choose File, Open or File, Import to navigate to the file you exported from Fireworks, and click Open.

Copying and Pasting Vectors

You can use the Copy Path Outlines option to copy selected Fireworks paths to FreeHand and other vector-based graphic programs. Copy Path Outlines copies only Fireworks paths.

To copy selected Fireworks paths, follow these steps:

1. Choose Edit, Copy Path Outlines or Quick Export, FreeHand, Copy Path (see Figure 14.16).

2. Switch to an open document in your desired graphic program.

3. Choose Edit, Paste to paste the paths.

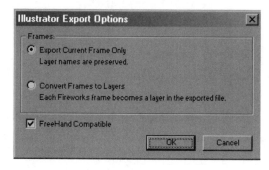

Figure 14.16   Exporting for vector-based graphic programs.

Exporting to Adobe Photoshop

In addition to vector-based graphic applications, Fireworks also provides excellent support for the bitmap-based program, Photoshop. The integration between these two applications allows you to retain layers, masks, and editable text as you move back and forth between the two programs.

Fireworks provides extensive support for exporting files in Photoshop format. Export settings let you control options for editability, appearance, and file size when you bring your Fireworks document into Photoshop.

To export a file in Photoshop format, follow these steps:

1. Choose File, Export or Quick Export, Other, Export to Photoshop (see Figure 14.17).

2. Enter a filename and choose Photoshop PSD from the Save As menu.

3. In the Settings menu, specify a grouped export setting. These settings provide preset combinations of individual export options for objects, effects, and text in the Fireworks file:

- If you plan to edit the image extensively in Photoshop and do not need to preserve the exact appearance of the Fireworks image, select Maintain Editability over Appearance. This method converts objects to layers, keeps effects editable, and converts the text to editable Photoshop text layers.

- If you want to maintain control over the Fireworks objects in Photoshop, but also want to maintain the original appearance of the Fireworks image, select Maintain Fireworks Appearance. This method converts each object into an individual Photoshop layer and effects and text become noneditable.

- If you are exporting a file containing a large number of Fireworks objects, select Smaller Photoshop File to flatten each layer into a fully rendered image.

- Select Custom to choose for yourself from the following object, effect, and text properties:
  - **Object Properties**—Convert to Photoshop Layers converts individual Fireworks objects to Photoshop layers and Fireworks masks to Photoshop layer masks.

    Flatten Each Fireworks Layer flattens all Fireworks objects into a single Photoshop layer. When you choose this option, you lose the ability to edit the Fireworks objects in Photoshop. You also lose features, such as blending modes, that are associated with the Fireworks objects.

  - **Effects Properties**—Maintain Editability converts Fireworks live effects to their equivalent in Photoshop. If the effects do not exist in Photoshop, they are discarded.

    Render Effects flattens effects into their objects. When you choose this option, you preserve the appearance of the effects at the expense of the ability to edit them in Photoshop.

  - **Text Properties**—Maintain Editability converts text to an editable Photoshop layer. Text formatting that's not supported by Photoshop is lost.

    Render Text turns text into an image object. When you choose this option, you preserve the appearance of the text at expense of the ability to edit it.

4. Click Save.

Note

Photoshop 5.5 and earlier cannot open files with more than 100 layers. You must delete or merge objects if the Fireworks document that you are exporting contains more than 100 objects.

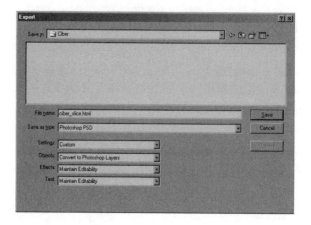

Figure 14.17   Exporting for Photoshop.

Summary

Whether you are using Fireworks to create a full-color print brochure or a highly complex interactive movie, knowing the wide range of export options available to you can greatly improve the quality and efficiency of your work. In particular, familiarity with the powerful new Quick Export feature greatly enhances the export process and allows for smooth integration across multiple applications and within Fireworks itself.

Automation

In web design production, there are many repetitive tasks. In this array are optimizing images, scaling images to fit a predetermined area, changing typefaces, and so on. Fireworks MX has tools that make many of these processes appealing, if not tolerable.

This chapter covers the Find and Replace tools, the batch-processing capabilities, and the use of the Project Log. All these capabilities can work on single files or multiple files.

Find and Replace

Fireworks has a Find and Replace panel that allows you to find text (including regular expressions), fonts, colors (including non web-safe colors), and URLs in any number of places—from the current selection, frame, document, the Project Log, or a range of specified documents. This feature is helpful when you want to locate all the occurrences of a certain color or font and then replace them with something else. Find and Replace only works for text, URL links, and vector objects. It does not work with bitmap objects.

After you get a design finished, usually something needs to be changed…either the client doesn't like a color, the art director decides to change the font he agreed upon, or one of the URLs that the page linked to changed. The Find and Replace feature helps you locate and change the formatting of vector and text objects or change one URL to another.

You can access the Find and Replace panel in three ways (see Figure 15.1):

- Press Ctrl-F (Windows) or Command-F (Macintosh)
- Choose Edit, Find and Replace
- Choose Window, Find and Replace

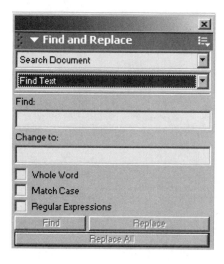 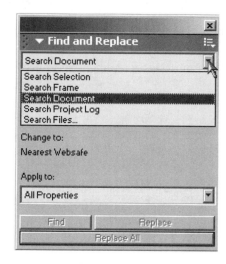

Figure 15.1   The Find and Replace panel shows the Search pop-up menu.

The Search choices are:

- **Search Selection**—Looks through all the currently selected objects.

- **Search Frame**—Searches all the elements in the selected frame.

- **Search Document**—Examines the entire document.

- **Search Project Log**—Searches all the files referenced in the Project Log. This is usually used for multiple file searches.

- **Search Files**—Searches selected files. A dialog box for specifying which files to search opens when required.

The Find attributes, whose options change depending on which attribute is chosen, include the following (see Figure 15.2):

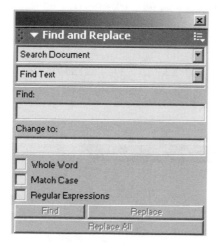 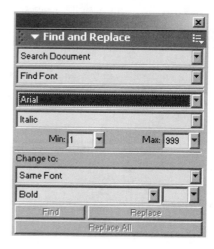

Figure 15.2   The Find Text and Find Font choices and their options. The Find URL has the same options as Find Text. The Find Font can also change just a font attribute.

- Find Text
- Find Font
- Find Color
- Find URL
- Find Non-Web216 (Colors)

The middle section of the panel shows different attributes, depending on the kind of object for which you are searching.

At the bottom of the panel, you can find three buttons:

- **Find**—Finds the next instance of the element. The found element is selected in the document. You can now choose whether to replace it. To skip changing this element, click Find again to go to the next instance of the element.

- **Replace**—Replaces the found element with the specified change. You must have completed a valid Find before you can do a Replace. After the Replace, Fireworks immediately executes the next Find.

- **Replace All**—Replaces all occurrences of the found element with the Change To options.

Exercise 15.1   Find and Replace Color in a Single File

You just finished your design for ciber. The client wants the dark-gray type on the buttons to match the purple in the logo. Instead of groaning in despair, you know that making that change is a simple process in Fireworks:

1. Open the file `ciber.png` from the `Exercise/15` folder on the CD-ROM (see Figure 15.3). Hide the slices by clicking the Hide Slices and Hotspots button on the Tools panel.

Figure 15.3   The original ciber navigation bar. The client wants the dark gray letters in the buttons to be changed to the purple in the ciber logo.

2. Select the navigation buttons in the top row (see Figure 15.4).

Figure 15.4   The text in the navigation buttons is selected.

3. Open the Find and Replace panel by choosing Window, Find and Replace or Ctrl-F (for Windows) or Command-F (for a Macintosh).

4. Open the Search pop-up menu and select Search Selection.

5. Open the Find pop-up menu and select Find Color. Click the upper color well to choose the Find color and the bottom color well to choose the Replace color.

6. Choose Fills and Strokes from the Apply To pop-up menu (see Figure 15.5). You only need to apply it to fills. Text color is a fill property.

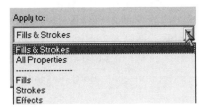

Figure 15.5   The Apply To pop-up menu.

This option allows you to identify how the new color will be applied. The choices are obvious:

- **Fills & Strokes**—Replaces the color in both the fill and the stroke.
- **All Properties**—Finds and replaces all occurrences of the color.
- **Fills**—Just works on the fill. Pattern fills are ignored, however.
- **Strokes**—Finds and replaces just strokes.
- **Effects**—Just changes the colors in effects.

7. Click Replace All. Fireworks acknowledges that the search is complete and tells how many changes were made. Click OK and close the Find and Replace panel.

   The dark-gray letters in the navigation bar are now purple. This didn't affect the rollovers, however. Those letters remain white. (Check it out using the Preview tab.)

8. Now that the colors are changed, the graphics need to be exported again so that the GIFs properly reflect the change. Choose File, Export and click OK when asked if you want to replace the existing images.

Note

The HTML doesn't change, so you only have to export the images. In fact, you could select the changed slices and limit the export to those files.

Find and Replace with Multiple Files

Find and Replace can be used to make changes in multiple files as well as single files. The files don't have to be opened; the Find and Replace dialog box asks what files to use. Also, this capability backs up files before making changes. All the attributes described earlier can be specified with multiple files.

To make a change to multiple files, open the Find and Replace panel by choosing Windows, Find and Replace, or Ctrl-F (for Windows) or Command-F (for a Macintosh) and select Search Files from the Search pop-up menu. The Open dialog box appears (see Figure 15.6), which allows you to select the files to search. Shift-select the files to be examined on Windows; this selects a contiguous range of files. To select a non-contiguous range of files, Ctrl-click the files that you want to examine. On a Macintosh, Shift-clicking allows you to select non-contiguous files in the window.

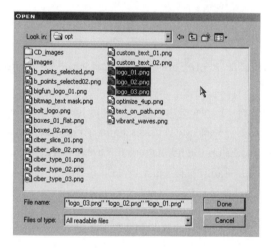

Figure 15.6   The Open dialog box with three files selected.

With multiple files, you can choose if a backup of the original file needs to be made, and what kind of a backup that must be (see Figure 15.7).

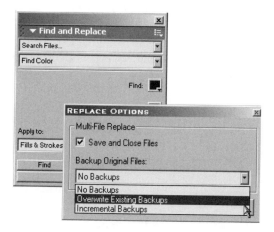

Figure 15.7   The Replace options pop-up menu shows the choices.

If the Save and Close Files check box is checked, each file is opened and searched, replacements are made if appropriate, and the file is saved and closed. If this check box is not checked, each file is processed and left open.

Note

If you are working with many or complex files, Fireworks can run out of memory and abort the process, so be safe and always check the Save and Close Files check box.

If the Save and Close Files check box is checked, the Backup Original Files options are available:

- **No Backups**—Just saves the files using the original filename, which overwrites the existing file.

- **Overwrite Existing Backups**—Backs up each file, which overlays an existing backup (if one exists).

- **Incremental Backups**—Makes a new backup for each file each time it's processed. An incremental number is appended to each filename.

To complete the operation, click the Find, Replace, or Replace All button.

The Project Log

The *Project Log* is a panel with multiple uses. The Project Log records changes made with Find and Replace and batch processing, and can export changed files. It can also select files for various operations. (See Figure 15.8.)

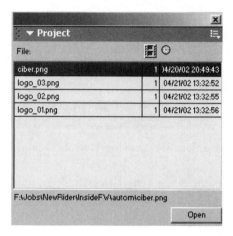

Figure 15.8   The Project Log shows the files that have been changed, the frame on which the change occurred, and the date and time of the action. Clicking the Open button at the bottom right opens the selected file.

The Project Log's Options pop-up menu provides options for exporting, adding files to the Project Log, removing files from the Project Log, and removing all files from the Project Log. The Export Again option is usually used with Find and Replace; it exports any selected files using the last export settings.

The remaining options manage the Project Log itself, accessing the Help system, grouping the Project Log with other panels, renaming the current panel group, and closing the Project Log or panel group.

Exporting Changed Files

To activate the Project Log for Find and Replace operations, open the Find and Replace panel's Options pop-up menu and make sure that Add Files to Project Log is checked before you start the operation. This is the default setting. (See Figure 15.9.)

Figure 15.9   The Find and Replace panel's Options pop-up menu with Add Files to Project Log checked.

After the Find and Replace operation is complete, all files that were changed are listed in the Project Log (choose Window, Project Log). You can easily export the changed files by selecting (or Shift-selecting or Ctrl-selecting) the file(s) that you want to export, and choosing Export Again from the Project Log's Options pop-up menu.

Note

Doing this exports the files using the last optimization and export settings.

Selecting Files for Searches

The Project Log can select files for Find and Replace or batch-processing operations. This is a good way to perform a series of operations on a select group of files.

If the Project Log already has a list of files, decide if you want to use them. Using the Project Log's Options pop-up menu, you can do the following:

- **Add Files to Log**—The Open dialog box appears. Navigate to and select the file(s) that you want to add. Click Done. The selected file(s) will be added to the Project Log.

- **Clear Selection**—First, select or Shift-select the file(s) that you want to eliminate from the Project Log. Then, open the Options pop-up menu and click Clear Selection.

- **Clear All**—Clears out the Project Log.

Viewing and Printing the Project Log

The latest version of the Project Log is stored as an HTML file. To view or print it, open the file in a web browser. You can find the `Project_Log.htm` file on your system. On Windows NT/2000/XP, it is in the `C:\Documents   and   Settings\<username>\ Application Data\Macromedia\Fireworks MX\` folder. On Windows 98, it is in the `Fireworks MX\Configuration\` folder. On Macintosh OS X, it is in the `Macintosh HD:Users:<username>:Library:Application Support:Macromedia:Fireworks MX` folder. On Mac OS 9.x, it is in the `Macintosh  HD:System  Folder:Application Support:Macromedia:Fireworks MX` folder.

Batch Processing

Doesn't it drive you crazy to have a number of images that all have to be sized to fit in an image block, and then each exported to a web format such as a JPG? Open the file, change the image size (make sure that it keeps its proportions), choose the export format, export it, and start all over again.

Batch processing in Fireworks is the way that you can combine commands such as these into a megacommand and apply it to multiple files in one step. Available commands, such as export, scale, find and replace, and rename, can include commands that you created from the History panel and others you can download from the Macromedia Exchange. After you delve into batch processing for making changes on multiple images, you can see the power behind this tool.

The Batch Process Window

To start using the batch-processing feature, open the Batch Process window by choosing File, Batch Process (see Figure 15.10).

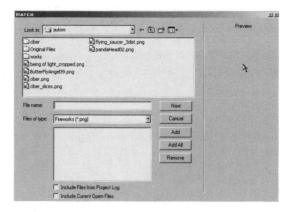

Figure 15.10   The Batch Process window where you choose the files to process.

You can select files for a batch-processing operation in three ways. You can use one, or any combination of, the following methods:

- **Using the Open dialog box**—Navigate to the directory that contains the files to be processed. Click or Shift-click or Ctrl-click (for Windows) to select the file(s) and then click Add. Alternatively, you can add all valid files in a folder by clicking Add All or by selecting the folder and clicking Add. The Batch panel's Files of Type dialog box defaults to Fireworks (*.png), but can be changed by clicking the down arrow to open the pop-up menu. Repeat this process until all desired files are listed in the box at the bottom of the window.

- **Include Files from Project Log**—Check this box to include all valid files listed in the Project Log. Make sure that the desired files are in the Project Log list by choosing Window, Project Log. You can change the contents of the Project Log as previously described in the section, "Selecting Files for Searches."

- **Include Current Open Files**—Check this box to process any files that are currently open.

  The files in the Project Log and/or the Current Open Files are not listed in the box at the bottom of the window, but they are included in the batch process if their respective boxes are checked.

If you want to remove a file, select it and click the Remove button.

After you select all the files to process, click Next.

The Batch Process Window

The Batch Process window's second dialog box defines the actions that will be applied to the selected files (see Figure 15.11).

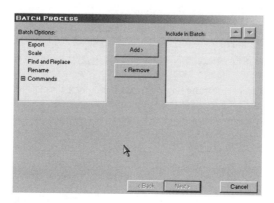

Figure 15.11   The Batch Process window's second dialog box defines the actions to be performed on the selected files.

There are five Batch Options. To include an option in the batch, select it and click the Add button. That option is reflected in the Include in Batch box. The lower half of the Batch Process panel changes to reflect the applicable options.

To remove an action from the Include in Batch box, select that option and click the Remove button.

To reorder the options, select one from the Include in Batch box and move it up or down by using the up and down arrow buttons in the upper-right part of the panel. The Export option is always going to be the last operation performed, despite the order of the included options.

The options are as follows:

- **Export**—When you select Export and click the Add button, you can use the Export Settings pop-up menu to do the following:
  - Select from one of the preset Export options.
  - Set the custom options.
  - Use the settings from each file (the optimization settings at the time the file was saved).

  To access more options, click the Edit button to open the Export Preview panel and modify the export settings (see Figure 15.12).

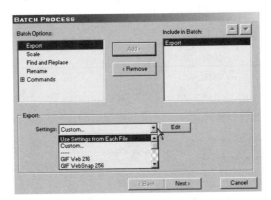

Figure 15.12   The lower half of the Batch Process dialog box changes to reflect the selected option. The Export Settings pop-up menu reflects the choices available for exporting the files in the batch.

- **Scale**—When you select the Scale option, you can scale your artwork (see Figure 15.13):

    - **Scale to Size**—Modifies each file to the specified width and height, regardless of its current dimensions.

    - **Scale to Fit Area**—Considers the file's proportions when modifying it to the specified width and height, and fits the image's largest x or y dimension inside the specified image size while constraining the proportions of the image.

    - **Scale to Percentage**—Increases or decreases the size of the image according to the specified percentage.

Figure 15.13   The options for Scale.

- **Find and Replace**—When you select Find and Replace and click the Add button, the Batch Replace dialog box appears so that you can set up the search and replace actions (see Figure 15.14). The box works like the Find and Replace panel (described in the beginning of this chapter).

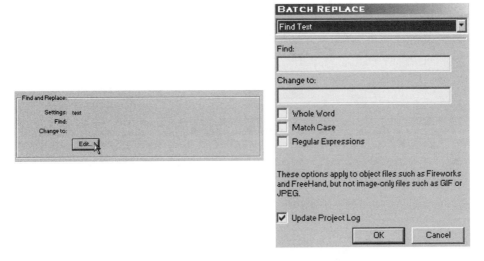

Figure 15.14   The Find and Replace options in the Batch Process dialog box. Clicking the Edit button opens the Batch Replace dialog box.

- **Rename**—When you select Rename and click the Add button, you can use the Rename pop-up menu to add a prefix or suffix to your selected documents' file-names (see Figure 15.15).

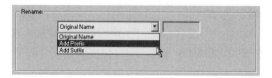

Figure 15.15   The choices for the Rename option.

- **Commands**—To add a command or commands to the Batch Process, first click the small plus sign (for Windows) or triangle (for a Macintosh) next to the Commands option in the Batch Options box to expand the list of available commands. These are the JavaScript commands that come with Fireworks and any other commands that you created or added to Fireworks. Then, select the command and click the Add button.

  Note that there are no options for these commands, and the commands cannot be edited here.

After you select the Batch Process options and set the order of processing, click the Next button.

The Batch Process Output Options

The last thing to do before you start the batch processing is to set up the output options (see Figure 5.16).

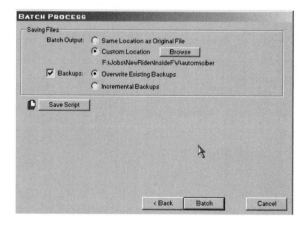

Figure 15.16   The Batch Process Output options dialog box.

In the Batch Output area of the dialog box, you can either save your files to their original location, which overwrites the current version, or save them to a custom location. Click the appropriate radio button and, if necessary, navigate to the new file location.

Click the Backups check box if you want to save the original files. You can either overwrite the existing backups or make incremental backups. Backups are saved in a folder named `Original  Files` in the same directory as the files you are processing. Incremental backups are suffixed with a number that identifies the backup (for example, `filename-1.png`).

If a file is being exported in a different format, the original file is not overwritten. A new file is created in the new format.

Saving the Batch Process

You can save this script to be executed at a later time by clicking the Save Script button and entering a name for the script. The default location is the `Commands` folder. If you save the script in the `Commands` folder, its name appears in any future command lists.

You can then run it anytime by choosing Commands, Run Script and selecting which script to run.

Running the Batch Process

After you finish, click the Batch button to run the batch process. Each of the selected documents is opened, acted upon, and saved according to your specifications. When the process is finished, a message box appears. Click OK.

Exercise 15.2   Combining Automated Functions

In this exercise, you combine a number of options that we have discussed to output a series of TIF files in the format needed to make a disjointed rollover. You want to output them as JPEGs, sized so that they fit in a 200 × 200-pixel space:

1. If the Project Log panel isn't showing, display it by choosing Window, Project Log. Clear any existing entries by selecting Clear All from the Project Log's Options pop-up menu. You do not want to accidentally process files.

2. From the Options pop-up menu, choose Add Files to Log and navigate to the `Exercises/15` folder on the CD-ROM. Using the Files of Type pop-up menu, choose All Files (*.*).

3. Select the five TIF files in the folder and click Done. The files are added to the Project Log (see Figure 15.17).

Figure 15.17   The Project Log panel with the five files to be included in the batch process.

4. You're ready to begin the batch process. Open the panel by choosing File, Batch Process. In the Open panel, check the Include Files from Project Log box and click Next. You can ignore the rest of the dialog box because you just want to process those five files.

5. Two steps are necessary to get these files in the shape you want: scale and export. Select Scale and click the Add button. From the Scale Options pop-up menu, choose Scale to Fit Area. This keeps the files' original proportions within the new size.

6. Enter **200** in the Max Width and Max Height text boxes. The Scale options should look like Figure 15.18.

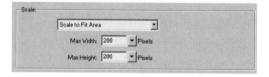

Figure 15.18   The Scale options chosen for the batch process.

7. Select Export from the Batch Options box and click the Add button. Select JPG—Smaller file from the presets and click the Edit button.

8. In the Export Preview panel that appears, change the Smoothing option to No Smoothing and click the Progressive check box. Click OK.

    The Batch window should look like Figure 15.19.

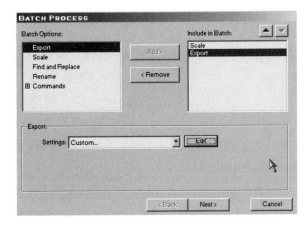

Figure 15.19   The Batch Process window is ready to process the selected documents.

9. Click Next to bring up the output options.

10. In the Saving Files options, click the Custom Location radio button and click Browse. Navigate to a folder on your hard drive to save the exported files.

   You must choose a folder on your hard drive because you cannot write to the folder on the CD-ROM.

11. Deselect the Backups check box. The original files on the CD-ROM cannot be overwritten.

12. If you want to save these actions for future processing, click the Save Script button. Call your script `export_tif` and click Save.

13. Click Batch. Each file is opened and processed. At the end, you can see the completion box that's shown in Figure 15.20.

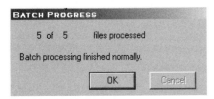

Figure 15.20   The Batch Process finished normally.

14. Click OK. Then, choose File, Open and navigate to the folder where you saved the JPEGs. Select all the JPEGs and click the Open as Animation check box. When the file opens, click the Next Frame button on the bottom of the Document window to display each of the images in their frame.

When you want to insert the disjoint rollovers into a file, just open that file, click Frame 2 in the Frames panel and choose File, Import. The PNG file, with all its frames, is imported into the document with the first image appearing in Frame 2, the second in Frame 3, and so on. Choose Edit, Insert, Slice, and you are ready to use the drag-and-drop behaviors to create your disjoint rollovers.

You just successfully completed a batch process!

Summary

Although it's essential to learn the fundamentals of Fireworks, such as optimizing images, working with color, using masks, adding text, and so on, you can save yourself time and effort by learning to automate everyday tasks. With a little practice, you can maximize the time you need for creativity by putting Fireworks' features to use, such as Find and Replace, the Project Log, and the ability to batch process.

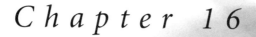

Chapter 16

Integrating Fireworks and Dreamweaver

I think it is safe to say that, as a group of readers, you come from diverse backgrounds and skill sets. Some of you have come to this book with prior understanding and knowledge of graphic applications;

some of you have no prior knowledge of graphic applications. Others are programmers who want to get a better handle on creating your graphics for your web pages. For many readers, this is a pioneer experience: learning a graphic application for the first time and even considering what web graphics and what generating HTML code with a graphical tool is all about.

Whether you are already a professional or if you are an emerging web developer or designer, you must be concerned not just about the web graphics, but about the layout and the functionality with which they operate. In terms of real-world production flow for creating web graphics and web-page layout, a couple of work-flow models are commonly used.

One method has designers create only the imagery and work closely with the programmers to create designs that will be good looking and performance sensitive when in the final HTML document. Because web graphics and web pages rely heavily on optimum production techniques and proper maintenance, the more efficiently one can create and modify images and page layouts, the more satisfying an experience it is for everyone involved, especially for the end user.

Although Fireworks has the capability to generate perfectly useable HTML, it is not meant to be a total web-page design and production solution. Because you will be publishing the images that you create in Fireworks on the web, and because you will probably want to create multiple pages within your web site or project, you will want to manage your web-authoring process.

Web Authoring with Dreamweaver and Fireworks

Enter Dreamweaver. *Dreamweaver* is the premiere web-authoring tool from Macromedia. It is the companion, or collaborative partner, of Fireworks. Both programs contain the new Macromedia MX user interface. They also both create and read JavaScript commands, and Dreamweaver interprets Fireworks-created behaviors along with its own. Because Dreamweaver can recognize images, either whole or sliced, as coming from Fireworks, it enables you to easily optimize images with Fireworks controls from inside Dreamweaver. Dreamweaver can also launch PNG, GIF, or JPEG images from Fireworks, where they can be edited and returned into Dreamweaver for updating. Suffice to say that this chapter certainly could warrant a book of its own. Many splendid variations, amazing tricks, and really cool techniques are based on the main topics that this chapter covers.

One key issue that web designers face is that of appropriate download time for their pages. Because a web page is generally a combination of text, graphics, and sometimes animation or movies, page download times vary. Times might arise when you have a simple web page with only a few graphics or images for the interface or illustrations, while at other times, your pages might contain more hefty amounts of content. Through testing your pages, analyzing the download time of its component parts, and optimizing your graphics and going back into your layout program and retesting, you can arrive at the proper combination and optimization settings to enable your pages to be seen in a reasonable amount of time on the modem speed with which you expect your users to browse.

Without the streamlined integration between Fireworks and Dreamweaver, this back-and-forth process becomes tiresome. In my mind, this dynamic duo is hard to beat. The combination of creation, production, and maintenance that these tools enable is, by far, the best on the market.

Exporting from Fireworks into Your Site in Dreamweaver

Exporting from Fireworks to Dreamweaver is a two-step process. First, you create some graphics in Fireworks and export it as HTML and images to your local site. Then, you insert the HTML code that you generated from Fireworks into a Dreamweaver document.

Exercise 16.1   Exporting an Image to Dreamweaver

In this exercise, you're going to export the file ciber.png so that the HTML file and the images can be used by Dreamweaver to build the complete page:

1. Create a folder on your hard drive to store the files for this exercise. I called mine ciber. Then, open ciber.png from the Base Files subfolder of the Exercises/16 folder on the CD-ROM. Save it in this folder.

2. Choose File, Export. Click the Options button on the right side of the Export dialog box to open the HTML Setup dialog box. Note: If the Save as Type pop-up box is set to Images Only, the Options button is grayed out. Make sure that the Save as Type pop-up box is set to HTML and Images. Also, you can access the HTML Setup from within the program by choosing File, HTML Setup.

3. Under the General tab, select Dreamweaver from the HTML Style pop-up menu (see Figure 16.1).

Figure 16.1   The General tab of the HTML Setup dialog box.

4. Under the Table tab, select Nested Tables—No Spacers from the Space With pop-
   up menu (see Figure 16.2). Check the Use Canvas Color check box under Empty
   Cells.

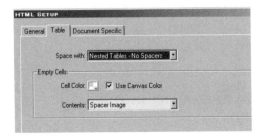

Figure 16.2   The Table tab of the HTML Setup dialog box.

5. Click OK to return to the Export dialog box. Navigate to the `ciber` folder that
   you created in step 1 for the Save In text box. Name the file `ciber` and select the
   other options as shown in Figure 16.3.

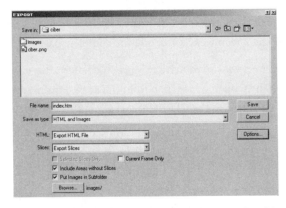

Figure 16.3   The Export dialog box shows the responses for exporting this graphic.

6. Click Save to complete this process.

You now have all the elements necessary to create this graphic in Dreamweaver.

Starting Dreamweaver

You can launch Dreamweaver in a number of ways, depending on how your computer is set up. Because this book is about Fireworks, we'll open Dreamweaver from within Fireworks. From the Quick Export button on any document, select Dreamweaver and choose Launch Dreamweaver (see Figure 16.4). Dreamweaver opens with an untitled document, ready for your web page.

Figure 16.4   You can launch Dreamweaver by using the Quick Export button in Fireworks.

The first true step to using the features in Dreamweaver is to set up your web site. Dreamweaver's Site panel allows you to manage your web page files, graphics, movies, and any other assets, including color, as well as control and management of the linking of files for your web site. The structure of your web site is important because its hyperlinks are directly related to the location of those files within their folders. Links tell your browser how to move from one HTML page to another. Links include a path that specifies the location of your linked file in its relationship to the original page or structure of the web site.

Exercise 16.2   Defining a Site

This exercise shows the distinction between opening a web page in Dreamweaver and opening up a page within an entire site or project:

1. In Dreamweaver, open the Site panel (see Figure 16.5). There are many ways to accomplish an action in Dreamweaver, so choose the one that is easiest for you:
    *   Choose Site from the top menu and then choose Site Files.
    *   Press F8.
    *   Click the Site button in the Launcher at the bottom right of the Document window.

- Choose Window, Site.
- Expand the Files panel group and click the Site tab.

I prefer jumping right into the new MX user interface, so I use the last option.

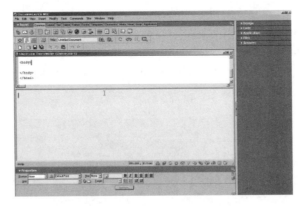

Figure 16.5   The Dreamweaver MX user interface. Actions can be started in a number of
ways. For example, selecting from the top menu bar, using one of the panel
groups, or clicking an icon in the Launcher.

2. To define a new site, choose Site from either the Site panel menu or the top
menu and then select New Site. The New Site dialog box appears.

Two tabs are at the top of the Site Definition panel: Basic and Advanced (see
Figure 16.6). The Basic tab opens a wizard that walks you through the site-
definition process. Let's use the Advanced tab and get the definition done
all at once.

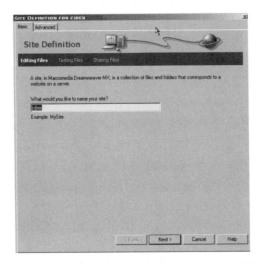

Figure 16.6   The Site Definition dialog box has two tabs: Basic and Advanced.

3. Click the Advanced tab to display the Advanced Site Definition dialog box (see Figure 16.7).

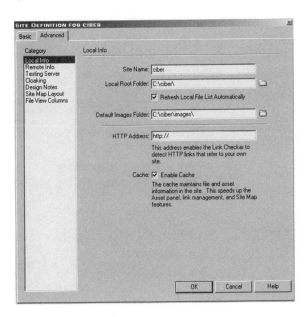

Figure 16.7   The Advanced Site Definition dialog box shows this exercise's definitions for the Local Info.

4. In the Site Name field, name your project. This is a pet name for your project; it does not have to follow any specific conventions. I named my project `ciber`.

5. Click the yellow folder icon after the Local Root Folder field and browse for the `ciber` folder that you just created. This points the site definition into the proper directory where the files you will be using are stored. Click Select.

6. Check the Refresh Local File List Automatically. Then, every time you add, change, or delete a file from the site, it is reflected in the file list.

7. Click the yellow folder icon after the Default Images Folder field and browse to the `ciber` folder. Then, using the Create New Folder icon at the top of the dialog box, create another folder below the `ciber` folder. Name this folder `images`. Click Select.

8. If you want to use Dreamweaver to upload your site to the web, fill in the URL in the HTTP Address text box. This box can be left blank if you do not want to specify a URL yet.

9. Click the Enable Cache check box. This needs to always be set unless you are extremely low on memory.

10. Click OK. This is all that's required to get started.

Note

For more information on defining sites in Dreamweaver, refer to the Dreamweaver Help files or to the *Inside Dreamweaver MX* book by New Riders Publishing.

Now the Site panel's file list shows all the files in your `ciber` folder (see Figure 16.8).

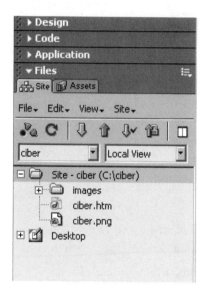

Figure 16.8   The Site panel now shows the list of files used in the web site.

The pop-up menu on the left side shows the site name. Click the arrow to see a pop-up menu of all the defined sites. The pop-up menu on the right shows the version of the site files that you are viewing. Click the arrow to change the location.

Inserting Fireworks HTML

After you define your site, you can build the ciber web page in Dreamweaver.

Exercise 16.3   Inserting Fireworks HTML

Use the images and HTML file that you created in Exercise 16.1 to insert Fireworks HTML:

1. If there is already an untitled document open in Dreamweaver, you can use it. Otherwise, select File, New and choose a basic page from the General tab in the New Document dialog box.

2. Name the page ciber—what we do by typing in the Title text box (near the top of the Dreamweaver window). Save the page in the ciber folder as index.htm.

3. The navigation bar and the left-hand side design were developed in Fireworks, so you want to insert that code. Click the Fireworks HTML button on the Insert panel. In the Insert Fireworks HTML dialog box that appears (see Figure 16.9), click Browse to navigate to the ciber folder. Select the ciber.htm file and click OK.

Figure 16.9   The Dreamweaver user interface (as I have it set up).

4. The Dreamweaver document now shows the top navigation bar and the left-side graphics for your index.htm page. Save it. You can view it in your web browser by pressing F12. Move your cursor over the navigation buttons to see that all of the rollover code is there.

Dreamweaver's Property Inspector (see Figure 16.10) reflects the table parameters that Fireworks built. It also shows the location and name of the Fireworks source file, which can be edited through Dreamweaver.

Figure 16.10   Dreamweaver's Property Inspector.

Updating Fireworks HTML

The real beauty of the interaction between Dreamweaver and Fireworks is reflected when you want to change a graphic. Without Dreamweaver, you have to open the graphics program, make the change, export the graphic in web format, and make any necessary changes in the HTML page. In Dreamweaver, you only have to click a button and make the change.

Exercise 16.4   Editing Graphics Within Dreamweaver

To edit a graphic within Dreamweaver, follow these steps:

1. In the Dreamweaver Property Inspector, click the Edit button next to the Src text box. You are going to change the subheading of the ciber page. If the Property Inspector doesn't show the Fireworks table, click anywhere in the area generated by Fireworks so that the HTML tags show at the bottom left in the status bar (see Figure 16.11). Click the first table tag. The tag is seen in bold.

Figure 16.11   Click the first table tag in the status bar to set the Property Inspector to the Fireworks table. Then, click the Edit button in the Property Inspector.

2. Navigate to the ciber folder (you're probably already there) and select ciber.png. When the file opens in Fireworks, it has an Editing from Dreamweaver icon at the top of the Document window along with a Done button to return to Dreamweaver after you finish (see Figure 16.12).

Figure 16.12   When entering Fireworks from Dreamweaver, a Done button and an Editing from Dreamweaver icon appears at the top of the Document window.

3. You are going to change the background color of the subhead ABOUT US and What We Do from gray to the purple color of the "i" in "ciber." The background is the last object in the Base Art layer, named subhead wedge. Click it in the Layers panel to activate the object.

4. In the Fireworks Property Inspector, click the Fill Color box. The cursor becomes an eyedropper. With the eyedropper, click the "i" in the ciber logo to sample the color. The background changes to purple.

5. Click the Done button to update the affected files and return to Dreamweaver. The files affected by the color change are automatically updated, exported, and reflected in the ciber web page.

This is a prime example of the power behind round-trip editing with Dreamweaver and Fireworks, otherwise known as updating Fireworks HTML. The combination of these programs makes a powerful tool for web development.

Inserting More Fireworks HTML Files

Frequently, more than one graphic appears in a web page, and all must be imported from Fireworks into the appropriate areas of the web page. Again, the integration between Fireworks and Dreamweaver simplifies this task.

Exercise 16.5   Importing a Table

In this exercise, you add another section to the ciber web page in place of part of the left gray bar. Ciber is promoting special pricing on graphics courses, and it wants an ad displayed on it's page:

1. You must prepare the ad. (The graphic has been prepared for you.) So, copy the file named summerSave.png from the Base Files subfolder of the Exercises/16 folder into the ciber folder. Open it in Fireworks.

2. Export the file into the `ciber` folder as you did the `ciber.png` file. Name the HTML file `savings.htm`, and output the images into the `images` folder.

The exported files are available in the `savings` subfolder of the `Exercise` folder on the CD-ROM. If you don't want to perform the export step, just copy all the files in the `savings` folder to the `ciber` folder, and from the `savings\images` folder to the `ciber\images` folder.

3. In Dreamweaver MX, open the `index.htm` document if it's closed. Click the middle of the left-side gray bar. The cell is named `gray_panel.gif` (see Figure 16.3).

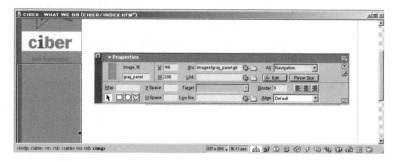

Figure 16.13   The `gray_panel.gif` graphic in the middle of the left panel is selected.

4. Delete that graphic by pressing the Delete key. Click the Fireworks HTML button on the Insert panel. Choose the `savings.htm` file that you just created and click OK. The Sizzling Summer Savings ad replaces the gray panel.

While the table is still selected, notice that the Property Inspector displays the attributes of the Savings table (see Figure 16.14).

Figure 16.14   The Fireworks table is seamlessly inserted into the `index.htm` web page.

This table can also be updated. Maybe the Sizzling Summer Savings text and the exclamation point would attract more attention if it were moved to the upper left of the ad.

5. Select the table again if you moved off of it. The source of the Fireworks graphic is summerSave.png. Click the Edit button at the bottom of the Property Inspector and open the file summerSave.png in Fireworks.

   Caution: If you make and save changes to a Fireworks document outside of Dreamweaver, you might get a warning message when you try to edit again from Dreamweaver. If this is what you want, just click OK. Otherwise, back out gracefully by clicking OK and immediately clicking the Done button (before making any changes) to return to Dreamweaver (see Figure 16.15).

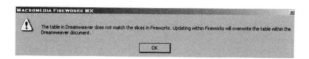

Figure 16.15   The Fireworks warning message.

6. Shift-click the Sizzling Summer Savings text object and the exclamation point object and reposition them to the upper left-hand corner of the artwork (see Figure 16.16).

Figure 16.16   Move the two selected objects to the upper left-hand corner.

7. Click Done. Your changed table object updates when you return to Dreamweaver.

Caution

When you are editing a table built in Fireworks, be sure to select the entire table before you click the Edit button. (You did this to select the entire Ciber table in step 1 of Exercise 16.4.) Dreamweaver can get "confused" when reloading a table.

You may want to avoid changing a lower-level table after nesting another table. We just did this when we nested the Savings table into a cell of the Ciber table. At this point you will need to make any changes to the outer table in Dreamweaver as opposed to opening it in Fireworks again.

If you want to change a piece of a nested table within a Fireworks table, you can make the change in Fireworks and then replace just that chunk of code in Dreamweaver. Once a nested table has been added, you cannot use this method to change the structure of the outer table without then replacing the nested table manually.

Editing an Object in Fireworks for Dreamweaver

Click each of the graphics within the `index.htm` document in Dreamweaver and notice that the filename, width, and height attributes, source, and link (if they contain one) are displayed in the Property Inspector (see Figure 16.17).

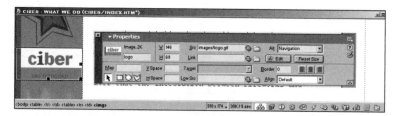

Figure 16.17   The graphic `logo.gif` is selected in Dreamweaver, and the Property Inspector reflects the attributes of that graphic.

Exercise 16.6   Editing in Fireworks

I don't like the position change of the Sizzling Summer Savings text and exclamation point, so let's change it back. This time, instead of selecting the entire table, you just work with that one piece. We don't want to fool with the table structure because the page is looking good, so make the change in Fireworks without going through Dreamweaver:

1. Select the table cell that contains the Sizzling Summer Savings text and exclamation point. You should see the image name of `a_r1_c1.jpg`. Remember that name.

2. Go to Fireworks and open the summerSave.png file (the source file for this graphic).

   In this case, you can't just edit the JPG. It's a bitmap and has no objects. You must go back to the original Fireworks file, which is summerSave.png.

3. Shift-select the Sizzling Summer Savings text object and the exclamation point object and move them back to the middle. Expand the Web layer in the Layers panel by clicking the small + sign (for Windows) or arrow (for a Macintosh) and selecting the large slice (see Figure 16.18). This is the only area that has changed, so it is all that you need to export.

Figure 16.18   Expand the Web layer in the Layers panel and select the large slice.

4. Open the Export dialog box by choosing File, Export (see Figure 16.19). Enter the name from step 1 (a_r1_c1.jpg) in the Save as Type text box, select Images Only from the pop-up menu, and check the Selected Slices Only box. Click Save.

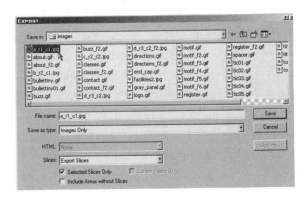

Figure 16.19   The Export panel settings to export just the selected slice from the Fireworks document.

5. Return to Dreamweaver. Select the image and click Reset Size in the Property Inspector. This just refreshes the image because you didn't change the size. The text returns to the middle.

Exercise 16.7   Finishing the Site

It's time to complete the web page. The finished product is shown in Figure 16.20. As you can see, you have much text to add to it and some more graphics. To save time, I prepared a snippet for you so that you won't have to type it all:

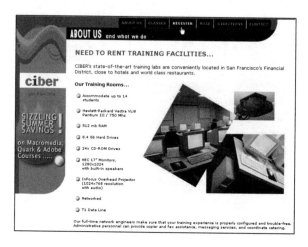

Figure 16.20   The completed `index.htm` page for ciber.

1. To fill in the middle cell, you need some more files. From the `Exercises/16` folder on the CD-ROM, copy the files `facilities2.jpg` and `bullettiny.gif` to the `ciber/images` folder on your hard drive. Next, copy the file `ciberText.csn` to the `Content_Tables` subfolder of the `Snippets` folder for Dreamweaver MX. The default location is `Program Files/Macromedia/Dreamweaver MX/Configuration/Snippets/Content_Tables`. If you can't locate the folder, search your hard drive for "snippets" to locate the proper folder.

Note: If you haven't built the `index.htm` file in the earlier exercises, or just want to use a standard version, copy the file `index_half.htm` to the ciber folder, rename it `index.htm`, and open it in Dreamweaver.

2. Open the Snippets panel by choosing Window, Snippets or clicking the Snippets tab of the Code panel group. Select the file `ciberText.csn` (see Figure 16.21).

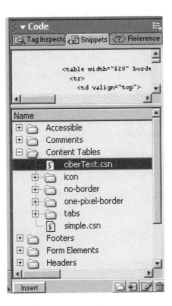

Figure 16.21   The Snippets panel shows the supplied folders and the `ciberText.csn`.

3. Go to the `index.htm` window and select the `spacer.gif` in the large cell. Delete it.

4. With the cursor in the large cell, click the Insert button on the Snippets panel. Voila! The page is finished. Save your file.

Optimizing Graphics from Within Dreamweaver

At the beginning of this chapter, I remarked on the necessity of keeping your web pages "lean" to minimize download time. (Many people have dial-up connections, particularly if your site is international.) Because of this, Dreamweaver gives you the ability to optimize graphics using Fireworks techniques while staying in Dreamweaver.

Exercise 16.8   Optimizing the Images

The pictures of the facilities in the right center might be able to be optimized further because it isn't necessary to have a really sharp picture here. Let's see if you can shave off a little download time by following these steps:

1. Select the `facilities2.jpg` graphic. It's the one with all the computers in it (the main image on the page).

2. In Fireworks, you can activate the optimization process in two ways:

    - Choose Commands, Optimize.
    - Right-click the image and select Optimize.

3. The next dialog box is Find Source, which asks if you want to use an existing Fireworks document (.png) as the source for `facilities2.jpg` or just use the named file. Clicking Yes opens a browsing window so that you can select the .png file. Clicking No opens the Optimize Image dialog box with the .jpg or .gif image. Click No.

4. The Optimize Images dialog box looks like the Fireworks Export preview (see Figure 16.22). Notice that, instead of the Next button at the lower right-hand corner, there is an Update button. The slices, HTML settings, and so on have already been determined. Set the preview to two windows so that you can see the original and the changed image. By changing the compression to 50, you can save nearly 4K without a significant loss in image quality.

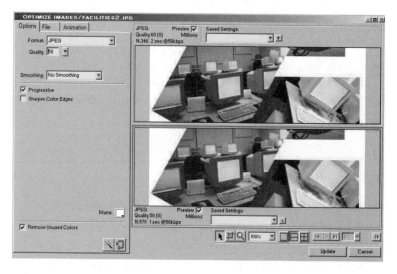

Figure 16.22   The Optimize Images dialog box shows the original and a more compressed `facilities2.jpg` image.

5. Click the Update button to save your changes and return to Dreamweaver.

Changing an Individual Graphic Using the Round-Trip Method

When you want to do more than just change the optimization settings, you need to use a different method for integrating Dreamweaver and Fireworks. Image-editing procedures can be streamlined quite efficiently. For resizing, redesigning, editing, cropping, or in other ways manipulating your graphics from Dreamweaver into Fireworks and back again, you'll want to use the round-trip method.

Exercise 16.9   Finessing the Design

The little bullets that set off each feature of the training rooms have an orange background and a blue border surrounding the yellow center. It is ugly. So, let's change the orange background to white and the blue border to orange so that the little bullet matches the button on the Savings ad:

1. Click one of the bullets that are positioned along the left side under Our Training Rooms. It is named `bullettiny.gif`. With the graphic selected, click the Edit button in the Property Inspector to launch Fireworks.

2. Fireworks shows the Open Files dialog box so that you can select the Fireworks `.png` file if you want. In this case, we only have the GIF, so click Cancel. The Fireworks Document window with the Editing from Dreamweaver caption opens with the `bullettiny.gif` ready for editing.

3. Zoom in until the graphic is big enough to work with. I used 800 percent. Then, using the elliptical marquee, drag a circle around the outside edge of the blue border (see Figure 16.23).

4. With this area selected, choose Select, Select Inverse to select the orange background. Change the background from orange to white using the Bucket tool with the Fill set to white.

5. To change the blue border, choose Select, Select Inverse again to eliminate the background from the selection. Then, using the Magic Wand tool and holding down the Alt key (for Windows) or the Command key (for a Macintosh), subtract the yellow center from the blue border.

Figure 16.23   The `bullettiny.gif` zoomed to 800 percent. The first shows the orange changed to white and the blue border selected. The second figure shows part of the web page with the changed bullets.

6. Set the Fill color to orange (I used #FF6633 to match the button) and use the Paintbucket tool to fill the selection.

7. Click Done. You are back in Dreamweaver. All the bullets look nice and clean with their orange backgrounds removed. Convenient, eh?

The web page is now complete. The finished version is in the `ciber` subfolder in the `Exercises/16` folder on the CD-ROM.

Exporting a Fireworks File to a Dreamweaver Library

Another timesaving feature is saving Fireworks files as Dreamweaver Library items. This is ideal for frequently used components, such as logos, an image map that is used on multiple pages, and so on. When you export Dreamweaver Library code from Fireworks, you export not only graphics and possibly an HTML table, but the code that you need to make your graphic easily updated. Library items are special in the way that they handle and contain code and enable you to focus your efforts on the design and layout of your graphics and pages.

Exercise 16.10   Building a Dreamweaver Library Object

To build a Dreamweaver Library object, you first must create the object in Fireworks that you want to export. Make sure to include whatever frames, rollovers, or URLs that you want the object to contain. For this exercise, use the ciber logo because it will be used on all the pages of the site. You'll build a `logo.png` file with a hotspot link to the `index.htm` page:

> **Note**
> Note: You cannot save a Fireworks file containing a pop-up menu as a LBI and retain the pop-up menu code! Instead, save it as an HTML and then open in Dreamweaver. Then save the file as an LBI file.

1. Open `ciber.png` in Fireworks.

2. Select the logo by clicking it on the document or by selecting the logo object in the Base Art layer in the Layers panel. Copy the logo (by choosing Edit, Copy or Ctrl-C). Create a new document (by choosing File, New) and click OK to accept the suggested size. Paste the logo into the new document.

3. Select the rectangular Hotspot tool in the Tools panel and draw a rectangle around the word "ciber." The rectangle can cover the entire image.

4. In the Property Inspector, type **index.htm** into the Link text box and **ciber logo** into the Alt text box.

5. Using the Optimize panel, set the parameters to Gif, WebSnap Adaptive, 16 colors, No Dither, and No Transparency.

6. Save the file as `ciberlogo.png` (by choosing File, Save As).

7. Export the file as a Dreamweaver Library item. Choose File, Export, and from the Save as Type pop-up menu, select Dreamweaver Library (`.lbi`).

8. If this is the first time that you have exported a Dreamweaver Library object in this site, you get the warning message that's shown in Figure 16.24.

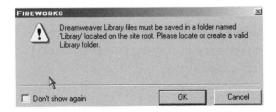

Figure 16.24   There must be a folder named `Library` in the site root.

9. Click OK and create the folder. The Select Folder dialog box appears next. Navigate to the root folder, ciber, and click the Create New Folder button (see Figure 16.25). Name the new folder Library and click Open.

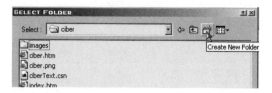

Figure 16.25   Click the Create New Folder button to create a Library folder within the root/ciber folders.

10. Save the ciber logo as a Dreamweaver Library item. The Export dialog box is still open (see Figure 16.26). Navigate to the library folder, and type **ciberlogo** into the Filename text box. The Dreamweaver Library (.lbi) should still be in the Save as Type text field. Click Save.

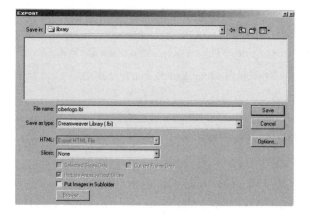

Figure 16.26   The Export dialog box is set up to export ciberlogo as a Dreamweaver Library item.

11. Return to Dreamweaver. Open the Assets panel by clicking the Assets tab in the Files panel group or choose Window, Assets (see Figure 16.27). Click the Library button on the bottom left of the panel. You see your library item.

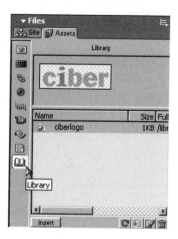

Figure 16.27   The Dreamweaver Assets panel with the library asset selected. It shows the `ciberlogo` Library item that you just created.

12. To add the item to a page, place your cursor on the page where you want the item inserted, select the item, and click the Insert button at the bottom left of the Assets panel. You can also drag and drop the item from the preview area of the Assets panel into your page.

The object retains the link to `index.htm` as a hotspot on an image map. If you choose the code view in Dreamweaver, you can see that the image map definition is stored in the Library along with the graphic.

Much of the power behind the Dreamweaver Library feature is its ability to update graphics after they are edited. If you edit the Library item once, Dreamweaver can update it everywhere that you have used it throughout your web pages.

Summary

What can I say except "POWER!" It's all up to your imagination now. With this arsenal of tools at your control, your web design dreams are secured!

Part IV

Appendix

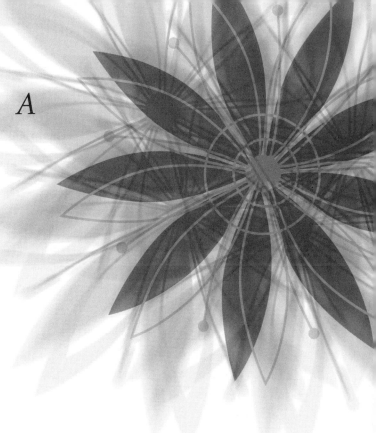

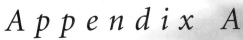
Appendix A

What's on the CD-ROM

The accompanying CD-ROM is packed
with all sorts of exercise files and products
to help you work with this book and
with Fireworks MX. The following sections
contain detailed descriptions of the CD's
contents.

For more information about the use of this CD, please review the ReadMe.txt file in the root directory. This file includes important disclaimer information, and information about installation, system requirements, troubleshooting, and technical support.

Certain projects may call for a particular font. The font being used is for illustration purposes only. You may substitute a different font as the font selected is not the important part of the project.

Technical Support Issues

If you have any difficulties with this CD, you can access the New Riders Publishing web site at www.newriders.com.

Loading the CD Files

To load the files from the CD, insert the disc into your CD-ROM drive. If autoplay is enabled on your machine, the CD-ROM setup program starts automatically the first time you insert the disc. You can copy the files to your hard drive or use them right off the disc.

Note

This CD-ROM uses long and mixed-case filenames, requiring the use of a protected-mode CD-ROM driver.

Exercise Files

This CD contains all the files you need to complete the exercises in *Fireworks MX Fundamentals*. These files can be found in the root directory's Chapters folder. To use these files, you must copy the individual projects to your hard drive; you are prompted to do so at the beginning of each exercise.

Software Folder

To save time downloading from the Internet, we included copies of the following demo software for you. You might want to try the new version of Fireworks because it's used throughout each of this book's projects.

Read This Before Opening the Software

By opening the CD package, you agree to be bound by the following agreement:

You may not copy or redistribute the entire CD-ROM as a whole. Copying and redistribution of individual software programs on the CD-ROM is governed by terms set by individual copyright holders.

The installer, code, images, actions, and brushes from the author(s) are copyrighted by the publisher and the authors.

This software is sold as-is, without warranty of any kind, either expressed or implied, including but not limited to the implied warranties of merchantability and fitness for a particular purpose. Neither the publisher nor its dealers or distributors assumes any liability for any alleged or actual damages arising from the use of this program. (Some states do not allow for the exclusion of implied warranties, so the exclusion may not apply to you.)

Index

Solutions from experts you know and trust.

www.informit.com

OPERATING SYSTEMS

WEB DEVELOPMENT

PROGRAMMING

NETWORKING

CERTIFICATION

AND MORE...

**Expert Access.
Free Content.**

New Riders has partnered with **InformIT.com** to bring technical information to your desktop. Drawing on New Riders authors and reviewers to provide additional information on topics you're interested in, **InformIT.com** has free, in-depth information you won't find anywhere else.

- **Master the skills you need, when you need them**
- **Call on resources from some of the best minds in the industry**
- **Get answers when you need them, using InformIT's comprehensive library or live experts online**
- **Go above and beyond what you find in New Riders books, extending your knowledge**

As an **InformIT** partner, **New Riders** has shared the wisdom and knowledge of our authors with you online. Visit **InformIT.com** to see what you're missing.

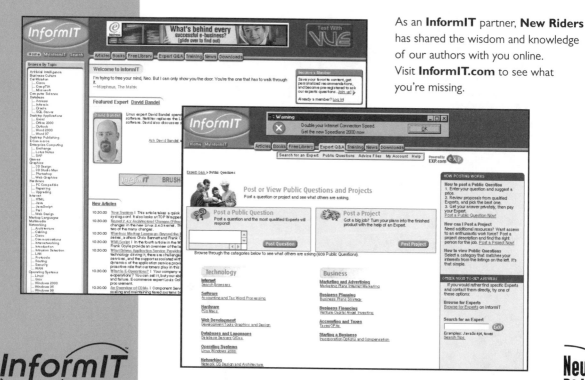

Publishing
the Voices
that Matter

OUR AUTHORS

PRESS ROOM

| web development | design | photoshop | new media | 3-D | server technologies |

EDUCATORS

ABOUT US

CONTACT US

You already know that New Riders brings you the **Voices That Matter**.

But what does that mean? It means that New Riders brings you the

Voices that challenge your assumptions, take your talents to the next

level, or simply help you better understand the complex technical world

we're all navigating.

Visit **www.newriders.com** to find:

- ▸ **10% discount** and **free shipping** on all book purchases
- ▸ Never before published chapters
- ▸ Sample chapters and excerpts
- ▸ Author bios and interviews
- ▸ Contests and enter-to-wins
- ▸ Up-to-date industry event information
- ▸ Book reviews
- ▸ Special offers from our friends and partners
- ▸ Info on how to join our User Group program
- ▸ Ways to have your Voice heard

New Riders

WWW.NEWRIDERS.COM

Fireworks MX Magic
0735711402
Lisa Lopuck
US$39.99

Inside Dreamweaver MX
073571181X
Laura Gutman
Patty Ayers
Donald Booth
US$45.00

Dreamweaver MX Magic
0735711798
Brad Halstead,
Josh Cavalier, et al.
US$39.99

Building Web Sites with Studio MX
0735712727
Tom Green
Jordan Chilcott
Chris Flick
US$49.99

Inside Flash MX
0735712549
Jody Keating
Fig Leaf Software
US$49.99

Flash MX Magic
0735711607
Matthew David
US$45.00

New Riders

Colophon

This book was written and edited in Microsoft Word, and laid out in QuarkXPress. The fonts used for the body text are Bembo and Digital. The book was printed on 50# Husky Offest Smooth paper at R. R. Donnelley & Sons in Crawfordsville, Indiana. Prepress consisted of PostScript computer-to-plate technology (filmless process). The cover was printed at Moore Langen Printing in Terre Haute, Indiana, on Carolina, coated on one side.